W9-BKK-128

Taking
SIDES

Clashing Views on
Controversial Issues in
World Civilizations
Volume II
From the Rise of National
States to the Present

Taking
SIDES

Clashing Views on
Controversial Issues in
World Civilizations
Volume II
From the Rise of National
States to the Present

Edited, Selected, and with Introductions by

Joseph R. Mitchell
Howard Community College

Helen Buss Mitchell
Howard Community College

William K. Klingaman
University of Maryland, Baltimore County

and

R. K. McCaslin

Dushkin/McGraw-Hill
A Division of the McGraw-Hill Companies

To our families

Cover Art Acknowledgment

Charles Vitelli

Library of Congress Cataloging-in-Publication Data

Main entry under title:
Taking sides: clashing views on controversial issues in world civilizations, volume ii from the rise of national states to the present/edited, selected, and with introductions by Joseph R. Mitchell and Helen Buss Mitchell.—1st ed.
Includes bibliographical references and index.
1. Civilization. I. Mitchell, Joseph R., *comp.* II. Mitchell, Helen Buss, *comp.* III. Klingaman, William K., *comp.* IV. McCaslin, R. K., *comp.*

901

0-697-42300-X   ISSN: 1094-7590

 Printed on Recycled Paper

PREFACE

In *Taking Sides: Clashing Views on Controversial Issues in World Civilizations*, we identify the issues that need to be covered in the teaching of world civilizations and the scholarly and readable sources that argue these issues. We have taken care to choose issues that will make these volumes multicultural, gender-friendly, and current with historical scholarship, and we frame these issues in a manner that makes them user-friendly for both teachers and students. Students who use these volumes should come away with a greater understanding and appreciation of the value of studying history.

One of the valuable aspects of this book is its flexibility. Its primary intended use is for world civilization courses, world history courses, and other courses that pursue a global/historical perspective. However, since more than half the issues in this volume focus on Western civilizations, teachers of Western civilization will be able to use these issues within the framework of their teaching and then assign the non-Western civilization issues as comparative studies or supplements for placing the Western materials in a wider context.

Plan of the book   This book is made up of 17 issues that argue pertinent topics in the study of world civilizations. Each issue has an issue *introduction*, which sets the stage for the debate as it is argued in the pro and con selections. Each issue concludes with a *postscript* that makes some final observations and points the way to other questions related to the issue. In reading the issue and forming your own opinions, you should not feel confined to adopt one or the other of the positions presented. There are positions in between the given views or totally outside them, and the *suggestions for further reading* that appear in each issue postscript should help you to find resources to continue your study of the subject. We have also provided Internet site addresses (URLs) in the *On the Internet* page that accompanies each part opener. At the back of the book is a listing of all the *contributors to this volume*, which will give you information on the historians and commentators whose views are debated here.

A word to the instructor   An *Instructor's Manual With Test Questions* (multiple-choice and essay) is available through the publisher. A general guidebook, *Using Taking Sides in the Classroom*, which discusses methods and techniques for integrating the pro-con approach into any classroom setting, is also available. An online version of *Using Taking Sides in the Classroom* and a correspondence service for Taking Sides adopters can be found at www.cybsol.com/usingtakingsides/. For students, we offer a field guide to analyzing argumentative essays, *Analyzing Controversy: An Introduc-*

tory Guide, with exercises and techniques to help them to decipher genuine controversies.

Taking Sides: Clashing Views on Controversial Issues in World Civilizations, Volume 1, is only one title in the Taking Sides series. If you are interested in seeing the table of contents for any of the other titles, please visit the Taking Sides Web site at http://www.dushkin.com/takingsides/.

Acknowledgments   We would like to thank Larry Madaras of Howard Community College, fellow teacher, good friend, and coeditor of *Taking Sides: Clashing Views on Controversial Issues in American History,* for suggesting we pursue a Taking Sides volume in world civilizations and for introducing us to the editorial team at Dushkin/McGraw-Hill. We are also grateful for the assistance of Jean Soto, Susan Myers, James Johnson, Keith Cohick, and the entire staff of the Howard Community College Library for their assistance with this volume.

Special thanks go to David Dean, list manager for the Taking Sides series; David Brackley, developmental editor; and Tammy Ward, administrative assistant, for their assistance in this project. Without their professionalism, encouragement, and cooperation, this volume would not have been the manageable pleasure that it has been.

We hope you enjoy using this book. Please send us any comments you have on its contents, especially suggestions for additions and deletions, to Taking Sides, Dushkin/McGraw-Hill, Sluice Dock, Guilford, CT 06437 or to tsides@mcgraw-hill.com.

Joseph R. Mitchell
Howard Community College

Helen Buss Mitchell
Howard Community College

CONTENTS IN BRIEF

CONTENTS

Professor of history William H. McNeill states that in 1500, western Europe began to extend its influence to other parts of the world, bringing about a revolution in world relationships in which the West was the principal benefactor. History professor Steven Feierman argues that because historians have viewed modern history in a unidirectional (European) manner, the contributions of non-European civilizations to world history have gone either undiscovered or unreported.

Historian of ideas Herbert Butterfield argues that the late sixteenth and early seventeenth centuries witnessed a radical break with the past and the emergence of dramatically new ways of understanding both knowledge and the world—in short, a Scientific Revolution. Professor of sociology and historian of science Steven Shapin questions the idea of a Scientific Revolution, suggesting that there was no philosophical break with the past and rejecting the existence of a single event that might be called a Scientific Revolution.

Political and military historian Edward L. Dreyer maintains that the Ming emperor's attempt to balance expansionist aims with Confucian ideals proved incompatible with sustaining the Chinese age of exploration in the fifteenth century. Dun J. Li, a historian of China, argues that the culture of northern China brought an inevitable end to the remarkable voyages of admiral Cheng Ho.

Peter Kropotkin (1842–1921), a Russian prince, revolutionary, and anarchist, argues that the French Revolution eradicated both serfdom and absolutism and paved the way for France's future democratic growth. History professor Simon Schama argues that not only did the French Revolution betray its own goals, but it produced few of the results that it promised.

Historian Edward Shorter argues that employment opportunities outside the home that opened up with industrialization led to a rise in the illegitimacy rate, which he attributes to the sexual emancipation of unmarried, working-class women. Historians Louise A. Tilly, Joan W. Scott, and Miriam Cohen counter that unmarried women worked to meet an economic need, not to gain personal freedom, and they attribute the rise in illegitimacy rates to broken marriage promises and the absence of traditional support from family, community, and the church.

History professor John King Fairbank makes the case that conservative forces, rooted in the Confucian virtues, subverted attempts by some to bring China into the modern world. History professor Jonathan D. Spence offers an economic analysis that draws on the ideas of Adam Smith and Karl Marx to explain China's initial failure to modernize and the role that foreign powers played in its eventual modernization.

Former U.S. ambassador to Japan Edwin O. Reischauer contends that the rulers of Meiji Japan forsook Japan's feudal heritage in favor of pragmatic policies to modernize the nation. Professor of history Thomas C. Smith asserts that the Meiji leaders explicitly promoted traditional Japanese values to ease the transition from feudalism to a modern state.

Turn-of-the-century British journalist J. A. Hobson provides a classic argument for the economic motivation of the "New Imperialism" of the late nineteenth century. History professors Ronald Robinson and John Gallagher, with Alice Denny, turn the tables on the Marxist interpretation of nineteenth-century imperialism, arguing that it was the bureaucrats who manipulated the capitalists into pursuing imperial adventure overseas.

University College curator Hartmut Pogge von Strandmann contends that the German government launched a war of conquest against France and Russia in August 1914. Historian Sidney Bradshaw Fay argues that every European nation that was involved in World War I bore a measure of responsibility for the outbreak of war.

History professor Richard Stites argues that in the early years of the Bolshevik Revolution, the Zhenotdel, or Women's Department, helped many working women take the first steps toward emancipation. Film historian Françoise Navailh contends that the Zhenotdel had limited political influence and could do little to improve the lives of Soviet women in the unstable period following the revolution.

Professor of government Daniel Jonah Goldhagen states that due to the nature of German society in the twentieth century—with its endemic, virulent anti-Semitism—thousands of ordinary German citizens became willing participants in the implementation of Holocaust horrors. Professor of history Fritz Stern argues that, in spite of the legitimacy of some of his arguments, Goldhagen's approach to Holocaust causation is deliberately provocative and overly simplistic in its treatment of the subject.

George F. Kennan, a former high-ranking official in the U.S. Department of State, under the pseudonym "X," argues that the Soviet Union started the cold war by adopting an expansionist policy in post–World War II Europe. Gar Alperovitz, president of the National Center for Economic and Security Alternatives, contends that American policymakers acted aggressively toward the Soviet Union in 1945, secure in the knowledge that the United States had the atomic bomb and the Soviets did not.

Professor of Middle East studies John L. Esposito sees the Iranian Revolution against Western-inspired modernization and Egypt's "holy war" against Israel as examples of the Islamic quest for a more authentic society and culture, which challenges a stable world order. Albert Hourani, an emeritus fellow of St. Antony's College, Oxford, finds hope for a stable world order in modern Islam's moderate position, which blends the traditional religious commitment to social justice with a more secular strain of morality and law.

Professor of politics Archie Brown asserts that Mikhail Gorbachev deserves credit for reforming the Soviet Union and ending the cold war and that he may have had a greater impact on the twentieth century than any other individual. Robert G. Kaiser, a member of the Council of Foreign Relations, contends that Gorbachev ultimately failed in his efforts to remake the Soviet Union because he shrank from the drastic, thoroughgoing changes that complete reform required.

Economics professor George B. N. Ayittey contends that since achieving independence, many African countries' interests have been betrayed by their own incompetent, corrupt, power-hungry leaders. Political science professor Ali A. Mazrui argues that colonialism's legacy is at the root of many of the problems facing African countries today.

Saadia Touval, a Peace Fellow at the United States Institute of Peace, maintains that the United Nations contains inherent defects that severely limit its effectiveness as a mediator and peacekeeper. Editorial writer Rosemary Righter argues that the increasing dependence upon multilateral action among the world's nations will enhance the United Nations' effectiveness.

Samuel P. Huntington, a professor of the science of government, maintains that due to internal weaknesses and threats from potential rivals organized along civilizational lines, the West is in danger of losing its status as the world's preeminent power base in the twenty-first century. Francis Fukuyama, a former deputy director with the U.S. State Department, argues that with the end of the cold war and the absence of alternatives to liberal democracy, the West is in a position to maintain and expand its role as the world's primary power base.

INTRODUCTION

World Civilizations and the Study of History

Helen Buss Mitchell

WHAT IS A CIVILIZATION?

What do we mean by the term *civilization?* Usually it designates a large group of people, spread out over a vast geographical area. In the modern world, we typically think in terms of nations or states, but these are a relatively recent development, traceable to sixteenth-century Europe. Before the rise of national states, the land that we call Europe belonged to a civilization known as Christendom—the unity of people ruled by the spiritual and temporal power of the Christian Church. At that time, other great civilizations of the world included China, Africa, India, Mesoamerica, and the Islamic Empire.

Civilization began about 5,000 years ago, when humans reached high levels of organization and achievement. When we look at world civilizations, we are considering the ancient and the contemporary versions of human alliances. Even in this age of national states, perhaps it makes sense to think of the West (Europe and North America) as a civilization. And the movement for European unity, which includes attempts to create a common currency, suggests that Europe may be thought of as a civilization despite its division into many separate nations. Postcolonial Africa is a continent of separate countries, and yet, in some ways, it remains a unified civilization. China, once a vast and far-flung group of kingdoms, has united as a civilization under communism. And Islam, which united the warring tribes of the Arabian Peninsula in the seventh century, is again defining itself as a civilization. What would be gained and what would be lost by shifting our focus from the national state to the much larger entity civilization?

Civilizations are systems for structuring human lives, and they generally include the following components: (1) an economic system by which people produce, distribute, and exchange goods; (2) a social system that defines relationships between and among individuals and groups; (3) a political system that determines who governs, who makes the laws, and who provides services for the common good; (4) a religious and/or intellectual orientation by which people make sense of the ordinary and extraordinary events of life and history—this may appear as a formal religious system, such as Judaism, Christianity, Islam, Buddhism, or Hinduism, or as an intellectual/values system, such as communism, Confucianism, or democracy; and (5) a cultural system, which includes the arts, and symbol systems, which give expression and meaning to human experience. Some of these components stand out more clearly than others in the selections in this volume, but all of them are present to one degree or another in every civilization.

WHAT IS HISTORY?

History is a dialogue between the past and the present. As we respónd to events in our own world, we bring the concerns of the present to our study of the past. What seems important to us, where we turn our attention, how we approach a study of the past—all these are rooted in the present. It has been said that where you stand determines what you see. This is especially true with history. If we stand within the Western tradition exclusively, we may be tempted to see its story as the only story, or at least the only one worth telling. And whose perspective we take is also critical. From the point of view of the rich and powerful, the events of history take one shape; through the lens of the poor and powerless, the same events can appear quite different. If we take women as our starting point, the story of the past may present us with a series of new surprises.

Presentism

Standing in the present, we must be wary of what historians call *presentism*, that is, reading the values of the present back into the past. For example, if we live in a culture that values individualism and prizes competition, we may be tempted to see these values as good even in a culture that preferred communalism and cooperation. And we may miss a key component of an ancient civilization because it does not match what we currently consider to be worthwhile. We cannot and should not avoid our own questions and struggles; they will inform our study of the past. Yet they must not warp our vision. Ideally, historians engage in a continual dialogue in which the concerns but not the values of the present are explored through a study of the past.

Revisionism

History is not a once-and-for-all enterprise. Each generation will have its own questions and will bring new tools to the study of the past, resulting in a process called *revisionism*. Much of what you will read in this book is a product of revisionism in that the featured historians have reinterpreted the past in the light of the present. You will find that whereas one generation might value revolutions, the next might focus on their terrible costs. Likewise, one generation might assume that great men shape the events of history, while the next might look to the lives of ordinary people to illuminate the past. There is no final answer, but where we stand will determine which interpretation seems more compelling to us.

As new tools of analysis become available, our ability to understand the past improves. Bringing events into clearer focus can change the meanings that we assign to them. Many of the selections in this book reflect new attitudes and new insights made possible by the tools that historians have recently borrowed from the social sciences.

The New Social History
Proponents of the new social history reject what they call "history from the top down." This refers to the previous generation of historians who had sometimes acted as if only the influential—often referred to as the "great man"—had a role in shaping history. Social historians assume that all people are capable of acting as historical agents rather than being passive victims to whom history happens. With this shift in attitude, the lives of slaves, workers, all women, and children become worthy of historical investigation. Social historians call this technique of examining ordinary people's lives "history from the bottom up."

Tools of the New Social History
Because the poor and powerless seldom leave written records, other sources of information must be analyzed to understand their lives. Applying the methods of social scientists to their own discipline, historians have broadened and deepened their field of study. Archaeological evidence, DNA analysis, the tools of paleoanthropology, and computer analysis of demographic data have allowed the voiceless to speak across centuries. Analyzing "material culture" (the objects that the people discarded as well as the monuments and other material objects they intended to leave as markers of their civilizations), for example, reveals to historians the everyday lives of people. At certain points in human history, to own a plow made the difference between merely surviving and having some surplus food to barter or sell. What people left to their heirs can tell us how much or how little they had while they lived. Fossil evidence and the analysis of mitochondrial DNA—the structures within cells that we inherit only from our mothers—may each be employed, sometimes with strikingly different results, to trace the migrations of preliterate peoples. As we continue to dig, for instance, we find our assumptions confirmed or denied by the fossils of once-living organisms. Evidence of sea life on the top of a mountain lets us know that vast geologic changes have taken place. And, in another example, our genetic material—our DNA—has information scientists are just now learning to decode and interpret that may settle important questions of origin and migration.

The high-speed comparative functions of computers have allowed historians to analyze vast quantities of data and to look at demographic trends. Consider this question: At what age do people marry for the first time or have a child? Looking at the time between marriage and the birth of a first child can help us to calculate the percentage of pregnant brides and to gain some insight into how acceptable or unacceptable premarital sex may have been to a certain population at a certain time in the context of an expected future marriage. If we study weather patterns and learn that certain years were marked by periods of drought or that a glacier receded during a particular time period, we will know a little more about whether the lives of the people who lived during these times were relatively easier or more difficult than those of their historical neighbors in earlier or later periods.

Broadening the Perspective

Stepping outside the Western tradition has allowed historians to take a more global view of world events. Accusing their predecessors of Eurocentrism, some historians have adopted a view of world history that emphasizes Africa's seminal role in cultural evolution. Also, within the Western tradition, women have challenged the male-dominated perspective that studied war but ignored the family. Including additional perspectives complicates our interpretations of past events but permits a fuller picture to emerge. We must be wary of universalism—for example, the assumption that patriarchy has always existed or that being a woman was the same for every woman no matter what her historical circumstances. If patriarchy or the nuclear family has a historical beginning, then there must have been a time when some other pattern existed. If cultures other than the West have been dominant or influential in the past, what was the world like under those circumstances?

Race, Class, and Gender

The experience of being a historical subject is never monolithic. That is, each of us has a gender, a race, a social class, an ethnic identity, a religion (even if it is atheism or agnosticism), an age, and a variety of other markers that color our experiences. At times, the most important factor may be one's gender, and what happens may be more or less the same for all members of a particular gender. Under other circumstances, however, race may be predominant. Being a member of a racial minority or of a powerful racial majority may lead to very different experiences of the same event. At other times social class may determine how an event is experienced; the rich may have one story to tell, the poor another. And other factors, such as religion, ethnic identity, or even age, can become the most significant pieces of a person's identity, especially if prejudice or favoritism is involved. Historians generally try to take into account how race, class, and gender (as well as a host of other factors) intersect in the life of a historical subject.

Ethnocentrism

All cultures are vulnerable to the narrow-mindedness created by *ethnocentrism*—the belief that one culture is superior to all others. From inside a particular culture, certain practices may seem normative—that is, we may assume that all humans or all rational humans must behave the way that we do or hold the attitudes that we hold. When we meet a culture that sees the world differently than we do, we may be tempted to write it off as inferior or primitive. An alternative to ethnocentrism is to enter the worldview of another and see what we can learn from expanding our perspective. The issues in this book will offer you many opportunities to try this thought experiment.

Issues of Interpretation

Often historians will agree on what happened but disagree about why or how something occurred. Sometimes the question is whether internal or external factors were more responsible for a happening. Both may have contributed to an event but one or the other may have played the more significant role. Looking at differing evidence may lead historians to varying interpretations. A related question considers whether it was the circumstances that changed or the attitudes of those who experienced them. For example, if we find that protest against a situation has been reduced, can we conclude that things have gotten better or that people have found a way to accommodate themselves to a situation that is beyond their control?

Public or Private?

Another consideration for historians is whether we can draw firm lines between public and private worlds. For instance, if a person is highly respected in private but discriminated against in public, which is the more significant experience? Is it even possible to separate the two? In the postindustrial world, women were able to exercise some degree of autonomy within the sphere of home and family. This might have compensated for their exclusion from events in the wider world. On the other hand, can success in the public sphere make up for an emotionally impoverished or even painful personal life? Every person has both a public and a private life; historians are interested in the balance between the two.

Nature or Nurture?

It seems plausible that our experiences within the private sphere, especially those we have as children, may affect how we behave when we move outside the home into a more public world. However, some of what we are in both worlds may be present at birth—that is, programmed into our genes. When historians look at the past, they sometimes encounter one of the puzzles of psychology and sociology: Are we seeing evidence of nature or nurture? That is, does biology or culture offer the more credible explanation for people's behavior through history? Do women and men behave in particular ways because their genetic makeup predisposes them to certain ways of acting? Or is behavior the result of an elaborate system of socialization that permits or rewards some actions while forbidding or punishing others? If people in the past behaved differently than those in the present do, what conclusions may we draw about the relative influence of nature and nurture?

Periodization

The student of the past must wonder whether or not the turning points that shape the chapters in history books are the same for all historical subjects. The process of marking turning points is known as *periodization*. This is the more or less artificial creation of periods that chunk history into manageable segments by identifying forks in the road that took people and events in new directions. Using an expanded perspective, we may find that the traditional turning points hold for men but not for women or reflect the experiences of one ethnic group but not another. And when periodization schemes conflict, which one should we use?

It is also important to keep in mind that people living at a particular moment in history are not aware of the labels that later historians will attach to their experiences. People who lived during the Middle Ages, for example, were surely not aware of living in the middle of something. Only long after the fact were we able to call a later age the Renaissance. To those who lived during what we call the Middle Ages or the Renaissance, marriage, childbirth, work, weather, sickness, and death were the primary concerns, just as they are for us today. Our own age will be characterized by future historians in ways that might surprise and even shock us. As we study the past, it is helpful to keep in mind that some of our assumptions are rooted in a traditional periodization that is now being challenged.

Continuity or Discontinuity?

A related question concerns the connection or lack of connection between one event or set of events and another. When we look at the historical past, we must ask ourselves whether we are seeing continuity or discontinuity. In other words, is the event we are studying part of a normal process of evolution, or does it represent a break from a traditional pattern? Did the Industrial Revolution take the lives of workers in wholly new directions, or did traditional behaviors continue, albeit in a radically different context? Questions of continuity versus discontinuity are the fundamental ones on which the larger issue of periodization rests.

Sometimes events appear continuous from the point of view of one group and discontinuous from the point of view of another. Suppose that factory owners found their world and worldview shifting dramatically, whereas the lives and perspectives of workers went on more or less as they had before. When this is the case, whose experience should we privilege? Is one group's experience more historically significant than another's? How should we decide?

The Power of Ideas

Can ideas change the course of history? People have sometimes been willing to die for what they believe in, and revolutions have certainly been fought, at least in part, over ideas. Some historians believe that studying the clash of ideas or the predominance of one idea or set of ideas offers the key to understanding the past. What do you think? Would devotion to a political or religious cause lead you to challenge the status quo? Or would poor economic conditions be more likely to send you into the streets? Historians differ in ranking the importance of various factors in influencing the past. Do people challenge the power structure because they feel politically powerless, or because they are hungry, or because of the power of ideas?

A related question might be, What makes a person feel free? Is it more significant to have legal and political rights, or is the everyday experience of personal autonomy more important? If laws restrict your options but you are able to live basically as you choose, are you freer than someone who has guaranteed rights but feels personally restricted? And, again, does the public sphere or the private sphere exert the greater influence? Suppose that you belong to a favored class but experience gender discrimination. Which aspect of your experience has a greater impact? On the other hand, suppose you are told that you have full political and economic rights and you are treated with great respect but are prevented from doing what you like. Will you feel freer or less free than the person who is denied formal status but acts freely? In the quest to understand the past, these questions are interconnected, and they are becoming increasingly difficult to answer.

THE TIMELINESS OF HISTORICAL ISSUES

If you read the newspaper or listen to the news, you will find that there are a confusing number of present-day political, economic, religious, and military clashes that can be understood only by looking at their historical contexts. The role of the United States in world events, the perennial conflicts in the Middle East, China's emerging role as an economic superpower, the threat posed by religious fundamentalism, Africa's political future, the question of whether revolutions are ever worth their costs—these concerns of the global village all have roots in the past. Understanding the origins of conflicts increases the possibility of envisioning their solutions. The issues in this book will help you to think through the problems that are facing our world and give you the tools to make an informed decision about what you think might be the best courses of action.

In a democracy, an informed citizenry is the bedrock on which a government stands. If we do not understand the past, the present will be a puzzle to us and the future may seem to be out of our control. Seeing how and why historians disagree can help us to determine what the critical issues are and where informed interpreters part company. This, at least, is the basis for forming our own judgments and acting upon them. Looking critically at clashing views also hones our analytic skills and makes us thoughtful readers of textbooks as well as magazines and newspapers.

WHY STUDY WORLD CIVILIZATIONS?

At times it seems that the West's power and dominance in the world make its story the only one worth studying. History, we are sometimes told, is written by the winners. For the Chinese, the Greeks, the Ottoman Turks, and many other victors of the past, the stories of other civilizations seemed irrelevant, unimportant, and not nearly as valuable as their own triumphal sagas. The Chinese considered their Middle Kingdom the center of the world; the Greeks labeled all others barbarians; and the Ottoman Turks never expected to lose their position of dominance. From our perspective in the present, these stories form a tapestry. No one thread or pattern tells the tale, and all stories seem equally necessary for a complete picture of the past to emerge.

Any single story—even that of a military and economic superpower—is insufficient to explain the scope of human history at a given moment in time. Your story is especially interesting to you. However, as we are learning, any one story achieves its fullest meaning only when it is told in concert with those of other civilizations, all of which share an increasingly interconnected planet. As communications systems shrink the Earth into a global village, we may be ignoring the rest of the world at our own peril. At the very least, the study of civilizations other than our own can alert us to events that may have worldwide implications. And, as we are beginning to learn, no story happens in isolation. The history of the West, for example, can be accurately told only within a global context that takes into account the actions and reactions of other civilizations as they share the world stage with the West. As you read the issues that concern civilizations other than those of your heritage, stay alert for what you can learn about your own civilization.

On the Internet . . .

HyperHistory Online

HyperHistory presents 3,000 years of world history via a combination of colorful graphics, life lines, time lines, and maps. Its main purpose is to convey a perspective of world historical events and to enable the reader to hold simultaneously in mind what was happening in widely separated parts of the world.
http://www.hyperhistory.com/online_n2/History_n2/a.html

Information Office of the State Council of the People's Republic of China

This official site of China's government contains policy statements by the government related to human rights.
http://www.cityu.edu.hk/HumanRights/index.htm

France During the French Revolution and Under Napoleon Bonaparte

A chronology of events and battles centered around the life of Napoleon Bonaparte and a bibliography list can be found at this Web site, which includes information on the Egypt campaign.
http://www.txdirect.net/users/rrichard/napoleo1.htm/

PART 1

The Early Modern World

Using the Age of Exploration as a starting point, this part shows how and why one civilization, the West, began to expand and influence the development of the rest of the world, and how other civilizations responded to it. It also traces the rise of capitalism and democracy and the influence that they had on the entire early modern world.

■ Did the Rise of the West Define the Modern World?

■ Was the Scientific Revolution Revolutionary?

■ Did Internal Political Factionalism End Chinese Overseas Expansion in the Fifteenth Century?

■ Was the French Revolution Worth Its Human Costs?

■ Did the Industrial Revolution Lead to a Sexual Revolution?

■ Was Confucianism Responsible for China's Failure to Modernize?

■ Did the Meiji Restoration Destroy Traditional Japanese Values?

■ Was Economic Motivation the Key Factor Behind Nineteenth-Century Imperialism?

ISSUE 1

Did the Rise of the West Define the Modern World?

YES: William H. McNeill, from *The Rise of the West: A History of the Human Community* (University of Chicago Press, 1991)

NO: Steven Feierman, from "African Histories and the Dissolution of World History," in Robert H. Bates, V. Y. Mudimbe, and Jean O'Barr, eds., *Africa and the Disciplines: The Contributions of Research in Africa to the Social Sciences and Humanities* (University of Chicago Press, 1993)

ISSUE SUMMARY

YES: Professor of history William H. McNeill states that in 1500, western Europe began to extend its influence to other parts of the world, bringing about a revolution in world relationships in which the West was the principal benefactor.

NO: History professor Steven Feierman argues that because historians have viewed modern history in a unidirectional (European) manner, the contributions of non-European civilizations to world history have gone either undiscovered or unreported.

It seems to be widely accepted that beginning in 1500, western Europe embarked on a course of world domination, the effects of which are still with us today. Due to factors such as superior military technology, immunity to diseases that ravaged others, and a strong will to succeed, Europeans were able to extend their influence over peoples in other parts of the world. The trans-Atlantic slave trade and the age of European imperialism were two major results of this cataclysmic movement.

Many have assumed that the capitalism and democracy that are so prominent among the world's nations today are part of the legacy that non-Western nations inherited from their contact with the West. In this view, the Western way was the wave of the future. Also, the West's technological and military superiority over the past 500 years have naturally led generations of Western historians to look at the last half-millennium through the eyes of their world. When the civilizations of the non-Western world were considered at all, they were simply included in a secondary and ancillary manner.

All of this changed with the end of colonialism, an important result of World War II. The former colonies, mandated territories, and Western-controlled areas were now free and independent nations, ready to determine their own destinies—and interpret their own histories. In this process, they were joined by a generation of new Western historians, who did not see the world through Eurocentric-colored glasses. Together, they are forcing the historical profession to reevaluate the Eurocentric interpretation of the last 500 years.

William H. McNeill's book *The Rise of the West*, first published in 1962, has achieved classic status among world history books. In the following selection from that book, McNeill operates from the thesis that from the earliest historical times, world civilizations have had contact with one another. He argues that this has profoundly shaped the history of humankind, although it is the West—as the title of his book implies—that has had the most profound influence on our world today. McNeill concludes that this superiority began during the Age of Exploration of the sixteenth century and continues to the present.

Steven Feierman represents the new generation of historians, who are not wedded to a Western analysis of the world's history. He utilizes African social and intellectual history (his area of expertise) to argue for the need to explain the past through non-Western eyes. This will require not only a more inclusionary approach to the study of the world's past, Feierman asserts, but also new tools and attitudes to be used in analyzing and evaluating non-Western sources, many of which might be considered nontraditional from a Western perspective. But it will mainly require work on the part of future historians to move away from the unidirectional view of the past that has dominated the historical profession for so long.

YES

William H. McNeill

THE FAR WEST'S CHALLENGE TO THE WORLD, 1500–1700 A.D.

The year 1500 A.D. aptly symbolizes the advent of the modern era, in world as well as in European history. Shortly before that date, technical improvements in navigation pioneered by the Portuguese under Prince Henry the Navigator (d. 1460) reduced to tolerable proportions the perils of the stormy and tide-beset North Atlantic. Once they had mastered these dangerous waters, European sailors found no seas impenetrable, nor any ice-free coast too formidable for their daring. In rapid succession, bold captains sailed into distant and hitherto unknown seas: Columbus (1492), Vasco da Gama (1498), and Magellan (1519–22) were only the most famous.

The result was to link the Atlantic face of Europe with the shores of most of the earth. What had always before been the extreme fringe of Eurasia became, within little more than a generation, a focus of the world's sea lanes, influencing and being influenced by every human society within easy reach of the sea. Thereby the millennial land-centered balance among the Eurasian civilizations was abruptly challenged and, within three centuries, reversed. The sheltering ocean barrier between the Americas and the rest of the world was suddenly shattered, and the slave trade brought most of Africa into the penumbra of civilization. Only Australia and the smaller islands of the Pacific remained for a while immune; yet by the close of the eighteenth century, they too began to feel the force of European seamanship and civilization.

Western Europe, of course, was the principal gainer from this extraordinary revolution in world relationships, both materially and in a larger sense, for it now became the pre-eminent meeting place for novelties of every kind. This allowed Europeans to adopt whatever pleased them in the tool kits of other peoples and stimulated them to reconsider, recombine, and invent anew within their own enlarged cultural heritage. The Amerindian civilizations of Mexico and Peru were the most conspicuous victims of the new world balance, being suddenly reduced to a comparatively simple village level after the directing classes had been destroyed or demoralized by the Spaniards. Within the Old World, the Moslem peoples lost their central position in the ecumene as ocean routes supplanted overland portage. Only in the Far East were the

From William H. McNeill, *The Rise of the West: A History of the Human Community* (University of Chicago Press, 1991). Copyright © 1991 by University of Chicago Press. Reprinted by permission. Notes omitted.

effects of the new constellation of world relationships at first unimportant. From a Chinese viewpoint it made little difference whether foreign trade, regulated within traditional forms, passed to Moslem or European merchants' hands. As soon as European expansive energy seemed to threaten their political integrity, first Japan and then China evicted the disturbers and closed their borders against further encroachment. Yet by the middle of the nineteenth century, even this deliberate isolation could no longer be maintained; and the civilizations of the Far East—simultaneously with the primitive cultures of central Africa—began to stagger under the impact of the newly industrialized European (and extra-European) West.

The key to world history from 1500 is the growing political dominance first of western Europe, then of an enlarged European-type society planted astride the north Atlantic and extending eastward into Siberia. Yet until about 1700, the ancient landward frontiers of the Asian civilizations retained much of their old significance. Both India (from 1526) and China (by 1644) suffered yet another conquest from across these frontiers; and the Ottoman empire did not exhaust its expansive power until near the close of the seventeenth century. Only in Central America and western South America did Europeans succeed in establishing extensive land empires overseas during this period. Hence the years 1500–1700 may be regarded as transitional between the old land-centered and the new ocean-centered pattern of ecumenical relationships—a time when European enterprise had modified, but not yet upset the fourfold balance of the Old World.

The next major period, 1700–1850, saw a decisive alteration of the balance in favor of Europe, except in the Far East. Two great outliers were added to the Western world by the Petrine conversion of Russia and by the colonization of North America. Less massive offshoots of European society were simultaneously established in southernmost Africa, in the South American pampas, and in Australia. India was subjected to European rule; the Moslem Middle East escaped a similar fate only because of intra-European rivalries; and the barbarian reservoir of the Eurasian steppes lost its last shreds of military and cultural significance with the progress of Russian and Chinese conquest and colonization.

After 1850, the rapid development of mechanically powered industry enormously enhanced the political and cultural primacy of the West. At the beginning of this period, the Far Eastern citadel fell before Western gunboats; and a few of the European nations extended and consolidated colonial empires in Asia and Africa. Although European empires have decayed since 1945, and the separate nation-states of Europe have been eclipsed as centers of political power by the melding of peoples and nations occurring under the aegis of both the American and Russian governments, it remains true that, since the end of World War II, the scramble to imitate and appropriate science, technology, and other aspects of Western culture has accelerated enormously all round the world. Thus the dethronement of western Europe from its brief mastery of the globe coincided with (and was caused by) an unprecedented, rapid Westernization of all the peoples of the earth. The rise of the West seems today still far from its apogee; nor is it obvious, even in the narrower political sense, that the era of Western dominance is past. The American and

Russian outliers of European civilization remain militarily far stronger than the other states of the world, while the power of a federally reorganized western Europe is potentially superior to both and remains inferior only because of difficulties in articulating common policies among nations still clinging to the trappings of their decaying sovereignties.

* * *

From the perspective of the mid-twentieth century, the career of Western civilization since 1500 appears as a vast explosion, far greater than any comparable phenomenon of the past both in geographic range and in social depth. Incessant and accelerating self-transformation, compounded from a welter of conflicting ideas, institutions, aspirations, and inventions, has characterized modern European history; and with the recent institutionalization of deliberate innovation in the form of industrial research laboratories, universities, military general staffs, and planning commissions of every sort, an accelerating pace of technical and social change bids fair to remain a persistent feature of Western civilization.

This changeability gives the European and Western history of recent centuries both a fascinating and a confusing character. The fact that we are heirs but also prisoners of the Western past, caught in the very midst of an unpredictable and incredibly fast-moving flux, does not make it easier to discern critical landmarks, as we can, with equanimity if not without error, for ages long past and civilizations alien to our own.

... Fortunately, a noble array of historians has traversed the ground already, so that it is not difficult to divide Western history into periods, nor to characterize such periods with some degree of plausibility. A greater embarrassment arises from the fact that suitable periods of Western history do not coincide with the benchmarks of modern world history. This is not surprising, for Europe had first to reorganize itself at a new level before the effects of its increased power could show themselves significantly abroad. One should therefore expect to find a lag between the successive self-transformations of European society and their manifestations in the larger theater of world history....

THE GREAT EUROPEAN EXPLORATIONS AND THEIR WORLD-WIDE CONSEQUENCES

Europeans of the Atlantic seaboard possessed three talismans of power by 1500 which conferred upon them the command of all the oceans of the world within half a century and permitted the subjugation of the most highly developed regions of the Americas within a single generation. These were: (1) a deep-rooted pugnacity and recklessness operating by means of (2) a complex military technology, most notably in naval matters; and (3) a population inured to a variety of diseases which had long been endemic throughout the Old World ecumene.

The Bronze Age barbarian roots of European pugnacity and the medieval survival of military habits among the merchant classes of western Europe, as well as among aristocrats and territorial lords of less exalted degree, [are worth emphasizing.] Yet only when one remembers the all but incredible courage, daring, and brutality of Cortez and Pizarro in the Americas, reflects upon the ruthless aggression of Almeida and Albuquerque in the Indian Ocean, and discovers the disdain of even so cultivated a European as Father Matteo Ricci for the civility of the Chinese, does the full force of European warlikeness, when compared with the attitudes and aptitudes of other major civilizations of the earth, become apparent. The Moslems and the Japanese could alone compare in the honor they paid to the military virtues. But Moslem merchants usually cringed before the violence held in high repute by their rulers and seldom dared or perhaps cared to emulate it. Hence Moslem commercial enterprise lacked the cutting edge of naked, well-organized, large-scale force which constituted the chief stock-in-trade of European overseas merchants in the sixteenth century. The Japanese could, indeed, match broadswords with any European; but the chivalric stylization of their warfare, together with their narrowly restricted supply of iron, meant that neither *samurai* nor a sea pirate could reply in kind to a European broadside.

Supremacy at sea gave a vastly enlarged scope to European warlikeness after 1500. But Europe's maritime superiority was itself the product of a deliberate combination of science and practice, beginning in the commercial cities of Italy and coming to fruition in Portugal through the efforts of Prince Henry the Navigator and his successors. With the introduction of the compass (thirteenth century), navigation beyond sight of land had become a regular practice in the Mediterranean; and the navigators' charts, or *portolans*, needed for such voyaging showed coasts, harbors, landmarks, and compass bearings between major ports. Although they were drawn freehand, without any definite mathematical projection, *portolans* nevertheless maintained fairly accurate scales of distances. But similar mapping could be ap-

plied to the larger distances of Atlantic navigation only if means could be found to locate key points along the coast accurately. To solve this problem, Prince Henry brought to Portugal some of the best mathematicians and astronomers of Europe, who constructed simple astronomical instruments and trigonometrical tables by which ship captains could measure the latitude of newly discovered places along the African coast. The calculation of longitude was more difficult; and, until a satisfactory marine chronometer was invented in the eighteenth century, longitude could be approximated only be dead reckoning. Nevertheless, the new methods worked out at Prince Henry's court allowed the Portuguese to make usable charts of the Atlantic coasts. Such charts gave Portuguese sea captains courage to sail beyond sight of land for weeks and presently for months, confident of being able to steer their ships to within a few miles of the desired landfall.

The Portuguese court also accumulated systematic information about oceanic winds and currents; but this data was kept secret as a matter of high policy, so that modern scholars are uncertain how much the early Portuguese navigators knew. At the same time, Portuguese naval experts attacked the problem of improving ship construction. They proceeded by rule of thumb; but deliberate experiment, systematically pursued, rapidly increased the seaworthiness, maneuverability, and speed of Portuguese and presently (since improvements in naval architecture could not be kept secret) of other European ships. The most important changes were: a reduction of hull width in proportion to length; the introduction of multiple masts (usually three or four); and the substitution of several smaller, more manageable sails for the single sail per mast from which the evolution started. These innovations allowed a crew to trim the sails to suit varying conditions of wind and sea, thus greatly facilitating steering and protecting the vessel from disaster in sudden gales.

With these improvements, larger ships could be built; and increasing size and sturdiness of construction made it possible to transform seagoing vessels into gun platforms for heavy cannon. Thus by 1509, when the Portuguese fought the decisive battle for control of the Arabian Sea off the Indian port of Diu, their ships could deliver a heavy broadside at a range their Moslem enemies could not begin to match. Under such circumstances, the superior numbers of the opposing fleet simply provided the Portuguese with additional targets for their gunnery. The old tactics of sea fighting —ramming, grappling, and boarding— were almost useless against cannon fire effective at as much as 200 yards distance.

The third weapon in the European armory—disease—was quite as important as stark pugnacity and weight of metal. Endemic European diseases like smallpox and measles became lethal epidemics among Amerindian populations, who had no inherited or acquired immunities to such infections. Literally millions died of these and other European diseases; and the smallpox epidemic raging in Tenochtitlan when Cortez and his men were expelled from the citadel in 1520 had far more to do with the collapse of Aztec power than merely military operations. The Inca empire, too, may have been ravaged and weakened by a similar epidemic before Pizarro ever reached Peru.

On the other hand, diseases like yellow fever and malaria took a heavy toll of Europeans in Africa and India. But climatic conditions generally prevented new tropical diseases from penetrating Europe itself in any very serious fashion. Those which could flourish in temperate climates, like typhus, cholera, and bubonic plague, had long been known throughout the ecumene; and European populations had presumably acquired some degree of resistance to them. Certainly the new frequency of sea contact with distant regions had important medical consequences for Europeans, as the plagues for which Lisbon and London became famous prove. But gradually the infections which in earlier centuries had appeared sporadically as epidemics became merely endemic, as the exposed populations developed a satisfactory level of resistance. Before 1700, European populations had therefore successfully absorbed the shocks that came with the intensified circulation of diseases initiated by their own sea voyaging. Epidemics consequently ceased to be demographically significant. The result was that from about 1650 (or before), population growth in Europe assumed a new velocity. Moreover, so far as imperfect data allow one to judge, between 1550 and 1650 population also began to spurt upward in China, India, and the Middle East. Such an acceleration of population growth within each of the great civilizations of the Old World can scarcely be a mere coincidence. Presumably the same ecological processes worked themselves out in all parts of the ecumene, as age-old epidemic checks upon population faded into merely endemic attrition.

The formidable combination of European warlikeness, naval technique, and comparatively high levels of resistance to disease transformed the cultural balance of the world within an amazingly brief period of time. Columbus linked the Americas with Europe in 1492; and the Spaniards proceeded to explore, conquer, and colonize the New World with extraordinary energy, utter ruthlessness, and an intense missionary idealism. Cortez destroyed the Aztec state in 1519–21; Pizarro became master of the Inca empire between 1531 and 1535. Within the following generation, less famous but no less hardy conquistadores founded Spanish settlements along the coasts of Chile and Argentina, penetrated the highlands of Ecuador, Colombia, Venezuela, and Central America, and explored the Amazon basin and the southern United States. As early as 1571, Spanish power leaped across the Pacific to the Philippines, where it collided with the sea empire which their Iberian neighbors, the Portuguese, had meanwhile flung around Africa and across the southern seas of the Eastern Hemisphere.

Portuguese expansion into the Indian Ocean proceeded with even greater rapidity. Exactly a decade elapsed between the completion of Vasco da Gama's first voyage to India (1497–99) and the decisive Portuguese naval victory off Diu (1509). The Portuguese quickly exploited this success by capturing Goa (1510) and Malacca (1511), which together with Ormuz on the Persian Gulf (occupied permanently from 1515) gave them the necessary bases from which to dominate the trade of the entire Indian Ocean. Nor did they rest content with .these successes. Portuguese ships followed the precious spices to their farthest source in the Moluccas without delay (1511–12); and a Portuguese merchant-explorer traveling on a Malay vessel visited Canton as early as 1513–14. By 1557, a permanent Portuguese settlement was founded at Macao on the south China coast; and trade and missionary activity in Japan started in the 1540's. On the other side of the world, the Portuguese discovered Brazil in 1500 and began to settle the country after 1530. Coastal stations in both west and east Africa, established between 1471 and 1507, completed the chain of ports of call which held the Portuguese empire together.

No other European nations approached the early success of Spain and Portugal overseas. Nevertheless, the two Iberian nations did not long enjoy undisturbed the new wealth their enterprise had won. From the beginning, the Spaniards found it difficult to protect their shipping against French and Portuguese sea raiders. English pirates offered an additional and formidable threat after 1568, when the first open clash between English interlopers and the Spanish authorities in the Caribbean took place. Between 1516 and 1568 the other great maritime people of the age, the Dutch, were subjects of the same Hapsburg monarchs who ruled in Spain and, consequently, enjoyed a favored status as middlemen between Spanish and north European ports. Initially, therefore, Dutch shipping had no incentive to harass Iberian sea power.

This naval balance shifted sharply in the second half of the sixteenth century, when the Dutch revolt against Spain (1568), followed by the English victory over the Spanish armada (1588), signalized the waning of Iberian sea power before that of the northern European nations. Harassment of Dutch ships in Spanish ports simply accelerated the shift; for the Dutch responded by despatching their vessels directly to the Orient (1594), and the English soon followed suit. Thereafter, Dutch naval and commercial power rapidly supplanted that of Portugal in the southern seas. The establishment of a base in Java (1618), the capture of Malacca from the Portuguese (1641), and the seizure of the most important trading posts of Ceylon (by 1644) secured Dutch hegemony in the Indian Ocean; and during the same decades, English traders gained a foothold in western India. Simultaneously, English (1607), French (1608), and Dutch (1613) colonization of mainland North America, and the seizure of most of the smaller Caribbean islands by the same three nations, infringed upon Spanish claims to monopoly in the New World, but failed to dislodge Spanish power from any important area where it was already established.

* * *

The truly extraordinary *élan* of the first Iberian conquests and the no less remarkable missionary enterprise that followed closely in its wake surely mark a new era in the history of the human community. Yet older landmarks of that history did not crumble all at once. Movement from the Eurasian steppes continued to make political history—for example, the Uzbek conquest of Transoxiana (1507–12) with its sequel, the Mogul conquest of India (1526–1688); and the Manchu conquest of China (1621–83).

Chinese civilization was indeed only slightly affected by the new regime of the seas; and Moslem expansion, which had been a dominating feature of world history during the centuries before 1500, did not cease or even slacken very noticeably until the late seventeenth century. Through their conquest of the high seas, western Europeans did indeed outflank the Moslem world in India and southeast Asia, while Russian penetration of Siberian forests soon outflanked the Moslem lands on the north also. Yet these probing extensions of European (or para-European) power remained tenuous and comparatively weak in the seventeenth century. Far from being crushed in the jaws of a vast European pincer, the Moslems continued to win important victories and to penetrate new territories in southeast Europe, India, Africa, and southeast Asia. Only in the western and central steppe did Islam suffer significant territorial setbacks before 1700.

Thus only two large areas of the world were fundamentally transformed during the first two centuries of European overseas expansion: the regions of Amerindian high culture and western Europe itself. European naval enterprise certainly widened the range and increased the intimacy of contacts among the various peoples of the ecumene and brought new peoples into touch with the disruptive social influences of high civilization. Yet the Chinese, Moslem, and Hindu worlds were not yet really deflected from their earlier paths of development; and substantial portions of the land surface of the globe—Australia and Oceania, the rain forests of South America, and most of North America and northeastern Asia—remained almost unaffected by Europe's achievement.

Nevertheless, a new dimension had been added to world history. An ocean frontier, where European seamen and soldiers, merchants, missionaries, and settlers came into contact with the various peoples of the world, civilized and uncivilized, began to challenge the ancient pre-eminence of the Eurasian land frontier, where steppe nomads had for centuries probed, tested, and disturbed civilized agricultural populations. Very ancient social gradients began to shift when the coasts of Europe, Asia, and

America became the scene of more and more important social interactions and innovation. Diseases, gold and silver, and certain valuable crops were the first items to flow freely through the new transoceanic channels of communication. Each of these had important and far-reaching consequences for Asians as well as for Europeans and Amerindians. But prior to 1700, only a few isolated borrowings of more recondite techniques or ideas passed through the sea lanes that now connected the four great civilization of the Old World. In such exchanges, Europe was more often the receiver than the giver, for its people were inspired by a lively curiosity, insatiable greed, and a reckless spirit of adventure that contrasted sharply with the smug conservatism of Chinese, Moslem, and Hindu cultural leaders.

Partly by reason of the stimuli that flowed into Europe from overseas, but primarily because of internal tensions arising from its own heterogeneous cultural inheritance, Europe entered upon a veritable social explosion in the period 1500–1650—an experience painful in itself but which nonetheless raised European power to a new level of effectiveness and for the first time gave Europeans a clear margin of superiority over the other great civilizations of the world....

CONCLUSION

Between 1500 and 1700, the Eurasian ecumene expanded to include parts of the Americas, much of sub-Saharan Africa, and all of northern Asia. Moreover, within the Old World itself, western Europe began to forge ahead of all rivals as the most active center of geographical expansion and of cultural innovation. Indeed, Europe's self-revolution trans-formed the medieval frame of Western civilization into a new and vastly more powerful organization of society. Yet the Moslem, Hindu, and Chinese lands were not yet seriously affected by the new energies emanating from Europe. Until after 1700, the history of these regions continued to turn around old traditions and familiar problems.

Most of the rest of the world, lacking the massive self-sufficiency of Moslem, Hindu, and Chinese civilization, was more acutely affected by contact with Europeans. In the New World, these contacts first decapitated and then decimated the Amerindian societies; but in other regions, where local powers of resistance were greater, a strikingly consistent pattern of reaction manifested itself. In such diverse areas as Japan, Burma, Siam, Russia, and parts of Africa, an initial interest in and occasional eagerness to accept European techniques, ideas, religion, or fashions of dress was supplanted in the course of the seventeenth century by a policy of withdrawal and deliberate insulation from European pressures. The Hindu revival in India and the reform of Lamaism in Tibet and Mongolia manifested a similar spirit; for both served to protect local cultural values against alien pressures, though in these cases the pressures were primarily Moslem and Chinese rather than European.

A few fringe areas of the earth still remained unaffected by the disturbing forces of civilization. But by 1700 the only large habitable regions remaining outside the ecumene were Australia, the Amazon rain forest, and northwestern North America; and even these latter two had largely felt tremors of social disturbance generated by the approaching onset of civilization.

At no previous time in world history had the pace of social transformation been so rapid. The new density and intimacy of contacts across the oceans of the earth assured a continuance of cross-stimulation among the major cultures of mankind. The efforts to restrict foreign contacts and to withdraw from disturbing relationships with outsiders—especially with the restless and ruthless Westerners—were doomed to ultimate failure by the fact that successive self-transformations of western European civilization, and especially of Western technology, rapidly increased the pressures Westerners were able to bring against the other peoples of the earth. Indeed, world history since 1500 may be thought of as a race between the West's growing power to molest the rest of the world and the increasingly desperate efforts of other peoples to stave Westerners off, either by clinging more strenuously than before to their peculiar cultural inheritance or, when that failed, by appropriating aspects of Western civilization—especially technology—in the hope of thereby finding means to preserve their local autonomy.

NO

Steven Feierman

AFRICAN HISTORIES AND THE DISSOLUTION OF WORLD HISTORY

Once upon a time historians used to know that certain civilizations (Western ones) were their natural subject matter, that some political leaders (Thomas Jefferson, Napoleon, Charlemagne) were worth knowing about, and that particular periods and developments (the Renaissance, the Age of Enlightenment, the rise of the nation-state) were worthy of our attention. Other places, other people, other cultural developments less central to the course of Western civilization did not count. Now all of that has come into question. Historians no longer agree on the subjects about which they ought to write. . . .

The loss of agreement on history's subject is only one part of the change that provokes scholars to write about fragmentation and chaos. The debate on history's subject emerged at the same time that increasing numbers of historians began to doubt their own methods. Many now find it impossible to sustain the claims they might once have made that their choices of subject and method are based on objective knowledge. These historians have become acutely aware that their own writings, their ways of constructing a narrative, conceal some kinds of historical knowledge even while they reveal others, and that their choice of subject and method is a product of their own time and circumstances, not an inevitable outcome of the impersonal progress of historical science. This change, which has roots within contemporary philosophy, also emerges from the evolution of the historian's craft itself.

It is a profound paradox of history-writing in the most recent era that our faith in objective historical knowledge has been shaken precisely because of the advance of "knowledge" in its objective sense. The authoritative version of historical knowledge has been undermined because historians, in recent decades, have built bodies of knowledge about which their predecessors could only have dreamed. By carrying assumptions about historical knowledge through to their conclusions, historians have discovered some of the limits of those assumptions. . . .

One obvious consequence of the expansion of historical research in the years since 1960 has been to show just how limited were our earlier understandings. Much of the new specialized research focuses on people previously

From Steven Feierman, "African Histories and the Dissolution of World History," in Robert H. Bates, V. Y. Mudimbe, and Jean O'Barr, eds., *Africa and the Disciplines: The Contributions of Research in Africa to the Social Sciences and Humanities* (University of Chicago Press, 1993). Copyright © 1993 by University of Chicago Press. Reprinted by permission. Notes and references omitted.

excluded from the general history of humanity. The history of Africa is not alone in this respect. Alongside it are new bodies of knowledge on the history of medieval peasants, of barbarians in ancient Europe, of slaves on American plantations, and of women as the previously silent majority (silent, at least, in historians' accounts) in every time and place.

The very substantial dimensions of the gains in our knowledge have led to a sense of doubt rather than triumph. Historians now understand the dubious criteria according to which women and Africans, peasants and slaves were excluded from the histories of earlier generations. They therefore cannot help but wonder which populations, and which domains of human experience, they themselves are excluding today.

The previously excluded histories do not only present new data to be integrated into the larger narrative; they raise questions about the validity of that narrative itself. University historians integrate African history into the history of the eighteenth century, or the nineteenth, and yet many histories written or recited in Africa do not measure historical time in centuries. Academic historians appropriate bits of the African past and place them within a larger framework of historical knowledge which has European roots —the history of commodity exchange, for example. They rarely think of using bits of European history to amplify African narratives, about the succession of Akan shrines or the origin and segmentation of Tiv lineages.

Even before these more difficult issues began to trouble historians, the growth of knowledge about non-European societies began to undermine earlier histories, to bring into question narratives of academic history which, in the 1960s,

seemed to be beyond reproach. The new knowledge showed that what was once thought to be universal history was in fact very partial and very selective. The narrative of human history which Western historians held at that time could no longer stand. Its destruction contributed to the sense of fragmentation and lost coherence. ...

In the early 1960s it was still possible to describe human history in terms of a story with a single narrative thread, from the earliest periods until modern times. Now that possibility is gone. It is difficult for us to remember how profoundly our historical vision has changed unless we return to examine important works of that time. For example, William McNeill's *The Rise of the West*, published in 1963 when African history was just beginning to emerge, presented a unicentric and unidirectional narrative, of a kind that would not be acceptable today.

The Rise of the West divided the ancient world between "civilizations" and the land of "barbarians." The book focused on the diffusion of the techniques of civilization, originally from Mesopotamia, and then within the area McNeill calls the *ecumene*, as opposed to the land of the barbarians. *Oikoumenê* (one of Arnold Toynbee's terms) had been used also by the great anthropologist A. L. Kroeber to mean "the range of man's most developed cultures" and therefore "the millennially interrelated civilizations in the connected main land masses of the Eastern Hemisphere." This was an intercommunicating zone within which the basic techniques of civilization were created, and within which they spread. The zone's boundaries shifted with time, but its early core was in the ancient Near East.

The origin of civilization, in McNeill's narrative, grows out of the introduction of agriculture. On this subject he takes contradictory positions but tries to maintain a single narrative thread. Even though the introduction explains that agriculture was introduced more than once, the book's narrative focuses on the central role of Mesopotamia, making a partial exception only for the introduction of agriculture in China. About the Americas, McNeill wrote, "Seeds or cuttings must have been carried across the ocean by human agency at a very early time." Then a bit later he explained that "contacts were far too limited and sporadic to allow the Amerindians to borrow extensively from the more advanced cultures of the Old World. As a result, the Andean and Mexican civilizations developed belatedly and never attained a mastery of their environment that could rival the levels attained by their contemporaries in Eurasia." He saw no possibility that domestication had independent beginnings in Africa and wrote that agriculture came to eastern and southern Africa only within the past five centuries. Until then, "primitive hunters roamed as their forefathers had done for untold millennia."

This statement is itself incorrect by millennia. We now know, as scholars of that generation did not, that animal domestication came very early to Africa (possibly earlier than to Southwest Asia), and that there were autonomous centers of crop domestication in Africa south of the Sahara.

Historians of McNeill's generation knew that great empires had grown up in sub-Saharan Africa by the first half of the present millennium—Ghana, Mali, Songhay, and other kingdoms in West Africa, and a great many kingdoms in eastern, central, and southern Africa, of which Zimbabwe was famous because of its great stone ruins. McNeill saw all of these as borrowings. The more advanced of Africa's societies, he wrote, "were never independent of the main civilizations of Eurasia." Islam, in his view, played a central role in bringing Eurasia's civilization to Africa. Even the southward migration of Bantu-speaking agriculturalists "may have been reinforced by the migration of tribes fleeing from Moslem pressures in the northwest."

Recent archaeological research in West Africa has shown that urbanism based on commerce came to West Africa before the birth of Islam. By about A.D. 500, Jenne, on the Niger River, emerged as a town built on local trade in agricultural surpluses drawn from lands flooded by the river. In this case, West Africans built their own town, which then grew further when Islam became important.

In central and southern Africa, also, kingdoms grew out of local roots. Zimbabwe is only one among the region's many stone ruins built in similar styles. These were sited so as to make farming and transhumant cattle-keeping possible as well as long-distance trade. As in West Africa, the evidence points to the growth of locally rooted centers which came ultimately to participate in long-distance trade. History can no longer be written as a single clear narrative of the spread of civilization's arts from the *ecumene*, the historical heartland, to Africa and other parts of the world.

Accounting for the new patterns challenged historians to find new ways of defining the spatial boundaries of important processes in world history. In this, as in so much else, the development of the *Annales* school of history writing in France interacted in creative ways with the development of African history. The creators of *Annales* history had a fresh historical vision; they challenged the orthodoxies of a style of history (associated with the legacy of Leopold von Ranke) that focused on the critical study of archival documents, especially as they related to the minutiae of political events. The early *Annalistes* reacted against the narrowly political definition of the historian's subject matter. Marc Bloch, in his early work, wrote about collectively held understandings of the world, in what seems to us now like an anthropological approach. Bloch, Lucien Febvre, and others were concerned with the history of society more generally, and not only with that narrow stratum to which the main political documents referred.

Fernand Braudel, the great leader of second-generation *Annales* historians, opened up the boundaries of historical space in a way that made it easier for us to understand Africa in world history. Many earlier scholars had limited themselves to national histories, of France, or of Italy, or of Spain. Others moved beyond national boundaries to continental ones. Braudel in his masterpiece saw the Mediterranean, with its palms and olive trees, as a significant historical unit, even though it took in parts of Europe and parts of Africa and Asia. It was tied together by its sea routes, but then extended wherever human communication took it: "We should imagine a hundred frontiers, not one," he wrote, "some political, some economic, and some cultural."

A flexible approach to spatial boundaries gives us a tool with which to break out of narrow definitions of core and periphery in world history. We do not need to see West African Muslims in a narrow framework which casts them only as bearers of culture from the center of civilization to the periphery. We can see them as West Africans, in economy, in

language, and in many elements of discursive practice, and yet at the same time Muslims. We do not read from a single historical map that inevitably separates Africans from Middle Easterners. We read many maps side by side, some for language, some for economy, some for religion. Similarly, when we define the boundaries of African healing practices we do not need to stop at the continent's edge; our history can extend to the Americas. If we adopt a flexible and situationally specific understanding of historical space, the plantation complex, which is often seen as narrowly American, as a phenomenon of the Caribbean, Brazil, and the southern United States, can now be understood as extending to the East Coast of Africa and to northern Nigeria.

Braudel, along with the other *Annales* historians, insisted on asking how representative our historical knowledge is in relation to the totality of the universe that might be described, if only we knew the full story. He saw the economy as studied by economists, for example, as only one small part of a much larger and more shadowy sphere of economic activity. He observed that "The market economy still controls the great mass of transactions *that show up in the statistics*," as a way of arguing that the historian ought to be concerned also with what does not show up in the statistics. A concern with the representativeness of historical knowledge was at the heart of African history's growth, which in this sense can be seen as Braudelian in its inspiration. African historians were saying that even if conventional sources were silent on Africa, this could not be taken as evidence that nothing had happened in Africa. If the contours of world history were determined by the silence of our sources, and not by the shape of history's subject matter, then we needed to find new sources.

Yet Braudel himself could not break out of a unidirectional history of the world with Europe at its center. *Civilisation matérielle, économie et capitalisme,* his three-volume history of the world between the fifteenth and eighteenth centuries, is driven by a tension between Braudel's disciplined attempt to find the correct spatial frame for each phenomenon (to explain the eighteenth-century rise of population on a worldwide basis, for example), and his definition of modern world history as the rise of a dominant Europe.

Civilisation matérielle, as a world history, touches on Africa's place in comparative context. The first volume is concerned with the history of everyday material life: food, clothing, crops, housing, furniture, and so on. Braudel's weakness in understanding sub-Saharan Africa does not undermine his more general analysis, except as it shapes his most general reflections on the full range of human experience. The same is true of the second volume, on the techniques by which people exchanged goods in various parts of the world. In the third volume, however, the question of Africa's place in history (and Latin America's) comes closer to the center of the analysis. This volume, which draws heavily on the thought of Immanuel Wallerstein, asks about the process by which a dominant capitalist world economy emerged, with its core in the West. In 1750, he says, the countries which were later to become industrialized produced 22.5 percent of the world's gross product. In 1976 the same countries produced 75 percent of that product. What were the origins of this movement from the relative eco-nomic parity of the world's parts to the dominance of the capitalist core? ...

Braudel adopted this framework, with its concern for the systematic character of inequality between the people he called "les *have* et les *have not.*" He was interested in how the dominance of the capitalist center grew out of developments within Europe, and out of relations among local world-economies. These latter were the spatial units which achieved a certain organic integration because of the density of exchange relations within them. The Mediterranean of the sixteenth century was a world-economy in this sense.

Braudel tried to make a serious assessment of the degree to which wealth drawn from outside Europe contributed to the rise of capitalism, but he treated Africans, and to a lesser extent people of the Americas, as historical actors only to the extent that they met European needs:

> While we might have preferred to see this "Non-Europe" on its own terms, it cannot properly be understood, even before the eighteenth century, except in terms of the mighty shadow cast over it by western Europe.... It was from all over the world... that Europe was now drawing a substantial part of her strength and substance. And it was this extra share which enabled Europeans to reach superhuman heights in tackling the tasks encountered on the path to progress.

This is a rather strange statement, lumping together much of the world simply on the basis that it is not Europe and proposing to ignore non-Europe on its own terms.

Braudel describes African developments, in particular, in terms of racial essences. In his view all civilization originated from the north, radiating southwards. He writes, "I should like now to concentrate on the heartland of Black Africa, leaving aside the countries of the Maghreb—a 'White Africa' contained within the orbit of Islam." Braudel's understanding of historical space is usually a subtle one in which each spatial frame is carefully differentiated. Here, however, he merges several frames in an inflexible and inaccurate way. Firstly, he merges race ("White" or "Black") with religion (Islamic or non-Islamic), even though many of the Muslims were people he would otherwise have described as "Black."

Secondly, he characterizes "Black Africa" as passive and inert. He writes that European ships on the West Coast met "neither resistance nor surveillance" and that the same thing happened on the shores of the desert: "Islam's camel-trains were as free to choose their entry-points as Europe's ships." This is demonstrably incorrect. A very large body of historical literature explores the complex interactions between West African kings or traders and those who came across the desert from the north. The spread of Islam and of the trans-Saharan trade was shared by initiatives taken on both sides of the desert.

According to Braudel, all movement was in a single direction. "Curiously, no black explorers ever undertook any of the voyages across either the desert or the ocean which lay on their doorstep.... To the African, the Atlantic was, like the Sahara, an impenetrable obstacle." He writes this despite the knowledge (with which he was certainly acquainted) that many Muslims who traded across the desert, or who went on the pilgrimage to Mecca from the West African Sudan, were Africans he would describe as black,

carrying the cultural heritage of West Africa with them. Black African rulers are reported as having made the pilgrimage to Mecca as early as the eleventh century. Mansa Musa of Mali traveled from West Africa to Cairo and then to Mecca in the fourteenth century with a retinue reported to number 60,000. Even though the correct number is likely to be smaller, there is no question that thousands of Africans crossed the desert to visit the world of the Mediterranean and the Red Sea, and others (from the East Coast) crossed the Indian Ocean to reach the Persian Gulf and India.

Finally, it appears to be the case that Braudel's characterization of the difference between "Black Africa" and "White Africa" is based on his understanding of race. In *Grammaire des civilisations* he acknowledges that Ethiopia (in this case Christian) was a civilization, explaining that it "undeniably possess white ethnic elements, and is founded on a *métisse* population, very different, however, from those of the true Melano-Africans." At times he denies the existence of facts in order to preserve the clear distinction between a Black Africa that is uncivilized and a White Africa that is civilized. In a 1963 book he acknowledges that the region near the Gulf of Guinea was urbanized very early. But then in a later book which argues that towns were one of the distinguishing marks of civilization, he writes that there were no towns on the fringes of the Gulf of Guinea....

Because historians have come to a fuller understanding of African urbanization, and of African initiatives in intercontinental exchange, it is now easy to see the weakness of this small part of Braudel's work. A central question remains, however: whether his unidirectional interpretation of Africa is merely an unfortunate idiosyncracy of an otherwise great historian, or whether it is a sign of deeper problems in the way many historians construct their narratives....

A reading of McNeill, Braudel, Bennassar and Chaunu, Wolf, Curtin, and others points to a larger and more general development: that the emergence of African history (and of Asian and Latin American history) has changed our understanding of general history, and of Europe's place in the world, in profound ways. It is no longer possible to defend the position that historical processes among non-European peoples can be seen as the consequence of all-encompassing influences emerging from a dominant European center. This shift in our understanding is uncomfortable for those who see history as the spread of civilization from a European center, and it is equally uncomfortable for those who sketch history in terms of an all-determining system of capitalist exploitation.

The shift away from historical narratives that originate in Europe has been both accompanied and enabled by innovations in methods for constructing knowledge about people who had previously been left out of academic histories. These renovated methods, some of which achieved their fullest early development among historians of Africa, include oral history, historical archaeology, and historical linguistics, as well as anthropologically informed historical analysis. The new methods and modes of interpretation made it possible for scholars to approach the history of non-literate people, and in many cases powerless ones, without departing from the accepted critical canons of historical research. Scholars were able to know histories they had never known before. The consequences were, once again, paradoxical. These significant advances in the range and quality of historical knowledge helped to shake historians' faith in the quality of their knowledge. To glimpse whole regions of history previously unknown, to see the dark side of the moon, inevitably shook scholars' faith in their own omniscience.

The methodological advances were not narrowly African ones. They had an impact in a number of historical fields, but many of them emerged with particular clarity and power amongst historians of Africa. The impact of oral history was bound to be great in studies of sub-Saharan Africa, where many societies were ideally suited for this form of research: their people transmitted substantial bodies of knowledge from one generation to the next and sustained complex political and economic hierarchies, all without practicing writing. Oral traditions were still alive (in many cases *are* still alive) when the historians of the 1960s and 1970s went about their work. Unlike Latin America, where the colonial period had begun several centuries earlier, it was only in the late nineteenth century that most of sub-Saharan Africa experienced conquest. Before this Europeans did not, in most cases, intervene directly in the transmission of knowledge....

The amplified range of methods employed by African historians has proven useful not only in societies that lack writing, but also for studying the underclasses of societies with a considerable range of literacy. Historians have used these amplified methods to construct rich accounts of the African majority in colonial society and especially to bring us magnificent accounts of peasant resistance to colonial domination....

The sense that we can no longer tell history as a single story, from a single consistent point of view or from a unified perspective, strikes deep resonances in recent social and cultural thought. Michel Foucault wrote, in *Language, Countermemory, Practice*, that the idea of the whole society "arose in the Western world, in this highly individualized historical development that culminates in capitalism. To speak of the 'whole of society' apart from the only form it has ever taken is to transform our past into a dream." The very categories by which we understand universal experience originate in the particular experience of the core of the capitalist world.

This is the same lesson taught by an examination of African history: the categories which are ostensibly universal are in fact particular, and they refer to the experience of modern Europe. That we have learned this lesson in two different ways—through philosophically based writings on Europe and through histories of non-Europeans—forces us to ask about the relationship between the two sets of developments. A central question which has not yet been fully addressed is the relationship between the crisis of historical representation that came about when historians began to hear the voices of those who had been voiceless, and the more general epistemological crisis affecting all the social sciences and humanities....

We are left, then, with an enormously expanded subject matter, with historical narratives originating in Africa that must be given full weight alongside those originating in Europe. We have seen, however, that this is not a simple process of adding one more body of knowledge to our fund, of increasing the balance in the account. The need for historians to hear African voices originates with the same impulse as the need to hear the voices that had been silent within European history. Since that is so, it hardly feels satisfying to listen to a single authoritative African voice, leaving others silent, or to read African texts without seeking marks of power, or without asking about the authority of the historian (African or American, European or Asian) who presumes to represent history. Historians have no choice but to open up world history to African history, but having done so, they find that the problems have just begun.

POSTSCRIPT

Did the Rise of the West Define the Modern World?

Changes in the historical profession in the last quarter-century can be seen clearly in the 25th anniversary edition of McNeill's *Rise of the West*. In a retrospective essay entitled "The Rise of the West After Twenty-Five Years," McNeill states that the first edition of his book was influenced by the postwar imperial mood in the United States, which was then at the apex of its power and ability to influence world affairs. He now urges historians to "construct a clear and elegant discourse with which to present the different facets and interacting flows of human history as we now understand them." McNeill expands the focus of the world's history in two published lecture series: *The Human Condition: An Ecological and Historical View* (Princeton University Press, 1979) and *Polyethnicity and National Unity in World History* (University of Toronto Press, 1985). The rise in the number of world civilization courses in college curricula (replacing the traditional Western civilization ones) is a notable part of the fruits of new historical labors.

The work of the Annales School of historical writing, with its effect of broadening the scope of historical research by encouraging the use of unorthodox and unconventional sources, played a major role in the creation of the multidirectional view of world history. Fernand Braudel's *Civilization and Capitalism, Fifteenth–Eighteenth Centuries, vol.3, The Perspective of the World* (University of California Press, 1992) has been instrumental in making these changes possible. In *Europe and the People Without History* (University of California Press, 1982), Eric Wolf seeks to present a history of the modern world from the perspective of "the people without history"—those whose stories have not yet received adequate historical coverage.

The future is likely to see a rapid increase in the number of works relating to the creation of a new world history—a history that is suited to the needs of a new multicultural, civilizational world.

ISSUE 2

Was the Scientific Revolution Revolutionary?

YES: Herbert Butterfield, from *The Origins of Modern Science, 1300–1800*, rev. ed. (Free Press, 1957)

NO: Steven Shapin, from *The Scientific Revolution* (University of Chicago Press, 1996)

ISSUE SUMMARY

YES: Historian of ideas Herbert Butterfield argues that the late sixteenth and early seventeenth centuries witnessed a radical break with the past and the emergence of dramatically new ways of understanding both knowledge and the world—in short, a Scientific Revolution.

NO: Professor of sociology and historian of science Steven Shapin questions the idea of a Scientific Revolution, suggesting that there was no philosophical break with the past and rejecting the existence of a single event that might be called a Scientific Revolution.

When you open a world history or Western civilization textbook, you will likely find that it is conveniently divided into chapters and units with titles that mark the major turning points of history. One of those titles is likely to be "The Scientific Revolution." Known as *periodization*, this tendency of historians to interpretatively group events has recently been subjected to reappraisal. If "where you stand determines what you see," then the very act of labeling periods of history makes judgments about what is important and valuable. Traditional schemes of periodization, for instance, have taken the experiences of white men as the standard and ignored the often quite different lives of women and minorities. However, if only the concerns of the powerful provide the interpretation of historical significance, then much of history will be left out.

The assumption behind periodization is that there are moments when the path of history is rerouted, when a sharp break with the past leads to a new kind of experience or a new way of understanding the world. One of the questions historians must ask, therefore, is whether a particular event or series of events represents continuity with the past or discontinuity from it. Traditional periodization has seen the Scientific Revolution —a period in the late sixteenth and early seventeenth centuries in which the medieval Aristotelian model of scientific explanation was largely abandoned in favor of modern scientific methods—as a classic example of discontinuity, or as a sharp break with the medieval past and the ushering in of the modern world. Recently, however, historians have taken a fresh look at this period and wondered how scientific and how revolutionary it actually was.

A danger historians must also remain alert to is called *presentism*, the tendency to judge and interpret the past by the standards and concerns of the present. From the perspective of the late twentieth century, for example, we might be tempted to view the Industrial Revolution positively because it made it possible for backbreaking labor to be accomplished through the power of machines. People living through what we have come to call the Industrial Revolution, by contrast, might have focused on the negative consequences: the breakup of the family, as individuals left the home to do wage work, and the substitution of the factory for the productive unit in the home. The questions we must ask ourselves are these: Did the people living in the seventeenth century think that something revolutionary was going on? And how much of a break with the past did the scientific discoveries represent?

For Herbert Butterfield there is no question that a Scientific Revolution occurred, even if that fact did not become obvious to historians until the twentieth century. In the following selection, he contends that there is a discrete entity called science and that scientists such as Francis Bacon and philosophers such as René Descartes broke with medieval Christendom to create the modern world. A strong sense of discontinuity with the past leads Butterfield to rate the Scientific Revolution as one of the strongest turning points in the periodization of world history.

Steven Shapin, in response, begins with a bold statement: "There was no such thing as the Scientific Revolution." Reflecting a postmodern view of the world, Shapin questions whether or not it is even possible to speak about an "essence" of something called "science." Instead of a single, discrete entity, he sees a wide variety of ways of understanding, explaining, and controlling the natural world. If we list the characteristics of the so-called revolution, Shapin believes, we will find that the experimental method, mathematical approaches, and even mechanical conceptions of nature were both advocated and rejected by people who thought of themselves as scientists. Furthermore, Shapin sees continuity with the medieval past rather than a radical break from it.

Both historians agree that some people living at the time certainly thought of themselves as doing something revolutionary. The question seems to be whether or not most people, even most educated people, shared the beliefs of this tiny minority. Is it possible for the world to be transformed in a dramatic way at any single moment in time?

YES

Herbert Butterfield

THE ORIGINS OF MODERN SCIENCE, 1300–1800

BACON AND DESCARTES

It is comparatively easy for people today to accommodate their minds to changes that may take place in upper regions of the different sciences—changes which from year to year may add further weight to the curriculum of the undergraduate student of the subject. It is not clear what the patriarchs of our generation would do, however, if we were faced with such a tearing-up of the roots of science that we had to wipe out as antiquated and useless the primary things said about the universe at the elementary school—if we had even to invert our attitudes, and deal, for example, with the whole question of local motion by picking up the opposite end of the stick. The early seventeenth century was more conscious than we ourselves (in our capacity as historians) of the revolutionary character of the moment that had now been reached. While everything was in the melting-pot—the older order undermined but the new scientific system unachieved—the conflict was bitterly exasperated. Men were actually calling for a revolution—not merely for an explanation of existing anomalies but for a new science and a new method. Programmes of the revolutionary movement were put forward, and it is clear that some men were highly conscious of the predicament in which the world now found itself. They seemed to be curiously lacking in discernment in one way, however, for they tended to believe that the scientific revolution could be carried out entirely in a single lifetime. It was a case of changing one lantern-slide of the universe for another, in their opinion—establishing a new system to take the place of Aristotle's. Gradually they found that it would need not merely one generation but perhaps two to complete the task. By the close of the seventeenth century they had come to see that they had opened the way to an indefinitely expanding future, and that the sciences were only in their cradle still.

Before the seventeenth century had opened, the general state of knowledge in regard to the physical universe had been conducive to the production of a number of speculative systems—these not founded upon scientific enquiry

From Herbert Butterfield, *The Origins of Modern Science, 1300–1800*, rev. ed. (Free Press, 1957). Copyright © 1957 by G. Bell and Sons, Ltd. Reprinted by permission of Simon & Schuster.

as a rule, but generally compounded out of ingredients taken from classical antiquity. Already in the sixteenth century, also, attention had been directed to the question of a general scientific method, and in the seventeenth century this problem of method came to be one of the grand preoccupations, not merely of the practising scientist, but, at a higher level, amongst the general thinkers and philosophers. The principal leaders in this seventeenth-century movement were Francis Bacon in the first quarter of the century, who glorified the inductive method and sought to reduce it to a set of regulations; and Descartes, whose work belongs chiefly to the second quarter of the century and who differed from Bacon not only in his glorification of mathematics as the queen of the sciences, but in the emphasis which he placed on a deductive and philosophical mode of reasoning, which he claimed to have screwed up to such a degree of tightness that it possessed all the discipline and certainty of mathematical reasoning. In the time of Newton and well into the eighteenth century, there was a grand controversy between an English school, which was popularly identified with the empirical method, and a French school, which glorified Descartes and came to be associated rather with the deductive method. In the middle of the eighteenth century, however, the French, with a charm that we must describe as Mediterranean, not only submitted to the English view of the matter, but in their famous *Encyclopédie* made even too ample a return, placing Bacon on a pedestal higher perhaps than any that had been given him before. It would appear that their excess of graciousness or charity brought some confusion into historical science at a later stage in the story.

Attacks on Aristotle had been increasingly common and sometimes exceedingly bitter in the sixteenth century. In 1543—a year which we have already seen to be so important in connection with Copernicus and Vesalius as well as the revival of Archimedes—Pierre Ramus produced his famous *Animadversions on Aristotle*. This work, which was known to Francis Bacon, and which attacked Aristotle without ever really understanding him, proposed an alternative method which was rather that of a humanist and professor of Belles Lettres—namely, studying nature through the best writers, and then applying deductive and syllogistic procedures to the result. In 1581 another writer, François Sanchez, produced a further attack on Aristotle, and more particularly on the modern followers of Aristotle—a work which provides a remarkable anticipation of Descartes. He said:

> I questioned the learned men of bygone centuries; then I consulted those who were my contemporaries... but none of their replies was satisfactory.... So I turned in upon myself & put everything to doubt, as though I had never been told anything by anybody. I began to examine things myself in order to discover the true way of gaining knowledge—Hence the thesis which is the starting-point of my reflections: the more I think, the more I doubt.

He attacked the syllogistic reasoning of the prevalent Aristotelian school, because it turned men away from the study of reality and encouraged them to play a sophistical game of verbal subtlety. He promised to expound the true method of science, but in the fifty years of life that were left to him he never fulfilled the promise. One participant in the controversies over scientific method, Everard

Digby, was teaching Logic in the University of Cambridge when Francis Bacon was there in his youth; and a German scholar has shown that at certain points Bacon appears to have followed the ideas of this man.

Bacon held that if Adam, owing to the Fall, had lost for the human race that domination over the created world which it had originally been designed to possess, still there was a subordinate command over nature, available if men worked sufficiently hard to secure it, though this had been thrown away by human folly. There had been only three short periods of genuine scientific progress throughout the whole course of human history, he said—one in Greek times, one in the Roman period, and the third which was being enjoyed in the seventeenth century. In each of the two ancient periods the era of scientific progress had been confined to two hundred years. The earlier Greek philosophers had set the course of enquiry on the right lines, but Plato and Aristotle had supervened, and they had come to prevail precisely because, being of light weight, they had managed to ride much farther down upon the stream of time. They had survived the storms of the Barbarian Invasions precisely because they had been shallow and buoyant, and Aristotle, in particular, had owed his remarkable sway in the world to the fact that, like the Ottoman sultans, he had pursued the policy of destroying all rivals. As for the scholastics of the middle ages, they had had "subtle and strong capacities, abundance of leisure, and but small variety of reading, their minds being shut up in a few authors"; and therefore they had "with infinite agitation of wit, spun out of a small quantity of matter those laborious webs

of learning which are extant in their books." Bacon was impressed by the fact that scientific knowledge had made such extraordinarily little progress since the days of antiquity. He begins by saying that men ought to "throw aside all thought of philosophy, or at least to expect but little and poor fruit from it, until an approved and careful natural and Experimental History be prepared and constructed."

For to what purpose are these brain-creations and idle display of power.... All these invented systems of the universe, each according to his own fancy [are] like so many arguments of plays... every one philosophises out of the cells of his own imagination, as out of Plato's cave.

He uses the term "history" in the sense that we have in mind when we speak of natural history, and he regards it as comprising a collection of data, the fruits of enquiry.

He believed that many men had been led away by allowing their scientific work to become entangled in a search for final causes, which really belonged rather to philosophy, and which he said corrupted the sciences, except those relating to the intercourse of man with man. In education he thought that scholars were introduced too early to logic and rhetoric, which were the cream of the sciences since they arranged and methodised the subject-matter of all the others. To apply the juvenile mind to these before it had been confronted with the subject-matter of the other sciences was like painting and measuring the wind, he said—on the one hand it degraded logic into childish sophistry, on the other hand it had the effect of making the more concrete sciences superficial. In his reaction against the older ways of discussing science, Bacon carried the attack beyond the bounds of prudence on occasion—denying the value of syllogistic modes of reasoning in a way that the modern philosopher would disapprove of; though the general line of attack was understandable, and very useful in view of the situation of things at that time. Bacon wanted men to close in on nature and get to grips with her, bringing their minds to mix in its actual operations. "The secrets of nature," he said, "betray themselves more readily when tormented by art than when left to their own course." "It is best to consider matter, its conformation, and the changes of that conformation, its own action, and the law of this action in motion." He did not support a dead kind of empiricism; the empirics, he said, were like ants merely heaping up a collection of data. The natural philosophers still generally current in the world, however, were rather like spiders spinning their webs out of their own interior. He thought that the scientists ought to take up an intermediate position, like that of the bees, which extracted matter from the flowers and then re-fashioned it by their own efforts. Existing interpretations of nature, he said, were generally "founded on too narrow a basis of experiment." "In any case," he insisted, "the present method of experiment is blind and stupid"—men did it as though they were schoolboys engaged "as it were in sport." He talked of "desultory, ill-combined experiment." The alchemists, he said, had theoretical preconceptions which hindered them from either carrying out their experiments along useful lines or extracting anything important from their results. Men in general glanced too hastily at the result of an experiment,

and then imagined that the rest could be done by sheer contemplation; or they would fly off into the skies with a hasty first impression and attempt to make this square with the vulgar notions already existing in their minds. Even Gilbert working on the magnet had no unity or order in his experiments—the only unity in his treatise lay in the fact that he had been ready to try out anything that there was to try out with a magnet.

Now it was Bacon's firm principle that if men wanted to achieve anything new in the world, it was of no use attempting to reach it on any ancient method—they must realise that new practices and policies would be necessary. He stressed above all the need for the direction of experiments—an end to the mere haphazard experimenting—and he insisted that something far more subtle and far-reaching could be achieved by the proper organisation of experiments. It is quite clear that he realised how science could be brought to a higher power altogether by being transported away from that ordinary world of common-sense phenomena in which so much of the discussion had hitherto been carried on. He insisted on the importance of the actual recording of experiments, a point which, as we have already seen, was now coming to be of some significance. He urged that experimenters in different fields should get together, because they would knock sparks off one another; and things done in one field would give hints to people working in another field. In this sense he anticipated the point of Professor Whitehead who shows how, precisely in this period, the knowledge of several different branches of science at once might have an enriching effect on each. Also, suggestions which are scattered in various parts of Bacon's work seem to have served as an inspiration to some of the men who founded the Royal Society....

PLACE OF SCIENTIFIC REVOLUTION IN HISTORY

... The changes which took place in the history of thought in this period, however, are not more remarkable than the changes in life and society. It has long been our tendency to push back the origins of both the industrial revolution and the so-called agrarian revolution of the eighteenth century, and though ... we can trace back the origin of anything as far as we like, it is towards the end of the seventeenth century that the changes are becoming palpable. The passion to extend the scientific method to every branch of thought was at least equalled by the passion to make science serve the cause of industry and agriculture, and it was accompanied by a sort of technological fervour. Francis Bacon had always laid stress on the immense utilitarian possibilities of science, the advantages beyond all dreams that would come from the control of nature; and it is difficult, even in the early history of the Royal Society, to separate the interest shown in the cause of pure scientific truth from the curiosity in respect of useful inventions on the one part, or the inclination to dabble in fables and freakishness on the other. It has become a debatable question how far the direction of scientific interest was itself affected by technical needs or preoccupations in regard to shipbuilding and other industries; but the Royal Society followed Galileo in concerning itself, for example, with the important question of the mode of discovering longitude at sea. Those who wish to trace the development of the steam-engine will find that it is a story which really begins to be vivid and lively in this period. Apart from such developments, the possibilities of scientific experiment were likely themselves to be limited until certain forms of production and technique had been elaborated in society generally. Indeed, the scientific, the industrial and the agrarian revolutions form such a system of complex and interrelated changes, that in the lack of a microscopic examination we have to heap them all together as aspects of a general movement, which by the last quarter of the seventeenth century was palpably altering the face of the earth. The hazard consists not in putting all these things together and rolling them into one great bundle of complex change, but in thinking that we know how to disentangle them—what we see is the total intricate network of changes, and it is difficult to say that any one of these was the simple result of the scientific revolution itself....

It is always easy for a later generation to think that its predecessor was foolish, and it may seem shocking to state that even after the first World War good historians could write the history of the nineteenth century with hardly a hint of the importance of Socialism, hardly a mention of Karl Marx—a fact which we should misinterpret unless we took it as a reminder of the kind of faults to which all of us are prone. Because we have a fuller knowledge of afterevents, we today can see the nineteenth century differently; and it is not we who are under an optical illusion—reading the twentieth century back unfairly into the nineteenth—when we say that the student of the last hundred years is missing a decisive factor if he overlooks the rise of Socialism. A man of insight could have recognised the importance of the phenomenon long before the end of the nineteenth century. But we, who have seen the implications worked out in the events of our time, need no insight to recognise the importance of this whole aspect of the story.

Something similar to this is true when we of the year 1957 take our perspective of the scientific revolution—we are in a position to see its implications at the present day much more clearly than the men who flourished fifty or even twenty years before us. And, once again, it is not we who are under an optical illusion-reading the present back into the past—for the things that have been revealed in the 1950s merely bring out more vividly the vast importance of the turn which the world took three hundred years ago, in the days of the scientific revolution. We can see why our predecessors were less conscious of the significance of the seventeenth century— why they talked so much more of the Renaissance or the eighteenth-century Enlightenment, for example—because in this as in so many other cases we can now discern those surprising overlaps and time-lags which so often disguise the direction things are taking. Our Graeco-Roman roots and our Christian heritage were so profound—so central to all our thinking—that it has required centuries of pulls and pressures, and almost a conflict of civilisations in our very midst, to make it clear that the centre had long ago shifted. At one time the effects of the scientific revolution, and the changes contemporary with it, would be masked by the persistence of our classical traditions and education, which still decided so much of the character of the eighteenth century in England and in France, for example. At another time these effects would be concealed through that popular attachment to religion which

so helped to form the character of even the nineteenth century in this country. The very strength of our conviction that ours was a Graeco-Roman civilisation— the very way in which we allowed the art-historians and the philologists to make us think that this thing which we call "the modern world" was the product of the Renaissance—the inelasticity of our historical concepts, in fact—helped to conceal the radical nature of the changes that had taken place and the colossal possibilities that lay in the seeds sown by the seventeenth century. The seventeenth century, indeed, did not merely bring a new factor into history, in the way we often assume—one that must just be added, so to speak, to the other permanent factors. The new factor immediately began to elbow the other ones away, pushing them from their central position. Indeed, it began immediately to seek control of the rest, as the apostles of the new movement had declared their intention of doing from the very start. The result was the emergence of a kind of Western civilisation which when transmitted to Japan operates on tradition there as it operates on tradition here—dissolving it and having eyes for nothing save a future of brave new worlds. It was a civilisation that could cut itself away from the Graeco-Roman heritage in general, away from Christianity itself—only too confident in its power to exist independent of anything of the kind. We know now that what was emerging towards the end of the seventeenth century was a civilisation exhilaratingly new perhaps, but strange as Nineveh and Babylon. That is why, since the rise of Christianity, there is no landmark in history that is worthy to be compared with this.

NO

Steven Shapin

THE SCIENTIFIC REVOLUTION

THE SCIENTIFIC REVOLUTION: THE HISTORY OF A TERM

There was no such thing as the Scientific Revolution, and this [selection is from] a book about it. Some time ago, when the academic world offered more certainty and more comforts, historians announced the real existence of a co-herent, cataclysmic, and climactic event that fundamentally and irrevocably changed what people knew about the natural world and how they secured proper knowledge of that world. It was the moment at which the world was made modern, it was a Good Thing, and it happened sometime during the period from the late sixteenth to the early eighteenth century. In 1943 the French historian Alexandre Koyré celebrated the conceptual changes at the heart of the Scientific Revolution as "the most profound revolution achieved or suffered by the human mind" since Greek antiquity. It was a revolution so profound that human culture "for centuries did not grasp its bearing or meaning; which, even now, is often misvalued and misunderstood." A few years later the English historian Herbert Butterfield famously judged that the Scientific Revolution "outshines everything since the rise of Christianity and reduces the Renaissance and Reformation to the rank of mere episodes.... [It is] the real origin both of the modern world and of the modern mentality." It was, moreover, construed as a conceptual revolution, a fundamental reorder-ing of our ways of *thinking* about the natural. In this respect, a story about the Scientific Revolution might be adequately told through an account of radical changes in the fundamental categories of thought. To Butterfield, the mental changes making up the Scientific Revolution were equivalent to "putting on a new pair of spectacles." And to A. Rupert Hall it was nothing less than "an *a priori* redefinition of the objects of philosophical and scientific inquiry."

This conception of the Scientific Revolution is now encrusted with tradi-tion. Few historical episodes present themselves as more substantial or more self-evidently worthy of study. There is an established place for accounts of the Scientific Revolution in the Western liberal curriculum, and this [se-lection] is an attempt to fill that space economically and to invite further curiosity about the making of early modern science. Nevertheless, like many twentieth-century "traditions," that contained in the notion of the Scientific Revolution is not nearly as old as we might think. The phrase "the Scientific Revolution" was probably coined by Alexandre Koyré in 1939, and it first became a hook title in A. Rupert Hall's *The Scientific Revolution* of 1954. Before that time there was no event to be studied in the liberal curriculum, nor any discrete object of historical inquiry, called the Scientific Revolution. Although many seventeenth-century practitioners expressed their intention of bringing about radical intellectual change, the people who are said to have made the revolution used no such term to refer to what they were doing.

From antiquity through the early modern period, a "revolution" invoked the idea of a periodically recurring cycle. In Copernicus's new astronomy of the mid-sixteenth century, for example, the planets completed their revolutions round the sun, while references to political revolutions gestured at the notion of ebbs and flows or cycles—fortune's wheel—in human affairs. The idea of revolution as a radical and irreversible reordering developed together with linear, unidirectional conceptions of time. In this newer conception revolution was not recurrence but its reverse, the bringing about of a new state of affairs that the world had never witnessed before and might never witness again. Not only this notion of revolution but also the beginnings of an idea of revolution in science date from the eighteenth-century writings of French Enlightenment philosophes who liked to portray themselves, and their disciplines, as radical subverters of ancien régime culture. (Some... seventeenth-century writers... saw themselves not as bringing about totally new states of affairs but as restoring or purifying old ones.) The notion of a revolution as epochal and irreversible change, it is possible, was first applied in a systematic way to events in science and only later to political events. In just this sense, the first revolutions may have been scientific, and the "American," "French," and "Russian Revolutions" are its progeny.

As our understanding of science in the seventeenth century has changed in recent years, so historians have become increasingly uneasy with the very idea of "the Scientific Revolution." Even the legitimacy of each word making up that phrase has been individually contested. Many historians are now no longer satisfied that there was any singular and discrete event, localized in time and space, that can be pointed to as "the" Scientific Revolution. Such historians now reject even the notion that there was any single coherent cultural entity called "science" in the seventeenth century to undergo revolutionary change. There was, rather, a diverse array of cultural practices aimed at understanding, explaining, and controlling the natural world, each with different characteristics and each experiencing different modes of change. We are now much more dubious of claims that there is anything like "a scientific method"—a coherent, universal, and efficacious set of procedures for making scientific knowledge—and still more skeptical of stories that locate its origin in the seventeenth century, from which time it has been unproblematically passed on to us. And many historians do not now accept that the changes wrought on scientific beliefs and practices during the seventeenth century were as "revolutionary" as has been widely portrayed. The continuity of seventeenth-century natural philosophy with its medieval past is now routinely asserted, while talk of "delayed" eighteenth- and nineteenth-century revolutions in chemistry and biology followed hard upon historians' identification of "the" original Scientific Revolution.

WHY WRITE ABOUT THE SCIENTIFIC REVOLUTION?

There are still other reasons for historians' present uneasiness with the category of the Scientific Revolution as it has been customarily construed. First, historians have in recent years become dissatisfied with the traditional manner of treating ideas as if they floated freely in conceptual space. Although previous accounts framed the Scientific Revolution in terms of autonomous ideas or disembodied mentalities, more recent versions have insisted on the importance of situating ideas in their wider cultural and social context. We now hear more than we used to about the relations between the scientific changes of the seventeenth century and changes in religious, political, and economic patterns. More fundamentally, some historians now wish to understand the concrete human *practices* by which ideas or concepts are made. What did people *do* when they made or confirmed an observation, proved a theorem, performed an experiment? An account of the Scientific Revolution as a history of free-floating concepts is a very different animal from a history of concept-making practices. Finally, historians have become much more interested in the "who" of the Scientific Revolution. What kinds of people wrought such changes? Did everyone believe as they did, or only a very few? And if only a very few took part in these changes, in what sense, if at all, can we speak of the Scientific Revolution as

effecting massive changes in how "we" view the world, as the moment when modernity was made, for "us"? The cogency of such questions makes for problems in writing as unreflectively as we used to about the Scientific Revolution. Responding to them means that we need an account of changes in early modern science appropriate for our less confident, but perhaps more intellectually curious, times.

Yet despite these legitimate doubts and uncertainties there remains a sense in which it is possible to write about the Scientific Revolution unapologetically and in good faith. There are two major considerations to bear in mind here. The first is that many key figures in the late sixteenth and seventeenth centuries vigorously expressed *their* view that they were proposing some very new and very important changes in knowledge of natural reality and in the practices by which legitimate knowledge was to be secured, assessed, and communicated. They identified *themselves* as "moderns" set against "ancient" modes of thought and practice. Our sense of radical change afoot comes substantially from them (and those who were the object of their attacks), and is not simply the creation of mid-twentieth-century historians. So we can say that the seventeenth century witnessed some self-conscious and large-scale attempts to change belief, and ways of securing belief, about the natural world. And a book about the Scientific Revolution can legitimately tell a story about those attempts, whether or not they succeeded, whether or not they were contested in the local culture, whether or not they were wholly coherent.

But why do we tell *these* stories instead of others? If different sorts of seventeenth-century people believed different things about the world, how do we assemble our cast of characters and associated beliefs? Some "natural philosophers," for example, advocated rational theorizing, while others pushed a program of relatively atheoretical fact collecting and experimentation. Mathematical physics was, for example, a very different sort of practice from botany. There were importantly different versions of what it was to do astronomy and believe as an astronomer believed; the relations between the "proper sciences" of astronomy and chemistry and the "pseudosciences" of astrology and alchemy were intensely problematic; and even the category of "nature" as the object of inquiry was understood in radically different ways by different sorts of practitioners. This point cannot be stressed too strongly. The cultural practices subsumed in the category of the Scientific Revolution—however it has been construed—are not coextensive with early modern, or seventeenth-century, science. Historians differ about which practices were "central" to the Scientific Revolution, and participants themselves argued about which practices produced genuine knowledge and which had been fundamentally reformed.

More fundamentally for criteria of selection, it ought to be understood that "most people"—even most educated people—in the seventeenth century did not believe what expert scientific practitioners believed, and the sense in which "people's" thought about the world was revolutionized at that time is very limited. There should be no doubt whatever that one could write a convincing history of seventeenth-century thought about nature without even *mentioning* the Scientific Revolution as traditionally construed.

The very idea of the Scientific Revolution, therefore, is at least partly an expression of "our" interest in our ancestors, where "we" are late twentieth-century scientists and those for whom what they believe counts as truth about the natural world. And this interest provides the second legitimate justification for writing about the Scientific Revolution. Historians of science have now grown used to condemning "present-oriented" history, rightly saying that it often distorts our understanding of what the past was like in its own terms. Yet there is absolutely no reason we should not want to know how we got from there to here, who the ancestors were, and what the lineage is that connects us to the past. In this sense a story about the seventeenth-century Scientific Revolution can be an account of those changes that we think led on—never directly or simply, to be sure—to certain features of the present in which, for certain purposes, we happen to be interested. To do this would be an expression of just the same sort of legitimate historical interest displayed by Darwinian evolutionists telling stories about those branches of the tree of life that led to human beings—without assuming in any way that such stories are adequate accounts of what life was like hundreds of thousands of years ago. There is nothing at all wrong about telling such stories, though one must always be careful not to claim too much scope for them. Stories about the ancestors as ancestors are not likely to be sensitive accounts of how it was in the past: the lives and thoughts of Galileo, Descartes, or Boyle were hardly typical of seventeenth-century Italians, Frenchmen, or Englishmen, and telling stories about them geared solely to their ancestral role in formulating the currently accepted law of free fall, the optics of the rainbow, or the ideal gas law is not likely to capture very much about the meaning and significance of their own careers and projects in the seventeenth century.

The past is not transformed into the "modern world" at any single moment: we should never be surprised to find that seventeenth-century scientific practitioners often had about them as much of the ancient as the modern; their notions had to be successively transformed and redefined by generations of thinkers to become "ours." And finally, the people, the thoughts, and the practices we tell stories about as "ancestors," or as the beginnings of our lineage, always reflect some present-day interest. That we tell stories about Galileo, Boyle, Descartes, and Newton reflects something about our late twentieth-century scientific beliefs and what we value about those beliefs. For different purposes we could trace aspects of the modern world back to philosophers "vanquished" by Galileo, Boyle, Descartes, and Newton, and to views of nature and knowledge very different from those elaborated by our officially sanctioned scientific ancestors. For still other purposes we could make much of the fact that most seventeenth-century people had never heard of our scientific ancestors and probably entertained beliefs about the natural world very different from those of our chosen forebears. Indeed, the overwhelming majority of seventeenth-century people did not live in Europe, did not know that they lived in "the seventeenth century," and were not aware that a Scientific Revolution was happening. The half of the European population that was female was in a position to participate in scientific culture scarcely at all, as was that overwhelming majority —of men and women—who were illiter-ate or otherwise disqualified from entering the venues of formal learning.

SOME HISTORIOGRAPHICAL ISSUES

I mean this [selection] to be historiographically up to date—drawing on some of the most recent historical, sociological, and philosophical engagements with the Scientific Revolution. On the other hand, I do not mean to trouble readers with repeated references to methodological and conceptual debates among academics. This [selection] is not written for professional specialized scholars.... There is no reason to deny that this story about the Scientific Revolution represents a particular point of view, and that, although I help myself freely to the work of many distinguished scholars, its point of view is my own. Other specialists will doubtless disagree with my approach— some vehemently—and a large number of existing accounts do offer a quite different perspective on what is worth telling about the Scientific Revolution. The positions represented here on some recent historiographic issues can be briefly summarized:

1. I *take for granted* that science is a historically situated and social activity and that it is to be understood in relation to the *contexts* in which it occurs. Historians have long argued whether science relates to its historical and social contexts or whether it should be treated in isolation. I shall simply write about seventeenth-century science as if it were a collectively practiced, historically embedded phenomenon, inviting readers to see whether the account is plausible, coherent, and interesting.

2. For a long time, historians' debates over the propriety of a sociological and

a historically "contextual" approach to science seemed to divide practitioners between those who drew attention to what were called "intellectual factors" —ideas, concepts, methods, evidence— and those who stressed "social factors" —forms of organization, political and economic influences on science, and social uses or consequences of science. That now seems to many historians, as it does to me, a rather silly demarcation, and I shall not waste readers' time here in reviewing why those disputes figured so largely in past approaches to the history of early modern science. If science is to be understood as historically situated and in its collective aspect (i.e., sociologically), then that understanding should encompass all aspects of science, its ideas and practices no less than its institutional forms and social uses. Anyone who wants to represent science sociologically cannot simply set aside the body of what the relevant practitioners *knew* and how they went about obtaining that knowledge. Rather, the task for the sociologically minded historian is to display the structure of knowledge making and knowledge holding *as social processes*.

3. A traditional construal of "social factors" (or what is sociological about science) has focused on considerations taken to be "external" to science proper— for example, the use of metaphors from the economy in the development of scientific knowledge or the ideological uses of science in justifying certain sorts of political arrangements. Much fine historical work has been done based on such a construal. However, the identification of what is sociological about science with what is external to science appears to me a curious and a limited way of going on. There is as much "society" inside the scientist's laboratory, and internal to the development of scientific knowledge, as there is "outside." And in fact the very distinction between the social and the political, on the one hand, and "scientific truth," on the other, is partly a cultural product of the period [I discuss]. What is commonsensically thought of as science in the late twentieth century is in some measure a product of the historical episodes we want to understand here. Far from matter-of-factly treating the distinction between the social and the scientific as a resource in telling a historical story, I mean to make it into a topic of inquiry. How and why did we come to think that such a distinction is a matter *of course?*

4. I do not consider that there is anything like an "essence" of seventeenth-century science or indeed of seventeenth-century reforms in science. Consequently there is no single coherent story that could possibly capture all the aspects of science or its changes in which we late twentieth-century moderns might happen to be interested. I can think of no feature of early modern science that has been traditionally identified as its revolutionary essence that did not have significantly variant contemporary forms or that was not subjected to contemporary criticism by practitioners who have also been accounted revolutionary "moderns." ...

* * *

The confrontation over Newton's optical work can stand as an emblem of the fragmented knowledge-making legacies of the seventeenth century. A theoretically cautious and experience-based conception of science was here juxtaposed to one that deployed mathematical as well as experimental tools to claim theoretical certainty. Diffidence was opposed to ambition, respect for the concrete particularities of nature to the quest for universally applicable idealizations, the modesty of the fact gatherer to the pride of the abstracted philosopher. Do you want to capture the essence of nature and command assent to representations of its regularities? Do you want to subject yourself to the discipline of describing, and perhaps generalizing about, the behavior of medium-sized objects actually existing in the world?

Both conceptions of science persist in the late twentieth century, and both can trace elements of their formation back to the seventeenth century. The one is not necessarily to be regarded as a failed version of the other, however much partisans may defend the virtues of their preferred practice and condemn the vices of another. These are, so to speak, different games that natural philosophers might wish to play, and decisions about which game is best are different in kind from decisions about what is a sensible move within a given game: an accurate pass from midfield to the winger in soccer is not a bad jump shot in basketball. In the seventeenth century natural philosophers were confronted with differing repertoires of practical and conceptual skills for achieving various philosophical goals and with choices about which ends they might work to achieve. The goal was always some conception of proper philosophical knowledge about the natural world, though descriptions of what that knowledge looked like and how it was to be secured varied greatly.

POSTSCRIPT

Was the Scientific Revolution Revolutionary?

The question of whether or not the Scientific Revolution was revolutionary is a philosophical as well as a historical one. At issue is how we understand key terms such as *science* and *revolution* as well as how we interpret what philosophers call "epistemology," or knowledge theory. Both historians agree that key people in the past understood that what they were doing represented a break with the past. Where they disagree is over how to evaluate the past in the context of what we know in the present. Butterfield assumes that we can all agree on the meaning of science, but Shapin questions his definition. In the 40 years between Butterfield's and Shapin's books, knowledge theory has changed. Taking apart texts to reveal their hidden meanings has led many to question whether or not it is possible to have a single, universal meaning for a term like *science*. What the word may have meant to people practicing it in the seventeenth century may be worlds away from what it means to people practicing it today. And those of us outside the scientific community in either period generally have even less idea what may be at stake.

Thomas Kuhn, whose widely read book *The Structure of Scientific Revolutions* (University of Chicago Press, 1962, 1970) has shed some light on this controversy, combines continuity with discontinuity. Revolutions, Kuhn contends, are occasional, dramatic breaks from periods of what he calls "normal science," when everyone in the scientific community operates from within an accepted paradigm. Revolutions occur when experiments repeatedly do not yield the expected results or when data do not conform to predicted outcomes. Scientists struggle to make the new material fit the old paradigm; those who challenge the paradigm are marginalized or forced to conform. When it becomes clear that the paradigm has broken down, a new paradigm is accepted. Then everything is explained in terms of the new paradigm. Students are educated in the new paradigm; textbooks are written to reflect it; and research takes it as its starting point. Has the world changed or only our way of explaining it to ourselves?

A selection from Kuhn's book is the concluding essay in Vern L. Bullough, ed., *The Scientific Revolution* (Holt, Rinehart & Winston, 1970). The opening essay is an excerpt from Andrew Dickson White's classic *A History of the Warfare of Science With Theology*, which was first published in 1896. A more modern collection of essays appears in *Reappraisals of the Scientific Revolution* edited by David C. Lindberg and Robert S. Westman (Cambridge University Press, 1990). In it, essays by philosophers of science and historians consider conceptions of science and the relationship between philosophy and science.

ISSUE 3

Did Internal Political Factionalism End Chinese Overseas Expansion in the Fifteenth Century?

YES: Edward L. Dreyer, from *Early Ming China: A Political History, 1355–1435* (Stanford University Press, 1982)

NO: Dun J. Li, from *The Ageless Chinese: A History,* 2d ed. (Charles Scribner's Sons, 1971)

ISSUE SUMMARY

YES: Political and military historian Edward L. Dreyer maintains that the Ming emperor's attempt to balance expansionist aims with Confucian ideals proved incompatible with sustaining the Chinese age of exploration in the fifteenth century.

NO: Dun J. Li, a historian of China, argues that the culture of northern China brought an inevitable end to the remarkable voyages of admiral Cheng Ho.

In 1368 a Chinese peasant led a rebellion that not only captured Beijing, the capital of his Mongol overlord, but also established a new dynasty, the Ming. Considered one of the most brilliant and dynamic periods of Chinese history, the Ming dynasty is best known for its accomplishments in the arts, particularly the ceramics that were created to grace the imperial court. However, from the time of the dynasty's founding to the year 1433, the course of Chinese politics experienced one of its most dramatic and unusual shifts, as intrigue and bureaucracy mixed at the highest levels of imperial government.

Immediately upon taking the throne, the Yung-lo emperor, Zhu Di (1402–1424), began a project to expand the tribute system from its Tang dynasty borders—namely, Tibet, Vietnam, and Korea—to include the rest of Asia and, for all intents and purposes, the rest of the world. This tribute system demanded that foreign nations recognize themselves as vassals to the Chinese ruler and confirm this relationship periodically with substantial payments to the emperor and the exchanging of gifts. At this juncture in history, China was well placed to assert its dominance because Arab international expansion and trade were in decline. Therefore, Zhu Di sponsored the establishment of an imperial navy and merchant fleet consisting of thousands of coastal boats, 400 armed vessels, and another 400 oceangoing ships. Nine of these ocean vessels were the famed "treasure ships," the most technologically advanced sailing ships of the day and four times as large as Christopher Columbus's *Santa Maria*. This fleet was commanded by the celebrated admiral Cheng Ho (Zheng He).

Cheng Ho, a Muslim by birth and faith, represented a particular class of advisers in the Ming court, the eunuchs. These men were taken as war captives when they were very young, castrated, and, if they survived, sent to serve in the capital at the imperial court. They were often trained as military officers or to serve in diplomatic positions on the frontiers of the Chinese Empire. Consequently, they came to exert tremendous influence over policy, especially in foreign affairs. Cheng Ho led the emperor on a course of overseas Chinese expansionism, taking his fleet across the Indian Ocean, up into the Persian Gulf, and even along the coast of East Africa. However, in 1433 the treasure ships and much of the Chinese naval and merchant fleet were dismantled as the Ming court looked inward, emphasizing domestic concerns over the goal of foreign domination.

Why did the voyages of the Chinese treasure ships cease? Had they continued, the course of world history might have been quite different. The rise of Western sea power in the fifteenth century might have taken a different route if a formidable Chinese navy were maintained. Undoubtedly, the answers are complex, varied, and deeply rooted in Chinese cultural attitudes and political rivalries. China was a self-sufficient country with little need for international trade. The ideological and ostentatious motives for the Ming voyages had little to do with commerce and materialism. At the same time, anticommercialist attitudes were fostered by the eunuchs' chief rivals for the imperial ear, the Confucian bureaucrats.

The Ming emperors reestablished the civil service entry examination system that had been discarded by the Mongols. This system opened up the bureaucracy to highly educated scholars versed in the Confucian classics, allowing them to gain great power and influence both locally and imperially. It is clear that the Confucians felt threatened by the gains made by the eunuchs during the early years of the Ming dynasty and that they desired to undercut the eunuchs' increasing influence. Was it political factionalism that destroyed the Chinese opportunity to dominate world trade, or did the Confucians simply reflect inherent cultural prejudices that had already doomed Chinese expansion? This question is taken up by Edward L. Dreyer and Dun J. Li in the following selections.

YES

Edward L. Dreyer

YUNG-LO: EMPEROR ON HORSEBACK, 1402–1424

[The year 1403 was] the first year of Yung-lo ("Perpetual Happiness"). Emperor Yung-lo's previous experience had been as a soldier, and this was the life he preferred, but political considerations kept him in Nanking for several years. As ruler, Yung-lo dealt both ruthlessly and subtly with individuals he considered enemies, but he tried to conciliate the classes they represented. Although the individual ministers and generals who had supported Chien-wen mostly either suffered execution or committed suicide while facing criminal charges, civil officials and military officers as classes benefited from his continuation of the examinations and revival of the military nobility. The princes lost their troop commands, but they regained their titles and properties.

Yung-lo attempted to live up to both the Chinese and the Mongol versions of the imperial ideal. The former involved the enhancement of the Confucian ideal through government-sponsored literary projects and the conscientious administration of famine relief and the criminal law. The latter required the military conquest of adjoining countries and the opening of diplomatic and commercial relationships with other lands. Yung-lo's reign recalls Qubilai's in its outstanding events: the conquest of the south, the establishment of the capital at Peking, the opening of relations with Japan (peaceful, this time), an ultimately abortive attempt to conquer Vietnam, and naval expeditions to Southeast Asia and the Indian Ocean. But in contrast to the repeated fiascos of Qubilai's reign (the failure to crush Qaidu and the botched invasions of Japan, Vietnam, and Java), Yung-lo was everywhere successful in his projects —or so it seemed when he died (1424), since the collapse of the Chinese position in Vietnam was then still three years in the future.

Nevertheless, Yung-lo was the heir of the native Chinese imperial tradition, and his attempts to follow two paths at the same time resulted in hopeless contradictions. As a model Confucian emperor, Yung-lo enhanced the position of the civil officials, restoring them to a place in the central government comparable, if not quite equal, to that which they had enjoyed prior to 1380. Moreover, many of the officials whom he favored were distinguished by both scholarship and principle. Naturally they opposed all of his military,

Excerpted from Edward L. Dreyer, *Early Ming China: A Political History, 1355–1435* (Stanford University Press, 1982). Copyright © 1982 by the Board of Trustees of the Leland Stanford Junior University. Reprinted by permission of Stanford University Press. Some notes omitted.

diplomatic, and commercial ventures. He tolerated their criticisms as his father never would have done, occasionally jailing some of them but usually afterwards relenting. Meanwhile, he allowed them to run the government with little imperial supervision, turning the projects connected with his plans of aggrandizement over to eunuchs and generals whom he could trust to carry out his orders. Yung-lo's contradictory objectives thus led to the division of the Ming state into two different sets of institutions: a civil bureaucracy that opposed the emperor's policies and looked to the crown prince to reverse them, and an establishment of eunuchs and military officers that carried out the emperor's policies and was sustained in power only by the emperor's favor. The spectacular achievements of his reign were in conflict with the line of institutional development that he himself promoted, but for the most part his successor was able to reverse the policies the civil officials opposed and embrace without reservation the ideology of the Confucian state....

EUNUCH ADMIRALS AND THE TRIBUTARY TRADE

Yung-lo's military expeditions and his attempt to conquer Vietnam both showed a conception of foreign relations radically different from Hung-wu's. Instead of attempting to preserve Chinese society by sealing it off from both foreign invasion and foreign trade, Yung-lo followed a policy of active counteroffensive. As applied to Southeast Asia, where expectations of a revival of commerce with China had been dashed by Hung-wu in the 1370's, Yung-lo's active policy took the form of naval expeditions led by the eunuch admiral Cheng Ho. On seven oc-

casions between 1405 and 1433 Chinese fleets visited the countries of East and Southeast Asia, and crossed the Indian Ocean to reach Ceylon, the Persian Gulf, and the East Coast of Africa. Although they resorted to force to gain their ends on a few occasions, the Chinese expeditions in general were peaceful, unlike the later Portuguese depredations. The Ming emperor was not interested in conquering or looting the countries reached by his fleet, but rather in exploring and expanding commerce and diplomatic relations within the tribute system. Rumors that Emperor Chien-wen had escaped and fled to Southeast Asia played a part in Yung-lo's decision to launch the expeditions. The geographical knowledge derived from these expeditions was the basis of Chinese understanding of the maritime world until the nineteenth century. The naval expeditions formed the main channel for the promotion of trade with the countries of the south, and tributary trade with Japan also was resumed —at Japanese initiative. For a while the diplomatic and commercial policies forbidden by Hung-wu were revived.

The first of the naval expeditions (1405–7) involved 27,800 men sailing in sixty-two great "treasure ships" (*pao-ch'uan*) of which the largest carried nine masts and were 440 feet in length and 180 feet in the beam. Sailing down the South China Sea, this fleet visited Champa and then Java before going on to Sumatra. There they found that the court and dynasty of Shrivijaya had deserted the harbor of Palembang, partly in response to the difficulties in the Malay world wrought by Hung-wu's policies. The harbor had been taken over by a Chinese pirate leader, Ch'en Tsu-yi, who made a surprise attack on Cheng Ho's ships but was himself captured and later sent to

Nanking and executed. The fleet went on to visit Ceylon and Calicut on the western coast of India. The second expedition (1407–9) visited the same places and also Thailand and Cochin in India.

By the time of the third expedition (1409–11) a regular pattern of visits had been established, with the fleets using Malacca as their base and dividing into squadrons assigned to particular missions. This expedition visited the same places as the previous two, plus Quilon in southwestern India. In Ceylon in 1410, the main body of the expedition ran into trouble. Cheng Ho and his guards were lured into the interior by the Sinhalese king, who demanded exorbitant presents and sent troops to attack the Chinese ships. Undaunted, Cheng Ho pushed on and took the capital, captured the offending monarch, and defeated his army. The king was taken to Nanking and treated kindly there, though the Chinese insisted on his being replaced as ruler by his cousin.

The fourth expedition (1413–15) made stops at the Southeast Asian countries visited previously. At Lambri in northwestern Sumatra, Cheng Ho's troops fought and captured Sekandar, a pretender to the local throne who was dissatisfied with his share of the Chinese gifts. He was sent to Nanking and ultimately executed; this was the last incident involving the use of force in the history of the Ming naval expeditions. However, the main objective of the fourth expedition was the further exploration of the Indian Ocean. The main fleet based itself on Ceylon, and squadrons were sent to Bengal, the Maldives, and throughout the Arabian Sea as far as the sultanate of Ormuz on the Persian Gulf. The prosperity of the many city-states of the Arabian peninsula and the east coast of Africa depended on maritime trade, which in turn depended on normal patterns of West Asian commerce that had not yet recovered from the disruptions caused by the career of Tamerlane. The news of the Chinese armada in Indian waters caused the rulers of these city-states to apprehend danger even as they hoped for an expansion of trade. Their response was to send ambassadors, who converged upon Nanking in a swarm in 1416.

Returning these ambassadors to their homes provided the occasion for a fifth expedition (1417–19), whose ships visited the Liuch'ius, Brunei, and the usual Southeast Asian countries before sailing into the Indian Ocean and exploring the Arabian coast from Ormuz to Aden and the African coast from Somaliland to Zanzibar. It was on this voyage that giraffes were brought back for the emperor's zoo; they were identified with the mythical *ch'i-lin* beast, whose appearance was a sign of good government. The sixth expedition (1421–22) also concentrated its attentions on the Arabian and African coasts. Thus, by the death of Yung-lo in 1424 the naval voyages based on Nanking under eunuch leadership had developed into an ongoing enterprise, as had the military expeditions from Peking into Mongolia. Yung-lo's successor, Hung-hsi, reversed both programs, cancelling the voyage scheduled for 1424, but his successor Hsüante allowed Cheng Ho to lead a seventh and final voyage (1431–33) before retiring honorably as military commandant (*shou-pei*) of Nanking.

Chinese naval capabilities had been highly developed for three centuries preceding the Yung-lo reign, ever since the great Southern Sung emperor Kao-tsung (r. 1126–62)—intent on patching together a regime from the debris left behind by the Jurchen invasions—removed himself to Hangchow, resolved to make the taxation of maritime trade one of the pillars of his empire, and so created a navy. This navy grew to control the East China Sea, and its ability to defend the Yangtze River and assure communications with Korea was a major factor in the successful resistance of the Southern Sung to Jurchen attack. The Yüan emperor Qubilai inherited this naval capability when he conquered the Southern Sung, and he employed it to launch expeditions aimed at the conquest of Japan (1274 and 1281), Champa (1282), the Liuch'ius (1291), and Java (1292). These expeditions were consistent failures, but they were several times more numerous in ships and men than any of Cheng Ho's voyages. Although they had possessed the organizational and technical abilities for a long time, it was nevertheless only in the Yung-lo reign that the Chinese were motivated to launch Cheng Ho's powerful but peaceful naval expeditions.

Yung-lo's motivations in launching the voyages were twofold. First, he was never certain that the charred corpse found among the ruins of the Nanking imperial palace in 1402 really was that of Emperor Chien-wen. Rumors that Chien-wen had escaped grew quickly into folk legends, and as late as 1440 a man was executed and his accomplices exiled because he claimed to be Chien-wen. The most persistent rumor had Chien-wen escaping Nanking in the guise of an itinerant Buddhist monk and fleeing to Southeast Asia, so Cheng Ho was ordered to search there for news of him. This was not the sole motive for the expeditions, but it explains the timing of the first one. After about two years on the throne, whose seizure even his most ingenious advisers could not

justify ideologically, Yung-lo faced up to the fact that legends concerning Chien-wen's escape were spreading among the population and sent Cheng Ho to find out the truth.

Second, Yung-lo was motivated by diplomatic, commercial, and explorational interests that were never clearly differentiated, but that became dominant as the expeditions progressed. Yung-lo, born in 1360, went to his northern fief only in 1380; before then he was in Nanking, a witness to the heyday of early Ming trade with Southeast Asia. Naturally no record of his personal impressions survives, but the sight of foreign ambassadors bringing exotic wares as tribute evidently made a deep impression on him, and to the end of his life he was always pleased to receive strange things from distant lands. Beyond that, Yung-lo's intentional reversal of the generally passive and isolationist foreign policies of his father's later years implied an active search for diplomatic relationships as well. The show of submission required of countries desiring to enter into diplomatic relations quite frankly dramatized the superior majesty and power of the Chinese emperor, but many foreign countries were happy to accept this precondition in order to increase their trade.

In Southeast Asia the Ming expeditions visited the mainland countries and Majapahit on Java, all of which had for political reasons sent tribute more or less regularly during the Hung-wu period. By demonstrating the scale of Chinese naval power and securing new statements of submission from these kingdoms, Cheng Ho's armada laid the foundations for a revival of the China trade carried on by the maritime Malay principalities within the tributary system. Majapahit and Thailand were ordered not to interfere, and states such as Sulu and Brunei, Pahang and Kelantan on the Malay Peninsula, and Jambi and Lambri on Sumatra now sent envoys directly to the Ming court. But the most important state in this category was Malacca, where the former dynasty of Shrivijaya had removed itself in 1401 (turning Moslem in the process), after a stay at Singapore. A Chinese diplomatic mission headed by the eunuch Yin Ch'ing in 1403 led to Malaccan friendship throughout the period of the naval voyages. The Ming fleets based themselves on Malacca, and in 1411 the ruler of Malacca came to Nanking in person. Under the Chinese umbrella, Malaccan sea power grew, and after the cessation of the Chinese voyages, Malacca maintained control of the straits, naval hegemony in the South China Sea, and a predominant position in the trade with China. The peace provided by Malaccan hegemony in turn provided an opportunity for Chinese merchants to trade throughout Southeast Asia—and for Chinese emigrants to settle—even after the Ming government withdrew from the naval scene.

As the attention of Cheng Ho's expeditions shifted westward into Indian and then African waters, exploration instead of commerce or diplomacy became the driving force. Here the Chinese, like the Europeans later in the century, entered areas about which nothing was known and of which anything could be believed. Medical doctors accompanied the voyages and, especially in Africa, compiled catalogues and collected examples of plants and animals and gems and minerals, some for use as medicines, others merely as objects of wonder. Yung-lo's infatuation with this aspect of the voyages roused the stuffy Confucian intellectuals into paroxysms of peevishness. Reciting the same arguments used by Han Yü in the ninth century, they held that the emperor's quest for strange and useless foreign things portended the collapse of the Ming empire. In view of the seemingly clear precedent afforded by the T'ang, the Confucian position was bitter and nonnegotiable; hostility toward the eunuch establishment that was managing the voyages merely intensified their already hard ideological stance. The voyages were doomed the moment the Confucians gained a clear ascendancy in the state.

Confucian hostility later resulted in the deliberate destruction of the plans for Cheng Ho's treasure ships. The official Ming history gives the dimensions of the largest, the nine-masted "treasure ships," as 440 feet long and 180 feet in the beam; the second largest, the eight-masted "horse ships" (ma-ch'uan), are described in another source as 370 feet long and 150 feet in the beam. The accuracy of these figures was confirmed in 1962 when the excavation of the Lung-chiang shipyard at Nanking turned up the rudderpost of one of the treasure ships; calculations based on its measurements yielded even larger dimensions for the ships than those given in the sources. They suggest shallow draft vessels with flat bottoms and watertight bulkheads, and without the keel-and-frame construction that imposed smaller size limits on western wooden ships. A displacement of 3,100 tons has been suggested for the treasure ships, which are said to have carried between 450 and 500 men, not an excessive complement for such a large ship; if the number refers to the military personnel manning the ship, there would have been much additional space for passengers and cargo. The 27,800 men of the first expedition, when divided among its sixty-two ships, yields almost exactly 450 men per ship, so the treasure ships and other large classes may have predominated in the Cheng Ho fleets. The treasure ships were three decks high at the stern, which calls to mind Ch'en Yu-liang's river warships of 1363, but the Chinese had been sailing the seas in great ships capable of carrying several hundred men since the days of Marco Polo and before.

The ships employed in the Cheng Ho voyages were built in the Lung-chiang shipyard in Nanking, were manned by troops from the Nanking guards, and sailed under the direction of the court eunuchs. The voyages are the most spectacular example of Yung-lo's use of eunuchs to supervise and military personnel to carry out large-scale activities, particularly of the sort disapproved of by Confucian opinion. Other examples include the refurbishing of Peking and the management of the timber-cutting operations in the southwest that provided lumber for both palaces and fleets.

The site of the Lung-chiang shipyard, hard by the wall of Nanking on the Ch'inhuai River, had been the headquarters of Ming naval activities since the capture of Nanking in 1356 and the creation of the Ch'inhuai wing soon afterwards. From 1403 on shipbuilding was a high priority matter and between then and 1419 the Lung-chiang shipyard, aided by other yards in Chekiang, Fukien, and Kwangtung, built a total of 2,149 seagoing vessels of all types, including 94 treasure ships of the large type described above; it also converted 381 freighters of the oceangoing grain-transport service for service in Indian and African waters. At the peak of this activity, Taoists were ordered to select auspicious days for beginning new construction, and the best artisans were posted to the shipyards from all other projects. In 1420 the shipyards were placed under a new administrative agency called the Ta-t'ung-kuan superintendency (t'i-chü-szu).

After 1419 very few seagoing ships were constructed, and the subsequent expeditions were carried out by already existing vessels. Having laid firm foundations for high-seas naval power, Yung-lo spent the last several years of his reign undermining them. In 1411 Sung Li finished the section of the Grand Canal from the Yellow River to Peking, and until 1415 canal and oceangoing transport of grain to the north coexisted. However, in 1415 ocean transport was suspended, and Ch'en Hsüan, earl of P'ingchiang, was ordered to build three thousand grain transports for use on the Grand Canal. The regime no longer had an economic need to maintain a deep-water fleet, a need that the oceangoing grain-transport system had provided. The connection between that system and the revival of naval expeditions was not lost on the civil officials, who thereafter consistently opposed the revival of oceangoing grain transport.

The Ming navy was not sharply distinguished institutionally from the army; ships were assigned as part of the regular military equipment of guards and battalions located along coasts or rivers. As of 1420 an estimated 1,350 small patrol craft and an equal number of large warships were distributed among the appropriate provincial garrisons. These were backed up by a main fleet, based in the Nanking areas, composed of about four hundred large warships and four hundred grain freighters plus two hundred fifty treasure ships and other large vessels used in Cheng Ho's voyages. Presumably many of these were laid up at any give time, but the ships in commission were manned largely by troops from the Nanking garrison. Of the ten guards under the chief military commissions at Nanking that were not transferred to Peking, four bear names that show that they specialized in naval affairs.[1] Virtually all of the Nanking guards were still operating at least a few ships even as late as the sixteenth century, and the men in the Nanking garrison who were not skilled as sailors would nevertheless have been useful as marines. Even after the 1420 troop transfers the strength of the Nanking garrison was eighty thousand men or more, easily sufficient to provide the personnel for the Cheng Ho voyages, though levies from the provincial garrisons probably participated as well.

Cheng Ho's fleets were of a size that would have required a noble as commander during the Hung-wu period. Although Hung-wu was willing to use eunuchs in confidential assignments, and Yung-lo had begun the practice of assigning eunuchs to some of the military command positions usually reserved for nobles, even in this respect the fleets were exceptional. In the great camps and the regional defense commands the eunuchs shared control with nobles, and in the field armies the nobles predominated, but in the fleets eunuchs' control was not qualified by the presence of nobles or military officers higher in rank than regional military commissioner. Both the main fleet and its squadrons were led by eunuchs, and in addition to Cheng Ho, who was accredited as the emperor's envoy to the various countries he visited, numerous lesser eunuch envoys led diplomatic missions to the other states in the region. These eunuchs were always grand directors (t'ai-chien) in the twenty-four offices into which the eunuch establishment had been organized during the Yung-lo reign. Eunuch control over the fleets was paralleled by eunuch control over the Nanking garrison. The absence of the emperor on his Mongolian campaigns and the withdrawal of his eldest son and eldest grandson to Peking in 1420 had left the Nanking chief military commissions and the guards of the emperor's personal army, all nominally directly under the emperor, in fact without any common superior in the city. The gap was filled by creating the position of military commandant to take charge of the forces at Nanking in lieu of the emperor. Though often held by a noble, the position was also often held by a eunuch, especially in the early period. The naval voyages and the Nanking establishment that supported them were eunuch-managed to an extent that was unusual even in the Yung-lo reign.

NOTES

1. The four were the Right and Left Shui-chün ("Marine Forces") Guards, the Kuang-yang ("Ocean-covering") Guard, and the Heng-hai ("Sea-spanning") Guard.

NO

Dun J. Li

THE AGELESS CHINESE: A HISTORY

PREFACE

In writing this book I hope to meet what I have considered as an important need in Chinese history: a one-volume book covering China's past from the very beginning to the present. Many books on modern China have been published in the United States in recent years, but there are few that relate modern China to its ancient past. It is my belief that modern China can be better understood by analyzing China's historical forces as well as forces that are mostly Western in origin. Aside from whatever merits it might have as a complete history, this book, I hope, will help students to understand contemporary China from a historical perspective and perhaps in a more profound manner. Since most of the basic forces that shape modern China have been accumulative and were in operation many centuries before the modern period, I have chosen to title the book *The Ageless Chinese....*

Maritime Expeditions

... Believing that all peoples on earth should be brought under the benevolent influence of the Son of Heaven, the first Ming emperor sent envoys overseas demanding the acknowledgement of his overlordship shortly after his accession. For reasons of their own, many of China's peripheral states and some in faraway South and Southeast Asia allowed themselves to be persuaded to join Ming's tribute system. Korea, Japan, Li-ch'iu, Annam (Vietnam), Cambodia, Siam (Thailand), Borneo, Java, Sumatra, several Malay states, and some small kingdoms on the southeast coat of India, directly or by implication, acknowledged Ming's overlordship at one time or another. Hung-wu's efforts along this line were continued by his son Yung-lo. It was during the latter's reign that Chinese influence was expanded overseas in a manner never before accomplished.

Under Yung-lo and his two immediate successors the Chinese launched a series of maritime expeditions on an unprecedented scale. From 1405 to 1431 Chinese armadas led by the court eunuch Cheng Ho made seven voyages to the "Western Ocean" (a term used during this period to cover the general

From Dun J. Li, *The Ageless Chinese: A History*, 2d ed. (Charles Scribner's Sons, 1971). Copyright © 1971 by Charles Scribner's Sons. Reprinted by permission of Prentice-Hall, Inc., Upper Saddle River, NJ.

area of South and Southeast Asia) for the ostensible purpose of "glorifying Chinese arms in the remote regions and showing off the wealth and power of the Central Kingdom." In 1405 when the first expedition began, a powerful fleet of 62 vessels carrying 27,800 men sailed from Fukien, visited many Southeast Asian countries, and went as far as India. In the places it visited, it "proclaimed publicly the decree of the Son of Heaven" (of demanding their submission), and "if they refused to submit, force was used to coerce them." On the other hand, if the local chieftains decided to cooperate, gold, silk, and other valuables were showered on them as rewards. The first expedition, successfully accomplished, was followed by six others, and most of them went as far as the Persian Gulf or Aden at the southeastern end of the Red Sea. In at least two of the voyages Chinese vessels personally commanded by Cheng Ho called on some of the small kingdoms on the east coast of Africa. As a result of these expeditions it was reported that altogether thirty-six countries in the "Western Ocean" sent tribute missions to China and acknowledged Ming's overlordship. These thirty-six countries included eight from the East Indies, eleven from India and Ceylon, five from Persia and Arabia, and five from the east coast of Africa.

Cheng Ho's voyages were the most spectacular maritime expeditions the world had yet seen. From a historian's point of view, they raise more questions than have ever been satisfactorily answered. First, what were the motives behind this adventure? What did it try to achieve? Second, what seamanship did the Chinese then possess which made these expeditions not only possible but also remarkably successful? Third, why did not the Chinese follow up their initial success, as later the Western Europeans did, with the establishment of a commercial and perhaps a political maritime empire? Lastly, what was the true meaning of the tribute system which, the Chinese insisted, was the only proper basis in their relations with non-Chinese countries?

Chinese sources give two reasons for this unprecedented maritime adventure: first, to trace the whereabouts of Ming Hui-ti who was believed by some to have escaped from Nanking and who might be somewhere in Southeast Asia, and second, to "impress people overseas with Ming's power and wealth" and to "bring ten thousand nations to bear tribute missions to the Central Kingdom." The first reason might have had something to do with the first voyage, but even then it was secondary at best, for there were no extensive efforts made during any of the seven voyages to find the ex-emperor. If this were a genuine reason, there would have been no need for these voyages to go as far as the Near East or Africa. The second reason was more plausible, since so far no other motives have been found. In other words, these expeditions were launched for ideological reasons and prestige. The material or commercial motive which prompted European expansion at a later date was notably absent.

Ideologically, the Ming emperors regarded themselves as the Sons of Heaven, thus representing all people on earth. Once such an assumption was made, it seemed logical that they should wish to bring as many foreign nations under their overlordship as they physically could. While the Han and T'ang emperors looked northward and overland for the extension of their pretensions, the Ming emperors looked southward and overseas for the same purpose. Perhaps by then history had shown them the futility of expansion across the grasslands and deserts on account of geographical and cultural factors. If a southern expansion was to be equally unprofitable, as later it did turn out to be, they had no historical lessons to guide them at that time. The word "profit," of course, should not be interpreted in its material sense, since the Chinese did not believe that material profit should be a primary factor in governing the relationships among nations. Traditionally against commercialism which seemed to be the only practical reason for such an adventure, they undertook one of the most costly operations in history for nonmaterial purposes.

Despite the basic attitude of anticommercialism on the part of the Chinese government and most of the Chinese people, the fact that China had a long coastline indented with many fine bays and harbors should explain why a certain portion of its people became orientated to the sea and depended on the sea to earn a livelihood. Regardless of what other people thought of them and their activities, the people on the southeast coast had long been engaged in commercial endeavors overseas. Since they lived far away from the Yellow River basin where more important history was made and since the Chinese had traditionally looked down upon trade and commerce, what they did in the faraway areas of Fukien and Kwangtung was only scantily recorded by the agriculturally minded historians. On the southeast coast where the rugged terrain dropped abruptly into the sea to form an irregular coastline with many bays and harbors, the land was poor and arable areas were few. As the pressure of population increased with the passage of time, people were forced by necessity to look beyond the blue horizon for a livelihood. With or without government approval, they sailed abroad with Chinese products and brought home goods of exotic origins. Many perished on the high seas or on remote islands; others brought back uncountable wealth. For every family that succeeded, many others mourned the loss of their beloved ones. Merchants who had found a more rewarding existence overseas settled down there permanently and never returned. Early in the 1560's it was reported that tens of thousands of Chinese resided in Luzon, and a Chinese community of several thousand families had been established in the city of Palembang (Sumatra).

As overseas trade expanded, numerous trade ports on the southeast coast flourished. The most important among them was Ch'üanchou which remained the leading shipping and trading center throughout the Sung, Yüan, and Ming dynasties. Government posts in charge of merchant marine and shipping were so lucrative that they were eagerly sought after, and officials who occupied them grew in power and wealth. One of them, P'u Shou-keng, became so powerful that his change of loyalty shortened the life of the South Sung regime, as has been mentioned before. Despite a basic anticommercial attitude, overseas trade was so profitable and prosperous that both government and people benefited from it. The large amount of wealth that could be acquired from overseas trade and the great risk involved in it gave birth to a new custom in Fukien province, the adoption of foster children. Abandoned children and orphans were adopted by families even when they had children of their own. They were sent abroad for commercial enterprise after they had grown up, while the true sons were generally kept at home. If they made good, the whole family benefited; if they were lost forever, their families would be somewhat comforted by the thought that they were not true sons in the first place.

Since seafaring had a long history on the southeast coast, seamanship improved with the passage of each generation. The merchants who roved the seven seas for profit could be easily converted into naval captains for manning warships, once their government demanded their service. When Kublai Khan decided to invade Japan again in 1281, enough seamen and ships to transport 140,000 troops were gathered in short order. When Yung-lo ordered his men to venture into the south seas, the people on the east coast were equally ready to provide what he needed. Generations of experiments and improvement enabled the Chinese to manufacture ships that were among the most seaworthy the world had yet seen. Some of the vessels used in Cheng Ho's first voyage, for instance, had a length of 44 *chang* (c. 517 feet), and a width of 18 *chang* (c. 212 feet), built with four decks and water tight compartments. With favorable winds they could make as fast as six knots an hour. The compass, which had been used for centuries to locate proper burial places for the dad, was now an indispensable instrument in navigation. Early during the fifteenth century when Chen Ho made his voyages, the Chinese had the men and the skill to undertake such feats of seamanship as had never before been seen in world history.

Despite their monumental success in seamanship, the maritime expeditions of the Ming dynasty were discontinued as suddenly as they had been launched. Cheng Ho goes down in history as an earlier Columbus who was not followed by a Cortes or a Pizarro, and his overseas voyages turned out to be the first and the only large-scale maritime adventure ever undertaken by a Chinese government. If the Chinese had continued his efforts, the economic and political structure of the world in the subsequent centuries, or at least that in Asia, would have changed considerably. The immediate causes of their discontinuance were rather obvious. First, these maritime expeditions were extremely costly, and yet they brought back nothing except dubious prestige. The Ming regime simply could not continue them indefinitely. Second, other areas began to demand more attention from the government after the 1430's, especially the northern frontier where the Mongols again threatened an invasion. The real causes, however, went much deeper. Had the maritime region on China's southeast coast constituted an independent state acting in observance of its own interests, it could have been another Portugal or Spain, one of the first maritime nations in the world. Its sailors, having touched the east coast of Africa early in the fifteenth century, could conceivably have reached the Cape of Good Hope later, and eventually might have been able to "discover" such strange places as England and France. This, however, was not to be the case. China remained land-centered and anticommercial. Instead of discovering more new territories, China and its tributary states were "discovered" by Western Europeans in a later age.

The reasons for the failure to follow up Cheng Ho's initial success with sustained interest and effort can be found in the nature of Chinese culture itself. In other words, the sense of values contained in the Chinese cultural system would not allow maritime success on a sustained basis. The Chinese lacked the motivations that prompted Western Europe to discover and explore new areas in a later period. First, as a people the Chinese were unusually self-centered. Separated from other centers of civilization by oceans and almost impassable mountains and deserts, the Chinese developed their culture independently. They had been little affected by foreign influence, except Buddhism from India, until modern times. The result was a self-centered "culturalism" which regarded the Chinese culture as the most unique and incomparably great. While foreigners were welcome to come to China to be Sinicized and, in the opinion of the Chinese, civilized, it was considered improper for the Chinese to go overseas for the sole purpose of propagating Chinese beliefs. Active proselyting was to be avoided because it could not serve any purpose except to place doubt on the advocated beliefs. In the Chinese mind, true values needed no persuasion, and if the Chinese culture were truly great (as they believed it was), foreigners would follow it out of their own accord. Throughout Chinese history individual Confucians might go to foreign countries to teach if they were invited, but there were no organized efforts on the part of the Chinese or their government to send missionaries overseas. Thus the missionary zeal which played such an important role in Europe's discovery and exploration of new territories during the age of commercial revolution was singularly absent so far as the Chinese were concerned. Second, there was the traditional anticommercialism in China. Ever since the Han dynasty the merchants had been regarded as exploitative and parasitic, and despite the useful functions they performed, they were discriminated against socially and occasionally even

persecuted. During the Ming dynasty the fact that the seafaring merchants generally came from the lower strata of the population and were the least cultured in Confucian learning strengthened further an ancient prejudice. In the minds of most Chinese, the merchants who voluntarily left their parents and their ancestors' graves to seek fortunes overseas were the most contemptible because by doing so they neglected to observe two cardinal virtues of Confucianism, i.e., filial piety and ancestor worship. Third, rightly or wrongly the Chinese believed that they were economically self-sufficient and that they needed nothing from foreign lands. That Cheng Ho's expeditions brought back nothing remarkable except such curiosities as ostriches, zebras, and giraffes further convinced them that while foreigners depended upon trade with China for the improvement of their livelihood, China had nothing to gain in trading with foreigners. This belief was strengthened in a later period by the insistence of Western Europeans on opening China to trade.

Spectacular as Cheng Ho's expeditions were, they did not represent a basic need from the Chinese point of view. Many Confucian scholars regarded this maritime adventure as being wasteful and unnecessary and merely "a eunuch's enterprise" with which they would have nothing to do. Though they had no objection to bringing many foreign lands into the tribute system, they believed that this should be done on a voluntary basis and that no coercion or "persuasion" should be applied for that purpose. The tribute system, as they saw it, was based upon a cultural relationship between superior and inferiors. China, being culturally superior, extended its benevolent influence to its neighbors, and its neighbors sent tribute missions to China out of gratitude and appreciation. Foreign countries that sent tribute missions should be given Chinese products in return that were worth more in monetary value than the tributes they sent in order to show "the generosity and abundance of the Central Kingdom." There should not be any motive for material gain in the operation of the tribute system. The tribute system, enshrined in tradition and history, was the only basis of international relations Confucian scholars would recognize. Clearly they did not believe in equality among sovereign nations because in their mind no nation except China was truly sovereign. This self-centered "culturalism," as one might call it, had worked fairly well throughout Chinese history until modern times when China was brought into contact with Western Europeans.

The actual performance of the tribute system fell far short of the ideal as conceived by Confucian scholars. The material motive, theoretically absent, played an important role as early as the tribute system began. The gifts given by Chinese emperors to foreign rulers and their emissaries were often subsidies and bribes in disguise; the Chinese hoped that foreigners, given the choice of obtaining what they needed by peaceful means, would not resort to the use of more violent methods. On the other hand, foreign countries perhaps had no objection to being considered as inferiors so long as the manifestation of inferiority did not extend beyond the nominal, ritualistic gestures such as the adoption of the Chinese calendar and the receiving of Chinese ranks and titles. Moreover, tribute embassies were often foreign trade missions in disguise and brought material benefits to the countries that sent them. Thus the tribute system rationalized foreign trade and gave it an aura of respectability which otherwise it would not have had. Traditionally anticommercial, the Chinese government would have been hard put to sanction foreign trade if it were not disguised as tribute missions. During the Ming dynasty the so-called tribute bearers were often the representatives of foreign trade interests. In many cases these representatives were Chinese exiles who had been chosen by foreign traders to represent them because of their expert knowledge of Chinese affairs. Oftentimes, the Chinese government threw these exiles into jail or even executed them, once their identity was established. From the government's point of view, the fact that these exiles left their ancestors' graves for foreign lands spoke eloquently of their rascality for which, it believed, they deserved no mercy. Needless to say, the government did not favor Chinese emigration overseas.

POSTSCRIPT

Did Internal Political Factionalism End Chinese Overseas Expansion in the Fifteenth Century?

In attempting to balance the political philosophies of the Chinese and their defeated foreign rulers, the Mongols, Emperor Yung-lo was playing a difficult and contradictory game, according to Dreyer. While continuing to expand the borders of the empire, Yung-lo restored the Confucian officials to central imperial positions. By doing so, says Dreyer, he laid the groundwork for the political rivalry that condemned his overseas adventures and plans for expansion to failure. As a result of the Confucians' "paroxysms of peevishness," the developing Chinese maritime empire collapsed. From the end of Yung-lo's reign, the Confucian bureaucracy continued to erode imperial support for the eunuchs' position. Even before this, argues Dreyer, the completion of the Grand Canal lessened the necessity for an oceangoing fleet. Although the eunuchs continued to play a role as military leaders afterwards, the accomplishments of eunuch admiral Cheng Ho were suppressed and the treasure ships were scuttled.

Dun Li, on the other hand, argues that the deep division between the eunuchs and Confucians was indicative of an already inherent division in China, both geographically and culturally, between the north and the south. He points out that the southern region had an ongoing dependence on maritime trade, while northern China, where political power resided, was overwhelmingly anticommercial, sinocentric (Chinese-centered), and suspicious of foreign influence. The Ming voyages were unsustainable because, according to Dun Li, the Chinese did not have the motivations necessary to sustain a prolonged program of exploration. With no missionary impulse in religion, no desire to promote international trade, and no interest in acquiring international prestige through overseas conquest, the Ming voyages were consigned to merely being a curious aberration in Chinese history.

Those who are interested in this period in Chinese history and the Ming voyages in particular should see Louise Leviathes, *When China Ruled the Seas: The Treasure Fleet of the Dragon Throne 1405–1433* (Simon & Schuster, 1994), which dramatically details not only the exploits of Admiral Cheng Ho but also the deceptions and duplicity practiced by the Confucians within the Ming court. Also, J. J. L. Duyvendak's older book *China's Discovery of Africa*, although difficult to obtain, is well worth the search.

ISSUE 4

Was the French Revolution Worth Its Human Costs?

YES: Peter Kropotkin, from *The Great French Revolution, 1789–1793* (Schocken Books, 1971)

NO: Simon Schama, from *Citizens: A Chronicle of the French Revolution* (Alfred A. Knopf, 1989)

ISSUE SUMMARY

YES: Peter Kropotkin (1842–1921), a Russian prince, revolutionary, and anarchist, argues that the French Revolution eradicated both serfdom and absolutism and paved the way for France's future democratic growth.

NO: History professor Simon Schama argues that not only did the French Revolution betray its own goals, but it produced few of the results that it promised.

Few historical eras have created the emotional responses and concomitant debates as has the French Revolution. Taking advantage of one of the largest bodies of historical data ever gathered, historians of the past two centuries have analyzed, synthesized, and evaluated every facet of this seminal event in the history of the Western world.

From this scholarship has come a myriad of important questions regarding the political, economic, social, religious, cultural, and intellectual aspects of the Revolution—questions involving causation, behavior, outcomes, and assessments. Each generation of historians has taken the work of its predecessors and used it to shape an understanding of the Revolution that emanates from the uncovering of new sources of information, the creation of new tools to assist in the process, and the development of new schools of thought that attempt to give a more contemporary, relevant slant to this important event. To list the major questions raised by this debate could well cover most of the pages in a work devoted to the subject.

But of all the questions that the French Revolution has raised, a double-edged one that is both elemental and significant is, What were its outcomes, and were they worth the price that was paid to achieve them?

The debate began before anyone knew what course the Revolution would take. In a 1790 treatise entitled *Reflections on the Revolution in France*, English statesman Edmund Burke (1729–1797) uncannily predicted the future course of the Revolution and its catastrophic consequences for both France and

Europe. He also argued in favor of the slow, evolutionary style of change that was taking place in his own country, rather than the sudden, spasmodic one that was beginning to envelop France. Burke's message was simple: the revolution in France will be costly and counterproductive.

A year later, the French Revolution gained its first articulate defender, an English-born American citizen named Thomas Paine (1737–1809). In *Common Sense* (1776), a stirring call-to-arms for American colonists to throw off the yoke of English oppression, Paine acquired a reputation as a foe of tyrannical government and as a strong supporter of human freedom and equality. In Part 1 of his political pamphlet *The Rights of Man*, published in 1791, Paine argued that revolution was necessary to purge civilization of those elements that stood in the way of societal reform. According to Paine, no price was too high to pay for the realization of these cherished goals.

As generations passed, the basic question debated by Burke and Paine faded into the background as historians began to explore other fertile areas of historical research. There was either a general acceptance of the French Revolution's value in changing the course of human history or a quiet acquiescence in its outcomes, regardless of the consequences.

The following selection is by Peter Kropotkin, an early historical defender of the French Revolution. Obviously influenced by his radical, anarchistic background and his desire to see all people freed from the yoke of oppression, his view of the Revolution was somewhat simplistic and uncritical. Coming from a ninteenth-century environment, in which revolutions were common and seen by many as an inevitable part of political evolution, his opinions on the French Revolution are representative for his time—and for generations to come.

Of all the books written about the French Revolution in recent years, none have been as popular as Simon Schama's *Citizens: A Chronicle of the French Revolution*, which is excerpted in the second selection of this issue. Published in the midst of the Revolution's bicentennial celebration, the book aroused much controversy for many reasons; among them was his view that the French Revolution was not worth its human costs. Seeing violence as an endemic part of the revolutionary process, Schama states that the French Revolution produced few of the results that it had promised.

YES

Peter Kropotkin

THE GREAT FRENCH REVOLUTION, 1789–1793

When one sees that terrible and powerful Convention wrecking itself in 1794–1795, that proud and strong Republic disappearing, and France, after the demoralising *régime* of the Directory, falling under the military yoke of a Bonaparte, one is impelled to ask: "What was the good of the Revolution if the nation had to fall back again under despotism?" In the course of the nineteenth century, this question has been constantly put, and the timid and conservative have worn it threadbare as an argument against revolutions in general.

... Those who have seen in the Revolution only a change in the Government, those who are ignorant of its economic as well as its educational work, those alone could put such a question.

The France we see during the last days of the eighteenth century, at the moment of the *coup d'état* on the 18th Brumaire, is not the France that existed before 1789. Would it have been possible for the old France, wretchedly poor and with a third of her population suffering yearly from dearth, to have maintained the Napoleonic Wars, coming so soon after the terrible wars of the Republic between 1792 and 1799, when all Europe was attacking her?

The fact is, that a new France had been constituted since 1792–1793. Scarcity still prevailed in many of the departments, and its full horrors were felt especially after the *coup d'état* of Thermidor, when the maximum price for all foodstuffs was abolished. There were still some departments which did not produce enough wheat to feed themselves, and as the war went on, and all means of transport were requisitioned for its supplies, there was scarcity in those departments. But everything tends to prove that France was even then producing much more of the necessaries of life of every kind than in 1789.

Never was there in France such energetic ploughing, Michelet tells us, as in 1792, when the peasant was ploughing the lands he had taken back from the lords, the convents, the churches, and was goading his oxen to the cry of *"Allons Prusse! Allons Autriche!"* Never had there been so much clearing of lands—even royalist writers admit this—as during those years of revolution. The first good harvest, in 1794, brought relief to two-thirds of France—at least in the villages, for all this time the towns were threatened with scarcity of food. Not that it was scarce in France as a whole, or that the *sans-culotte* municipalities neglected to take measures to feed those who could not find employment, but from the fact that all beasts of burden not actually used in tillage were requisitioned to carry food and ammunition to the fourteen armies of the Republic. In those days there were no railways, and all but the main roads were in the state they are to this day in Russia—well-nigh impassable.

A new France was born during those four years of revolution. For the first time in centuries the peasant ate his fill, straightened his back and dared to speak out. Read the detailed reports concerning the return of Louis XVI. to Paris, when he was brought back a prisoner from Varennes, in June 1791, by the peasants, and say: "Could such a thing, such an interest in the public welfare, such a devotion to it, and such an independence of judgment and action have been possible before 1789?" A new nation had been born in the meantime, just as we see to-day a new nation coming into life in Russia and in Turkey.

It was owing to this new birth that France was able to maintain her wars under the Republic and Napoleon, and to carry the principles of the Great Revolution into Switzerland, Italy, Spain, Belgium, Holland, Germany, and even to the borders of Russia. And when, after all those wars, after having mentally followed the French armies as far as Egypt and Moscow, we expect to find France in 1815 reduced to an appalling misery and her lands laid waste, we find, instead, that even in its eastern portions and in the Jura, the country is much more prosperous than it was at the time when

Pétion, pointing out to Louis XVI. the luxuriant banks of the Marne, asked him if there was anywhere in the world a kingdom more beautiful than the one the King had not wished to keep.

The self-contained energy was such in villages regenerated by the Revolution, that in a few years France became a country of well-to-do peasants, and her enemies soon discovered that in spite of all the blood she had shed and the losses she had sustained, France, in respect of her *productivity*, was the richest country in Europe. Her wealth, indeed, is not drawn from the Indies or from her foreign commerce: it comes from her own soil, from her love of the soil, from her own skill and industry. She is the richest country, because of the subdivision of her wealth, and she is still richer because of the possibilities she offers for the future.

Such was the effect of the Revolution. And if the casual observer sees in Napoleonic France only a love of glory, the historian realises that even the wars France waged at that period were undertaken to secure the fruits of the Revolution—to keep the lands that had been retaken from the lords, the priests and the rich, and the liberties that had been won from despotism and the Court. If France was willing in those years to bleed herself to death, merely to prevent the Germans, the English, and the Russians from forcing a Louis XVIII. upon her, it was because she did not want the return of the emigrant nobles to mean that the *ci-devants* would take back the lands which had been watered already with the peasant's sweat, and the liberties which had been sanctified with the patriots' blood. And France fought so well for twenty-three years, that when she was compelled at last to admit the Bourbons, it was she who imposed conditions on them. The Bourbons might reign, but the lands were to be kept by those who had taken them from the feudal lords, so that even during the White Terror of the Bourbons they dared not touch those lands. The old *régime* could not be re-established.

This is what is gained by making a Revolution.

* * *

There are other things to be pointed out. In the history of all nations a time comes when fundamental changes are bound to take place in the whole of the national life. Royal despotism and feudalism were dying in 1789; it was impossible to keep them alive; they had to go.

But then, two ways were opened out before France: reform or revolution.

At such times there is always a moment when reform is still possible; but if advantage has not been taken of that moment, if an obstinate resistance has been opposed to the requirements of the new life, up to the point when blood has flowed in the streets, as it flowed on July 14, 1789, then there must be a Revolution. And once the Revolution has begun, it must necessarily develop to its conclusions—that is to say, to the highest point it is capable of attaining— were it only temporarily, being given a certain condition of the public mind at this particular moment.

If we represent the slow progress of a period of evolution by a line drawn on paper, we shall see this line gradually though slowly rising. Then there comes a Revolution, and the line makes a sudden leap upwards. In England the line would be represented as rising to the Puritan Republic of Cromwell; in France it rises to the *Sans-culotte* Republic of 1793. However, at this height

progress cannot be maintained; all the hostile forces league together against it, and the Republic goes down. Our line, after having reached that height, drops. Reaction follows. For the political life of France the line drops very low indeed, but by degrees it rises again, and when peace is restored in 1815 in France, and in 1688 in England—both countries are found to have attained a level much higher than they were on prior to their Revolutions.

After that, evolution is resumed: our line again begins to rise slowly: but, besides taking place on a very much higher level, the rising of the line will in nearly every case be also much more rapid than before the period of disturbance.

This is a law of human progress, and also a law of individual progress. The more recent history of France confirms this very law by showing how it was necessary to pass through the Commune to arrive at the Third Republic.

The work of the French Revolution is not confined merely to what it obtained and what was retained of it in France. It is to be found also in the principles bequeathed by it to the succeeding century —in the line of direction it marked out for the future.

A reform is always a compromise with the past, but the progress accomplished by revolution is always a promise of future progress. If the Great French Revolution was the summing up of a century's evolution, it also marked out in its turn the programme of evolution to be accomplished in the course of the nineteenth century.

It is a law in the world's history that the period of a hundred or a hundred and thirty years, more or less, which passes between two great revolutions, receives its character from the revolution in which this period began. The nations endeavour to realise in their institutions the inheritance bequeathed to them by the last revolution. All that this last could not yet put into practice, all the great thoughts which were thrown into circulation during the turmoil, and which the revolution either could not or did not know how to apply, all the attempts at sociological reconstruction, which were born during the revolution, will go to make up the substance of evolution during the epoch that follows the revolution, with the addition of those new ideas to which this evolution will give birth, when trying to put into practice the programme marked out by the last upheaval. Then, a new revolution will be brought about in some other nation, and this nation in its turn will set the problems for the following century. Such has hitherto been the trend of history.

Two great conquests, in fact, characterise the century which has passed since 1789–1793. Both owe their origin to the French Revolution, which had carried on the work of the English Revolution while enlarging and invigorating it with all the progress that had been made since the English middle classes beheaded their King and transferred his power to the Parliament. These two great triumphs are: the abolition of serfdom and the abolition of abosolutism, by which personal liberties have been conferred upon the individual, undreamt of by the serf of the lord and the subject of the absolute king, while at the same time they have brought about the development of the middle classes and the capitalist *régime.*

These two achievements represent the principal work of the nineteenth century, begun in France in 1789 and slowly spread over Europe in the course of that century.

The work of enfranchisement, begun by the French peasants in 1789, was continued in Spain, Italy, Switzerland, Germany, and Austria by the armies of the *sans-culottes.* Unfortunately, this work hardly penetrated into Poland and did not reach Russia at all.

The abolition of serfdom in Europe would have been already completed in the first half of the nineteenth century if the French *bourgeoisie,* coming into power in 1794 over the dead bodies of Anarchists, Cordeliers, and Jacobins, had not checked the revolutionary impulse, restored monarchy, and handed over France to the imperial juggler, the first Napoleon. This ex-*sans-culotte,* now a general of the *sans-culottes,* speedily began to prop up aristocracy; but the impulsion had been given, the institution of serfdom had already received a mortal blow. It was abolished in spain and Italy in spite of the temporary triumph of reaction. It was closely pressed in Germany after 1811, and disappeared in that country definitively in 1848. In 1861, Russia was compelled to emancipate her serfs, and the war of 1878 put an end to serfdom in the Balkan peninsula.

The cycle is now complete. The right of the lord over the person of the peasant no longer exists in Europe, even in those countries where the feudal dues have still to be redeemed.

This fact is not sufficiently appreciated by historians. Absorbed as they are in political questions, they do not perceive the importance of the abolition of serfdom, which is, however, the essential feature of the nineteenth century. The rivalries between nations and the wars resulting from them, the policies of the Great Powers which occupy so much of the historian's attention, have all sprung from that one great fact—the abolition of serfdom and the development of the wage-system which has taken its place.

The French peasant, in revolting a hundred and twenty years ago against the lord who made him beat the ponds lest croaking frogs should disturb his master's sleep, has thus freed the peasants of all Europe. In four years, by burning the documents which registered his subjection, by setting fire to the châteaux, and by executing the owners of them who refused to recognise his rights as a human being, the French peasant so stirred up all Europe that it is to-day altogether free from the degradation of serfdom.

On the other hand, the abolition of absolute power has also taken a little over a hundred years to make the tour of Europe. Attacked in England in 1648, and vanquished in France in 1789, royal authority based on divine right is no longer exercised save in Russia, but there, too, it is at its last gasp. Even the little Balkan States and Turkey have now their representative assemblies, and Russia is entering the same cycle.

In this respect the Revolution of 1789–1793 has also accomplished its work. Equality before the law and representative government have now their place in almost all the codes of Europe. In theory, at least, the law makes no distinctions between men, and every one has the right to participate, more or less, in the government.

* * *

The absolute monarch—master of his subjects—and the lord—master of the soil and the peasants, by right of birth—have both disappeared. The middle classes now govern Europe.

But at the same time the Great Revolution has bequeathed to us some other principles of an infinitely higher import; the principles of communism. We have seen how all through the Great Revolution the communist idea kept coming to the front, and how after the fall of the Girondins numerous attempts and sometimes great attempts were make in this direction. Fourierism descends in a direct line from L'Ange on one side and from Chalier on the other. Babeuf is the direct descedant of ideas which stirred the masses to enthusiasm in 1793; he, Buonarotti, and Sylvain Maréchal have only symtematised them a little or even merely put them into literary form. But the secret societies organized by Babeuf and Buonarotti were the origin of the *communistes matérialistes* secret societies through which Blanqui and Barbès conspired under the *bourgeois* monarchy of Louis-Philippe. Later on, in 1866, the International Working Men's Association appeared in the direct line of descent from these societies. As to "socialism" we know now that this term came into vogue to avoid the term "communism," which at one time was dangerous because the secret communist societies became societies for action, and were rigorously suppressed by the *bourgeoisie* then in power.

There is, therefore, a direct filiation from the *Enragés* of 1793 and the Babeuf conspiracy of 1795 to the International Working Men's Association of 1866–1878.

There is also a direct descent of ideas. Up till now, modern socialism has added absolutely nothing to the ideas which were circulating among the French people between 1789 and 1794 and which it was tried to put into practice in the Year II. of the Republic. Modern socialism has only systematised those ideas and found arguments in their favour, either by turning against the middle-class economists certain of their own definitions, or by generalising certain facts noticed in the development of industrial capitalism, in the course of the nineteenth century.

But I permit myself to maintain also that, however vague it may have been, however little support it endeavoured to draw from arguments dressed in a scientific garb, and however little use it made of the pseudo-scientific slang of the middle-class economists, the popular communism of the first two years of the Republic saw clearer, and went much deeper in its analyses, than modern socialism.

First of all, it was communism in the consumption of the necessaries of life—not in production only; it was the communalisation and the nationalisation of what economists know as consumption—to which the stern republicans of 1793 turned, above all, their attention, when they tried to establish their stores of grain and provisions in every commune, when they set on foot a gigantic inquiry to find and fix the true value of the objects of prime and secondary necessity, and when they inspired Robespierre to declare that *only the superfluity of food stuffs should become articles of commerce, and that what was necessary belonged to all.*

Born out of the pressing necessities of those troublous years, the communism of 1793, with its affirmation of the right of all to sustenance and to the land for its production, its denial of the right of any one to hold more land than he and his family could cultivate—that is, more than a farm of 120 acres—and its attempt to communalise all trade and industry—this communism went straighter to the heart of things than all the minimum programmes of our own time, and even all the maximum preambles of such programmes.

In any case, what we learn to-day from the study of the Great Revolution is, that is was the source of origin of all the present communist, anarchist, and socialist conceptions. We have but badly understood our common mother, but now we have found her again in the midst of the *sans-culottes,* and we see what we have to learn from her.

Humanity advances by stages and these stages have been marked for several hundred years by great revolutions. After the Netherlands came England with her revolution in 1648–1657, and then it was the turn of France. Each great revolution has in it, besides, something special and original. England and France both abolished royal absolutism. Beut in doing so England was chiefly interested in the personal rights of the individual, particularly in matters of religion, as well as the local rights of every parish and every community. As to France, she turned her chief attention to the land question, and in striking a mortal blow at the feudal system she struck also at the great fortunes, and sent forth into the world the idea of nationalising the soil, and of socialising commerce and the chief industries.

Which of the nations will take upon herself the terrible but glorious task of the next great revolution? One may have thought for a time that it would be Russia. But if she should push her revolution further than the mere limitation of the imperial power; if she touches the land question in a revolutionary spirit—how far will she do? Will she know how to avoid the mistake made by the French Assemblies, and will she socialise the land and give it only to those who want to cultivate it with their own hands? We know not: any answer to this question would belong to the domain of prophecy.

The one thing certain is, that whatsoever nation enters on the path of revolution in our own day, it will be heir to all our forefathers have done in France. The blood they shed was shed for humanity —the sufferings they endured were borne for the entire human race; their struggles, the ideas they gave to the world, the shock of those ideas, are all included in the heritage of mankind. All have borne fruit and will bear more, still finer, as we advance towards those wide horizons opening out before us, where, like some great beacon to point the way, flame the words—LIBERTY, EQUALITY, FRATERNITY.

NO

Simon Schama

CITIZENS: A CHRONICLE OF THE FRENCH REVOLUTION

Asked what he thought was the significance of the French Revolution, the Chinese Premier Zhou En-lai is reported to have answered, "It's too soon to tell." Two hundred years may still be too soon (or, possibly, too late) to tell.

Historians have been overconfident about the wisdom to be gained by distance, believing it somehow confers objectivity, one of those unattainable values in which they have placed so much faith. Perhaps there is something to be said for proximity. Lord Acton, who delivered the first, famous lectures on the French Revolution at Cambridge in the 1870s, was still able to hear firsthand, from a member of the Orléans dynasty, the man's recollection of "Dumouriez gibbering on the streets of London when hearing the news of Waterloo."

Suspicion that blind partisanship fatally damaged the great Romantic narratives of the first half of the nineteenth century dominated scholarly reaction during the second half. As historians institutionalized themselves into an academic profession, they came to believe conscientious research in the archives could confer dispassion: the prerequisite for winkling out the mysterious truths of cause and effect. The desired effect was to be scientific rather than poetic, impersonal rather than impassioned. And while, for some time, historical narratives remained preoccupied by the life cycle of the European nation-states—wars, treaties and dethronements—the magnetic pull of social science was such that "structures," both social and political, seemed to become the principal objects of inquiry.

In the case of the French Revolution this meant transferring attention away from the events and personalities that had dominated the epic chronicles of the 1830s and 1840s. De Tocqueville's luminous account, *The Old Regime and the Revolution*, the product of his own archival research, provided cool reason where before there had been the burning quarrels of partisanship. The Olympian quality of his insights reinforced (albeit from a liberal point of view) the Marxist-scientific claim that the significance of the Revolution was to be sought in some great change in the balance of social power. In both these views, the utterances of orators were little more than vaporous claptrap, unsuccessfully disguising their helplessness at the hands of impersonal historical forces. Likewise, the ebb and flow of events could only be made intelligible by being displayed to reveal the *essential*, primarily social, truths of the Revolution. At the core of those truths was an axiom, shared by liberals, socialists and for that matter nostalgic Christian royalists alike, that the Revolution had indeed been the crucible of modernity: the vessel in which all the characteristics of the modern social world, for good or ill, had been distilled.

By the same token, if the whole event was of this epochal significance, then the causes that generated it had necessarily to be of an equivalent magnitude. A phenomenon of such uncontrollable power that it apparently swept away an entire universe of traditional customs, mentalities and institutions could only have been produced by contradictions that lay embedded deep within the fabric of the "old regime." Accordingly, weighty volumes appeared, between the centennial of 1889 and the Second World War, documenting every aspect of those structural faults. Biographies of Danton and Mirabeau disappeared, at least from respectable scholarly presses, and were replaced by studies of price fluctuations in the grain market. At a later stage still, discrete social groups placed in articulated opposition to each other—the "bourgeoisie," "sans-culottes,"—were defined and anatomized and their dialectical dance routines were made the exclusive choreography of revolutionary politics.

In the fifty years since the sesquicentennial, there has been a serious loss of confidence in this approach. The drastic social changes imputed to the Revolution seem less clear-cut or actually not apparent at all. The "bourgeoisie" said in the classic Marxist accounts to have been the authors and beneficiaries of the event have become social zombies, the product of historiographical obsessions rather than historical realities. Other alterations in the modernization of French society and institutions seem to have been anticipated by the reform of the "old regime." Continuities seem as marked as discontinuities.

Nor does the Revolution seem any longer to conform to a grand historical design, preordained by inexorable forces of social change. Instead it seems a thing of contingencies and unforeseen consequences (not least the summoning of the Estates-General itself). An abundance of fine provincial studies has shown that instead of a single Revolution imposed by Paris on the rest of a homogeneous France, it was as often determined by local passions and interests. Along with the revival of place as a conditioner have come people. For as the imperatives of "structure" have weakened, those of individual agency, and especially of revolutionary utterance, have become correspondingly more important.

… I have pressed one of the essential elements in de Tocqueville's argument—his understanding of the destabilizing effects of modernization *before* the Revolution—further than his account allows it to go. Relieved of the revolutionary coinage "old regime," with its heavy semantic freight of obsolescence, it may be possible to see French culture and society in the reign of Louis XVI as troubled more by its addiction to change than by resistance to it. Conversely, it seems to me that much of the anger firing revolutionary violence arose from hostility towards that modernization, rather than from impatience with the speed of its progress.

... [I attempt] to confront directly the painful problem of revolutionary violence. Anxious lest they give way to sensationalism or be confused with counter-revolutionary prosecutors, historians have erred on the side of squeamishness in dealing with this issue. I have returned it to the center of the story since it seems to me that it was not merely an unfortunate by-product of politics, or the disagreeable instrument by which other more virtuous ends were accomplished or vicious ones were thwarted. In some depressingly unavoidable sense, violence *was* the Revolution itself....

* * *

The tenth to the twelfth of March [1793] saw the first stage in the uprising, when spontaneously assembled crowds in villages and *bourgs* attacked the offices and houses of mayors, *juges de paix, procureurs* and dangerously isolated units of the National Guard. The riot at Machecoul was repeated, with less murderous consequences, in Saint-Florent-le-Veil, Sainte-Pazanne, Saint-Hilaire-de-Chaléons and Clisson. The leaders who emerged from this first wave of violence were often, like the gamekeeper and ex-soldier Stofflet, men who had long been identified in their locality with resistance to the revolutionary authorities. Once they had evicted their enemies and taken their weapons, the crowds coalesced with each other, forming processions towards larger towns and snowballing in size as they traveled along the roads.

At this stage, the riots in the Vendée seemed no different from similar antirecruitment riots taking place in many other parts of France from the Calvados in Normandy to the Côte d'Or in Burgundy and the Puy in the southern Massif Central. Some of the worst upheavals occurred north of the Loire in Brittany. But there the government had been so obsessed by the possibility of counter-revolutionary plots, it had in place sufficient force to take rapid and decisive action against the centers of resistance. The Vendée, in contrast, was dangerously depleted of troops. At Challans, for example, there were just two hundred Patriot Guards who had to face more than a thousand insurgents on the twelfth of March. By the time that reinforcements could be provided, the several riots had already fused into a general insurrection. Moreover, even of the fifty thousand republican soldiers who were eventually concentrated in the Vendée by the third week of March, only a tiny proportion—perhaps fewer than two thousand—were veterans of the "line"—the old royal army. The remainder were unseasoned volunteers, badly fed and equipped and, more critically for the situation they faced, extremely apprehensive about the rebels. None of the armies of France in the spring and summer of 1793 showed such propensity to take to panic and break ranks as the *bleus* of the Vendée. Perhaps they feared the fate of the republicans of Machecoul. As it was, many of them were dispersed in small units of fifty or some hundreds, numerous enough to provide a target for the infuriated rebels but not substantial enough to overawe them.

By the time that the Republic understood the gravity of the situation, the rebels had already taken many of the larger centers, in particular Cholet, Chemillé and Fontenay-le-Comte. On the fourteenth of March, Stofflet joined his forces with those attached to another gamekeeper, Tonnelet, and men following the wagoner-vendor Cathelineau. After failing to persuade the republican troops, commanded by the citizen-marquis de Beauveau, to lay down their arms, the rebels overwhelmed the *bleus* in a great barrage of fire, mortally wounding de Beauveau....

* * *

The second half of March brought a steady drumbeat of calamity to republican France. Within the same week, the Convention heard of the defeat at Neerwinden, a further military collapse near Louvain, Custine's abrupt retreat in the Rhineland and the Vendéan uprising. Report after report described Republican armies dissolving on contact with the enemy (especially in the Vendée); volunteers demoralized and disorderly, deserting or taking to their heels; the tricolor trampled in the mud. When Delacroix returned from the Belgian front, he brought with him a gloom as deep and as dark as the weeks before Valmy. French troops had fallen back on Valenciennes, but if that fortress fell, he warned, there was nothing between the Allied armies and Paris. To many deputies, and not just those of the Mountain, there could be only one explanation for this sorry trail of disasters: conspiracy. The commissioners with General Marcé's defeated army in the Vendée accused him of either "the most cowardly ineptness" or, worse, "the most cowardly treason." His son; his second-in-command, Verteuil; and another Verteuil presumed to be *his* son (but in fact a distant relative) were all arrested for being "in treasonable contact with the enemy." ...

Faced with this military landslide, the Convention, with very few exceptions, acknowledged that it had to strengthen the powers of the state. Without an effective executive and a coherent chain of command, centrifugal forces would pull France apart. For the first time since the beginning of the Revolution, the legislature set about creating strong organs of central authority authorized to do the Republic's work without endless reference to the "sovereign body." On March 6 it dispatched eighty of its own members (known, from April on, as "representatives on mission") to the departments to ensure compliance with the central government's will. They were, in effect, a revolutionary version of the old royal *intendants*, traveling embodiments of sovereignty. Much of their work was meant to concern itself with judicial and punitive matters. On March 11 a special Revolutionary Tribunal was established in Paris to try suspects accused of counter-revolutionary activities. On March 20, with the rebellions in the Vendée and Brittany in mind, the Convention adopted Cambacérès' proposal giving military courts jurisdiction over anyone who had been employed in public positions (including clergy and nobles) and who was found with the white royalist cockade or fomenting rebellion. If guilty, they were to be shot within twenty-four hours. A day later, every commune in the country was equipped with committees of surveillance and all citizens were encouraged to denounce anyone they suspected of uncertain loyalties. Predictably, the law rapidly became a charter for countless petty dramas of revenge.

Finally, on April 6, it was decided to replace the Committee of General Defense, set up in January as a body of twenty-five to coordinate the work of the several committees of the Convention. In its place was to be a much tighter committee of just nine members, to be known as the Committee of Public Safety....

On October 10 Saint-Just came before the Convention to issue a report in the name of the Committee of Public Safety on the "troubles affecting the state." He took the righteously self-scrutinizing line of declaring that the people had only one enemy, namely the government itself, infected as it was with all sorts of spineless, corrupt and compromised creatures of the old regime. The remedy was unremitting austerity of purpose, implacable punishment for the backsliders and the hypocrites. The charter of the Terror—the Law of Suspects, enacted on September 17, which gave the Committee and its representatives sweeping powers of arrest and punishment over extraordinarily broad categories of people defined as harboring counter-revolutionary designs—should be applied with the utmost rigor. "Between the people and their enemies there can be nothing in common but the sword; we must govern by iron those who cannot be governed by justice; we must oppress the tyrant.... It is impossible for revolutionary laws to be executed unless the government itself is truly revolutionary." ...

*   *   *

The Terror went into action with impressive bureaucratic efficiency. House searches, usually made at night, were extensive and unsparing. All citizens were required to attach to their front doors a notice indicating all residents who lived inside. Entertaining anyone not on that list, even for a single night, was a serious crime. Denunciations poured into the Commission. People were accused of defaming Chalier, of attacking the liberty tree, secreting priests or émigrés, making speculative fortunes and—one of the standard crimes of the year II—writing or uttering *"merde à la république."* From early December the guillotine went into action at a much greater tempo. As in Paris, pride was taken in its mechanical efficiency. On the eleventh of Nivôse, according to the scrupulous accounts kept, thirty-two heads were severed in twenty-five minutes; a week later, twelve heads in just five minutes.

For the most eager Terrorists, though, this was still a messy and inconvenient way of disposing of the political garbage. Citizens in the Streets around the place des Terreaux, on the rue Lafont, for example, were complaining about the blood overflowing the drainage ditch that led from beneath the scaffold. A number of the condemned, then, were executed in mass shootings on the Plaine des Brotteaux—the field beside the Rhone where Montgolfier had made his ascent. Yet another ex-actor, Dorfeuille, presided over some of these *mitraillades*, in which as many as sixty prisoners were tied in a line by ropes and shot at with cannon. Those who were not killed outright by the fire were finished off with sabers, bayonets and rifles. On the fourth of December, Dorfeuille wrote to the President of the Convention that a hundred and thirteen inhabitants of "this new Sodom" had been executed on that single day and in those that followed he hoped another four to five hundred would "expiate their crimes with fire and shot." ...

By the time that the killings in "Ville-Affranchie" had finished, one thousand nine hundred and five people had met their end. ...

*   *   *

The violence did not stop, however, with the Terror. Richard Cobb has written eloquently of the waves of the Counter-Terror, especially brutal in the Midi and the Rhone Valley; of anarchic murder gangs picking off selected targets implicated in Jacobinism. Republican officials; army officers; members of departmental administrations; conspicuous militants of the popular societies; and, in the south, Protestant farmers and merchants—all became prey for the *sabreurs* of the year III. Corpses were dumped in front of cafés and inns in the Midi or thrown into the Rhone or Saône. In many areas, the Counter-Terrorists would gather together at an inn as if for a day's hunting, and go off in search of their quarry.

Considerable areas of the country—the Midi and Rhone Valley, Brittany and western Normandy—remained in a virtual state of civil war, though the violence now proceeded in a haphazard, hit-and-run fashion rather than by organized insurrection. The great engines of capitalist prosperity in late eighteenth-century France, the Atlantic and Mediterranean ports, had been broken by antifederalist repression and British naval blockade. When Samuel Romilly returned to Bordeaux during the peace of 1802, he was dismayed to find the docks silent and ghostly and grass growing tall between the flagstones of the quai des Chartrons. Marseille and Lyon only recovered as the Revolution receded and the reorientation of the Bonapartist state towards Italy offered new markets and trade routes.…

What had the Revolution accomplished to balance these penalties? Its two great social alterations—the end of the seigneurial regime and the abolition of the guilds—both promised more than they delivered. Though many artisans were undoubtedly happy to be free of the hierarchy of the corporations that constrained their labor and reward, they were, if anything, even more nakedly exposed to the economic inequities that per-sisted between masters and journeymen. Likewise the abolition of feudalism was more in the way of a legal than a social change and merely completed the evolution from lords to landlords that had been well under way in the old regime. There is no question that peasants were thankful for the end of seigneurial exactions that had imposed a crushing burden of payments on static rural incomes. Equally certainly, they were determined at all costs to oppose their reimposition. But it is hard to say whether the mass of the rural population were measurably better off in 1799 than they had been in 1789. Though the redemption tariff for feudal dues had been abolished outright in 1793, landlords often compensated themselves by various rent strategies that deepened the indebtedness of share-cropping *métayers*. Moreover, the taxes demanded by the Republic —among them the single land tax, the *impot fôncier*—were certainly no lighter than those exacted by the King. Before long the Consulate and Empire would revert to indirect taxes on at least as onerous a scale as under the old regime. All that they were spared, fiscally, were extraordinary poll taxes, including the old *capitation* and the *vingtième*, but this relief was only a consequence of the ever-expanding military frontier. Taxes lifted from the shoulders of the French were now dropped on those of the Italians, Germans and Dutch. When that frontier suddenly retreated in 1814, back to the old limits of the hexagonal *patrie*, the French were stuck with the bill, which, just as in 1789, they adamantly refused to pay, thus sealing the Empire's fate.

Was the world of the village in 1799 so very different from what it had been ten years before? In particular regions of France where there had been heavy emigration and repression, rural life had indeed been emptied of noble dominance. But this obvious rupture disguises a continuity of some importance. It was exactly those sections of the population who had been gaining economically under the old regime that profited most from the sale of noble and church lands. Those sales were declared irreversible, so there was indeed a substantial transfer of wealth. But much of that transfer was *within* the landed classes—extending from well-to-do farmers up to "patriot" nobles who had managed to stay put and actually benefited from the confiscations. Fat cats got fatter.... There were, to be sure, many regions of France where the nobility as a group lost a considerable part of their fortune. But there were also others— in the west, the center and the south— where, as Jean Tulard has shown, lands that remained unsold could be recovered by families who returned in substantial numbers after 1796. Thus, while many of the leading figures in this history ended their lives on the guillotine, many others stayed put and reemerged as the leading notables of their department....

By contrast, the rural poor gained very little at all from the Revolution. Saint-Just's Ventôse laws remained a dead letter and it became harder than ever to pasture animals on common land or gather fuel from the open woods. In all these respects the Revolution was just an interlude in the inexorable modernization of property rights that had been well under way before 1789. No government—that of the Jacobins any more than that of the King —had really answered the cries for help that echoed through the rural *cahiers de doléances* in 1789....

Had the Revolution, at least, created state institutions which resolved the problems that brought down the monar-

chy? Here, too, as de Tocqueville emphasized, it is easier to discern continuities, especially of centralization, than any overwhelming change. In public finance, the creation of a paper currency came to be recognized as a catastrophe beside which the insolvencies of the old regime looked almost picayune. Eventually the Bonapartist Consultate (whose finances were administered overwhelmingly by surviving bureaucrats of the old regime) returned to a metallic system based on Calonne's important monetary reform of 1785 fixing the ratio of silver to gold. Fiscally, too, post-Jacobin France slid inexorably back to the former mixture of loans and indirect as well as direct taxes. The Republic and Empire did no better funding a large army and navy from these domestic sources than had the monarchy and depended crucially on institutionalized extortion from occupied countries to keep the military pump primed.

The Napoleonic prefects have always been recognized as the heirs of the royal *intendants* (and the revolutionary *représentants-en-mission*), brokering administration between central government priorities and the interest of the local notability. Without any question that notability had suffered a violent shock during the height of the Jacobin Terror, especially in the great provincial cities, where, after the federalist revolt, they were virtually exterminated. The constitution of the year III, however, with its reintroduction of tax qualifications for the electoral assemblies, returned authority to those who had, in many places, exercised it continuously between the mid-1780s and 1792. As we have seen, in some small towns, such as Calais, where adroit mayors paid lip service to passing regimes, there was unbroken continuity of office from 1789 through the Restoration.... For these men and countless others like them, the Revolution had been but a brutal though mercifully ephemeral interruption of their social and institutional power....

What killed the monarchy was its inability to create representative institutions through which the state could execute its program of reform. Had the Revolution done any better? On one level, the succession of elected legislatures, from the Estates-General to the National Convention, was one of the most impressive innovations of the Revolution. They took the intensive debate on the shape of governing institutions in France, which had been going on for at least half a century, into the arena of representation itself and articulated its principles with unparalleled eloquence. But for all their virtues as theaters of debate, none of the legislatures ever managed to solve the issue that had bedeviled the old regime: how to create a viable working partnership between the executive and the legislature? Once the Constituent had rejected Mounier and Mirabeau's "British" proposal of drawing ministers from the assembly, it regarded the executive not as the administration of the country, working in good faith, but as a fifth column bent on subverting national sovereignty. With this doomed beginning, the executive and legislative branches of the constitution of 1791 simply intensified the war with each other until their mutual destruction in 1792. The Terror effectively reversed matters by putting the Convention under the thrall of the committees, but still make it impossible to change governments except by violence.

The framers of the constitution of the year III (1795) obviously learned something from this unhappy experience. A two-chamber legislature was introduced, elected indirectly from colleges in which property was the criterion for membership. A governing council was in theory accountable to the legislature (as indeed the committees had been). In practice, however, the experiment remained darkened by the long shadow of the revolution itself, so that factions inevitably crystallized, not around specific issues of government but plans for the overthrow of the state, hatched either by royalists or neo-Jacobins. With the separate organs of the constitution in paralyzing conflict with each other, violence continued to determine the political direction of the state far more than did elections.

But the violence was, after the year III, no longer coming from the streets and *sections* but from the uniformed army. If one had to look for one indisputable story of transformation in the French Revolution, it would be the creation of the juridical entity of the citizen. But no sooner had this hypothetically free person been invented than his liberties were circumscribed by the police power of the state. This was always done in the name of republican patriotism, but the constraints were no less oppressive for that. Just as Maribeau—and the Robespierre of 1791—had feared, liberties were held hostage to the authority of the warrior state. Though this conclusion might be depressing, it should not really be all that surprising. The Revolution, after all, had begun as a response to a patriotism wounded by the humiliations of the Seven Years' War. It was Vergennes' decision to promote, at the same time, maritime imperialism and continental military power which generated the sense of fiscal panic that overcame the monarchy in its last days. A crucial element—perhaps, indeed, *the* crucial element—in the claim of the revolutionaries of 1789 was that they could better regenerate the *patrie* than could the appointees of the King. From the outset, then, the great continuing strand of militancy was patriotic. Militarized nationalism was not, in some accidental way, the unintended consequence of the French Revolution: it was its heart and soul. It was wholly logical that the multimillionaire inheritors of revolutionary power —the true "new class" of this period of French history—were not some *bourgeoisie conquérante* but *real* conquerors: the Napoleonic marshals, whose fortunes made even those of the surviving dynasts of the nobility look paltry by comparison.

For better or worse, the "modern men" who seemed poised to capture government under Louis XVI—engineers, noble industrialists, scientists, bureaucrats and generals—resumed their march to power once the irritations of revolutionary politics were brushed aside. *"La tragédie, maintenant, c'est la politique,"* claimed Napoleon, who, after the coup d'état that brought him to power in 1799, added his claim to that which had been made by so many optimistic governments before him, that "the Revolution is completed."

At other times, though, he was not so sure. For if he understood that one last achievement of the Revolution had been the creation of a military-technocratic state of immense power and emotional solidarity, he also realized that its *other* principal invention had been a political culture that perennially and directly challenged it. What occurred between 1789 and 1793 was an unprecedented explosion of politics—in speech, print, image and even music—that broke all the barriers that had traditionally circumscribed it. Initially, this had been the monarchy's own doing. For it was in the tens of thousands of little meetings convened to draft *cahiers* and elect deputies to the

Estates-General that French men (and occasionally women) found their voice. In so doing, they became part of a process that tied the satisfaction of their immediate wants into the process of redefining sovereignty.

That was both the opportunity and the problem. Suddenly, subjects were told they had become Citizens; an aggregate of subjects held in place by injustice and intimidation had become a Nation. From this new thing, this Nation of Citizens, justice, freedom and plenty could be not only expected but required. By the same token, should it not materialize, only those who had spurned their citizenship, or who were by their birth or unrepentant beliefs incapable of exercising it, could be held responsible. Before the promise of 1789 could be realized, then, it was necessary to root out Uncitizens.

Thus began the cycle of violence which ended in the smoking obelisk and the forest of guillotines. However much the historian, in the year of celebration, may be tempted to see that violence as an unpleasant "aspect" of the Revolution which ought not to distract from its accomplishments, it would be jejune to do so. From the very beginning—from the summer of 1789—violence was the motor of the Revolution. The journalist Loustalot's knowing exploitation of the punitive murder and mutilation of Foulon and Bertier de Sauvigny conceded nothing in its calculated ferocity to the most extreme harangues of Marat and Hébert. *"Il faut du sang pour cimenter la révolution"* (There must be blood to cement revolution), said Mme Roland, who would herself perish by the logical application of her enthusiasm. While it would be grotesque to implicate the generation of 1789 in the kind of hideous atrocities perpetrated under the Terror, it would be equally naive not to recognize that the former made the latter possible. All the newspapers, the revolutionary festivals, the painted plates; the songs and street theater; the regiments of little boys waving their right arms in the air swearing patriotic oaths in piping voices—all these features of what historians have come to designate the "political culture of the Revolution"—were the products of the same morbid preoccupation with the just massacre and the heroic death.

Historians are also much given to distinguishing between "verbal" violence and the real thing. The assumption seems to be that such men as Javogues and Marat, who were given to screaming at people, calling for death, gloating at the spectacle of heads on pikes or processions of men with their hands tied behind their backs climbing the steps to the rasoir national were indulging only in brutal rhetoric. The screamers were not to be compared with such quiet bureaucrats of death as Fouquier-Tinville who did their jobs with stolid, silent efficiency. But the history of "Ville-Affranchie," of the Vendée-Vengé, or of the September massacres suggests in fact a direct connection between all that orchestrated or spontaneous screaming for blood and its copious shedding. It contributed greatly to the complete dehumanization of those who became victims. As "brigands" or the "Austrian whore" or "fanatics" they became nonentities in the Nation of Citizens and not only could but had to be eliminated if it was to survive. Humiliation and abuse, then, were not just Jacobin fun and games; they were the prologues to killing.

Why was the French Revolution like this? Why, from the beginning, was it powered by brutality? The question might seem to be circular since if, in fact, reform had been all that had been required, there would have been no Revolution in the first place. The question nonetheless remains important if we are ever to understand why successive generations of those who tried to stabilize its course—Mirabeau, Barnave, Danton —met with such failure. Was it just that French popular culture was already brutalized before the Revolution and responded to the spectacle of terrifying public punishments handed out by royal justice with its own forms of spontaneous sanguinary retribution? That all naive revolutionaries would do, would be to give the people the chance to exact such retribution and make it part of the regular conduct of politics? This may be part of the explanation, but even a cursory look beyond French borders, and especially over the Channel to Britain, makes it difficult to see France as uniquely damaged, either by a more dangerous distance between rich and poor or indeed by higher rates of crime and popular violence, than places which avoided violent revolution.

Popular revolutionary violence was not some sort of boiling subterranean lava that finally forced its way onto the surface of French politics and then proceeded to scald all those who stepped in its way. Perhaps it would be better to think of the revolutionary elite as rash geologists, themselves gouging open great holes in the crust of polite discourse and then feeding the angry matter through the pipes of their rhetoric out into the open. Volcanoes and steam holes do not seem inappropriate metaphors here, because contemporaries were themselves constantly invoking them. Many of those who were to sponsor or become caught up in violent change were fascinated by seismic violence, by the great primordial eruptions which geologists now said were not part of a single Creation, but which happened periodically in geological time. These events were, to borrow from Burke, both sublime and terrible. And it was perhaps Romanticism, with its addiction to the Absolute and the Ideal; its fondness for the vertiginous and the macabre; its concept of political energy, as, above all, electrical; its obsession with the heart; its preference for passion over reason, for virtue over peace, that supplied a crucial ingredient in the mentality of the revolutionary elite: its association of liberty with wildness. What began with Lafayette's infatuation with the hyena of the Gévaudan surely ended in the ceremonies of the pike-stuck heads.

There was another obsession which converged with this Romanticization of violence: the neoclassical fixation with the patriotic death. The annals of Rome (and occasionally the doomed battles of Athens and Sparta) were the mirrors into which revolutionaries constantly gazed in search of self-recognition. Their France would be Rome reborn, but purified by the benison of the feeling heart. It thus followed, surely, that for such a Nation to be born, many would necessarily die. And both the birth and death would be simultaneously beautiful.

POSTSCRIPT

Was the French Revolution Worth Its Human Costs?

In many ways, Schama's book was revolutionary and was considered so by his peers in the historical profession. Covering a subject that had been dominated by Marxists, Annalistes, and social historians, he returned to the domain of the historical narrative as his vehicle of expression, something that had lost favor with many of the French Revolution's leading scholars. Secondly, according to the preface from *Citizens*, Schama's focus was "an unfashionable 'topdown' rather than 'bottom up' approach." Finally, although a scholar of impeccable credentials, he was considered an outsider in the field of French Revolution historiography because he had not "been a lifetime toiler in the vineyards of the Revolution," according to Alan Spitzer, in "Narrative's Problems: The Case of Simon Schama," *Journal of Modern History* (March 1993).

The most controversial feature of the French Revolution was the infamous Reign of Terror, and it is a subject that all toilers in the garden of the Revolution have to explain. The horrors of this century (some committed in the name of revolution) demand that the Terror gets the fullest treatment possible. Only then can the question of whether or not the Revolution was worth its human costs be answered. As always, the present and the search for relevance in the past will be the final arbiter. If Kropotkin's work speaks to the spirit of the ninteenth century's era of democratic revolutions, Schama's does the same to the dreams deferred and lives lost to that century's failed revolutions.

To list all of sources on the French Revolution is daunting. William Doyle, *The Oxford History of the French Revolution* (Oxford University Press, 1989) and Donald M. G. Sutherland, *France, 1789–1815: Revolution and Counter-Revolution* (Oxford University Press, 1986) are two scholarly, general accounts of the era. As always, much can be learned from Alexis de Tocqueville, whose *Old Regime and the French Revolution*, first published in the 1850s, could be a useful starting point for a study of French Revolutionary historiography. Finally, the 1984 film *Danton*, which deals with the French Revolution and especially the Terror gone mad, is worth seeing.

ISSUE 5

Did the Industrial Revolution Lead to a Sexual Revolution?

YES: Edward Shorter, from "Female Emancipation, Birth Control, and Fertility in European History," *The American Historical Review* (June 1973)

NO: Louise A. Tilly, Joan W. Scott, and Miriam Cohen, from "Women's Work and European Fertility Patterns," *Journal of Interdisciplinary History* (Winter 1976)

ISSUE SUMMARY

YES: Historian Edward Shorter argues that employment opportunities outside the home that opened up with industrialization led to a rise in the illegitimacy rate, which he attributes to the sexual emancipation of unmarried, working-class women.

NO: Historians Louise A. Tilly, Joan W. Scott, and Miriam Cohen counter that unmarried women worked to meet an economic need, not to gain personal freedom, and they attribute the rise in illegitimacy rates to broken marriage promises and the absence of traditional support from family, community, and the church.

Historians agree that between 1750 and 1850, the illegitimacy rate rose across Europe. In many of the European countries this time period coincides with industrialization. Did the arrival of capitalism change the living and working habits of unmarried women and introduce new attitudes that made them more interested in sex? When the result is agreed upon, what matters most is the evidence offered to explain the cause.

In the selection that follows, Edward Shorter boldly claims that a nineteenth-century sexual revolution that had its roots in industrial capitalism occurred. In his view the market economy, with its values of self-interest and competitiveness, changed the value system of the proletarian subculture— the young men and women working for wages in industrializing countries. Earning their own money, says Shorter, gave these workers the means to live independently. Young women in particular, he argues, declared their independence from family control, struck out in pursuit of personal freedom, and began to enjoy sex as a way of finding individual self-fulfillment. The predictable result was a rise in illegitimacy rates.

Louise A. Tilly, Joan W. Scott, and Miriam Cohen, in reply, fault Shorter for offering little or no hard evidence for his hypothesis. Citing the work of other historians, they assert that family interest rather than self-interest led women to work. Women moved very slowly into industrial work, and, even by the end of the period (1850), most women who were employed were doing domestic service, dressmaking, laundering, and tailoring, not factory work. Many women earned far too little to permit them to live independently. Those who did probably kept the traditional assumption that premarital intercourse with an intended bridegroom would be followed by marriage. Tilly, Scott, and Cohen argue that what changed was not the attitudes but the external context. In the absence of traditional pressures, young men moved on to other work or better opportunities, leaving the women they had impregnated behind.

As you read these two conflicting interpretations, look for the explanation offered by each essay and, most important, at what evidence is offered to support the interpretation. It may seem logical to assume that an increase in rates of illegitimacy must be due to a sexual revolution. But is that the only or the best explanation that existing information can support? There is a real temptation to use our "common sense" to fill in the gaps, but the historian insists on evidence.

For centuries history was written exclusively from the point of view of the rich, the powerful, and the literate. For some, understanding the "great man" —Alexander the Great, Julius Caesar, and Napoleon, for example—was the key to understanding the age in which he lived. This is often called history "from the top down." Many scholars, however, have begun to uncover the lives of the poor, the powerless, and the illiterate—what some call history "from the bottom up." Borrowing the methods of the social sciences, such as archaeology, anthropology, sociology, and psychology, and using quantitative analyses of economic and demographic data, historians are trying to fill in the missing pieces of the past. The essays in this issue take on the challenge of assessing the motives of people who left few, if any, written records. Since we cannot read their diaries and letters, we must use the evidence that we do have about the lives these women led and attempt to imagine how they might have seen the world.

In this issue, the chief question concerns continuity versus discontinuity. What changed? What remained the same? Did the attitudes of working women change as they entered the capitalist labor force, as Shorter claims? And did these attitudes lead them to pursue personal pleasures such as sex, which, in the absence of birth control, resulted in higher rates of illegitimacy? Or, as Tilly, Scott, and Cohen argue, did the attitudes stay the same (premarital sex, as usual, in the context of courtship and with the expectation of marriage), while the context changed, leaving women pregnant and with no expectation of marriage?

YES

Edward Shorter

FEMALE EMANCIPATION, BIRTH CONTROL, AND FERTILITY IN EUROPEAN HISTORY

The conventional wisdom about female emancipation is that it originated among upper-class women in the mid-nineteenth century, surfacing first in tandem with the movement for emancipation of the slaves, then moving forward independently as the suffrage movement. While this account may be substantially correct as involves women's participation in national political life, it is, in my opinion, inapplicable to family history.[1] I suggest that the position of women within the family underwent a radical shift starting late in the eighteenth century; furthermore, the change progressed form young and lowly women to older women of higher status.[2] The logic of this chronology sees involvement in the economy of the market place as the principal motor of emancipation.

What exactly is meant by "female emancipation"? General statements about the position of women within early modern European families are uncertain in the extreme because, at the same time, so many impressions of individual famous women are to be found in the literature and so little is known in a systematic, quantitative way about the cultural rules and norms of women in the popular classes. Yet one might fairly characterize the situation of most women as one of subordination. In the first place, both young men and women were subordinated to the authority of their parents, so that parental intervention in the mating market customarily replaced romantic love in bringing young couples together. In the second place, both social ideology and the force of events conspired to make the husband supreme over the woman in the household, his obligation being merely to respect her, hers, however, to serve and obey him. In most matters of sex, economics, or family authority the woman was expected to do the husband's bidding. Clearly individual exceptions existed, yet the rule seems to have been powerlessness and dependency for the woman.[3]

Thus female emancipation involves, quite simply, the replacement of this subordination with independence. In the nineteenth and twentieth centuries

From Edward Shorter, "Female Emancipation, Birth Control, and Fertility in European History," *The American Historical Review*, vol. 78, no. 3 (June 1973). Copyright © 1973 by The American Historical Association. Reprinted by permission.

married women acquired for themselves first, practical leverage on household political power, and second, a family ideology stressing their own rights to sexual gratification and emotional autonomy.[4] And unmarried women became increasingly convinced of the impropriety of family and community restraints upon social and sexual relations, so that they came to ignore the strictures of both parents and community in order to gratify their own personal needs. Therefore women's emancipation at the popular level means disregarding outside controls upon personal freedom of action and sexuality for the sake of individual self-fulfillment.[5]

What evidence exists that the years 1750–1850 saw a movement toward female emancipation among the popular classes? We are, alas, at the beginning of the investigation rather than the end, and so I can merely anticipate the findings of future research. Yet even within the existing literature strong hints may be found that crucial changes in the status and authority of women were under way after 1750 and that these changes were linked in some way to economic modernization. The search for evidence may be aided by considering the nature of the change in the relationship between married woman and husband as well as that between the young, unmarried woman and parental and communal authority. To demonstrate that there is in fact an *explicandum*, let us briefly review some previous findings on these questions.

Least studied to date has been the family life and authority relationships of lower-class women in the years before 1900. Save for tiny pinpricks of information here and there the subject is uncharted, yet those studies that exist converge to demonstrate a radical upheaval in popular family life in the wake of capitalism. Neil Smelser, in a classic study of the British cotton industry, describes "the reversal of traditional age and sex roles as wives and children went to the factory." Industrial growth fragmented the customary "family economy" by making individual producers of its separate members. And, for the children at least, independence accompanied wage labor. Peter Stearns has recently reviewed the German literature, finding toward the end of the nineteenth century (a period inconveniently late for the case I wish to present here) "recognition of greater independence for the woman.... There is suggested here a new sentiment within the family, the possibility of greater affection for the children, who were not underfoot all the time, and greater sensuality and equality in the relationship between man and wife." And Rudolf Braun, in his sensitive reconstruction of life among cottage and factory workers in the Zurich highlands, notes massive shifts in family patterns, starting with the eighteenth century. While Braun is silent on specific changes in the relationships between married men and women, he pulls back the canvas for a brief instant to reveal, for example, women forgetting how to cook. Why, Braun asks, were ready-made foods in such great demand in factory towns?

It was not merely the pressure to eat at the workplace that accelerated the demand for prepared dishes, nor the lack of time at home, but also the woman factory worker's lack of skill in cooking. Bound to the machine and the factory since earliest childhood, she inadequately learned the arts of cooking and homemaking. We have seen these complaints since the woman cottage workers of the *ancien régime*, but with factory workers they become even more urgent.[6]

One can imagine that the authority patterns among traditional petit-bourgeois families were as different from those of worker couples out on the frontier of economic advance as night is from day.

Evidence is more abundant that young unmarried women were rebelling against parental and social authority in the period from 1750 to 1850. To draw upon my own research, I noted in early nineteenth-century Bavaria an absolute squall of outrage from middle-class observers of popular life, seated for the most part in lower levels of the governmental bureaucracy, about a new spirit of independence among young women in agricultural labor and domestic service.[7] Through this chorus of complaints ran the themes of escape and experimentation, of throwing off old superordinates and codes, and of, in general, what a much later generation of emancipators was to call "liberation."

There was the theme of escape from old jobs. Young women wanted, when possible, to forsake domestic service for employment that would safeguard personal independence. The unpopularity of service may be seen in the cries about a shortage of rural labor (Dienstbotenmangel) that became a constant theme in social criticism from the mid-eighteenth century onward.[8] Or, to take another sort of example, Munich's police chief noted in 1815:

It is sad, and most difficult for the police to prevent, that so many young girls leave service when they grow tired of waiting on people and under one pretext or another take a room somewhere, living from their own industry. But they do little real work and let themselves be supported by boyfriends; they become pregnant and then are abandoned.[9]

And there was the theme of escape from old residences. Young women wanted to live alone, in their own quarters and away from the oppressive supervision of either parents or employers. In the late 1830s the indignant provincial government of Würzburg observed:

In our province the so-called practice of Eigenzimmern is quite customary, according to which the deflorated daughter leaves the parental house and rents a room elsewhere, not necessarily to avoid the reproaches of the parents for her misdeeds, but in order to move more freely, to accommodate the visit of the boyfriend [Zuhälter] and with him to live in concubinage [wilde Ehe].[10]

On the matter of escape from old personal styles, let Joseph Maria Johann Nepomuck Freiherr von Frauenberg, archbishop of Bamberg, speak:

A most detrimental alteration in the character of the female gender [has taken place]. Earlier, women distinguished themselves through their soft, withdrawn, modest, and chaste being, while nowadays they take part in all public entertainments, indeed providing some, set the tone [den Ton angeben], and so have entirely departed from their natural situation. Thus has female morality disappeared.

The archbishop noted this development had occurred principally in the cities. There were other complaints about how female servants and hired hands would squander their entire wages in buying expeditions to the cities, returning to the farm with clothes alien to native folkways. Still other laments were voiced about feminine indifference to pastoral authority and about newly grasping, calculating female attitudes to wage matters. All these threads led back in the opinion of contemporaries—and rightly so I think—to sexuality and thus ultimately to fertility: "In the countryside a young girl who has preserved her virgin purity until age twenty is exceptional, and moreover encounters even among her girlfriends no recognition."[11]

Perhaps Bavaria was not typical of the rest of Europe, though I believe that it was, for within its frontiers the kingdom harbored a remarkable diversity of social and economic arrangements. Perhaps, even more serious for the case I wish to make, male complaints about "moral breakdown" among young women reflected sooner the beholder's own libidinal preoccupations than a change in objective social conditions. Perhaps, too, nostalgia is close to being a historical constant, so that most men who search their own memories invariably see behind the outlines of a gray, disorganized present the golden harmony of an idealized past. Yet in this case I doubt it. And I suspect that future research will verify that this particular set of social critics at this particular point in time—the years 1800–40 —were onto something. The objective order of the real world was in fact changing, and a shift in the position of women was moving the ground directly from under the feet of these "patriarchs."

* * *

These changes in the mentalities and sexual comportment of women may ultimately be linked to a variety of changes in economic structure that one might summarize under the label "capitalism." Three salients of industrial advance mattered to fertility, and two of the three made more of a difference to women than to men....

First, capitalism meant the formation of a proletarian subculture. Large numbers of people who had in common the fact that they were wage laborers found themselves living together in the same communities. Because the material conditions of their lives differentiated them clearly from the surrounding social order of small proprietors, these newly aggregated workers in both agriculture and industry began to develop their own rules for doing cultural business, which is, after all, the essence of a subculture. A way of life specific to the working classes began to elaborate itself within the large farm areas of modernizing agriculture, upon the upland slopes where the putting out of textiles and nail manufacture was thriving, and within the newly blossoming industrial cities themselves.[12]

The subculture would sooner or later matter to fertility by providing alternative sets of rules for sexual comportment, target family sizes, and new techniques for contraception and abortion. But subcultures are especially important in the area of legitimation of behavior about which the individual might otherwise feel uneasy. It is now common knowledge that the charter culture of traditional Europe had internalized within young people a host of restraints against intercourse. So that if before 1750 there was relatively little premarital intercourse, it was not necessarily because external supervision was totalitarian in its strictness but because most people within the culture shared the belief that premarital sex was wrong. When in later years sex before marriage became commonplace, it was because a new generation of sexually active young men and women felt their behavior was socially accepted, at least by their peers. The point is that if an individual is going to bend the operating rules of the dominant culture, he must feel that members of his own group, whose good opinion he treasures, will support his venturesomeness.[13]

The proletarian subculture was, of course, indulgent of eroticism. Yet this particular indulgence must not be attributed without further argument to the industrial origins of the subculture. The fact that a subculture exists does not automatically mean that its specific operating rules must be libertine. Indeed many subculture with quite repressive sexual values have flourished in the past, such as the colonies of nineteenth-century pietists in the United States. Some additional aspect of industrialism must therefore be adduced to explain the expressly permissive sexual content of the European proletarian subculture.

The second important dimension of capitalism lay in the mentality of the market place. In the eighteenth and early nineteenth centuries the market economy encroached steadily at the cost of the moral economy, and the values of individual self-interest and competitiveness that people learned in the market were soon transferred to other areas of life. It was this process of the transfer of values that gave the proletarian subculture its libertine moral caste.

The years after 1750 saw the intrusion of the principles of the market place into popular life. In early modern Europe trade in foodstuffs and in most non-agricultural products was tightly regulated by communal and corporate bodies, so that the Continent was fragmented into countless tiny local markets, kept through a complot of regulation and poor transportation as hermetically sealed compartments. Of course long-distance trade existed, yet most of the labor force was involved in local production along noncapitalistic lines. German political

economists made a classic distinction between *Export-* and *Lokalgewerbe,* and most of the population lived form the latter. Then late in the eighteenth century these locally administered economies began to be engulfed by free markets of vast territorial scope. The struggle over free trade in grain in France has been often told; the losing battle of German guilds against pack pedlars, retail merchandise shops, unlicensed competitors, and the Customs Union is similarly familiar. Everywhere the moral economy regulated by the village fathers lost out to free competition regulated only by the invisible hand of the price mechanism.[14]

Contact with these new labor markets was the most direct source of personal autonomy. As women became immersed in the market, they learned its values. I have elsewhere suggested that capitalism's mental habits of maximizing one's self-interest and sacrificing community goals to individual profit transfer easily to other thought processes.[15] It seems a plausible proposition that people assimilate in the market place an integrated, coherent set of values about social behavior and personal independence and that these values quickly inform the noneconomic realms of individual mentalities. If this logic holds true, we may identify exposure to the market place as a prime source of female emancipation, for women who learned autonomy and maximization of self-interest in the economy would quickly stumble upon these concepts within the family as well. Men would also have learned these values, but then it was men who had traditionally been the dominant sex; a more sensitive attunement to questions of individuality left men, if anything, less able to defend themselves against the demands for autonomy of their wives and daughters.

The moral authority of traditional society was of a piece; the same communitarian principles that held together the moral economy also maintained the authoritarian family. And they crumbled together as well.

Thus a second crucial consequence of capitalism for women came in the area of personal values: an unwillingness to accept the dictates of superordinates and a new readiness to experiment with personal freedom and gratification. The reader should at this point bear in mind that we have to juggle simultaneously three different effects of capitalism:[16] the first dimension of subculture weakened traditional moral taboos and destroyed internalized antisexual values; the second dimension, which we have just considered, quickened interest in intercourse as an aspect of personality development; and the third dimension of capitalism, to which we now turn, removed many of the external controls upon female sexual emancipation.

This last principal salient of industrial advance worked in the interest of women by modifying with wage labor the balance of power in the family. Paid employment meant that women would bring a distinct, quantifiable contribution to the family's resources, and accordingly would probably be entitled to a greater voice in the disposal of these resources. As many sociologists of the family have noted, the wife's (or daughter's) influence within the conjugal unit is a direct function of the status she enjoys in the outside world and of the resources she is able to import from that world into the family circle. Richard F. Tomasson has convincingly explained the historical development and the present-day international singularity of the Swedish family with such an approach, arguing also that, "Where females have greater equality and are subject to less occupational and social differentiation, the premarital sex codes will be more permissive than where the female's status is completely or primarily dependent on the status of her husband."[17] Altogether, capitalism entailed a quite material source of female independence and autonomy, increasing vastly the leverage formerly obtained from customary, dependent, unpaid, "women's work."

Popular involvement in the market economy started with the young and the poor and ended with the older and more prosperous. It was the most marginal whom capitalism could first detach from their traditional economic moorings, and so in the eighteenth century the young members of the proletarian classes that population growth had been creating went first to the cottage looms and spinning wheels. Thereafter ever more prosperous groups of the traditional economy found themselves pulled into the flux of the market, so that by the late nineteenth century even the most isolated sectors of the old middle class had been plunged into price competition and profit rationality. Immersion in the market progressed by stages.

Early in the eighteenth century the putting-out system began its conquest of the countryside, drawing in the landless poor. Then, in the course of the century agricultural capitalism began to encroach upon traditional subsistence and manorial farming, recruiting from among the landless and especially from the youth, for often unmarried laborers would live in the farmer's house, or newly married couples in nearby cottages. Next came migration to the newly rising factories and mills. The timing varied from one region to another, but normally it was the youth whom the fresh modern sector pulled from small farms and craft shops into factories.

In the nineteenth century industrial growth created a prosperous new middle class of administrators and clerks, of technicians and professionals. Because these people had often to endure long delays before marriage, women entered their childbearing periods at relatively advanced ages and largely abstained from intercourse beforehand. Finally, in the nineteenth century capitalism tore at the heart of the traditional old middle class itself, rather than merely at the supernumary poor. Across the Continent the masters of craft shops had to accommodate themselves to industrial capitalism, either by servicing the new factories or by going to work in them. And the depopulation of the countryside on the threshold of the twentieth century is an oft-told tale. It was frequently as mature men and women that these families were forced out of the traditional sector, of which they had constituted the backbone.

Thus the market started with the youngest and lowliest on the age-status spectrum and concluded with the most established and mature. It was also in this order that, I suggest, the spirit of female emancipation spread, from young and poor to well to do and middle-aged.

* * *

How, precisely, did these massive shifts in economic structure, culture, and individual mentalities affect either marital or nonmarital fertility? The linkages between emancipation and the increase in illegitimacy seem crisp and strong; those between capitalism and marital fertility are largely artifacts.

For the unmarried woman capitalism meant personal freedom, which meant in turn sexual freedom. The young woman could withstand parental sanctions against her sexual and emotional independence because the modern sector promised employment, economic self-sufficiency, and if need be, migration from home to another town. Such independence meant often, as we have seen, a paramour and therewith, in the absence of birth control, illegitimacy.[18]

NOTES

1. J. A. and Olive Banks, *Feminism and Family Planning in Victorian England* (New York, 1964), is a sophisticated recasting of this conventional wisdom. Kate Millett's *Sexual Politics* (New York, 1970) has again documented the thesis, using belletristic evidence. I have attempted, in choosing the phrase "female emancipation" as a description of changes in women's mentalities, to avoid the connotations of either of two alternative terms: "women's liberation," which moves too much what's-happening-now explosive into the vicinity of a basically scholarly discussion, and "feminism," which refers specifically to the agitation of upper-middle-class women for equal educational opportunities and the like. Two new studies of these educated, politically motivated feminists are William L. O'Neill, *Everyone Was Brave: A History of Feminism in America* (Chicago, 1971), and David M. Kennedy, *Birth Control in America: The Career of Margaret Sanger* (New Haven, 1970). My argument, of course, takes issue with this literature in emphasizing the working-class origin of the female emancipation movement, in singling out family rather than national politics as the field of agitation, and in dating the beginning about a hundred years earlier than is customary.

2. In treating the "age-status" spectrum as a single continuum I am assuming that the young tend to behave like the lower classes do, the more mature like the middle classes. Subcultures of youth have in fact much in common with lower-class subcultures because the young, like the lower classes, tend to be present-oriented, while older people, like the middle classes, tend to be more oriented to the future. Maurice Agulhon's important study of Basse Provence shows this interaction between youth and lower-class cultures at work: "Thus it is adolescent sociability that probably served as model and point of departure for popular sociability in general, whose thoroughgoing diffusion took place in the nineteenth century, the Indian summer of the 'chambrées.' (The emotional affinity between

youth and proletariat, an article of faith for traditional paternalists, turns up here in the form of an observable though somewhat hazy social phenomenon.)" *Pénitents et francs-maçons de l'ancienne Provence* (Paris, 1968), 250.

3. I have relied partly on Helmut Möller's *Die kleinbürgerliche Familie im 18. Jahrhundert: Verhalten und Gruppenkultur* (Berlin, 1969), *passim*. See also J. M. Mogey, "A Century of Declining Paternal Authority," *Marriage and Family Living* 19 (1957): 234–39. Eugen Lupri, who characterizes the "traditional" German family as extremely patriarchal, postulates a change to female emancipation over time. But for Lupri "traditional" means the period around 1900, and he has no evidence on the years before the First World War. "The West German Family Today and Yesterday: A Study in Changing Family Authority Patterns" (Ph.D. dissertation, University of Wisconsin, 1967).

4. The powerful trend toward emancipation was reflected, at least for middle-class women, in the mirror of marriage-manual advice. See Michael Gordon, "From an Unfortunate Necessity to a Cult of Mutual Orgasm: Sex in American Marital Education Literature, 1830–1940," in James Henslin, ed., *Studies in the Sociology of Sex* (New York, 1971), 53–77; see also, Michael Gordon and M. Charles Bernstein, "Mate Choice and Domestic Life in the Nineteenth-Century Marriage Manual," *Journal of Marriage and the Family*, 32 (1970): 665–74.

5. Those observers familiar with working-class sexual patterns in North America will doubtless react with some incredulity to the notion of the lower classes in the vanguard of a sexual revolution. After all, on this side of the Atlantic it is precisely the working classes who count as most "repressed" sexually, who have the highest degree of role segregation and the least evident that the Continental pattern of working-class sexuality is entirely different: a close tie between coitus and romantic love, less pronounced sex roles for men and women, inventive and spontaneous styles of intercourse. Volkmar Sigusch and Gunter Schmidt, having discussed the "de-emotionalizing" of sexuality, or of extreme double standards with dissatisfaction and de-sexualization of the female —characteristics… typical of the American lower classes," continue: "The West German workers regard sexuality much more as a social activity involving reciprocity. Mutuality should definitely be present in the nonsexual areas as well. The strong tendency toward assimilating sexuality with personal and emotional bonds sets the conditions for a partner-centered sexuality, above all among women, in which 'love' and 'fidelity' are central values." If my own arguments are correct, Sigusch and Schmidt's comment that the workers are following the patterns of the "liberal bourgeoisie" appears mildly ironical, for it was after all the

workers who started the whole business off in the first place. "Lower-Class Sexuality: Some Emotional and Social Aspects in West German Males and Females," *Archives of Sexual Behavior*, 1 (1971): 29–44, quotation from 42. If Sigusch and Schmidt, H. L. Zetterberg, and other students of Europe are correct, an urgent problem for research is why American workers are so different. Sigusch and Schmidt drew upon Lee Rainwater for their characterization of working-class sexuality in the United States, especially upon his classic work *And the Poor Get Children: Sex, Contraception and Family Planning in the Working Class* (Chicago, 1960).

6. Neil Smelser, *Social Change in the Industrial Revolution: An Application of Theory to the British Cotton Industry* (Chicago, 1959), 209 and the chapter "Pressures on the Family Division of Labour," 180–224; Peter Stearns, "Adaptation to Industrialization: German Workers As a Test Case," *Central European History*, 3 (1970): 303–31, especially 307; Rudolf Braun, *Sozialer und Kultureller Wandel in einem ländlichen Industriegebiet (Zürcher Oberland) unter Einwirkung des Maschinen- und Fabrikwesens im 19. und 20. Jahrhundert* (Erlenbach-Zurich, 1965), 201. On the lack of domestic accomplishments among English working-class wives, see Margaret Hewitt, *Wives & Mothers in Victorian Industry* (London, 1958), ch. 6, "The Married Operative As a Home-Maker," 62–84.

7. See Edward Shorter, " *La Vie Intime'* Beiträge zu seiner Geschichte am Beispiel des kulturellen Wandels in den bayerischen Unterschichten im 19. Jahrhundert," *Kölner Zeitschrift für Soziologie*, 16 (1973): 530–49.

8. See, for example, Hanns, Platzer, *Geschichte der ländlichen Arbeitsverhältnisse in Bayern* (Munich, 1904).

9. "Auszug aus dem Tags-Berichte des k. Polizei-Directors dahier… 2 August 1815. Betreffend: Die vielen ledigen Weibspersonen dahier," Bayerisches Hauptstaatsarchiv, Munich, MI 46545.

10. Report from provincial government to interior ministry, "Das Verhältnis der unehelichen zu den ehelichen Geburten betr," Feb. 30, 1839, *ibid.*, MI 46556.

11. For the archbishop's statement, see petition to the king, Apr. 3, 1838, *ibid.*; the final quotation is from provincial government of the Obermainkreis, in "Auszüge aus den dreijährigen Verwaltungs-Berichte, 1830–33; Öffentliche Sitten," *ibid.*, MI 15396.

12. Least known about the formation of an industrial labor force in Europe is still how cultural patterns changed. Among recent works, however, are Rudolf Braun, *Industrialisierung und Volksleben: Die Veränderungen der Lebensformen in einem ländlichen Industriegebiet vor 1800 (Zürcher Oberland)* (Erlenbach-Zurich, 1960), especially 90–154, 181–212; R. P. Neuman, "Industrialization and

Sexual Behavior: Some Aspects of Working-Class Life in Imperial Germany," in Robert J. Bezucha, ed., *Modern European Social History* (Lexington, Mass., 1972), 270–98; and Jeffry Kaplow, "The Culture of Poverty in Paris on the Eve of the Revolution," *International Review of Social History*, 12 (1967): 277–91.

13. Michael Schofield has recently pointed out the interaction between peer-group membership and teenage sexual activation in contemporary Britain: "One of the strongest influences on a teenager's behaviour in any sphere is the desire to be like other teenagers, and sexual activities are no exception. Experienced boys spend more time in teenage groups and seek advice from friends rather than parents. They are influenced by other teenagers and by the entertainment industry and the flourishing commercial market directed towards teenage spending. Conformity with other teenagers is very important." The same is roughly true of girls, except that, additionally, girls are more in revolt against their families than are boys and so see sex as part of a domestic power struggle. Thus Schofield finds sex-specific differences precisely where my argument, based on historical material, would have predicted them: membership in a subculture is important for both sexes alike, but individual self-awareness and "taking off the lid" in revolt against the parents affected young women more than young men. See *The Sexual Behaviour of Young People* (Harmondsworth, Middlesex, 1968), 80, 133, 193–95, and especially 202–08; quotation from 204.

14. The literature on how the free market conquered the moral economy is enormous. Among recent work may be mentioned Louise A. Tilly, "The Food Riot As a Form of Political Conflict in France," *Journal of Interdisciplinary History*, 2 (1971): 23–57; Francois Furet, "Le catéchisme révolutionnaire," *Annales: Économies, Sociétés, Civilisations*, 26 (1971): 255–89, especially 265–66; E. J. Hobsbawm and George Rudé, *Captain Swing* (New York, 1968), especially pt. 1; Wilhelm Abel *et al.*, *Handwerksgeschichte in neuer Sicht* (Göttingen, 1970), especially the contribution by Friedrich-Wilhelm Henning, "Die Einführung der Gewerbefreiheit und ihre Auswirkungen auf das Handwerk in Deutschland," 142–72. Mack Walker has traced the disappearance of a whole way of life, once incubated in the hermetically sealed small German town, in *German Home Towns: Community, State, and General Estate, 1648–1871* (Ithaca, 1971), especially 108–42, 405–31.

15. This argument has been presented in greater detail in Shorter, "Sexual Revolution, Social Change and Illegitimacy." An important work linking social change to the search for personal autonomy (for men) is Fred Weinstein and Gerald M. Platt, *The*

Wish to be Free: Society, Psyche, and Value Change (Berkeley, 1969).

16. It seems a bit unfair to make capitalism carry the brunt of the analysis, in view of the fact that two of the three dimensions of industrial advance affecting sexual behavior would also occur under socialism. The agglomeration of a proletarian work force is an accompaniment of any form of modern industry, as is the increased leverage within family circles women get through participation in the labor force. Only the noneconomic personal values that people learned from the logic of the market place—that impersonal, "ruthless" device for allocating resources and mobilizing capital—would not necessarily be found under socialism. Yet European economic development took place under the aegis of capitalism, not socialism, and the phrase appears just.

17. Richard F. Tomasson, *Sweden: Prototype of Modern Society* (New York, 1970), 165–98, especially 180. In modern European agriculture, of course, the labor of peasant women is essential to the profit of the farm, and even though they do not have salaried jobs, such women supply vital resources to the family's economy. See, for example, Frederik Barth, "Family Life in a Central Norwegian Mountain Community," in T. D. Eliot and A. Nillman, eds., *Norway's Families: Trends, Problems, Programs* (Philadelphia, 1960), 81–107, on the equality of the contemporary peasant woman within the household. This "modern" pattern in Norway dates back to at least the 1850s and 1860s, when Eilert Sundt noted that the woman's contribution to farm labor might equal the man's. Sundt's writings are reviewed in Michael Drake, *Population and Society in Norway, 1735–1865* (Cambridge, 1969), 145. Drake, however, believes this Norwegian pattern of female labor input to have been unusual in Western Europe at that time.

18. Aggregate illegitimacy rates provide one way to test this hypothesis. If the modern sector promised greater freedom for women, one would expect a higher propensity to illegitimacy among, say, factory women than among women in occupations likely to be tied to middle-class life and family controls, such as small-shop merchandising. Yet such published data are rare, and what studies exist lead to divergent conclusions. Auguste Lange, for example, found that in Baden during the 1890s female factory workers had easily the highest propensity to illegitimacy, followed by domestic servants, and then, at a very distant remove, by women in agriculture and such genteel occupations as schoolteaching and nursing, results consistent with my argument. *Die unehelichen Geburten in Baden: Eine Untersuchung über ihre Bedingungen und ihre Entwicklung* (Karlsruhe, 1912), 96*–98*. L. Berger, on the other hand, determined that in Prussia in 1907 domestic servants had the

highest illegitimate fertility, followed closely by factory workers and peasants (who tied for second place once age is controlled for), and then far behind by commerce, the free professions, and women without an occupation. "Untersuchungen über den Zusammenhang zwischen Beruf und Fruchtbarkeit under besonderer Berücksichtigung des Königreichs Preussen," *Zeitschrift des königlich preussischen statistischen Landesamts*, 52 (1912): 225–58, especially 230–31. Of three French textile towns in 1840, factory women in Châlons-sur-Marne and Reims represented no higher a proportion of illegitimate mothers than they did of the population as a whole. Only in Troyes did factory women contribute considerably more of the illegitimacy than they did of the city's population. In 1840, fifty-three per cent of all illegitimate births came from the "classe manufacturière," a class that represented only one-third of the city's population. Ernest Bertrand, "Essai sur la moralité des classes ouvrières dans leur vie privée," *Journal de la société de statistique de Paris*, 13 (1872): 86–95.

NO

Louise A. Tilly, Joan W. Scott, and Miriam Cohen

WOMEN'S WORK AND EUROPEAN FERTILITY PATTERNS

According to [Edward] Shorter, a change in fertility rates can only mean a change in sexual practices, which has to mean a change in attitudes, particularly of women. The sequence must be linear and direct. As Shorter argues:

> It seems a plausible proposition that people assimilate in the market place an integrated, coherent set of values about social behavior and personal independence and that these values quickly inform the noneconomic realm of individual mentalities. If this logic holds true, we may identify exposure to the market place as a prime source of female emancipation.[1]

This statement, as its language clearly reveals, is based on a claim of reasoning, not on evidence. Shorter offers nothing to prove that more women worked in the capitalist marketplace in this period. He merely assumes that they did. Similarly, he assumes that women at the end of the eighteenth century had different family roles and attitudes from their predecessors. And he assumes as well that changes in work opportunities immediately changed values.[2] Ideas, in his opinion, instantly reflect one's current economic experience. Shorter employs a mechanistic notion of "value transfer" to explain the influence of changes in occupational structure on changes in collective mentalities: "In the eighteenth and early nineteenth centuries the market economy encroached steadily at the cost of the moral economy, and the values of individual self-interest and competitiveness that people learned in the market were soon transferred to other areas of life."[3]

For Shorter, sexual behavior echoes market behavior at every point. "Emancipated" women gained a sense of autonomy at work that the subordinate and powerless women of pre-industrial society had lacked. That work, created by capitalist economic development, necessarily fostered values of individualism in those who participated in it, and individualism was expressed in part by a new desire for sexual gratification. Young women working outside the home, Shorter insists, were by definition rebelling against parental authority. Indeed, they sought work in order to gain the independence and individual

Excerpted from Louise A. Tilly, Joan W. Scott, and Miriam Cohen, "Women's Work and European Fertility Patterns," *Journal of Interdisciplinary History*, vol. 6, no. 3 (Winter 1976), pp. 447–476. Copyright © 1976 by The Massachusetts Institute of Technology and the editors of the *Journal of Interdisciplinary History*. Reprinted by permission of MIT Press Journals. Some notes omitted.

fulfillment that could not be attained at home. It follows, in Shorter's logic, that sexual behavior, too, must have been defiant of parental restraint. As the market economy spread there arose a new, libertine, proletarian subculture "indulgent of eroticism." Once married, the independent young working women engaged in frequent intercourse because they and their husbands took greater pleasure in sex. Female "emancipation" thus began among the young and poor. In the absence of birth control, the sexual gratification of single working girls increased the illegitimate birthrate; that of married women (who worked or had worked) inflated the legitimate birthrate. In this fashion Shorter answers a central question of European historical demography. The fertility increase in the late eighteenth century was simply the result of the "emancipation," occupational and sexual, of working-class women.…

It is now time to examine the historical evidence that Shorter neglected on women's role in pre-industrial society; on the effects of industrialization on women's work and on their attitudes; and on the motives which sent young girls out into the "marketplace" at the end of the eighteenth and beginning of the nineteenth century. None of the evidence that we have found supports Shorter's argument in any way. Women were not powerless in "traditional" families; they played important economic roles which gave them a good deal of power within the family. Industrialization did not significantly modernize women's work in the period when fertility rates rose; in fact, the vast majority of working women did not work in factories, but at customary women's jobs. Women usually became wage earners during the early phases of industrial-

ization not to rebel against their parents or declare independence form their husbands, but to augment family finances. Indeed, women in this period must be studied in their family settings, for the constraints of family membership greatly affected their opportunities for individual autonomy. No change in attitude, then, increased the numbers of children whom working women bore. Rather, old attitudes and customary behavior interacted with greatly changed circumstances—particularly in the composition of populations—and led to increased illegitimate fertility.

Women eventually shed many outdated priorities, and by the end of the nineteenth century some working women had clearly adopted "modern" life styles. But these changes involved a more gradual and complex adaptation than Shorter implies. The important point, however, is that the years around 1790 were not a watershed in the history of women's economic emancipation—despite the fact that the locus of women's work began to move outside the home. These *were* the crucial years for the increases in fertility in Europe. All of the evidence is not in, by any means; what we offer, however, indicates that in this period, women of the popular classes simply were not searching for freedom or experiencing emancipation. The explanation for changed fertility patterns lies elsewhere.

WOMEN'S PLACE IN "TRADITIONAL" FAMILIES

In the pre-industrial family, the household was organized as a family or domestic economy. Men, women, and children worked at tasks which were differentiated by age and sex, but the work of all was necessary for survival. Artisans' wives assisted their husbands in their work as weavers, bakers, shoemakers, or tailors. Certain work, like weaving, whether carried on in the city or the country, needed the cooperation of all family members. Children and women did the spinning and carding; men ran the looms. Wives also managed many aspects of the household, including family finances. In less prosperous urban families, women did paid work which was often an extension of their household chores: They sewed and made lace; they also took odd jobs as carters, laundresses, and street cleaners.

Unmarried women also became servants. Resourcefulness was characteristic of poor women: When they could not find work which would enable them to contribute to the family income, they begged, stole, or became prostitutes. Hufton's work on the Parisian poor in the eighteenth century and Forrest's work on Bordeaux both describe the crucial economic contribution of urban working-class women and the consequent central role which these women played in their families.

In the country, the landowning peasant's family was also the unit of productive activity. The members of the family worked together, again at sex-differentiated tasks. Children—boys and girls—were sent to other farms as servants when their help was not needed at home. Their activity, nonetheless, contributed to the well-being of the family. They sent their earnings home, or, if they were not paid wages, their absence at least relieved the family of the burden of feeding and boarding them. Women's responsibilities included care of the house, barnyard, and dairy. They managed to bring in small net profits from marketing

of poultry and dairy products and from work in rural domestic industry. Management of the household and, particularly, of finances led to a central role for women in these families. An observer in rural Brittany during the nineteenth century reported that the wife and mother of the family made "the important decisions, buying a field, selling a cow, a lawsuit against a neighbor, choice of future son-in-law." For rural families who did not own land, women's work was even more vital: From agricultural work, spinning, or petty trading, they contributed their share to the family wage—the only economic resource of the landless family.

In city and country, among propertied and propertyless, women of the popular classes had a vital economic role which gave them a recognized and powerful position within the household. It is impossible to guess what sort of sexual relations were practiced under these circumstances. We *can* say, however, that women in these families were neither dependent nor powerless. Hence, it is impossible to accept Shorter's attempt to derive women's supposed sexual subordination from their place in the pre-industrial household.

WHY WOMEN WORKED

Shorter attributes the work of women outside the home after 1750, particularly that of young, single women, to a change in outlook: a new desire for independence from parental restraints. He argues that since seeking work was an individualistic rebellion against traditionalism, sexual behavior, too, reflected a defiance of parental authority. The facts are that daughters of the popular classes were most often sent into service or to work in the city by their families. Their work represented a continuation of practices customary in the family economy. When resources were scarce or mouths at home too numerous, children customarily sought work outside, generally with family approval. Industrialization and urbanization created new problems for rural families but generated new opportunities as well. In most cases, families strategically adapted their established practices to the new context. Thus, daughters sent out to work went farther away from home than had been customary. Most still defined their work in the family interest. Sometimes arrangements for direct payment in money or foodstuffs were made between a girl's parents and her employer. In other cases, the girls themselves regularly sent money home. Commentators observed that the girls considered this a normal arrangement—part of their obligation to the family.[4]

In some cases the conditions of migration for young working girls emphasized their ties to family in many ways limited their independence. In Italy and France, factory dormitories housed female workers, and nuns regulated their behavior and social lives. In the needle trades in British cities, enterprising women with a little capital turned their homes into lodging houses for piece-workers in their employ.[5] Of course, these institutions permitted employers to control their employees by limiting their mobility and regulating their behavior. The point is not that they were beneficent practices, but that young girls lived in households which permitted them limited autonomy. Domestic service, the largest single occupation for women, was also the most traditional and most protective of young girls. They would be sent from one household to another and thus be given secu-

rity. Châtelain argues that domestic service was a safe form of migration in France for young girls from the country. They had places to live, families, food, and lodgings and had no need to fend for themselves in the unknown big city as soon as they arrived.[6] It is true that servants often longed to leave their places, and that they resented the exploitation of their mistresses (and the advances of their masters). But that does not change the fact that, initially, their migration was sponsored by a set of traditional institutions which limited their individual freedom.

In fact, individual freedom did not seem to be at issue for the daughters of either the landed or the landless, although clearly their experiences differed. It seems likely that peasant families maintained closer ties with their daughters, even when the girls worked in distant cities. The family interest in the farm (the property that was the birthright of the lineage and not of any individual) was a powerful influence on individual behavior. Thus, farm girls working as domestics continued to send money home. Married daughters working as domestics in Norwegian cities sent their children home to be raised on the farm by grandparents. But even when ties of this sort were not maintained, it was seldom from rebellious motives. Braun describes the late eighteenth-century situation of peasants in the hinterland of Zurich. These peasants were willing to divide their holdings for their children because of new work opportunities in cottage industry. These young people married earlier than they would have if the farm had been held undivided, and they quickly established their own families. Braun suggests that the young workers soon lost touch with their parents. The process, as he describes it, however, was not rebellion; rather, the young people went into cottage industry to lessen the burden that they represented for the family. These motives were welcomed and encouraged by the parents. Family bonds were stretched and broken, but that was a consequence, not a cause, of the new opportunities for work.[7]

Similarly, among urban artisans, older values informed the adaptation to a new organization of work and to technological change. Initially, artisans as well as their political spokesmen insisted that the old values of association and cooperation could continue to characterize their work relationships in the new industrial society. Artisan subculture in cities during the early stages of industrialization was not characterized by an individualistic, self-seeking ideology, as Thompson, Hufton, Forrest, Soboul, Gossez, and others have clearly shown.[8] With no evidence that urban artisans adopted the values of the marketplace at work, Shorter's deduction about a "libertine proletarian subculture" has neither factual nor logical validity. It seems more likely that artisan families, like peasant families, sent their wives and daughters to work to help bolster their shaky economic situation. These women undoubtedly joined the ranks of the unskilled who had always constituted the urban female work force. Wives and daughters of the unskilled and propertyless had worked for centuries at service and manufacturing jobs in cities. In the nineteenth century there were more of them because the proportions of unskilled propertyless workers increased.

Eighteenth- and early nineteenth-century cities grew primarily by migration. The urban working class was thus constantly renewed and enlarged by a stream of rural migrants. Agricultural change drove rural laborers and peasants cityward at the end of the eighteenth century, and technological change drove many artisans and their families into the ranks of the unskilled. Women worked outside the home because they had to. Changed attitudes did not propel them into the labor force. Family interest and not self-interest was the underlying motive for their work.

WOMEN'S WORK

What happened in the mid-eighteenth century with the spread of capitalism, the growth of markets, and industrialization? Did these economic changes bring new work experiences for women, with the consequences which Shorter describes? Did women, earning money in the capitalist marketplace, find a new sense of self that expressed itself in increased sexual activity? In examining the historical evidence for the effects on women's work of industrialization and urbanization, we find that the location of women's work did change—more young women worked outside the home and in large cities than ever before. But they were recruited from the same groups which had always sent women to work.

The female labor force of nineteenth-century Europe, like that of seventeenth- and eighteenth-century Europe, consisted primarily of the daughters of the popular classes and, secondarily of their wives. The present state of our knowledge makes it difficult to specify precisely the groups within the working classes from which nineteenth-century women wage earners came. It is clear, however, that changes in the organization of work must have driven the daughters and wives of craftsmen out of the family shop. Similarly, population growth (a result of declining mortality and younger age at marriage due to opportunities for work in cottage industry) created a surplus of hands within the urban household and on the family farm. Women in these families always had been expected to work. Increasingly, they were sent away from home to earn their portion of the family wage.[9]

Shorter's notion that the development of modern capitalism brought new kinds of opportunities to working-class women as early as the middle of the eighteenth century is wrong. There was a very important change in the location of work from rural homes to cities, but this did not revolutionize the nature of the work that most women did. Throughout the nineteenth century, most women worked at traditional occupations. By the end of the century, factory employment was still minimal....

Shorter is also incorrect in his assumption that the working woman was able to live independently of her family because she had the economic means to do so. Evidence for British working women indicates that this was not the case. Throughout the nineteenth century, British working women's wages were considered supplementary incomes —supplementary, that is, to the wages of other family members. It was assumed by employers that women, unlike men, were not responsible for earning their own living. Female wages were always far lower than male. In the Lancashire cotton mills in 1833, where female wages were the highest in the country, females aged 16–21 earned 7/3.5 weekly, while males earned 10/3. Even larger differentials obtained among older workers. In London in the 1880s, there was a similar differential between the average earnings of the sexes: 72 percent of the males

in the bookbinding industry earned over 30/— weekly; 42.5 percent of women made less than 12/—. In precious metals, clocks, and watch manufacturing, 83.5 percent of the males earned 30/— or more weekly; females earned 9–12/—. Women in small clothing workshops earned 10–12/— weekly, while women engaged in outwork in the clothing trades made only 4/— a week. In Birmingham, in 1900, the average weekly wage for working women less than age 21 was 10/—, for men 18/—. Women's work throughout this period, as in the eighteenth century, was for the most part unskilled. Occupations were often seasonal and irregular, leaving women without work for many months during the year. Is it possible that there were many single women who could enjoy a life of independence when the majority could not even afford to live adequately on their personal wages?...

Women's work from 1750 to 1850 (and much later) did not provide an experience of emancipation. Work was hard and poorly paid and, for the most part, it did not represent a change from traditional female occupations. Those women who traveled to cities did find themselves free of some traditional village and family restraints. But, as we shall see, the absence of these restraints was more often burdensome than liberating. Young women with inadequate wages and unstable jobs found themselves caught in a cycle of poverty which increased their vulnerability. Having lost one family, many sought to create another.

THE ORIGINS OF INCREASED ILLEGITIMACY

The compositional change which increased the numbers of unskilled, propertyless workers in both rural and urban areas and raised their proportion in urban populations also contributed to an increase in rates of illegitimacy. Women in this group of the population always had contributed the most illegitimate births. An increase in the number of women in this group, therefore, meant a greater incidence of illegitimacy.

A recent article by Laslett and Oosterveen speaks directly to Shorter's speculations: "The assumption that illegitimacy figures directly reflect the prevalence of sexual intercourse outside marriage, which seems to be made whenever such figures are used to show that beliefs, attitudes and interests have changed in some particular way, can be shown to be very shaky in its foundations." Using data from Colyton, collected and analyzed by E. A. Wrigley, they argue that one important component in the incidence of illegitimacy is the existence of illegitimacy-prone families, which bring forth bastards generation after generation. Nevertheless, they warn, "this projected sub-society never produced all the bastards, all the bastard-bearers."[10]

The women who bore illegitimate children were not pursuing sexual pleasure, as Shorter would have us believe. Most expected to get married, but the circumstances of their lives— propertylessness, poverty, large-scale geographic mobility, occupational instability, and the absence of traditional social protection—prevented the fulfillment of this expectation. A number of pressures impelled young working girls to find mates. One was the loneliness and isolation of work in the city. Another was economic need: Wages were low and employment for women, unstable. The logical move for a single girl far from her family would be to find a husband with whom she might re-establish a family economy. Yet another pressure was the desire to escape the confines of domestic service, an occupation which more and more young women were entering.

Could not this desire to establish a family be what the domestic servants, described by the Munich police chief in 1815, sought? No quest for pleasure is inherent in the fact that "so many young girls leave service.... But they do little real work and let themselves be supported by boyfriends; they become pregnant and then are abandoned."[11] It seems a sad and distorted version of an older family form, but an attempt at it, nevertheless. Recent work has shown, in fact, that for many French servants in the nineteenth century, this kind of transfer to urban life and an urban husband was often successful.[12]

Was it a search for sexual fulfillment that prompted young women to become "engaged" to young men and then sleep with them in the expectation that marriage would follow? Not at all. In rural and urban areas premarital sexual relationships were common.[13] What Shorter interprets as sexual libertinism, as evidence of an individualistic desire for sexual pleasure, is more likely an expression of the traditional wish to marry. The attempt to reconstitute the family economy in the context of economic deprivation and geographic mobility produced unstable and stable "free unions."

... The central point here is that no major change in values or mentality was necessary to create these cases of illegitimacy. Rather, older expectations operating in a changed context yielded unanticipated (and often unhappy) results.... Women's work in the late eighteenth and early nineteenth centuries was not "liberating" in any sense. Most women stayed in established occupations. They were so poorly paid that economic independence was precluded. Furthermore, whether married or single, most women often entered the labor force in the service of the family interest. The evidence available points to several causes for illegitimacy, none related to the "emancipation" of women: economic need, causing women to seek work far from the protection of their families; occupational instability of men which led to *mariages manqués* (sexual intercourse following a promise of marriage which was never fulfilled). Finally, analysis of the effects of population growth on propertied peasants and artisans seems to show that the bifurcation of marriage and property arrangements began to change the nature of marriage arrangements for propertyless people.

NOTES

1. "Female Emancipation," 622.
2. The weakness of Shorter's evidence on these points is striking. For example, the source of his description of peasant and working-class women's roles in traditional society is Helmut Möller's study of the eighteenth-century petty bourgeois family in Germany *(Die kleinburgerliche Familie im 18. Jahrhundert: Verhalten und Gruppenkultur* [Berlin, 1966], 69). For his proposition about the free and easy sexuality of the early nineteenth-century European working class, Shorter draws his evidence from post-World War II West Germany.
3. "Female Emancipation," 621.
4. Rudolf Braun, "The Impact of Cottage Industry on an Agricultural Population," in David Landes (ed.), *The Rise of Capitalism* (New York, 1966), 61–63; R.-H. Hubscher, "Une contribution à la connaissance des milieux populaires ruraux au XIXᵉ siècle: Le livre de compte de la famille Flauhaut, 1881–

1887," *Revue d'histoire économique et sociale,* XLVII (1969), 395–396; Evelyne Sullerot, *Histoire et sociologie du travail féminin* (Paris, 1968), 91–94; Anderson, *Lancashire 22;* Peter Stearns, "Working Class Women in Britain, 1890–1914," in Martha Vicinus (ed.), *Suffer and Be Still* (Bloomington, Ind., 1972), 110; Marie Hall Ets, *Rosa, The Life of an Italian Immigrant* (Minneapolis, 1970), 138–140; Frédéric Le Play, *Les Ouvriers européens* (Paris, 1855–78), V, 122.
5. Ets, *Rosa,* 87–115; Italy, Ufficio del Lavoro, *Rapporti sulla ispezione del Lavoro (1 dicembre 1906–30 giugno 1908)* (Milan, 1909), 93–94; Sullerot, *Histoire,* 91–94, 100; Jules Simon, *L'Ouvrière* (Paris, 1871), 53–54. Eileen Yeo and E. P. Thompson, *The Unknown Mayhew* (New York, 1972), 116–180.
6. Abel Châtelain, "Migrations et domesticité feminine urbaine en France, XVIII siècle-XX siècle," *Revue d'histoire économique et sociale,* XLVII (1969), 508.
7. Drake, *Population,* 138; Braun, "Impact of Cottage Industry," 63–64.
8. Hufton, "Women in Revolution"; Forrest, "Condition of the Poor"; Albert Soboul, *Les Sans-Culottes parisiens en l'an II* (Paris, 1958); Rémi Gossez, *Les Ouvriers de Paris* (Paris, 1967), I; E. P. Thompson, *The Making of The English Working Class* (London, 1963).
9. For an elaboration of this see Joan W. Scott and Louise A. Tilly, "Women's Work and the Family in Nineteenth Century Europe," *Comparative Studies in Society and History,* XVII (1975), 36–64.
10. Laslett and Oosterveen, "Long-term Trends," 257–258, 284.
11. Quoted in Shorter, "Female Emancipation," 618. Sex ratios discussed in Weber, *Growth of Cities,* 285–300, 320, 325–327.
12. Theresa McBride, "Rural Tradition and the Process of Modernization: Domestic Servants in Nineteenth Century France," unpub. Ph.D. diss. (Rutgers University, 1973).
13. Shorter, Knodel, and van de Walle, "Decline of Non-Marital Fertility," 384; Le Play, *Les Ouvriers,* V, 150–154. Pierre Caspard attacks Shorter's notion of a sexual revolution as the cause of increased prenuptial conceptions in "Conceptions prénuptiales et développement due capitalisme dans la Principauté de Neuchâtel (1678–1820)," *Annales E.S.C.,* XXIX (1974), 989–1008.

POSTSCRIPT

Did the Industrial Revolution Lead to a Sexual Revolution?

In the world of the "great man," women, racial and ethnic minorities, and the poor are nearly invisible. They appear as passive participants in the historical drama; it is as if history happens to them. Revisionist historians, however, insist that even the apparently powerless have the potential to act as agents of historical change rather than as passive victims. Both Shorter and Tilley et al. assume that working-class, European women in the years between 1750 and 1850 made decisions and acted upon them. For reasons that may never be completely clear, there was a rise in illegitimacy rates, evidence that more babies than in the past were being born outside of marriage. What changed? A higher illegitimacy rate can mean that more sexual activity is taking place, but it can also mean that fewer unmarried, pregnant women are marrying.

To help you to make your own decision, you may wish to consider the evidence offered in the following books and essays. For a Marxist interpretation, see Friedrich Engels, *The Origin of the Family, Private Property and the State* (International Publishers, 1972). Ivy Pinchbeck, in *Women Workers and the Industrial Revolution, 1750–1850* (F. Cass, 1969), argues that occupational changes played a significant role in women's legal and political emancipation. In *The World We Have Lost* (Scribner's, 1965), Peter Laslett describes the household as the center of production, a place where everyone in the family both lived and worked. He concludes that the chief effect of the Industrial Revolution was to separate work from home and deprive the home of its traditional productive focus. Rudolf Braun, in "The Impact of Cottage Industry on an Agricultural Population," in David Landes, ed., *The Rise of Capitalism* (Macmillan, 1966), describes an economic system in rural Switzerland in which the daughters in a family learned to spin and weave, contributing their earnings to the family economic unit as a matter of course. Olwen Hufton makes a similar point about the Parisian poor in the eighteenth century in "Women in Revolution, 1789–1796," *Past and Present* (vol. 53, 1971) and about a broader segment of the population in "Women and the Family Economy in Eighteenth-Century France," *French Historical Studies* (vol. 9, 1975). Lutz K. Berkner describes the precapitalist family life cycle in "The Stem Family and the Developmental Cycle of the Peasant Household: An Eighteenth-Century Austrian Example," *American Historical Review* (April 1972). Whether or not young working women kept their own wages and had enough money to support an independent lifestyle is a key historiographic question. For more work by this issue's authors, students may wish to read "Women's Work and the Family in Nineteenth Century Europe," *Comparative Studies in Society and*

History (vol. 17, 1975) and *Women, Work, and Family* (Holt, Rinehart & Winston, 1978) by Joan W. Scott and Louise A. Tilly. Essays by Edward Shorter include "Illegitimacy, Sexual Revolution and Social Change in Modern Europe," *Journal of Interdisciplinary History* (vol. 2, 1971) and "Sexual Change and Illegitimacy: The European Experience," in Robert J. Bezucha, ed., *Modern European Social History* (D. C. Heath, 1972).

ISSUE 6

Was Confucianism Responsible for China's Failure to Modernize?

YES: John King Fairbank, from *The Great Chinese Revolution: 1800–1985* (Harper & Row, 1986)

NO: Jonathan D. Spence, from *The Search for Modern China* (W. W. Norton, 1990)

ISSUE SUMMARY

YES: History professor John King Fairbank makes the case that conservative forces, rooted in the Confucian virtues, subverted attempts by some to bring China into the modern world.

NO: History professor Jonathan D. Spence offers an economic analysis that draws on the ideas of Adam Smith and Karl Marx to explain China's initial failure to modernize and the role that foreign powers played in its eventual modernization.

Most China scholars would agree that China's failure to modernize may be traced to a combination of internal and external forces—the uniquely Chinese version of traditionalism rooted in classic texts attributed to the philosopher Confucius and the economic realities of a worldwide market economy. For centuries both China and Japan remained aloof from the rest of the world. China, in particular, thought of itself as the Middle Kingdom, the center of the universe, and its centuries of scholarship and high culture had convinced many that China had nothing to learn from upstarts in the "barbarian West." Whereas Japan chose to enter the modern world on its own terms in the late nineteenth century, China refused to do so. This decision has had far-reaching consequences for China and continues to puzzle historians.

To look at an internal cause thesis, we must consider the writings of Confucius, which date back to the sixth century B.C.E., and which became deeply embedded in Chinese society 2,000 years later. Focusing on proper behavior and patterns of deference, the Confucian system stressed the practice of virtue—especially the cardinal virtues of faithfulness, sincerity, earnestness, and respectfulness—as the route to a stable social order and a defense against forces of corruption. Children were schooled to obey parents, wives to submit to husbands, younger siblings to look to older siblings for guidance and ministers to be guided by rulers. The system of examinations—the path to civil service jobs that remained in effect until 1905—was based on knowledge of the Confucian classics. Some scholars hold that continuing to honor these premodern values accounts for China's failure to modernize.

However, external factors also may have played a role. When we look at China's history during the last century, we cannot fail to take into account its large land mass and growing population. Economists, beginning with Adam Smith in his influential book *The Wealth of Nations* (1776), noted that while China was not amassing further wealth, its population was continuing to expand, which cheapened both labor and the value of human life. In the nineteenth century, the German philosopher Karl Marx saw Asia as being outside the influence of the "World Spirit" in its march through history. As European powers invaded China and exploited its economic resources, some historians blamed China's failure to modernize on capitalist imperialism, a clearly external force.

Between 1860 and 1900 Japan abandoned its historic isolationism, selectively borrowed from the West, and began the economic development that would eventually make it a world power. The question that has puzzled Chinese observers and Western historians is why China failed to do the same. The same opportunities were available, but China nevertheless remained marginal in the modern world at least until the communist revolution of 1949.

In the following selection, retired historian John King Fairbank chooses to put the explanatory emphasis on conservative forces within China. He argues that ethnocentrism, the belief that one's own culture is superior to all others, made China smugly confident of its ability to keep its old ways and prosper. Confucian platitudes, combined with the conservatism of the imperial dynasty, subverted the forces of modernization and made China vulnerable to invasion by the Western powers.

In the second selection, historian Jonathan D. Spence summarizes the economic explanation that came into general acceptance during the first decades of the twentieth century. He notes that Marx, following the analysis of his mentor G. W. F. Hegel, had left Asia out of the historic development of world cultures under the guidance of the World Spirit. Left to its self-imposed isolation, China (according to Smith's analysis and Hegel's model) would never modernize. The only hope for China, Hegel and Marx agreed, would be for the Western powers to plant the seeds of their superior mode of production and more fully developed notion of freedom in Chinese soil.

YES

John King Fairbank

EFFORTS AT MODERNIZATION

The forty years beginning in 1860 form a distinct era in the buildup of the Chinese Revolution—a time when the old system seemed to work again and some Western ways were adopted, yet China's progress was so comparatively slow that she became a sitting duck for greater foreign aggression. The imperialist rivalry of the powers came to a terrifying climax in the 1898 "scramble for concessions," and the period ended with troops of eight nations occupying Peking in 1900. Obviously these were the four decades when China missed the boat. While Japan ended her seclusion, adroitly began to Westernize, got rid of her unequal treaties, and was prepared to become a world power, why did China fail to do the same?

This question has haunted Chinese patriots throughout the twentieth century. At first the explanation was found in Social Darwinism. China had simply lost out in the competition for survival among nations. Partly this was due to her tardiness in ceasing to be an ancient empire and becoming a modern nation. The fault lay within.

By 1920, however, a more satisfying explanation was offered by Marxism-Leninism. The fault lay with the capitalist imperialism of the foreign powers who invaded China, secured special privileges under the unequal treaties, exploited Chinese markets and resources, and suppressed the stirrings of Chinese capitalism. Since many foreigners announced loudly that they were going to do just that, all sides could agree. The same decades saw the triumph of colonialism all around China's periphery. Burma and Malaysia were taken over by Britain, Vietnam by France, Taiwan by Japan. Foreign aggression and exploitation were too plain to be denied.

Two generations of argument over these explanatory theories have come to rest in the 1980s on a "both... and" formula: internal weakness invited foreign invasion, just as Confucious said 2,500 years ago. The real argument has been over the proportions between the two and the timing of their influence. As the onward march of scholarship helps us to learn more abut China within, I believe the claims of Marxism-Leninism will be watered down as time goes on but no one can deny their validity in many important respects.

From John King Fairbank, *The Great Chinese Revolution: 1800–1985* (Harper & Row, 1986). Copyright © 1986 by John King Fairbank. Reprinted by permission of HarperCollins Publishers, Inc. Notes omitted.

How does this apply to 1861–94? The era began with a joint leadership of Manchus and Chinese, at Peking and in the provinces, who agreed on a general program of appeasing the Anglo-French invaders while suppressing the Chinese rebels. There are few better examples of how to turn weakness into strength, though sometimes at the expense of the Chinese populace.

By mid-1860 a revived Taiping offensive had invaded the Yangtze delta, taking the major cities of Hangchow and Soochow and threatening Shanghai, while at the same time an Anglo-French army arrived off Tientsin in two hundred ships, and fought its way to Peking. Facing this double disaster, the Manchu leadership executed a neat double appeasement: they finally gave Tseng Kuo-fan supreme command against the Taipings, abandoning the old rule that Chinese civil officials should not control armies in the provinces, and they accepted the Anglo-French demands to open China further to foreign trade and proselytism. As they put it in the dynastic councils, the rebels were an "organic disease," the foreigners merely an "affliction of the limbs." (This of course would be the way Chiang Kai-shek phrased his problems with Japanese invasion and Communist rebellion in the 1930s and 1940s.) All the British wanted was trade; so their opium trade was legalized and inland trade on the Yangtze promised them as soon as the Taipings (who stubbornly prohibited opium) should have been destroyed.

American and British mercenaries, like F. T. Ward of Salem, Massachusetts, were hired to use steamers and artillery in amphibious warfare around Shanghai. Having got the terms they wanted at Peking, the British and French abandoned neutrality and let officers like C. G. "Chinese"

Gordon fight the Taipings while, even more important, foreign merchants sold Remingtons and howitzers to the imperial armies. Anglo-French forces had returned from humbling Peking to defend Shanghai and the Yangtze delta, and so help save the dynasty.

In this way the Ch'ing restoration of the 1860s secured foreign help while still expounding the classical ideology of rule by virtue. Tseng Kuo-fan . . . set the tone of the restoration by his admirable strength of character and rather simple-minded faith in the Confucian ideals of proper behavior.

"Barbarian affairs are hard to manage," he wrote his understudy Li Hung-chang in 1862, "but the basic principles are no more than the four words of Confucius: *chung, hsin, tu,* and *ching* —faithfulness, sincerity, earnestness and respectfulness. . . . Hsin means merely not to tell a lie, but it is very difficult to avoid doing so. . . .

"Confucious says, 'If you can rule your own country, who dares to insult you?' If we are unified, strict and sober, and if hundreds of measures are fostered, naturally the foreigners will not insult and affront us without reason." (Obviously, a man so indoctrinated with the Confucian virtues could be entrusted with the fate of the dynasty.)

"In your association with foreigners," Tseng told Li, "your manner and deportment should not be too lofty, and you should have a slightly vague, casual appearance. Let their insults, deceitfulness, and contempt for everything appear to be understood by you and yet seem not understood, for you should look somewhat stupid."

What better prescription could one suggest for swallowing pride and appeasing an invader? The Manchus at court had quoted the ancient saying "Resort to peace and friendship when temporarily obliged to do so; use war and defense as your actual policy." The dynasty and its Chinese ruling class were in the soup together.

After Tseng Kuo-fan died in 1872 the lead in dealing with foreigners for the next thirty years was taken by Li Hung-chang, a tall (over six feet), vigorous, and extremely intelligent realist, who was eager to take responsibility and became adept at hanging on to power. He was devoted to the art of the possible and, working within that limitation, became the leading modernizer of his day. Although Li Hung-chang himself went around the world only toward the end of his career in 1896, he realized from the first moment his troops got their Remington rifles that foreign things were the key to China's defense and survival. He became the leading advocate of what Peking a century later under Deputy Premier Deng Hsiao-p'ing would call "modernization."

Li had benefited from the fact that his father had been a classmate of Tseng Kuo-fan in the top examination of 1838. After Li won his provincial degree, he studied under Tseng at Peking. He got his own top degree there in 1847, and in the early 1850s went back to his native place (Ho-fei in Anhwei) to organize militia against the rebels, much as Tseng was doing in Hunan. He assisted the provincial governor in campaigns and then in 1859 joined Tseng Kuo-fan's staff, became his chief secretary, and drafted his correspondence. When the Ch'ing court was finally obliged to give Tseng overall command in 1860, Li had his chance.

Backed by Tseng to organize his own Anhwei army on the model of Tseng's Hunan army, Li in April 1862 used seven foreign steamers hired by refugee gentry to bring his troops down the Yangtze to Shanghai. At age thirty-nine he now became governor of Kiangsu province at the fulcrum of Sino-foreign relations. Shanghai he found to be an Anglo-French military base, with foreign troops far better armed and trained than his Chinese forces. Troops so armed could take over China! Indeed, he feared "the hearts of the officials and of the people have long since gone over to the foreigners." He felt himself "treading on frost over ice." Could Shanghai be kept from a foreign takeover? Li rushed to buy Western arms and build up his Anhwei army. Within two years he had forty thousand men with ten thousand rifles and cannon using thirty-six-pound shells. He got Western cooperation against the Taipings but kept it strictly within limits.

In this way Li Hung-chang moved in on the ground floor of the late Ch'ing establishment. Having qualified first as a scholar, he won the dynasty's confidence as a general commanding troops. His Anhwei army helped surround and strangle the Taipings in the Lower Yangtze and then in the late 1860s finished off the Nien rebels, whose cavalry had been raiding all across North China. Purchasing foreign rifles, setting up arsenals, and drilling troops gave the dynasty the edge over dissident peasants from this time on. Simultaneously the British with their gunboats and troops at Hong Kong and the treaty ports and on the Yangtze became an integral part of China's power structure, helping to maintain political order in the interests of foreign trade....

Li Hung-chang's diplomatic efforts gave him high visibility, and Western journalists occasionally touted him as the

"Bismarck of the East." The comparison can be instructive. Li Hung-chang (1823–1901) no doubt had many of the abilities of his German contemporary Otto von Bismarck (1815–98). He was a big man, an astute diplomat and energetic administrator, above all a realistic practitioner of the possible, who for forty years played principal roles in China. But, while Bismarck between 1862 and 1890 engineered and won three wars to create the German empire and dominate central Europe, Li confronted rebellions at home and foreign aggression on China's borders that led the Ch'ing empire steadily downhill. While Bismarck was fashioning a new balance of power in Europe, Li had to deal with the breakup of the Ch'ing tribute system that had once provided a kind of international order in East Asia. The Iron Chancellor held central executive power among a people already leading the way in modern science, industrial technology, and military nationalism. Li Hung-chang never held central power but only represented Peking as a provincial governor-general. His influence hung by the thread of his loyalty to the regent for two boy emperors in succession, the Empress Dowager Tz'u-hsi, a clever, ignorant woman intent on preserving Manchu rule at all costs. Li's loyalty to his ruler had to be expressed in large gifts and unquestioning sycophancy, to the point where in 1888–94 Li's North China navy, racing against Japan's naval buildup, had to divert its funds to build Tz'u-hsi's new summer palace. In place of a Bleichroder, who financed Bismarck in the clinches, Li Hung-hang had to collect his own squeeze by the usual age-old filching from his official funds. After he negotiated the secret Russo-Chinese alliance in 1896 he received a personal gift of a million roubles. Some said he amassed a fortune worth $40 million. It is plain that he got some things done, but he led the late Ch'ing effort at modernization only by persistent pushing and constant manipulation of an intractable environment.

This was a two-front struggle, to find out the practical secrets of Western power and also to convince indoctrinated fellow officials that imitating the West was necessary. Tseng Kuo-fan, for example, supported the Shanghai Arsenal and it built a steamship, on which he even ventured to sail. But he opposed telegraphs, railways, and other uses of Western technology as likely to harm Chinese livelihood and give foreigners too much influence. Li had to steer a devious and indirect course. For instance, Tseng offered him the conventional Confucian wisdom (or balderdash) that "warfare depends on men, not weapons" (an old idea, but modified today by a thought of Mao Tse-tung's). Li countered by describing British and French warships he had visited. "I feel deeply ashamed," he said, at China's inferiority in weapons. "Every day I warn and instruct my officers to be humble-minded, to bear the humiliation, to learn one or two secret methods from the Westerners."

If we recall the American need in public discussions of the Cold War era to first reassure an audience that Communism, the enemy, was not for us, we can sympathize with Li Hung-chang's problem. To the court at Peking he wrote in 1863: "Everything in China's civil and military system is far superior to the West. Only in firearms it is absolutely impossible to catch up with them. Why? Because in China the way of making machines is for the scholars to understand the principles, while the artisans put them into practice. . . . The two do not consult each other.... But foreigners are different.... I have learned that when Western scholars make weapons, they use mathematics for reference."

Li also pointed to the Japanese success in learning to navigate steamships and make cannon. If China could stand on her own feet militarily, he prophesied, the Japanese "will attach themselves to us." But if not, "then the Japanese will imitate the Westerners and will share the Westerners' sources of profits."

By 1864 Li ventured to recommend that science and technology be added to the topics in the examination system. From today's point of view' this was surely the starting point for China's adaptation to the modern world. But the idea never had a chance. Even the proposal that regular degree holders be recruited to study Western science in the interpreters' college that Hart was financing at Peking, and in similar small government schools at Shanghai and Canton, was shot down.

The imperial tutor Wo-jen, a Mongol who dominated the Peking literary bureaucracy, spoke for the orthodox majority: "The way to establish a nation is to stress propriety and righteousness, not power and plotting... the minds of people, not technology.... The barbarians are our enemies. In 1860 they rebelled against us." They invaded Peking, he continued, burned the imperial summer palace, killed our people. "How can we forget this humiliation even for a single day?" Why, he asked, was it necessary to "seek trifling arts and respect barbarians as teachers?... Since the conclusion of the peace [in 1860], Christianity has been prevalent and half our ignorant people [the Taipings] have been fooled by it.... Now if talented scholars have to change from their regular course of study to follow the barbarians... it will drive the multitude of the Chinese people into allegiance to the barbarians.... Should we further spread their influence and fan the flame?"

These sentiments coincided with the vested interest of every scholar who taught, and every young man who studied, the classics. Modern learning was effectively kept out of the examinations until they were finally abolished in 1905.

The modernization of China thus became a game played by a few high officials who realized its necessity and tried to raise funds, find personnel, and set up projects in a generally lethargic if not unfriendly environment. Hope of personal profit and power led them on, but the Empress Dowager's court, unlike the Meiji Emperor's in Japan, gave them no firm or consistent backing. Tz'u-hsi on the contrary found it second nature to let the ideological conservatives like Wo-jen stalemate the innovators so that she could hold the balance. Since South China was as usual full of bright spirits looking for new opportunities, especially in the rapidly growing treaty-port cities, the late nineteenth century was a time of much pioneering but little basic change. Westernization was left to the efforts of a few high provincial officials partly because this suited the central-local balance of power—the court could avoid the cost and responsibility —and partly because treaty-port officials in contact with foreigners were the only ones who could see the opportunities and get foreign help.

On this piecemeal basis Li Hung-chang found allies in Cantonese entrepreneurs whose long contact with Westerners gave them new channels to climb up. For example there was a T'ang clan based ten miles from Macao who grew rich making shrimp sauce and selling it there. The clan steadily gained influence during the nineteenth century as its members passed local and provincial examinations. However, Tong King-sing (T'ang T'ing-shu, 1832–92) opened up a new channel. He learned English in a missionary school, became an interpreter in the Hong Kong police court and the Shanghai customs house, and after 1863 grew wealthy as Jardine's top comprador. From investing in pawn shops and native banks he moved on to shipping companies, insurance, and even a newspaper. Meanwhile he bought degree status and an official title, which the dynasty was now selling for revenue. From 1873 Li Hung-chang got Tong's assistance in his industrial-development projects.

Instead of battling his fellow Confucians on the intellectual front, Li found it easier to compete with foreign economic enterprise in China. China's domestic commerce in private hands was already actively expanding. Li pursued the traditional idea of enlisting Chinese merchant capital in projects that would be "supervised by officials but undertaken by merchants," something like the salt trade. After all, the proportion of China's national income that passed through the governments hands and sticky fingers was still very low.

Li in 1872 started a joint-stock steamship line, even calling it the China Merchants Steamship Company, and soon got Tong King-sing to be the manager. But merchant capital came forward only in small amounts. The crash of 1877 allowed Li to buy up the fleet of Russell and Company, the Boston firm that with Chinese merchant help had inaugurated steamboating on the Yangtze. But a majority of the funds had to come from official sources. When in 1885 Robert Hart lent one of his young customs commissioners (H. B. Morse, Harvard '74) to advise the China Merchants' managers, Morse found the company overloaded with personnel and being milked of its profits. It survived by hauling the tribute rice to Tientsin and making rate deals with the British lines of Jardine, Matheson & Company and Butterfield and Swire, who continued for the next fifty years under the unequal treaty system to dominate water transport within China.

When Li Hung-chang in 1876 started the Kaiping coal mine north of Tientsin to fuel his steamships and give them return cargo to Shanghai, he made Tong manager of the mining company. At Kaiping Tong brought in a dozen Western engineers and installed modern pumps, fans, and hoists. Soon Kaiping had a machine shop, telephones and telegraphs, and a small railway, and was producing 250,000 tons of coal a year. It was so successful that Peking could not keep its hands off. A Chinese squeeze artist from the court succeeded Tong, squeezed the company dry, and kept it going mainly on foreign loans. Finally in the Boxer crisis of 1900 a British company, represented by an up-and-coming American mining engineer named Herbert C. Hoover, got control of it. China's legal counsel in London later claimed that this takeover was almost indistinguishable from grand larceny. After 1912 the Kaiping mines were run by the Anglo-Chinese Kailan Mining Administration.

A similar spottiness marked Li's first venture in sending students abroad. This had been proposed by another Cantonese, a school classmate of Tong named Yung Wing, who had gone so far as to accept missionary support and make it to Yale. He became Yale's first

Chinese graduate, in 1854. Trying to make himself useful back in China, he was eventually sent out to buy the machinery for the Shanghai Arsenal. Finally in 1872 he was given charge of the Chinese educational mission that during the next decade brought 120 long-gowned Chinese youths to America. The first batch, selected by Tong King-sing, included seven of his relatives, and the third group, his nephew T'ang Shao-i.

On the advice of the Connecticut commissioner of education, Yung Wing set up headquarters in Hartford, but President Porter of Yale suggested the students should board with families up and down the Connecticut Valley. Soon they learned to tuck their queues under their caps and play very smart baseball, while Yung Wing himself married Mary Louise Kellogg of Avon, Connecticut. Yung Wing's co-supervisor, a proper long-gowned scholar, was horrified: the boys were becoming barbarized. They were not mastering the classics in preparation for their examinations back in China! In 1881 the project was abandoned. Chinese students came to America again only thirty years later, not as young teenagers, and without their queues and classics, after the end of the dynasty.

The 120 students from the Hartford project made their mark in China's foreign relations and industrialization after 1900. If the project had continued after 1881, China's modern history might have been different. . . .

When China's Ch'ing dynasty restoration after thirty years confronted Japan's Meiji restoration in warfare, the two protagonists were Li Hung-chang and one of Japan's founding fathers, Itō Hirobumi. They had first met in 1885 over the Korean question and agreed that Japan and China should both stay out of Korea, where they were backing rival factions. Li noted, however, "In about ten years, the wealth and strength of Japan will be admirable . . . a future source of trouble for China."

Sure enough, when the Japanese intervened in 1894, ostensibly to quell Korean rebels, they routed Li's North China army and in one of the first modern naval battles, off the Yalu River, sank or routed his fleet. It was commanded by an old cavalry general who brought his ships out line abreast like a cavalry charge, while the Japanese in two columns circled around them. Today when tourists visit the marble boat which stands in the summer palace lake outside Peking, they should be able to imagine a caption on it—"In memoriam: here lies what might have been the late Ch'ing navy."

In 1895 when Li was sent to Shimonoseki to sue for peace, he and Itō had a polite dialogue, which was recorded in English. Li said: "China and Japan are the closest neighbors and moreover have the same writing system. How can we be enemies? . . . We ought to establish perpetual peace and harmony between us, so that our Asiatic yellow race will not be encroached upon by the white race of Europe."

Itō said: "Ten years ago I talked with you about reform. Why is it that up to now not a single thing has been changed or reformed?"

Li could only reply, "Affairs in my country have been so confined by tradition that I could not accomplish what I desired. . . . I am ashamed of having excessive wishes and lacking the power to fulfill them."

From our perspective today, the startling thing is that China's first modern war should have been left on the shoulders of a provincial official as though it were simply a matter of his defending his share of the frontier. The Manchu dynasty has of course been blamed for its non-nationalistic ineptitude, but the trouble was deeper than the dynasty's being non-Chinese; the fault evidently lay in the imperial monarchy itself, the superficiality of its administration, its constitutional inability to be a modern central government.

NO

Jonathan D. Spence

THE SEARCH FOR MODERN CHINA

WESTERN IMAGES OF CHINA

Until the middle of the eighteenth century, China generally received favorable attention in the West. In large part this stemmed from the wide dissemination of books and published correspondence by Catholics, especially the Jesuits, who saw in the huge population of China a potential harvest of souls for the Christian faith. Although mindful of some of China's problems, most Catholic observers followed the example of the Jesuit missionary Matteo Ricci, who had lived in China from 1583 to 1610 and admired the industry of China's population, the sophistication of the country's bureaucracy, the philosophical richness of its cultural traditions, and the strength of its rulers.

The French Jesuits, who dominated the China missions late in Kangxi's reign, presented an even more laudatory picture of the early Qing state, one deliberately designed to appeal to the "Sun King," Louis XIV, and to persuade him to back the missionaries with money and personnel. Central to these flattering presentations was the idea that the ethical content of the Confucian Classics proved the Chinese were a deeply moral nation and had once practiced a form of monotheism not so different from that found in the Judaeo-Christian tradition. With a little effort, therefore, the Chinese could be brought back to the true values they had once espoused, and did not have to be forced to convert.

Although the Jesuits rapidly lost influence in China during the last years of Kangxi's reign, and declined in prestige in Europe during the eighteenth century until suppressed altogether in 1773, their books on Chinese government and society remained far the most detailed available. The German philosopher Gottfried Wilhelm von Leibnitz read them and became deeply interested in the structure of the hexagrams in the *Book of Changes*. Even the anticlerical philosopher Voltaire was intrigued by what he read about the Chinese. Since Voltaire was intent on attacking the power of the Catholic church in eighteenth-century France, he cleverly used the information about

From Jonathan D. Spence, *The Search for Modern China* (W. W. Norton, 1990). Copyright © 1990 by Jonathan D. Spence. Reprinted by permission of W. W. Norton & Company, Inc. Notes omitted.

China provided by the Catholics to disprove their more extreme claims. If, argued Voltaire, the Chinese really were so moral, intelligent, ethical, and well governed, and if this was largely attributable to the influence of Confucious, it followed that since Confucious had not been a Christian it was obviously possible for a country to get along admirably without the presence of Catholic clerical power.

In a series of influential works written between 1740 and 1760, Voltaire expounded his ideas about China. In one novel he presented his views on the parallelism of moral values in different societies, European and Asian. In a play he suggested that the innate moral strength of the Chinese had been able to calm even the Mongol conquerors led by Genghis Khan. And in an unusual historiographical gesture, Voltaire *began* his review of world history—*Essai sur les moeurs et l'esprit des nations* ("An Essay on the Customs and Spirit of Nations")—with a lengthy section on China. He did this to emphasize the values of differing civilizations and to put European arrogance in perspective: "The great misunderstanding over Chinese rites sprang from our judging their practices in light of ours: for we carry the prejudices that spring from our contentious nature to the ends of the world." Unable to find a "philosopher-king" in Europe to exemplify his views of religion and government, Voltaire believed Emperor Qianlong would fill the gap, and he wrote poems in the distant emperor's honor.

Voltaire's praise for Chinese institutions appeared in a cultural context that was intensely sympathetic to China. During this same brief period in the mid-eighteenth century, Europe was swept by a fascination with China that is usually described by the French word *chinois-*erie, an enthusiasm drawn more to Chinese decor and design than to philosophy and government. In prints and descriptions of Chinese houses and gardens, and in Chinese embroidered silks, rugs, and colorful porcelains, Europeans found an alternative to the geometrical precision of their neoclassical architecture and the weight of baroque design. French rococo was a part of this mood, which tended to favor pastel colors, asymmetry, a calculated disorder, a dreamy sensuality. Its popular manifestations could be found everywhere in Europe, from the "Chinese" designs on the new wallpapers and furnishings that graced middle-class homes to the pagodas in public parks, the sedan chairs in which people were carried through the streets, and the latticework that surrounded ornamental gardens.

Yet this cult of China, whether intellectual or aesthetic, faded swiftly as angry and sarcastic accounts like George Anson's became available. Voltaire's very enthusiasms made him the object of sarcasm or mockery as other great figures among the French Enlightenment philosophers began to find his picture of China unconvincing. Jean-Jacques Rousseau and the Baron de Montesquieu worried that the Chinese did not seem to enjoy true liberty, that their laws were based on fear rather than on reason, and that their elaborate educational system might lead to the corruption of Chinese morals rather than to their improvement. Other writers declared that China did not seem to be progressing, had indeed no notion of progress; from this it was but a short step to see the Chinese as, in fact, retrogressing. In the somber words of the French historian Nicolas Boulanger, written in 1763 and translated from the French the following year by the English radical John Wilkes:

All the remains of her ancient institutions, which China now possesses, will necessarily be lost; they will disappear in the future revolutions; as what she hath already lost of them vanished in former ones; and finally, as she acquires nothing new, she will always be on the losing side.

Reflecting on these arguments concerning China and the Chinese, some leading European thinkers labored to assess the country's prospects. One of these was the Scottish philosopher Adam Smith, who wrote on China in *The Wealth of Nations*, first published in 1776. In his analysis of the productive capacities of different countries, Smith found China useful for comparative purposes, especially with the nations of Europe and the developing societies of North America. Examining population growth as an index of development, he concluded that in Europe, where countries doubled their populations every five hundred years, growth was steady if undramatic. In North America, where the population doubled every twenty or twenty-five years, there was instant employment for the entire new work force; the New World was therefore "much more thriving, and advancing with much greater rapidity to the further acquisition of riches."

China, however, "long one of the richest, that is, one of the most fertile, best cultivated, most industrious, and most populous countries in the world," had reached that stage in the cycle of growth where it had "acquired that full complement of riches which the nature of its laws and institutions permits it to acquire." In such a situation, continued population growth brought serious economic reper-

cussions: "If in such a country the wages of labour had ever been more than sufficient to maintain the labourer, and to enable him to bring up a family, the competition of the labourers and the interest of the masters would soon reduce them to this lowest rate which is consistent with common humanity." The result was that "the poverty of the lower ranks of people in China far surpasses that of the most beggarly nations in Europe" and infanticide became an integral social practice. As Smith acidly phrased it: "Marriage is encouraged in China, not by the profitableness of children, but by the liberty of destroying them." China was exacerbating these problems, according to Smith, by refusing to consider change. By staying aloof from the growth of the world economy, China was sealing its fate: "A country which neglects or despises foreign commerce, and which admits the vessels of foreign nations into one or two of its ports only, cannot transact the same quantity of business which it might do with different laws and institutions."

In a famous series of lectures delivered by the German philosopher Georg Wilhelm Friedrich Hegel in the early 1820s, the various critical analyses explored by Boulanger, Rousseau, Montesquieu, and Smith were synthesized in such a way that "Oriental Civilizations"—China preeminent among them—came to be seen as an early and now by-passed stage of history. The view of "Asiatic Society" synthesized by Hegel was to have a profound influence on the young Karl Marx and other later nineteenth-century thinkers. History, to Hegel, was the development of what he called the ideas and practices of freedom throughout the world. Freedom was the expression of the self-realization of the "World Spirit," and that spirit was reaching its fullest manifestations in the Christian states of Europe and North America. Optimistic about his own time, Hegel developed a theory that downplayed China's past. He described China as dominated by its emperors or despots, as typical of the "oriental nations" that saw only *one* man as free. In the West, the Greeks and Romans had come to see that *some* men were free; and, centuries later, Hegel's generation had come to see that *all* humans were free. Lacking an understanding of the march of Spirit in the world, even the Chinese emperor's "freedom" was "caprice," expressed as either "ferocity—brutal recklessness of passion—or a mildness and tameness of the desires, which is itself only an accident of Nature."

Part of China's fate, Hegel wrote, turned on geographical factors: "The extensive tract of eastern Asia is severed from the general historical development." In a powerfully worded passage, Hegel explained that China had lacked the great boldness of the Europeans in exploring the seas and instead had stayed tied to the agricultural rhythms of her great plains. The soil presented only "an infinite multitude of dependencies," whereas the sea carried people "beyond these limited circles of thought and action.... This stretching out of the sea beyond the limitations of the land, is wanting to the splendid political edifices of Asiatic States, although they themselves border on the sea—as for example, China. For them the sea is only the limit, the ceasing of the land; they have no positive relation to it." Though such a statement would have startled the wealthy ocean-going merchants of Fujian had they seen it, Hegel was basically correct that the Qing state itself was not interested in maritime exploration.

In a series of bleak conclusions, Hegel consigned the Chinese permanently to their space outside the development of the World Spirit. Although China had historians galore, they studied their country within their own limited preconceptions, not realizing that China itself lay "outside the World's History, as the mere presupposition of elements whose combination must be waited for to constitute their vital progress." Although Chinese emperors may speak words of "majesty and paternal kindness and tenderness to the people," the Chinese people "cherish the meanest opinion of themselves, and believe that men are born only to drag the car of Imperial Power." In a passage that moved beyond anything Lord Macartney had opined about the fate of the Qing dynasty, Hegel mourned for the Chinese people themselves: "The burden which presses them to the ground, seems to them to be their inevitable destiny: and it appears nothing terrible to them to sell themselves as slaves, and to eat the bitter bread of slavery."

Yet perhaps China was not caught forever in a metaphysical and geographical isolation. In one of his most ambiguous asides, Hegel added that "a relation to the rest of History could only exist in their case, through their being sought out, and their character investigated by others." The question of by whom or how that seeking out was to be done was left open by Hegel, but the Western powers, with their ships, their diplomatic missions, and their opium, were rapidly beginning to provide an answer....

FOREIGN PRESSURES AND MARX'S VIEWS

One of many factors that helped the Qing overthrow the Taiping was the assistance of foreigners in the early 1860s, whether in the form of customs dues collected through the foreign-managed Shanghai Inspectorate of Customs or in the form of the Ever-Victorious Army, led in the field by Western officers. The reasons for that support had mainly to do with international affairs, in which, once again, the primary actors were the British. Disappointed at the results of the Nanjing treaty and frustrated by continued Qing intransigence, the British reacted with scant sympathy when the Qing were threatened by the spread of the Taiping rebellion. Instead the British made the highly legalistic decision to apply the most-favored-nation clause to the American treaty of 1844, which had stipulated that that treaty be renegotiated in twelve years. By applying that renewal stipulation to their own Nanjing treaty of 1842, British authorities forced the Chinese to renegotiate in 1854.

The British foreign secretary saw the speciousness of this argument, writing to the governor of Hong Kong that "the Chinese Authorities may perhaps and with some degree of plausibility object that the circumstances of the time are unsuitable for the commencement of such a work. But he nevertheless suggested that the Qing be presented with the following formidable list of requests: access for the British to the entire interior of China or, failing that, to all of coastal Zhejiang and the lower Yangzi up to Nanjing; legalization of the opium trade; cancellation of internal transit dues on foreign imports; suppression of piracy; regulation of Chinese labor emigration; residence in Peking for a British ambassador; and reliance on the English version rather than the Chinese in all disputed interpretations of the revised treaty.

Despite some caution because of their involvement in the Crimean War against Russia, the British moved jointly with the Americans and French to press for treaty revision, which the beleaguered Qing continued to oppose. The British finally took advantage of an allegedly illegal Qing search of a ship formerly of Hong Kong registry, the Arrow, to recommence military actions at Canton in late 1856. After some delays in getting reinforcements—the Indian mutiny was now raging, and the idea of a war in east Asia was not popular with the British people—the British seized Canton in December 1857 and exiled the consistently hostile governor-general of the region to Calcutta. Sailing north in a near repeat of the 1840 campaign, they took the strategic Dagu forts in May 1858 and threatened to seize Tianjin. In June, with the way to Peking now open to the British forces, the Qing capitulated and agreed to sign a new treaty. By the terms of the most-favored-nation clause, all British gains would also be shared by the other major foreign powers.

This "Treaty of Tianjin" of 1858 imposed extraordinarily strict terms on China. A British ambassador was henceforth to reside in Peking, accompanied by family and staff, and housed in a fitting residence. The open preaching of Christianity was protected. Travel anywhere inside China was permitted to those with valid passports, and within thirty miles of treaty ports without passports. Once the rebellions currently raging in China were suppressed, trade was to be allowed up the Yangzi as far as Hankou, and four new Yangzi treaty ports (Hankou, Jiujiang, Nanjing, and Zhenjiang) would be opened. An additional six treaty ports were to be opened immediately: one in Manchuria, one in Shandong, two on Taiwan, one in Guangdong, and one on Hainan Island in the far south. The Tianjin treaty also stipulated that all further interior transit taxes on foreign imports be dropped upon payment of a flat fee of 2.5 percent. Standard weights and measures would be employed at all ports and customshouses. Official communications were to be in English. The character for *barbarian* ... must no longer be used in Chinese documents describing the British. And British ships hunting pirates would be free to enter any Chinese port. A supplementary clause accompanying the various commercial agreements stated explicitly: "Opium will henceforth pay thirty taels per picul [approximately 130 pounds] Import Duty. The importer will sell it only at the port. It will be carried into the interior by Chinese only, and only as Chinese property; the foreign trader will not be allowed to accompany it." This condition was imposed despite the prohibition in the Chinese penal code on the sale and consumption of opium. Virtually the only British concession was to pull back from Tianjin and return the Dagu forts to Qing control.

The British evidently expected China's rulers to abandon the struggle at this point, but the Qing would not, and showed no intention of following the treaty clause that permitted foreign ambassadors to live in Peking. In June 1859, to enforce the new treaty terms, the British once more attacked the Dagu forts, now strengthened and reinforced by Qing troops. Fighting was heavy and the British were beaten back, even though the American naval commodore Josiah Tattnall, despite his country's declared neutrality, came to the aid of wounded British Admiral Hope with the ringing cry "Blood is thicker than water." Re-pulsed from the Dagu forts, the British sent a team of negotiators to Peking by a different route in 1860, but they were arrested by the Qing and some were executed. Determined now to teach the Qing a lessen they could not ignore, Lord Elgin, Britain's chief treaty negotiator, ordered his troops to march on Peking. On October 18, 1860, following Elgin's orders, the British burnt to the ground the Yuan Ming Yuan—the exquisite summer palace in the Peking suburbs built for Qianlong's pleasure using the plans of Jesuit architects. The British, however, spared the Forbidden City palaces within Peking, calculating that destruction of those hallowed buildings would be a disgrace so profound that the Qing dynasty would inevitably fall.

The emperor had already fled the city for Manchuria and named his younger brother, Prince Gong, to act as negotiator. But there was nothing left to negotiate, and on the very day the summer palace burned, Prince Gong reaffirmed the terms of the 1858 Tianjin treaty. In an additional "Convention of Peking," the emperor was stated to express his "deep regret" at the harassment of the British queen's representatives. He also promised a further 8 million taels in indemnity, permitted Chinese emigration on British ships, made Tianjin itself a treaty port, and ceded part of the mainland Kowloon peninsula to Hong Kong. Thus did the "treaty system" reach its fruition.

With these spectacular new gains firmly embedded in treaty form, and confident that Prince Gong would see to their enforcement, the British now swung to strong support for the Qing. The logic seemed clear: if the Qing beat back the Taiping, the foreigners would keep their new gains; if the Taiping defeated the Qing, even under the semi-Westernized aegis of Hong Ren'gan, then the West would have to start the tiresome process of negotiation—and perhaps wage fresh wars—all over again. A sardonic observer of these international shifts was Karl Marx, who had been following the progress of the Taiping rebellion and of British foreign policy with great interest. Marx, born in 1818 in Germany, had written the *Manifesto of the Communist Party* in 1848 with his friend Friedrich Engels. Expelled from both Germany and France for his radical views, he settled in London in 1849 and thereafter made England his home. By 1853, the revolutionary surge for which Marx had hoped in Europe had faded in the face of sustained opposition from reactionary government forces, and he turned to China to find reassurance for his belief that revolutionary change might still be possible.

That same year, as the Taiping seized Nanjing, Marx wrote that he now believed all of China's various dissident forces were at last "gathered together in one formidable revolution." Although he could not tell what "religious, dynastic, or national shape" the Taiping would take, he was confident in ascribing the rise of the Taiping movement to the British opium trade, reinforced by British cannon. Together, these had ended China's self-imposed isolation, wrecked the myth of Manchu authority, and involved China's once venerated mandarins in a cycle of smuggling and corruption. The upshot could only be that Qing "dissolution must follow as surely as that of any mummy carefully preserved in a hermetically sealed coffin, whenever it is brought into contact with the open air."

The result of China's collapse would be spectacular, thought Marx, since the Western powers had become so strongly committed to the balance of their Chinese trade with Indian opium production, and the taxation of that trade to maintain their own domestic revenues, that they could not do without it. Accordingly, Marx wrote, "it may safely be augured that the Chinese revolution will throw the spark into the overloaded mine of the present industrial system and cause the explosion of the long-prepared general crisis, which, spreading abroad, will be closely followed by political revolutions on the continent." It was an apocalyptic version of that dragging of China into the modern world that Hegel had speculated about thirty years before.

By the later 1850s, however, events in China had not had this kind of direct impact on European society. Still, Marx found his attention drawn to the new phase of British imperialism in China, which was represented by the *"Arrow war"* and the fighting that led first to the Treaty of Tianjin, and finally to the ratification of the Convention of Peking in 1860. He compared the British actions in bombarding Canton to the filibustering activities of "General" William Walker in California, Mexico, and Nicaragua, and wondered if it were possible that "the civilized nations of the world will approve this mode of invading a peaceful country, without previous declaration of war, for an alleged infringement of the fanciful code of diplomatic etiquette." Marx was intrigued when Parliament censured Lord Palmerston in March 1857 for initiating the war, leading to a dissolution of Parliament, a general election, and what Marx saw as the end of "Palmerston's dictatorship."

When Palmerston was vindicated in the elections and England returned to the fray in China, Marx could only reiterate his sense of the injustice of the entire enterprise and the dangers that it implied for constitutional government. But Marx shrewdly added that the China trade was not going to expand as much as the ever-hopeful British merchants expected, because the Chinese could not possibly afford *both* large imports of opium and large imports of British manufacturers' goods. He observed too that the nation with the most to gain in the protracted Chinese negotiations was Russia. Despite setbacks in the Crimean War, Russia had now expanded its railway network into east Asia, was strengthening its hold over the coastline north of Korea, and had seized for itself immense areas of territory along the Amur River, where it had been excluded ever since the Treaties of Nerchinsk and Kiakhta, negotiated by Emperors Kangxi and Yongzheng.

Following up on ideas suggested by Hegel thirty years before, Marx divided world history into four stages of the "modes of production"—namely, "Asiatic, ancient, feudal, and modern bourgeois." One might observe that the sequence of ancient-feudal-bourgeois has both chronological and analytical meaning in the European world. It provides, indeed, a way of summarizing the movement from Greco-Roman slave-owning empires, through the feudal epoch of medieval Europe, to the development of merchant guilds and municipal urban governments that spelled the start of bourgeois society. But the "Asiatic" mode is a geographical one; it lies outside the time Sequence of the other three. And although Marx wrote that the four modes represented "progressive epochs in the economic formation of society," in reality

he followed Hegel in placing China (and India) outside the development of world history. Asiatic modes had in no way been subsumed into later development—they had merely limped on alongside them.

One of Marx's powerful formulations in the *Critique of Political Economy*, which he wrote in 1859, was this: "No social order ever perishes before all the productive forces for which there is room in it have developed; and new, higher relations of production never appear before the material conditions of their existence have matured in the womb of the old society itself." Marx might have followed Adam Smith in seeing China as having exhausted its "room" for fresh productive forces, but he was also suggesting that Westerners had the power to implant the seeds of "new, higher relations of production," since China had (as Marx wrote elsewhere) "a fossil form of social life." Thus, in a sense, the destructive march of foreign imperialism had a constructive effect: in weakening China's traditional structures, it would speed the day of successful proletarian revolution.

Here Marx's speculations on China stop. By 1862 he was growing weary and sarcastic about continuing news of Taiping horrors. Nor did he draw solace from the rapid rise of a completely new rebellion, that of the Nian, which had begun raging in north China well before the Taiping had been suppressed. As he and Engels had written so vividly in the *Communist Manifesto*: although "the 'dangerous class,' the social scum, that passively rotting mass thrown off by the lowest layers of the old society," might be briefly swept up in revolutionary movements, it would inevitably revert to its logical role as the "bribed tool of reactionary intrigue." Yet one haunting and powerful idea continued to hang over Marx's various writings on China. Sometime in the future, he reflected, as the reactionaries fled Europe in the face of an enraged proletariat, seeking shelter in what they regarded as a last bastion of conservative power, they might find to their astonishment, written in bold letters upon the Great Wall, the words "Chinese Republic: Liberty, Equality, Fraternity."

POSTSCRIPT

Was Confucianism Responsible for China's Failure to Modernize?

China's failure to modernize in the last four decades of the nineteenth century was probably due to a combination of internal and external pressures. The tendency to gaze inward and to fear internal rebellion more than external aggression made China vulnerable to forces it did not yet understand. At the same time, the stagnation of its economy and the invasion of Western trade, especially the traffic in opium, corrupted China and opened the door to exploitative trade policies and even military intervention by the Western imperial powers. The Manchu dynasty, wanting above all to consolidate and maintain its power, failed to take into account the dangers that threatened it until it was too late.

Fairbank and Spence are among the best-known Western chroniclers of Chinese history. Fairbank's masterwork *China: A New History* (Harvard University Press, 1992) covers four millennia of Chinese history, and Spence's *God's Chinese Son* (W. W. Norton, 1996) recounts the bizarre story of Hong Xiuquan, leader of the Taiping uprising of 1845–1864. *Modernization and Revolution in China* (M. E. Sharpe, 1991) by June Grasso, Jay Corrin, and Michael Kort offers a readable survey of 4,000 years of Chinese history that is accessible to undergraduates and lay historians. Mary Clabaugh Wright's *Last Stand of Chinese Conservatism* (Stanford University Press, 1957) focuses on the T'ung-Chih Restoration of 1862–1874, which she considers the beginning of modern Chinese conservatism. For a positive analysis of the empress dowager, who some feel has been unfairly characterized as an iron-willed concubine who ruled through murder and intrigue, see Sterling Seagrave's strongly revisionist biography *Dragon Lady: The Life and Legend of the Last Empress of China* (Alfred A. Knopf, 1992). Students who wish to read something from Hegel should try *Reason in History* translated by Robert S. Hartman (Bobbs-Merrill, Inc., 1953), and those wishing to explore Marx might enjoy *Marx and Engels: Basic Writings on Politics and Philosophy* edited by Lewis S. Feuer (Doubleday, 1959). Any translation of the *Analects* provides a good introduction to Confucius.

A final recommendation is Bernardo Bertolucci's Academy Award–winning film *The Last Emperor*, which begins with the death of the empress dowager and takes us inside the Forbidden City, the official residence of the emperors of the Ming and Quing dynasties.

ISSUE 7

Did the Meiji Restoration Destroy Traditional Japanese Values?

YES: Edwin O. Reischauer, from *Japan: The Story of a Nation*, 3rd ed. (Alfred A. Knopf, 1981)

NO: Thomas C. Smith, from "Old Values and New Techniques in the Modernization of Japan," *Far Eastern Quarterly* (May 1955)

ISSUE SUMMARY

YES: Former U.S. ambassador to Japan Edwin O. Reischauer contends that the rulers of Meiji Japan forsook Japan's feudal heritage in favor of pragmatic policies to modernize the nation.

NO: Professor of history Thomas C. Smith asserts that the Meiji leaders explicitly promoted traditional Japanese values to ease the transition from feudalism to a modern state.

Commodore Matthew C. Perry, seeking diplomatic and trade relations with the Japanese, sailed into Edo Bay on July 8, 1853. By that time, the twin Tokugawa policies of isolation and stability were already disintegrating. For over two centuries, Japan had remained almost completely isolated from foreigners outside East Asia; now, however, the appearance of superior Western technology—in the form of steam-powered naval vessels—forced the leaders of imperial Japan to abandon their policies of isolation.

Chinese officials had not understood the threat posed by Western intrusions into East Asia, and China had paid the price, forced into unequal treaties that had already removed several of that nation's maritime ports from Chinese control. In an effort to forestall similar domination by the West, a group of young Japanese leaders carried out a relatively bloodless revolution, jettisoning the antiquated political institutions of the *bakufu*—literally, "tent government," the name by which the Tokugawa regime was known. Under Tokugawa rule, the nation was governed by the *shogun*, or supreme military commander of Japan. By 1868, however, the shogunate had been overthrown and replaced by the nominal restoration of power to the emperor Mutsuhito, who subsequently adopted the reign name "Meiji"—hence the term *Meiji Restoration*.

Real power, however, resided in the young reformers, who evinced a willingness to experiment, to try new methods in an attempt to build up Japan's military and industrial power. Their goal was to achieve equality with the

West, and when Japan handily defeated Russia in the Russo-Japanese War of 1904–1905, the reformers seemed to have accomplished their objective.

In the following summary of Japanese history, Edwin O. Reischauer notes that the antiquated feudal institutions of Tokugawa Japan had grown rotten by 1850, a conclusion that the appearance of Perry and his gunboats three years later made painfully clear. No longer could the Japanese rulers pretend that Japan was superior to all other nations, and the shock of this realization paved the way for the Meiji reformers. For Reischauer, the key to the success of the Meiji reformers lay in their pragmatism. One after another, the new government jettisoned traditional Japanese institutions. The cumulative effect of these reforms, Reischauer argues, amounted to a revolution in Japanese society.

In the second selection, Thomas C. Smith acknowledges the revolutionary impact of the Meiji reforms, but he argues that the reformers deliberately maintained traditional Japanese values to make their changes more palatable. Indeed, Smith claims that the reformers had no choice but to use traditional ideas to justify their reforms. Without the sanctions of the old values —particularly those of obedience to the throne and collective authority—the reformers could never have pushed through such radical alterations.

YES

Edwin O. Reischauer

THE TRANSITION TO A MODERN STATE

When Japan had closed its doors to the Europeans in the first half of the seventeenth century, it had stood abreast of the Occident technologically, but by the nineteenth century rapid scientific progress and the beginning of the Industrial Revolution had made the countries of the West incomparably stronger in military and economic power. After their expulsion from Japan, the Europeans had for a while all but forgotten this distant island nation, but now their own steady expansion brought them close once again to Japan's shores. Observant Japanese were not unaware of European colonial expansion and especially the military disasters and national humiliation the British inflicted on great China itself in 1839–1842 and again, together with the French, in 1856–1858....

In the first half of the nineteenth century the Americans, British, and Russians repeatedly sent expeditions to Japan in efforts to persuade the Japanese to open their ports to foreign ships, and the Dutch urged the Tokugawa to accede to these demands. But Edo stood firm on its old policy. A few students of "Dutch learning" bravely advocated the opening of Japan, but the vast majority of the people, long accustomed to isolation from the rest of the world, were bitterly opposed to allowing foreigners into their land.

The American government eventually decided to try to force the doors open. For this purpose, it dispatched under Commodore Matthew C. Perry a fair-sized fleet that steamed into what is now called Tokyo Bay in July 1853. After delivering a letter from the president of the United States demanding the inauguration of trade relations, Perry withdrew to Okinawa for the winter, with the promise that he would return early the next year to receive a reply. Edo was thrown into consternation over this sudden crisis, and the remaining decade and a half of Tokugawa rule, known as the *bakumatsu*, or the "end of the *bakufu*," was a period of great unrest. The Japanese were appalled at the size and guns of the American "black ships," as they called them, and they were amazed by the steam-powered vessels that moved up the bay against the wind. They realized that their own antiquated shore batteries were almost useless against them and that Edo and the coastal shipping which provisioned it lay defenseless.

From Edwin O. Reischauer, *Japan: The Story of a Nation*, 3rd ed. (Alfred A. Knopf, 1981). Copyright © 1970 by Edwin O. Reischauer. Reprinted by permission of Alfred A. Knopf, Inc.

The government split into two factions—conservatives who advocated resistance to the foreigners, and realists who saw that Japan could do nothing but bow to the American demands. In their own indecision, the Edo authorities did a most unusual thing. For the first time in over six centuries of military rule, the shogun's government asked the opinion of the emperor on an important problem of state. It also invited counsel from the daimyo [Japanese feudal barons]. Conservative Kyoto and many of the daimyo, most of whom were safely removed from the immediate threat, were of course strongly in favor of repelling the foreigners.

The Edo government was indeed caught on the horns of a dilemma when Perry's fleet returned to Tokyo Bay in February 1854. The emperor's court and the nation as a whole demanded a policy which the Tokugawa were quite incapable of carrying out. Under the threatening guns of the American ships, Edo had no choice but to sign a treaty with the United States, opening two ports to American ships and permitting a certain amount of closely regulated trade. The two ports were Shimoda, at the end of a peninsula near Edo, and Hakodate in Hokkaido, both insignificant ports in relatively remote places, but adequate for the provisioning of American ships. An American consul was also permitted to reside at Shimoda, and it was stipulated that any new concession granted other Western countries would automatically apply to the United States as well, a provision taken from the "unequal treaty" system then being forced on China.

Once the door had been opened a crack, there was no closing it. Within two years Edo had been forced to sign sim-

ilar treaties with the British, Russians, and Dutch. The Russian treaty added Nagasaki to the open ports and included another element of the Chinese "unequal treaty" system—extraterritoriality, or the right of Western residents in Japan to be tried by their own consular courts under their own national laws. In 1858 Townsend Harris, the first American consul, negotiated a full commercial treaty, using as his chief argument the threat of British naval power, which was far greater than American. Relatively free trade relations at six ports and the permanent residence of Westerners in the great cities of Edo and Osaka were to be permitted. The British, Russians, Dutch, and French immediately followed suit, adding in 1866 limitations, commonly of 5 percent, on the tariffs Japan would be allowed to impose on foreign imports. This was another key element of the "unequal treaty" system. Foreign merchants were particularly attracted to the newly opened deep-water ports of Yokohama near Edo and Kobe across the bay from Osaka, both of which were in time to develop into great cities, and British and French soldiers followed the Westerners to protect them from diehard samurai opponents to their presence. To observers of the time, Japan must have seemed well on the road to the semicolonial status into which China was already falling.

* * *

All Japan was thrown into turmoil by the sudden collapse of the policy of isolation. The differing rates between gold and silver in Japan and the rest of the world produced for a while a serious drain of gold. Textile markets were disrupted by cheap machine-made foreign imports. But, far worse, the credibility of the Edo government had been shattered by its inability to defend Japan and its meek acceptance of foreign policies that most politically conscious Japanese bitterly opposed. Edo had again consulted the daimyo before signing the commercial treaty with Harris in 1858, drawing as before largely negative reactions. There was no choice, however, but to go ahead with the treaties, and under the strong leadership of the chief "hereditary" daimyo, Ii Naosuke, Edo attempted to crush opposition by forcing the imperial court to give its assent and placing leading opposition daimyo under house arrest.

The nation, however, seethed with discontent and unrest over the national humiliation to which Edo had bowed. Unruly samurai, declaring themselves *ronin*, or "masterless samurai," attacked Westeners, killing Harris' secretary in 1859 and burning down the British legation in Edo in 1863. Another group, largely from Mito, one of the major "related" Tokugawa domains, waylaid Ii Naosuke in 1860 at a gate to the Edo castle and assassinated him. Still more flocked around the emperor's court in Kyoto, seeing in the emperor a symbol for united resistance to Tokugawa policies, and raised the double battle cry of *sonno*, "honor the emperor," and *joi*, "expel the barbarians." After Ii's death, Edo's control over the country rapidly disintegrated. Even the system of "alternate attendance" at Edo was abandoned in 1862, and the shogun humbly proceeded to Kyoto for consultations when summoned by the imperial court....

* * *

Most of the domains and the great bulk of the Japanese people passively watched, either irresolute, unconcerned, or financially paralyzed, while a small group of able young samurai from western Japan, mostly from flee lower ranks of that class, together with a handful of court nobles who never before had been involved in political power, seized control of the remains of the central government. Edo had for so long been the real political capital of Japan that the new leaders made it their own headquarters. In the autumn of 1868 it was renamed Tokyo, or "eastern capital," and the emperor and his court were moved to the great Edo castle the next spring. The new government was supported by the military power of Satsuma, Choshu, and their allies—only a small minority of the hereditary warrior class of Japan—but had as its chief financial base the land tax from the huge shogunal realm, which it appropriated largely for itself. It also resorted to forced loans from rich merchants, as the shogun and daimyo had done when in need.

To create an effective new administration on the ruins of the discredited and bankrupt *bakufu*, however, was no easy task. The chief assets of the new leaders were their control of the imperial symbol of political legitimacy, the armies of the few domains they personally controlled, and the political paralysis that gripped the other domains and the shogun's realm. The new leaders had already learned that trying to "expel the barbarians" was an objective they would have to abandon, at least for the present. They soon signaled this change of attitude, and in the spring of 1868 had the emperor receive the representatives of the foreign power in audience. The other slogan of the revolution, *sonno*, or "honor the emperor," remained central to their cause, however, since it was the only justification for their rule. They built their regime around the emperor, doing everything in his name, even though he was only fourteen years old at the time. In 1868 they changed the name of the "year period" to Meiji, meaning "Enlightened Rule," a name posthumously given to the emperor when he died in 1912, and the whole revolution and the tremendous changes of all sorts that followed it came to be known as the Meiji Restoration.

In theory the movement may have "restored" the imperial rule of antiquity, but nothing of the kind actually took place. While paying utmost deference to the emperor, the group of young samurai and court nobles who were in actual control ruled in a collegial manner, as had become customary in Japan, and they took their models for innovation not from ancient Japan, but from the contemporary West. They did revive ancient court titles and the names of old institutions, but the resurrection of such names did not signify their restoration as functioning institutions. The real changes they made were the abandonment of the feudal structure of Tokugawa society and government and the piecemeal adoption of Western institutions of modern centralized rule.

All these changes were made under the motto of *fukoku kyohei*, "a rich country and strong military," because it was clear that until Japan was militarily powerful on the basis of its own economic strength, it could not expect to "expel the barbarians," even in the modified sense of winning military and economic security from the West and diplomatic equality with it. The whole tenor of the effort was expressed in a Five Articles Oath (also called the Charter Oath), which the new leaders had the emperor issue on April 8, 1868. In it he promised that "evil customs of the past shall be broken off," careers shall be opened to all people equally, and "knowledge shall be sought throughout the world."

In traditional Japanese style, the chief posts in the new government were given to high court nobles and the daimyo of the domains who had cooperated in the overthrow of the Tokugawa, but these men were mainly figure-heads. Below them were the real leaders—the samurai and younger court nobles who had actually carried out the revolution. The main figure among them until his death in 1883 was the court noble Iwakura Tomomi, the oldest of the group at forty-three. The rest were mostly young samurai, among whom Kido Koin of Choshu and Okubo Toshimichi and Saigo Takamori of Satsuma were the most prominent. For the most part these men occupied posts as councilors and as vice ministers in the new ministries that were being formed. Falling back on the old Japanese technique of collective leadership, they made their important decisions through consultation and consensus, whatever the formal structure of government might be. Not once did any of them attempt to acquire dictatorial power for himself, quite unlike most of the revolutions that have occurred in modernizing countries in more recent times.

It was clear that something more than a coalition of a few domains was needed to produce a unified and powerful nation capable of staving off the Western menace and maintaining order in a land smoldering with resentment at the presence of foreigners and the seizure of power by a group of men who were representative of only a small part of the country. The new government had no difficulty in taking over the shogun's realm and dividing it into centrally controlled prefectures, a system well known from Japan's own past, but the real tasks were to gain control over the domains, which constituted three-fourths of the country, and to eliminate the class divisions that stood in the way of modernizing the government, the economy, and, most important, the military.

The new leaders began by persuading the daimyo of Satsuma, Choshu, Tosa, and Hizen, a domain in northern Kyushu, to symbolically restore their territories to the emperor on March 5, 1869, and receive them back as lands over which they were now considered to be governors, with one-tenth of their former domain revenues as personal incomes. Most of the other domains quickly followed suit for fear of being discriminated against, and the remainder were forced to accept the new system. Then quite suddenly, on August 29, 1871, the new government abolished all the domains, putting them under centrally appointed governors and paying off the daimyo fairly generously with government bonds; these, of course, would have no value unless the new regime survived. The domains were so demoralized that they put up no concerted opposition, and the daimyo, accustomed to being little more than figureheads, meekly complied. Their bonds became an important source of future banking capital, but they themselves faded away for the most part into genteel and affluent obscurity.

The abolition of the domains, most of which had been well-established political units for several centuries, was achieved with surprising ease, but depriving the samurai of their feudal privileges was a more difficult and dangerous undertaking. They formed a wide stratum of society that monopolized military and political power and enjoyed the privileges of hereditary, even if often niggardly, salaries. In 1871 the government lifted all class restrictions on roles in society and decreed legal equality for everyone, including the semi-outcast elements, once known as *eta* but now usually called *burakumin*, who constituted about 2 percent of the population. Then, early in 1873, the government carried out what was in the Japanese context perhaps its most revolutionary reform, decreeing universal conscription and hence putting an end to the concept of a privileged military class. The point was emphasized in 1876 when the samurai were denied the right to wear their swords, which were their badge of class distinction. Largely under the leadership of Yamagata Aritomo of Choshu, a new army of peasant conscripts was built up, at first on the French model and later on the Prussian, and the Prussian innovation of a general staff was adopted by the new army in 1878. Because of Yamagata's leadership, officers from Choshu were to dominate the army through World War I. To back the army up in maintaining domestic order, an efficient police force was also developed. Meanwhile, Satsuma had taken the lead in building a modern navy on the British model, and men from Satsuma remained at its head until well into the twentieth century.

The samurai's loss of his cherished position as an aristocratic warrior-administrator was accompanied by the loss of his privileged economic status. Hereditary stipends, inadequate though most of them were, had been cut in half in the reform of 1869, and finally in 1876 the government forced those samurai who had not already done so to commute their remaining stipends into lump sum payments of still further reduced value. Even then, the payments to samurai and daimyo constituted an extremely heavy financial burden on the new government. Completely cutting off the feudal aristocracy would have been cheaper in the short run, but perhaps this relatively generous treatment is one reason why modern Japan had no continuing problem with the *ancien régime,* as did France.

There were, of course, strong reactions to these drastic reforms. Because of their traditions of leadership and education, men of samurai origin virtually monopolized all the important posts in the new government, while others made for themselves new careers in business and intellectual pursuits. But the bulk of the samurai had neither the talents nor the flexibility to adjust to the new conditions, and they sank into obscure poverty. So large a privileged class could not be disinherited without some turmoil. Irreconcilable conservatives among the samurai often defied the new government in its first decade of rule. Significantly, these troubles occurred largely in the same western domains from which the new leaders had come. Perhaps the authority of these men seemed less valid in areas where their relatively lowly origins were well remembered. The final and most serious of the samurai revolts came in 1877 in Satsuma itself. There some 40,000 discontented conservatives rallied around Saigo, who had withdrawn from the government in dudgeon four years earlier. In bloody fighting, the government's new conscript army managed to crush the rebels, proving to the diehards that the old order had indeed passed.

* * *

Within ten years of coming to power, the new government had thus cleared away the antiquated Tokugawa political and social system and had achieved unchallenged control over the country. But the development of modern political institutions, a new social order, and a new economic system to support modern military power was a much slower and more difficult undertaking.

The pragmatic new leaders adopted piecemeal elements of Western political organization, trying them out cautiously to see how they would work in Japan. The finance ministry became the core of the government, since it determined the use of funds. A banking system was created, at first along decentralized American lines and later on the basis of the centralized banking system of Belgium. The currency was made uniform, and in 1871 the *yen* was adopted as the unit of value. In order to make budgeting possible, the land tax, the chief source of revenue, which had been paid in percentages of yield, was shifted to a fixed money tax in 1873, and the payers of this tax were recognized as the outright owners of the land. This measure clearly gave the land to the peasantry, but the fixed money tax as well as military conscription were at first unpopular with the peasants, who broke out in sporadic but localized riots. Another more lasting result of the new tax system was the foreclosure of mortgages in bad years, raising the proportion of tenant-operated land from around 25 percent to 45 percent by the end of the century. . . .

* * *

By the mid-1880s it was clear that Japan had succeeded in making the perilous transition from a feudally organized premodern society to a modern nation. It was strong enough to be safe from further Western encroachments; it was politically stable at home; and it was becoming economically secure from Western domination and even competitive in some world markets such as cotton thread. The magnitude of the achievement was not generally recognized at the time, when the ultimate outcome still seemed far from certain, but now that Japan is indeed one of the leading industrialized nations of the world and we have seen how hard comparable transitions have proved to be for most other premodern societies, Japan's success in the early Meiji period stands out as an extraordinary and perhaps unique story.

It is by no means easy to explain. Simply giving labels drawn from Western history is of little help and can be very misleading. To call the Meiji Restoration a bourgeois revolution is more confusing than helpful. The rich urban merchants provided loans to both sides in the struggle, but stood timidly aside in the contest between elements of the ruling feudal class. After the contest was decided, they were in large part replaced by a new business community drawn mostly from the samurai class. To compare Japan's transition to the triumph of absolutism in early modern Europe is even more inaccurate, since the Tokugawa system was already more absolutist than the kingdoms of early modern Europe, and the Meiji reforms led to liberalizing trends. To call the Restoration a counterrevolution is equally misleading. It is true that peasant and urban unrest rose to a crescendo in the decades immediately before and after 1868, but popular uprisings, except for the reactionary samurai revolts, were not aimed at changing the political system, only at correcting specific grievances over unduly heavy taxes or maladministration.

No European precedents are very useful in explaining the causes or the effects of the Meiji revolution. It was clearly forced on a peaceful, stable Japan by the threat of foreign domination. It was carried out largely by able young men drawn almost exclusively from the lower ranks of the dominant samurai class. It succeeded because of a number of characteristics the Japanese possessed, the relative importance of which is not easily measured. They shared some of these characteristics with their neighbors and others with the peoples of the West, but probably no other people had exactly their particular mix of traits. To sum up, the Meiji Restoration cannot be pigeonholed in some neat compartment of historical theory. Certainly what happened during these decades would not have transpired just at that time in Japanese history without the pressures from the West, nor would these pressures have produced the results they did without the specific historical experience and qualities of the Japanese people.

It is difficult to determine what aspects of premodern Japan were significant in shaping modern Japan and what their relative importance may have been. Certainly one important factor was the natural isolation of an island nation, which, strengthened by more than two centuries of artificially enforced isolation, helped make the Japanese a very homogeneous people, extremely conscious of their own identity and distinctiveness. They lacked important ethnic minorities and religious cleavages, which have been the bane of many modernizing countries. In addition, they had a sense of nationalism not unlike that of contemporary European nations, but largely lacking in most non-Western lands at that time. Though maintaining feudal autonomies and bitterly divided over policies toward the West, no Japanese for a moment thought of supporting some foreign power against his own countrymen.

Why nationalism should have appeared so early and developed so fully in Japan, long before it became significant in other Asian lands, is an interesting question. A sense of national identity seems to have been stirred as early as the first great period of cultural borrowing from China, probably inspired by a feeling of inferiority—the sharp contrast between a small and backward Japan and an in comparably larger, older, and more advanced China. One is reminded of the early nationalism of North Europe, which may have resulted from a similar inferiority complex toward the older and more developed cultures of the lands of the Mediterranean. This early awareness of the superiority of China had also produced a clear realization of the possibility of learning from abroad. Cultural imports to Japan had come by sea and had therefore been clearly identifiable. The Japanese, unlike most other peoples, East or West, had long been aware that much of their civilization had come from abroad. Therefore, unlike the Chinese and other non-Western peoples, they had no difficulty in realizing, in the nineteenth century, that there was much that not only could but must be learned from the West.

Japan's more than two centuries of enforced isolation had also made possible an equally long period of absolute peace and order, during which the Japanese had developed an extremely advanced and complex economy and society, high levels of education, an extraordinary degree of national economic and intellectual unity, and high standards of political competence. It was by no means a backward nation, and lagged appreciably behind the West only in technology. In group coordination and skills in cooperation, it probably was well ahead of most Western lands. Long experience with orderly and peaceful legal processes probably account for the relative lack of violence accompanying the great changes that took place in the 1860s and 1870s.

The Japanese, like the other peoples of East Asia, had a strong work ethic and a deeply ingrained drive for education, characteristics not widely shared among most currently modernizing nations. But unlike the other peoples of East Asia, who had centrally unified monarchies, they had a basically feudal political structure and, during their long period of peace, had developed an economic, social, and intellectual system that no longer fitted this political structure very well. The top feudal class was seriously in debt to the theoretically lowest merchant class. Ambitious samurai of low rank hungered for a political system that recognized ability and achievement over birth. Secure in their feudal niches, merchants and peasants enjoyed broad autonomies in running their own town or village affairs and often developed into vigorous entrepreneurs. Japanese society was riddled with inconsistencies, and unlike the monolithically solid social and political systems of China and Korea, was ripe for change. It required no prolonged period of destructive blows from the outside before it collapsed, clearing the way for new institutions.

NO

Thomas C. Smith

OLD VALUES AND NEW TECHNIQUES IN THE MODERNIZATION OF JAPAN

Modern technology was introduced into Japan under the sanction of traditional Japanese values. I do not suggest that there was logical necessity in this: that from the values we could infer modernization; nor do I suggest that nothing new was added. But despite amplification and reinterpretation, it was, none the less, traditional ideas that Japanese leaders used to justify change. Japanese mythology, long neglected by political theory, became the core of an ideology that made national power a necessity. At a time when Japan found herself impotent yet plunged into the middle of a world power struggle, mythology was called upon to endow the nation with one kind of greatness: the emperor was descended by unbroken lineage from divine ancestors, and he was father of a nation conceived as an extended family: what other nation could make *that* claim? A nation unique and precious as this was, could not fall behind others in power—economic and political as well as military—even if inherited institutions had to be scrapped wholesale to keep abreast. Otherwise the claim to greatness must eventually collapse. Belief in the claim, which was bolstered in everyday life by making a cult of the patriarchal family with its values of obedience and hierarchy, gave the nation the will and discipline to transform an almost purely agrarian society into a predominantly industrial one within a generation. No Asian nation has yet duplicated this feat.

Do we credit the old values with too much? I think not: telescoping centuries of social time into decades requires powerful sanctions that cannot be improvised. The alternative to building on the past was waiting for gunboats and ideas to destroy it and then there might be nothing to build with; in any case, for decades and perhaps generations, the envisioned forced march to modernization must be an agonizing crawl.

But if old loyalties provided the sanctions for change, they were not in turn strengthened by it. Having sanctioned technological and institutional change without themselves being able to change—how can a claim to divine origins be modified?—they gradually lost power to command belief. Let me cite a few examples of how their works robbed them of faith.

From Thomas C. Smith, "Old Values and New Techniques in the Modernization of Japan," *Far Eastern Quarterly*, vol. 14, no. 3 (May 1955). Copyright © 1974 by *Journal of Asian Studies*. Reprinted with permission of The Association for Asian Studies, Inc. Notes omitted.

Rationalist thought, which an educational system dedicated to the advancement of science and technology could not but promote, increasingly called into question the Japanese political myth. Modern industry gave rise to new and harsher class antagonisms that made the familial ideal of society harder to cherish. The authority of the family and the power of its symbols declined as the family lost economic functions to the market and as the difference in outlook between generations widened with accelerating change. Nevertheless, the primary old values—throne and family—did not collapse, for they were continuously reinforced by stronger and more efficient measures of indoctrination and thought control by the state.

The groups in control of the state had no choice but to sustain the old values as best they could. Without them there was no sanction for their monopoly of power or for the fearful and wrenching effort of industrialization. If that effort should collapse, so must Japan's always precarious international position, bringing loss of foreign markets, unemployment, perhaps even social revolution; for Japan's industrial economy was built in critical part on the exploitation of other peoples' resources, and the scope of exploitation had continuously to be extended to maintain the momentum of economic growth and allay deep-lying class conflicts. And because foreign aggrandizement brought resistance and moral condemnation from others, Japanese leaders insisted the more vehemently on judging themselves by their own unique standards. There was no way out: the weaker old values became, the more they were needed. To push ahead at any cost demanded either supreme nerve or blind faith, and in the end (as is so often the case) the two were

one. The price the nation paid for *these* qualities of leadership was frightful: to be led without enthusiasm into challenging half the world to arms by men whose belief in the old values was most nearly absolute and whose brush with the outside world and modern thought most superficial—men whose rural origins and army careers had kept them "pure."

But long before this the nation was paying a price in malaise. Japanese life was racked by the mounting tension of living by old values in a world to which they no longer belonged. Tension did not take the form of an ideological struggle between parties that stood by the old values and parties that would overthrow them. This might have relieved the tension; in any case, for some the tension would have been *between* them and others and not inside. But except for Marxist intellectuals, no important segment of the Japanese population openly disavowed the official ideology; no one could without becoming an enemy of the state and, worse, breaking with his cultural past. But fewer and fewer people wore the straight-jacket of orthodoxy comfortably: despite nearly universal protestations of loyalty and belief, there was secret or unconscious alienation.

It is easier to guess than to prove the existence of inner conflict because Japanese dissembled it. Still, there were unwitting flashes of candor and even some quite intentional. Take this passage from the novel *Sore kara*, by Natsume Sōseki, in which a young man reflects on his father:

His father had received the moral upbringing usual for *samurai* before the Restoration. This training was unsuited to the realities of contemporary life, but his father, who was true to its precepts neither in conduct nor feeling clung to it in theory and for appearances sake. He had gone into business and had been driven by egotism and avarice which over the years had corrupted him. He was quite unaware of this. Although he was not the man he had been, he was always professing that it was his same old self that acted and had brought his affairs so satisfactorily to their present state. But Daisuke felt that no man could satisfy the hourly demands of modern life and remain true to a feudal ethic. Whoever tired, whoever strove to maintain two disparate selfs, must suffer the torment of war between them.

Or consider the case of Ishikawa Takuboku, one of Japan's most popular modern poets. Takuboku wrote a novel in which the hero (who is himself) thinks existing society utter]y corrupt and worthy only of destruction. While writing this novel, Takuboku wrote to a friend that he badly needed money from its publication to discharge a long-neglected duty to his elder brother. What this duty was we do not know, but the term he used was *giri*—one of the central concepts of ethics as taught in Japanese schools; and Takuboku was at this time a teacher, and his hero was the principal of a village elementary school. I am convinced that conflicts like that of Takuboku, who seems both a rebel against society's conventions and a slave to them, went so deep and wide that few aspects of modern Japanese culture would not reveal them to analysis. Let me cite a few random and gross examples of what I mean.

Everyone knows that a recurring theme in Japanese drama is the inner struggle of the individual torn between duty and desire—between the imperatives of conventional morality and contrary impulses from experience. I am not about to suggest that this is a novel or uniquely Japanese theme; but when it becomes perhaps the dominant theme of a popular theatre we suspect that a great many people are tormented by the problems it treats, and we can see why this was so in Japan. *Kabuki* was the product of a wealthy merchant class which, deprived of political power and social honor by the warrior class, embroidered living with the enjoyment of the sharpest sensual pleasures—riotous color, melodrama, wine, women, and song. Pursuit of these pleasures was as contrary to the stern ethic of the dominant warrior class as the colorful ukiyoe prints of bourgeoise culture were different from the severe black and white paintings of Zen masters. And since the warrior ethic dominated Tokugawa society, pursuit of these pleasures involved the bourgeoisie in essentially the same conflict that assumed larger proportions and caught more people later on, as the warrior class modernized the country and sought at the same time to make its own moral code the ethic of the nation. I say it was essentially the same conflict, for, despite the drastic social changes modernization brought, *Kabuki* did not change its themes or its repertoire nor did it lose its popularity.

My second example is from the field of politics. Except on the far left, which did not count in the parliamentary struggle, no political party openly challenged the theory that all political authority derived from the emperor. For the "liberal" parties that embraced this theory as well as the conservative, it had serious disadvantages: it placed Japanese cabinets, whose ministers were responsible only to the emperor, ultimately beyond their control. To overcome this inconvenience, one party or another, almost continuously from 1880 to about 1935, advanced the view, strongly resisted by the military, the bureaucracy and the conservative political parties, that cabinet ministers should be responsible to parliament: the emperor would still appoint them but now from the majority party in the lower house. Those who held this view disclaimed any intention of encroaching on the power of the emperor, and they proved it to their own satisfaction by giving the doctrine of the emperor as father of the people an ingenious if unconvincing twist. Since the emperor was a wise and benevolent father who desired nothing but the welfare of his loving and filial subjects, there could be no conflict between throne and people. And to make the government responsible to parliament was to bring the two closer together and to make the single will of both, now sometimes frustrated by selfish (and presumably unfilial) ministers, more effective. This argument was advanced by parties that represented hardheaded modern businessmen who, while well aware of the stabilizing value of the throne, were from time to time embarrassed, frustrated, and bullied by the governments that manipulated its occult powers. The argument was in essence a radical attack on authoritarian government hidden in a statement of the purest and fussiest orthodoxy. There was no dishonesty in this; just divided minds and hearts.

We might give still other examples: the drive to rationalize operations in business firms organized on the family principle; indoctrination in the values of the hierarchical family in an essentially equalitarian educational system; emperor worship and class struggle in the labor movement. But we must go on to consider two problems our argument

raises. First, why did Japanese leaders combine beliefs upon which they placed the highest value with a technology destructive of them? Of course, they did not fully appreciate the contradiction; but holding the beliefs they did, why did they value the new technology at all? It is no answer to say that they saw in it a means of enhancing Japan's power and prestige; the question *still* remains, for there were fanatically patriotic men who sought these same ends by rejecting the new technology. Second, how was the combination of old values and new techniques, once effected, sustained? By action of the state, of course; but what sustained the purpose of the state as its social base was transformed? My answers to these questions must be very general, tentative, and incomplete.

As to the first question, consider the interests joined by the Meiji Restoration, the political revolution of 1867 that started Japan on her career of modernization. At that time Japan's feudal rulers were overthrown in the name of the emperor by dissatisfied low-ranking warriors backed by a developing capitalist class. The grievances of these warriors were in part grudges nursed by a centuries-old feudal vendetta between eastern and western barons and in part economic dissatisfactions bred of rising prices and falling incomes as the land economy, on which warrior wealth and position were based, gave way before commercial capitalism. There was *nothing* in either of these grievances that helps explain the revolutionary use low-ranking warriors made of power once they had it: why, for example, they swept away the feudal political structure by which warriors monopolized power to establish a modern bureaucratic state in its place. The answer I think is that the warrior's capitalist allies were not interested in substituting one group of feudal rulers for another. They were for the most part rural industrialists and merchants who found feudal government, with its closed class system, its manifold restrictions on enterprise, and its bias in favor of tamed city guild-merchants, hateful. These men not only backed the Restoration movement with money; they gave it direction, turning what might otherwise have been a struggle to reorganize the feudal system into a movement to destroy it.

But why, then, did the slogans and ideology of the revolution look to the past? Why not some native variant of "liberty, equality, and fraternity" instead of "revere the Emperor"? For one thing, the capitalist element, although able to influence the Restoration movement, was not strong enough to dominate it. Under Tokugawa feudal rule even very wealthy commoners did not have the self-confidence, freedom of movement, and prestige to organize and lead an opposition movement; they could do no better than follow warriors who did. And because the warriors, who were the elite carriers of the traditional virtues, led the revolution, it was justified in the only way it could be for them, not as a break with the past but as a spiritual return to it. But there was another reason for this: the warrior's allies had one foot in the future, but the other was firmly planted in the past. As merchants and industrialists, they looked forward to sweeping change. But they were also landlords who exploited land through a system of patriarchal tenant relationships based on protection and patronage, loyalty and obedience, the structures of which not only gave them dominant social and political power in the village but supported their mercantile

and industrial operations as well. While they wished to be free of the trammels and inequalities of feudalism, they did not wish to weaken the traditional structure and spirit of the village. What they wished was a more efficient and enlightened authoritarianism—one that would give them economic scope and opportunity for social advancement and at the same time stand as a bulwark against radical agrarian change.

This is what they got; but it became increasingly hard to preserve, for the enlightened efficiency of the new regime eventually weakened its authoritarian base. This brings me to the second question: what sustained authoritarian government?

Although modern technology must, it seems, ultimately transform the whole of a traditional society and all its values, it does not transform all sectors at the same rate. Typically, change in rural areas is slower than in cities, and in Japan it has been exceptionally slow. The reason for this, I think, is at least in part the character of Japanese agriculture.

One way industrial development may radically change agriculture is by depriving it of essential labor and so forcing the mechanization of farming. This has not occurred in Japan because rural population growth has offset—and in some areas more than offset—emigration to the city. No doubt this growth is due in part to the elimination or softening of Malthusian checks. But equally important in my opinion is that the typical holding in Japan is so small and badly fragmented that mechanization is blocked, and the peasant family faced with a labor shortage has no means of meeting it but natural increase. This is not always possible; biology sometimes lets the family down. But it is in most cases because the family adapts to the demands of biology—by adopting sons-in-law, permitting second wives, holding the young child-bearing generations in the family indefinitely. There is more than a hint of this adaptability and its consequences in the remarkably close correlation, confirmed by many demographic studies, between the size of the family and the size of its holding—that is, the amount of labor it needs.

Population growth, in part forced by the smallness of the holding, sustained the small holding in the face of a growing demand from industry for labor. Indeed, the average working holding has become somewhat smaller during the past century of industrial development and, as a result, although the family has been broken up as a unit of production elsewhere, it has *not* in agriculture. The typical family uses no more than a few days of hired labor a year, and all its adult members work at the same occupation-under closely similar conditions, as share-holders in a single enterprise. And because the enterprise operates on the narrowest margin—costs are high and income low with hand labor—solidarity, obedience, and authority are for the peasant family conditions of survival.

Since machines cannot supplant nor wage labor compete with family labor in agriculture, the development of capitalist farming is blocked even though, as farming becomes increasingly commercial, land ownership tends to concentrate (although typically on a small scale). The man who by lending and foreclosing lays field to field, acquiring more land than he can work with family labor, almost invariably lets the surplus to families of tenants. The result is increasingly sharp distinctions of wealth and income in the village, but the solidarity of the village

is never shattered, as that of the medieval English village was, by division of the population increasingly into capitalist farmers and agricultural laborers. With rare exceptions, the village remains predominantly a community of small farmers—some landlords, some tenants, and others owner-cultivators but all faced with essentially the same problems of small-scale farming. Not that conflicts of interest do not occur: but for the most part they take the form of personal quarrels, and although larger, class antagonisms undoubtedly exist, they are usually submerged by an overriding sense of community solidarity. I wish to comment further on this point after noting two other factors that contribute to the spirit of solidarity.

The first concerns landlord-tenant relations, a complex subject that I must unconscionably simplify. Before the occupation land reform the Japanese landlord rented a holding to a tenant who managed it; the landlord's return depended on the skill and resourcefulness of the tenant as a farmer; for he could not collect rent unless the tenant, who almost never had savings, made enough from current operations to pay it. He could normally evict the tenant for nonpayment of rent; but unless the tenant and not nature or the market were at fault, he rarely exercised this right, for there was no reason to think another tenant could do better, and it was not easy to deprive a whole family known to him and everyone else in the village of the means of life. So in bad years he reduced the rent instead and, the return from agriculture being highly variable from year to year, he made this concession repeatedly. Therefore, even when rent was theoretically a fixed payment in money or kind, it varied in practice from year to year with yields, so that the landlord was to some extent a partner of the tenant whose interests he could not infringe beyond a certain point without hurting his own. Moreover, such events in the tenant's family as sickness and death affected the tenant's ability to pay rent in full almost as directly as the weather, and the landlord had to make similar allowance for them. Since this forced him to take an interest in and assess events at the very center of the tenant's family life, landlord-tenant relations were social as well as economic. The relationship was not always friendly, but it was rarely overly hostile, for it was subject to conventions of polite and considerate conduct enforced by community opinion.

The second factor I wish to mention is the cultivation of rice. Rice is cultivated in Japan everywhere soil, climate, and terrain permit, which is to say on at least part of most holdings and all of some. And because rice must be made to stand in water during much of the growing season to get maximum yields, there is need in almost every village for a vast and complex system of ditches, dams, dikes, ponds, tunnels, and water gates that can be constructed and maintained only by community effort. No man who grows rice, therefore, owns or controls all of the essential means of production himself nor may make all of the more critical decisions of farming independently. A man may wish, for example, to turn an unirrigated field into paddy, but he will not be allowed to do so if this would impair the water supply of others; and he will refrain from insisting on his wish because he has been taught he must, and village opinion will be ranged solidly against him if he does not. The habit of bowing to group opinion where water is concerned carries over, we may suppose,

to other matters—if for no other reason than that any serious breach of harmony in the village strikes at the communal foundations of agriculture.

To return now to the significance for us of community solidarity: the sense of it makes the village a powerful agency for suppressing individualism and dissent, for blocking innovation and maintaining custom's hard cake into which most lives and personalities in rural Japan are molded.

I have one further point to make and it also concerns the concentration of Japanese agriculture on the cultivation of rice. This concentration is characteristic of individual holdings as well as agriculture as a whole, and consequently there is far less specialization in farming than one might think in a country with the large urban market of Japan. Most peasant families, therefore, supply all or nearly all of their own food, and since the labor force is large in relation to its output, what is consumed takes a very large part of what is produced. Of the total agricultural income of the average peasant family in 1935, about one-third was in kind—that is, was not marketed. This means that the peasant's involvement in the market, the limits on which seem absolute, is far from complete and that commercial values do not penetrate a very large area of his economic relations, which remain embedded in custom-bound social groupings.

It is perhaps possible now to see what permitted the state to sustain the old values. Among the urban population modernization generated new attitudes destructive of them—class consciousness, individualism, skepticism; but the peasantry remained a vast hinterland of conservatism. And, owing to the intensive use of labor in agriculture, the demographic ratio between city and country did not alter with industrialization as radically as in many countries: in 1930 agricultural labor in Japan was 50.3 per cent of the total labor force as compared to 18.8 per cent in the U.S. in 1940, 16.3 per cent in Germany in 1933, and 6.2 per cent in England in 1938. I am suggesting, of course, that the peasantry provided a social base by virtue of which the state was able to impose the worship of old gods upon the entire nation.

But why, we may ask, did the agrarian sector remain decisive politically when it had ceased to be so economically? This question brings us back to Japan's struggle against the West. Launching upon industrialization late and poorly endowed with resources, Japan was bound to build heavily on foreign markets and resources already preëmpted; so she was bound to intrude and intruding to face fierce resistance which she must either defy or retreat before. And since she could not

retreat—not without grave social risks and the risk of remaining powerless—she defied. Defiance brought success, but success intensified resistance, calling for a strengthening of old loyalties to overcome inner uncertainties and discipline the nation to a new effort. Pressure from the outside did not grow continuously; there were periods of relaxation; and nothing testifies so convincingly to the importance of foreign relations for the persistence of old values than the fact that in these periods the old values were seriously challenged by other values from the West. But the international honeymoon never lasted long and the '20's were invariably followed by the '30's. These wild oscillations between uncritical acclaim of the West and xenophobia were not mere fickleness: they were rooted in the real claims of two cultures that could not be reconciled because one was the foundation of a state always imperiled by states built on the other.

POSTSCRIPT

Did the Meiji Restoration Destroy Traditional Japanese Values?

In discussing the alienation that allegedly beset many Japanese in the early twentieth century, Smith calls upon Japanese literature to prove his point. The use of literature to obtain insights into national psychology can be quite rewarding, and it is a resource that is generally employed far too seldom by historians. Readers may track changes in Japanese thought in several excellent anthologies of modern Japanese literature, including Donald Keene's *Dawn to the West* (Holt, Rinehart & Winston, 1984); *The Showa Anthology* edited by Van C. Gessel and Tomone Matsumoto (Kodansha International, 1985); and *This Kind of Woman* edited by Yukiko Tanaka and Elizabeth Hanson (Stanford University Press, 1982).

Another intriguing angle on twentieth-century Japanese psychology is provided by Carol Gluck in *Japan's Modern Myths: Ideology in the Late Meiji Period* (Princeton University Press, 1985). In *Giving Up the Gun* (David R. Godine, 1979), Noel Perrin explores the persistence of one particular instrument of traditional Japanese culture: the samurai sword. The essays in *Meiji Japan's Centennial* edited by David Wurfel (University of Kansas Press, 1971) focus on various aspects of political thought and action during the Meiji Restoration.

ISSUE 8

Was Economic Motivation the Key Factor Behind Nineteenth-Century Imperialism?

YES: J. A. Hobson, from *Imperialism: A Study* (Ann Arbor, 1965)

NO: Ronald Robinson, John Gallagher, and Alice Denny, from *Africa and the Victorians: The Official Mind of Imperialism,* 2d ed. (Macmillan, 1981)

ISSUE SUMMARY

YES: Turn-of-the-century British journalist J. A. Hobson provides a classic argument for the economic motivation of the "New Imperialism" of the late nineteenth century.

NO: History professors Ronald Robinson and John Gallagher, with Alice Denny, turn the tables on the Marxist interpretation of nineteenth-century imperalism, arguing that it was the bureaucrats who manipulated the capitalists into pursuing imperial adventure overseas.

From 1870 to the early years of the twentieth century, the European nation-states engaged in an accelerated acquisition of colonial territory like no other period in history. Indeed, while Western imperialism can be documented even before the Crusades, this rush to annex or control more and more territory proved remarkable even to the people of the time. The continent that was most dramatically changed by this frenzy of conquest was Africa.

In some ways, the Partition of Africa, as this competition for African territory was called by competing nations, can be considered a product of the technological innovations that Europeans developed during the nineteenth century. Daniel R. Headrick, in his groundbreaking book *The Tools of Empire: Technology and European Imperialism in the Nineteenth Century,* points out that the opening of the Dark Continent became possible for Europeans once steam-powered gunboats were invented and designed to navigate the rivers, once quinine came to be accepted as a preventive against malaria, and once the efficient and reliable Maxim machine gun allowed them to overpower any resistance. Whether one is studying this period or the earlier ages of exploration, it is interesting to consider whether expansionist endeavors were a result of the invention of new technologies or whether the necessities of imperialism led to the development of new tools. Headrick and others have added an interesting twist to the ongoing and already fractious discussion of the rise of Western world dominance.

Classically, however, the chief bone of contention between historians of the "New Imperialism," as this late-nineteenth-century manifestation is called, is over the role that the economy of the Industrial Revolution played in instigating and driving European policies. Marxist historians, from the time of Lenin's *Imperialism: The Highest Stage of Capitalism* (1917) to the present, have argued that the rise of capitalism and the goals of its industrialists and financiers drove the decision-making processes of the industrial nations, leading them to intervene in foreign, especially underdeveloped, nations in order to acquire their natural resources and to exploit their labor. On the other hand, some scholars, most prominently Arthur Schumpeter, have asserted the exact opposite—that capitalism was inimicable to imperialism and ultimately contributed to the decline of the nineteenth-century empires. To these scholars, the New Imperialism was an atavism that the West continues to outgrow.

The following reading is an excerpt from one of the most often quoted theorists on the economic motivations for imperialism, J. A. Hobson. Hobson was an English journalist at the turn of the century who was opposed to British involvement in the Boer War. Writing primarily to a British audience, Hobson decided to use the example of the United States in the Spanish-American War (1898) and its annexation of the Philippines to make his point (rather than alienate his readers by making direct reference to his own country's actions). His attitude is that the economics of the late Industrial Revolution became manifest in imperial adventure, a view that became a compelling and comfortable model to accept.

However, in the early 1960s Ronald Robinson and John Gallagher published several articles and their most important book, *Africa and the Victorians*, with Alice Denny, disputing the economic model of causation for the New Imperialism and reframing the question in terms of international stability and modern bureaucracy. The second reading, an excerpt from the second edition of *Africa and the Victorians*, expands on this view.

Most recently, new ground has been broken in the study of popular culture and its endorsement of empire through advertising, literature, and theater. The responses of the victims of imperialism, their variety and forms, have also proved to be an enlightening and surprising endeavor of study.

YES

J. A. Hobson

THE ECONOMIC TAPROOT
OF IMPERIALISM

No mere array of facts and figures adduced to illustrate the economic nature of the new Imperialism will suffice to dispel the popular delusion that the use of national force to secure new markets by annexing fresh tracts of territory is a sound and a necessary policy for an advanced industrial country like Great Britain. It has indeed been proved that recent annexations of tropical countries, procured at great expense, have furnished poor and precarious markets, that our aggregate trade with our colonial possessions is virtually stationary, and that our most profitable and progressive trade is with rival industrial nations, whose territories we have no desire to annex, whose markets we cannot force, and whose active antagonism we are provoking by our expansive policy.

But these arguments are not conclusive. It is open to Imperialists to argue thus: "We must have markets for our growing manufactures, we must have new outlets for the investment of our surplus capital and for the energies of the adventurous surplus of our population: such expansion is a necessity of life to a national with our great and growing powers of production. An ever larger share of our population is devoted to the manufactures and commerce of towns, and is thus dependent for life and work upon food and raw materials from foreign lands. In order to buy and pay for these things we must sell our goods abroad. During the first three-quarters of the nineteenth century we could do so without difficulty by a natural expansion of commerce with continental nations and our colonies, all of which were far behind us in the main arts of manufacture and the carrying trades. So long as England held a virtual monopoly of the world markets for certain important classes of manufactured goods, Imperialism was unnecessary. After 1870 this manufacturing and trading supremacy was greatly impaired: other nations, especially Germany, the United States, and Belgium, advanced with great rapidity, and while they have not crushed or even stayed the increase of our external trade, their competition made it more and more difficult to dispose of the full surplus of our manufactures at a profit. The encroachments made by these nations upon our old markets, even in our own possessions, made

From J. A. Hobson, *Imperialism: A Study* (Ann Arbor, 1965). Copyright © 1965 by Routledge (Allen & Unwin). Reprinted by permission. Notes omitted.

it most urgent that we should take energetic means to secure new markets. These new markets had to lie in hitherto undeveloped countries, chiefly in the tropics, where vast populations lived capable of growing economic needs which our manufacturers and merchants could supply. Our rivals were seizing and annexing territories for similar purposes, and when they had annexed them closed them to our trade. The diplomacy and the arms of Great Britain had to be used in order to compel the owners of the new markets to deal with us: and experience showed that the safest means of securing and developing such markets is by establishing 'protectorates' or by annexation. The value in 1905 of these markets must not be taken as a final test of the economy of such a policy; the process of educating civilized needs which we can supply is of necessity of gradual one, and the cost of such Imperialism must be regarded as a capital outlay, the fruits of which posterity would reap. The new markets might not be large, but they formed serviceable outlets for the overflow of our great textile and metal industries, and, when the vast Asiatic and African populations of the interior were reached, a rapid expansion of trade was expected to result.

"Far larger and more important is the pressure of capital for external fields of investment. Moreover, while the manufacturer and trader are well content to trade with foreign nations, the tendency for investors to work towards the political annexation of countries which contain their more speculative investments is very powerful. Of the fact of this pressure of capital there can be no question. Large savings are made which cannot find any profitable investment in this country; they must find employment elsewhere, and it is to the advantage of the nation that they should be employed as largely as possible in lands where they can be utilized in opening up markets for British trade and employment for British enterprise.

"However costly, however perilous, this process of imperial expansion may be, it is necessary to the continued existence and progress of our nation; if we abandoned it we must be content to leave the development of the world to other nations, who will everywhere cut into our trade, and even impair our means of securing the food and raw materials we require to support our population. Imperialism is thus seen to be, not a choice, but a necessity."

The practical force of this economic argument in politics is strikingly illustrated by the later history of the United States. Here is a country which suddenly broke through a conservative policy, strongly held by both political parties, bound up with every popular instinct and tradition, and flung itself into a rapid imperial career for which it possessed neither the material nor the moral equipment, risking the principles and practices of liberty and equality by the establishment of militarism and the forcible subjugation of peoples which could not safely admit to the condition of American citizenship.

Was this a mere wild freak of spread-eaglism, a burst of political ambition on the part of a nation coming to a sudden realization of its destiny? Not at all. The spirit of adventure, the American "mission of civilization," were as forces making for Imperialism, clearly subordinate to the driving force of the economic factor. The dramatic character of the change is due to the unprecedented rapidity of the industrial revolution in the United States from the eighties onwards. During that period the United States, with her unrivalled natural resources, her immense resources of skilled and unskilled labour, and her genius for invention and organization, developed the best equipped and most productive manufacturing economy the world has yet seen. Fostered by rigid protective tariffs, her metal, textile, tool, clothing, furniture, and other manufactures shot up in a single generation from infancy to full maturity, and, having passed through a period of intense competition, attained, under the able control of great trust-makers, a power of production greater than has been attained in the most advanced industrial countries of Europe.

An era of cut-throat competition, followed by a rapid process of amalgamation, threw an enormous quantity of wealth into the hands of a small number of captains of industry. No luxury of living to which this class could attain kept pace with its rise of income, and a process of automatic saving set in upon an unprecedented scale. The investment of these savings in other industries helped to bring these under the same concentrative forces. Thus a great increase of savings seeking profitable investment is synchronous with a stricter economy of the use of existing capital. No doubt the rapid growth of a population, accustomed to a high and an always ascending standard of comfort, absorbs in the satisfaction of its wants a large quantity of new capital. But the actual rate of saving, conjoined with a more economical application of forms of existing capital, exceeded considerably the rise of the national consumption of manufactures. The power of production far outstripped the actual rate of consumption, and, contrary to the older economic theory, was unable to force a corresponding increase of consumption by lowering prices.

This is no mere theory. The history of any of the numerous trusts or combinations in the United States sets out the facts with complete distinctness. In the free competition of manufactures preceding combination the chronic condition is one of "over-production," in the sense that all the mills or factories can only be kept at work by cutting prices down towards a point where the weaker competitors are forced to close down, because they cannot sell their goods at a price which covers the true cost of production. The first result of the successful formation of a trust or combine is to close down the worse equipped or worse placed mills, and supply the entire market from the better equipped and better placed ones. This course may or may not be attended by a rise of price and some restriction of consumption: in some cases trusts take most of their profits by raising prices, in other cases by reducing the costs of production through employing only the best mills and stopping the waste of competition.

For the present argument it matters not which course is taken; the point is that this concentration of industry in "trusts," "combines," etc., at once limits the quantity of capital which can be effectively employed and increases the share of profits out of which fresh savings and fresh capital will spring. It is quite evident that a trust which is motived by cut-throat competition, due to an excess of capital, cannot normally find inside the "trusted" industry employment for that portion of the profits which the trust-makers desire to save and to invest. New inventions and other economies of production or distribution within the trade may absorb some of the new capital, but there are rigid limits to this absorption. The trust-maker in oil or sugar must find other investments for his savings: if he is early in the application of the combination principles to his trade, he will naturally apply his surplus capital to establish similar combinations in other industries, economising capital still further, and rendering it ever harder for ordinary saving men to find investments for their savings.

Indeed, the conditions alike of cutthroat competition and of combination attest the congestion of capital in the manufacturing industries which have entered the machine economy. We are not here concerned with any theoretic question as to the possibility of producing by modern machine methods more goods than can find a market. It is sufficient to point out that the manufacturing power of a country like the United States would grow so fast as to exceed the demands of the home market. No one acquainted with trade will deny a fact which all american economists assert, that this is the condition which the United States reached at the end of the century, so far, as the more developed industries are concerned. Her manufactures were saturated with capital and could absorb no more. One after another they sought refuge from the waste of competition in "combines" which secure a measure of profitable peace by restricting the quantity of operative capital. Industrial and financial princes in oil, steel, sugar, railroads, banking, etc., were faced with the dilemma of either spending more than they knew how to spend, or forcing markets outside the home area. Two economic courses were open to them, both leading towards an abandonment of the political isolation of the past and the adoption of imperialist methods in the future. Instead of shutting down inferior mills and rigidly restricting output to correspond with profitable sales in the home markets, they might employ their full productive power, applying their savings to increase their business capital, and, while still regulating output and prices for the home market, may "hustle" for foreign markets, dumping down their surplus goods at prices which would not be possible save for the profitable nature of their home market. So likewise they might employ their savings in seeking investments outside their country, first repaying the capital borrowed from Great Britain and other countries for the early development of their railroads, mines and manufactures, and afterwards becoming themselves a creditor class to foreign countries.

It was this sudden demand for foreign markets for manufactures and for investments which was avowedly responsible for the adoption of Imperialism as a political policy and practice by the Republican party to which the great industrial and financial chiefs belonged, and which belonged to them. The adventurous enthusiasm of President Theodore Roosevelt and his "manifest destiny" and "mission of civilization" party must not deceive us. It was Messrs. Rockefeller, Pierpont Morgan, and their associates who needed Imperialism and who fastened it upon the shoulders of the great Republic of the West. They needed Imperialism because they desired to use the public resources of their country to find profitable employment for their capital which otherwise would be superfluous....

The suddenness of this political revolution is due to the rapid manifestation of the need. In the last years of the nineteenth century the United States nearly trebled the value of its manufacturing export trade, and it was to be expected that, if the rate of progress of those years continued, within a decade it would overtake our more slowly advancing export trade, and stand first in the list of manufacture-exporting nations.

This was the avowed ambition, and no idle one, of the keenest business men of America; and with the natural resources, the labour and the administrative talents at their disposal, it was quite likely they would achieve their object. The stronger and more direct control over politics exercised in America by business men enabled them to drive more quickly and more straightly along the line of their economic interests than in Great Britain. American Imperialism was the natural product of the economic pressure of a sudden advance of capitalism which could not find occupation at home and needed foreign markets for goods and for investments.

The same needs existed in European countries, and, as is admitted, drove Governments along the same path. Over-production in the sense of an excessive manufacturing plant, and surplus capital which could not find sound investments within the country, forced Great Britain, Germany, Holland, France to place larger and larger portions of their economic resources outside the area of their present political domain, and then stimulate a policy of political expansion so as to take in the new areas. The economic sources of this movement are laid bare by periodic trade-depressions due to an inability of producers to find adequate and profitable markets for what they can produce. The Majority Report of the Commission upon the Depression of Trade in 1885 put the matter in a nutshell. "That, owing to the nature of the times, the demand for our commodities does not increase at the same rate as formerly; that our capacity for production is consequently in excess of our requirements, and

could be considerably increased at short notice; that this is due partly to the competition of the capital which is being steadily accumulated in the country." The Minority Report straightly imputed the condition of affairs to "over-production." Germany was in the early 1900's suffering severly from what is called a glut of capital and of manufacturing power: she had to have new markets; her Consuls all over the world were "hustling" for trade; trading settlements were forced upon Asia Minor; in East and West Africa, in China and elsewhere the German Empire was impelled to a policy of colonization and protectorates as outlets for German commercial energy.

Every improvement of methods of production, every concentration of ownership and control, seems to accentuate the tendency. As one nation after another enters the machine economy and adopts advanced industrial methods, it becomes more difficult for its manufacturers, merchants, and financiers to dispose profitably of their economic resources, and they are tempted more and more to use their Governments in order to secure for their particular use some distant undeveloped country by annexation and protection.

The process, we may be told, is inevitable, and so it seems upon a superficial inspection. Everywhere appear excessive powers of production, excessive capital in search of investment. It is admitted by all business men that the growth of the powers of production in their country exceeds the growth in consumption, that more goods can be produced than can be sold at a profit, and that more capital exists than can find remunerative investment.

It is this economic condition of affairs that forms the taproot of Imperialism.

If the consuming public in this country raised its standard of consumption to keep pace with every rise of productive powers, there could be no excess of goods or capital clamorous to use Imperialism in order to find markets: foreign trade would indeed exist, but there would be no difficulty in exchanging a small surplus of our manufactures for the food and raw material we annually absorbed, and all the savings that we made could find employment, if we chose, in home industries.

There is nothing inherently irrational in such a supposition. Whatever is, or can be, produced, can be consumed, for a claim upon it, as rent, profit, or wages, forms part of the real income of some member of the community, and he can consume it, or else exchange it for some other consumable with some one else who will consume it. With everything that is produced a consuming power is born. If then there are goods which cannot get consumed, or which cannot even get produced because it is evident they cannot get consumed, and if there is a quantity of capital and labour which cannot get full employment because its products cannot get consumed, the only possible explanation of this paradox is the refusal of owners of consuming power to apply that power in effective demand for commodities.

... [I]t may be asked, "Why should there be any tendency to over-saving? Why should the owners of consuming power withhold a larger quantity for savings than can be serviceably employed?" Another way of putting the same question is this, "Why should not the pressure of present wants keep pace with every possibility of satisfying them?" The answer to these pertinent questions carries us to the broadest issue of the distribu-

tion of wealth. If a tendency to distribute income or consuming power according to needs were operative, it is evident that consumption would rise with every rise of producing power, for human needs are illimitable, and there could be no excess of saving. But it is quite otherwise in a state of economic society where distribution has no fixed relation to needs, but is determined by other conditions which assign to some people a consuming power vastly in excess of needs or possible uses, while others are destitute of consuming power enough to satisfy even the full demands of physical efficiency. The following illustration may serve to make the issue clear. "The volume of production has been constantly rising owing to the development of modern machinery. There are two main channels to carry off these products—one channel carrying off the product destined to be consumed by the workers, and the other channel carrying off the remainder to the rich. The workers' channel is in rock-bound banks that cannot enlarge, owing to the competitive wage system preventing wages rising *pro rata* with increased efficiency. Wages are based upon cost of living, and not upon efficiency of labour. The miner in the poor mine gets the same wages per day as the miner in the adjoining rich mine. The owner of the rich mine gets the advantage—not his labourer. The channel which conveys the goods destined to supply the rich is itself divided into two streams. One stream carries off what the rich 'spend' on themselves for the necessities and luxuries of life. The other is simply an 'overflow' stream carrying off their 'savings.' The channel for spending, i.e. the amount wasted by the rich in luxuries, may broaden somewhat, but owing to the small number of those rich enough to indulge in whims it can never be greatly enlarged, and at any rate it bears such a small proportion to the other channel that in no event can much hope of avoiding a flood of capital be hoped for from this division. The rich will never be so ingenious as to spend enough to prevent over-production. The great safety overflow channel which has been continuously more and more widened and deepened to carry off the ever-increasing flood of new capital is that division of the stream which carried the savings of the rich, and this is not only suddenly found to be incapable of further enlargement, but actually seems to be in the process of being dammed up."

Though this presentation over-accentuates the cleavage between rich and poor and over-states the weakness of the workers, it gives forcible and sound expression to a most important and ill-recognised economic truth. The "overflow" stream of savings is of course fed not exclusively from the surplus income of "the rich"; the professional and industrial middle classes, and to some slight extent the workers, contribute. But the "flooding" is distinctly due to the automatic saving of the surplus income of rich men. This is of course particularly true of America, where multi-millionaires rise quickly and find themselves in possession of incomes far exceeding the demands of any craving that is known to them. To make the metaphor complete, the overflow stream must be represented as re-entering the stream of production and seeking to empty there all the "savings" that it carries. Where competition remains free, the result is a chronic congestion of productive power and of production, forcing down home prices, wasting large sums in advertising and in pushing for orders, and periodically causing a crisis followed by a collapse, during which quantities of capital and labour lie unemployed and unremunerated. The prime object of the trust or other combine is to remedy this waste and loss by substituting regulation of output for reckless over-production. In achieving this it actually narrows or even dams up the old channels of investment, limiting the overflow stream to the exact amount required to maintain the normal current of output. But this rigid limitation of trade, though required for the separate economy of each trust, does not suit the trust-maker, who is driven to compensate for strictly regulated industry at home by cutting new foreign channels as outlets for his productive power and his excessive savings. Thus we reach the conclusion that Imperialism is the endeavour of the great controllers of industry to broaden the channel for the flow of their surplus wealth by seeking foreign markets and foreign investments to take off the goods and capital they cannot sell or use at home.

NO

Ronald Robinson, John Gallagher, and Alice Denny

NATIONALISM AND IMPERIALISM

Did new, sustained or compelling impulses towards African empire arise in British politics or business during the Eighteen eighties? The evidence seems unconvincing. The late-Victorians seem to have been no keener to rule and develop Africa than their fathers. The business man saw no greater future there, except in the south; the politician was as reluctant to expand and administer a tropical African empire as the mid-Victorians had been; and plainly Parliament was no more eager to pay for it. British opinion restrained rather than prompted ministers to act in Africa. Hence they had to rely on private companies or colonial governments to act for them. It is true that African lobbies and a minority of imperialists did what they could to persuade government to advance. Yet they were usually too weak to be decisive. Measured by the yardstick of official thinking, there was no strong political or commercial movement in Britain in favour of African acquisitions.

The priorities of policy in tropical Africa confirm this impression. West Africa seemed to offer better prospects of markets and raw materials than east Africa and the Upper Nile; yet it was upon these poorer countries that the British government concentrated its efforts. These regions of Africa which interested the British investor and merchant least, concerned ministers the most. No expansion of commerce prompted the territorial claims to Uganda, the east coast and the Nile Valley.... [P]rivate enterprise was not moving in to develop them; and they were no more useful or necessary to the British industrial economy between 1880 and 1900 than they had been earlier in the century. Territorial claims here reached out far in advance of the expanding economy. Notions of pegging out colonial estates for posterity hardly entered into British calculations until the late Eighteen nineties, when it was almost too late to affect the outcome. Nor were ministers gulled by the romantic glories of ruling desert and bush. Imperialism in the wide sense of empire for empire's sake was not their motive. Their territorial claims were made for the sake of African empire or commerce as such.

They were little more than by-products of an enforced search for better security in the Mediterranean and the East. It was not the pomps or profits of

From Ronald Robinson, John Gallagher, and Alice Denny, *Africa and the Victorians: The Official Mind of Imperialism*, 2d ed. (Macmillan, 1981). Copyright © 1981 by Ronald Robinson, John Gallagher, and Alice Denny. Reprinted by permission of St. Martin's Press, Inc.

governing Africa which moved the ruling *élite*, but the cold rules for national safety handed on from Pitt, Palmerston and Disraeli.

According to the grammar of the policy-makers, their advances in Africa were prompted by different interests and circumstances in different regions. Egypt was occupied because of the collapse of the Khedivial *régime*. The occupation went on because the internal crisis remained unsolved and because of French hostility which the occupation itself provoked. Britain's insistent claims in east Africa and the Nile Valley and her yielding of so much in west Africa were largely contingent upon the Egyptian occupation and the way it affected European relations. In southern Africa, imperial intervention against the Transvaal was designed above all to uphold and restore the imperial influence which economic growth, Afrikaner nationalism and the Jameson fiasco had overthrown. Imperial claims in the Rhodesias, and to a lesser extent in Nyasaland, were contingent in turn upon Cape colonial expansion and imperial attempts to offset the rise of the Transvaal. The times and circumstances in which almost all these claims and occupations were made suggest strongly that they were called forth by crises in Egypt and south Africa, rather than by positive impulses to African empire arising in Europe.

To be sure, a variety of different interests in London—some religious and humanitarian, others strictly commercial or financial, and yet others imperialist —pressed for territorial advances and were sometimes used as their agents. In west Africa, the traders called for government protection; in Uganda and Nyasaland, the missionaries and the anti-slavery groups called for annexation; in Egypt, the bondholders asked government to rescue their investments; in south Africa, philanthropists and imperialists called for more government from Whitehall, while British traders and investors were divided about the best way of looking after their interests. Ministers usually listened to their pleas only when it suited their purpose; but commercial and philanthropic agitation seldom decided which territories should be claimed or occupied or when this should be done, although their slogans were frequently used by government in its public justifications.

It is the private calculations and actions of ministers far more than their speeches which reveal the primary motives behind their advances. For all the different situations in which territory was claimed, and all the different reasons which were given to justify it, one consideration, and one alone entered into all the major decisions. In all regions north of Rhodesia, the broad imperative which decided which territory to reserve and which to renounce, was the safety of the routes to the East. It did not, of course, prompt the claiming of Nyasaland or the lower Niger. Here a reluctant government acted to protect existing fields of trading and missionary enterprise from foreign annexations. In southern Africa the extension of empire seems to have been dictated by a somewhat different imperative. Here the London government felt bound as a rule to satisfy the demands for more territory which their self-governing colonials pressed on them. Ministers did this in the hope of conserving imperial influence. Nevertheless, the safety of the routes to India also figured prominently in the decision to uphold British supremacy in south Africa. It was the same imperative which after impelling the occupation of

Egypt, prolonged it, and forced Britain to go into east Africa and the Upper Nile, while yielding in most of west Africa. As soon as territory anywhere in Africa became involved, however indirectly, in this cardinal interest, ministries passed swiftly from inaction to intervention. If the papers left by the policy-makers are to be believed, they moved into Africa, not to build a new African empire, but to protect the old empire in India. What decided when and where they would go forward was their traditional conception of world strategy.

Its principles had been distilled from a century and more of accumulated experience, from far-reaching and varied experiments in the uses of power to promote trade and in the uses of trade to promote power. Much of this experience confirmed one precept: that Britain's strength depended upon the possession of India and preponderance in the East, almost as much as it did upon the British Isles. Therefore, her position in the world hung above all upon safe communications between the two. This was a supreme interest of Victorian policy; it set the order of priorities in the Middle East and Asia, no less than in Africa, and when African situations interlocked with it, they engaged the serious and urgent attention of the British government. At the first level of analysis, the decisive motive behind late-Victorian strategy in Africa was to protect the all-important stakes in India and the East.

An essentially negative objective, it has been attained hitherto without large African possessions. Mere influence and co-operation with other Powers had been enough to safeguard strategic points in north Africa; while in south Africa control of coastal regions had sufficed. The ambition of late-Victorian minis-ters reached no higher than to uphold these mid-Victorian systems of security in Egypt and south Africa. They were distinguished from their predecessors only in this: that their security by influence was breaking down. In attempting to restore it by intervention and diplomacy, they incidentally marked out the ground on which a vastly extended African empire was later to arise. Nearly all the interventions appear to have been consequences, direct or indirect, of internal Egyptian or south African crises which endangered British influence and security in the world. Such an interpretation alone seems to fit the actual calculations of policy. Ministers felt frankly that they were making the best of a bad job. They were doing no more than protecting old interests in worsening circumstances. To many, the flare-up of European rivalry in Africa seemed unreasonable and even absurd; yet most of them felt driven to take part because of tantalising circumstances beyond their control. They went forward as a measure of precaution, or as a way back to the saner mid-Victorian systems of informal influence. Gloomily, they were fumbling to adjust their old strategy to a changing Africa. And the necessity arose much more from altered circumstances in Africa than from any revolution in the nature, strength or direction of British expansion.

Hence the question of motive should be formulated afresh. It is no longer the winning of a new empire in Africa which has to be explained. The question is simpler: Why could the late-Victorians after 1880 no longer rely upon influence to protect traditional interests? What forced them in the end into imperial solutions? The answer is to be found first in the nationalist crises in Africa itself, which were the work of intensifying

European influences during previous decades; and only secondarily in the interlocking of these crises in Africa with rivalries in Europe. Together the two drove Britain step by step to regain by territorial claims and occupation that security which could no longer be had by influence alone. The compelling conditions for British advances in tropical Africa were first called into being, not by the German victory of 1871, nor by Leopold's interest in the Congo, nor by the petty rivalry of missionaries and merchants, nor by a rising imperialist spirit, nor even by the French occupation of Tunis in 1881—but by the collapse of the Khedivial *régime* in Egypt.

From start to finish the partition of tropical Africa was driven by the persistent crisis in Egypt. When the British entered Egypt on their own, the Scramble began; and as long as they stayed in Cairo, it continued until there was no more of Africa left to divide. Since chance and miscalculation had much to do with the way that Britain went into Egypt, it was to some extent an accident that the partition took place when it did. But once it had begun, Britain's over-riding purpose in Africa was security in Egypt, the Mediterranean and the Orient. The achievement of this security became at the same time vital and more difficult, once the occupation of Egypt had increased the tension between the Powers and had dragged Africa into their rivalry. In this way the crisis in Egypt set off the Scramble, and sustained it until the end of the century.

British advances in tropical Africa have all the appearances of involuntary responses to emergencies arising from the decline of Turkish authority from the Straits to the Nile. These advances were decided by a relatively close official circle. They were largely the work of men striving in more desperate times to keep to the grand conceptions of world policy and the high standards of imperial security inherited from the mid-Victorian preponderance. Their purposes in Africa were usually esoteric; and their actions were usually inspired by notions of the world situation and calculations of its dangers, which were peculiar to the official mind.

So much for the subjective views which swayed the British partitioners. Plainly their preconceptions and purposes were one of the many objective causes of the partition itself. There remain the ultimate questions: how important a cause were these considerations of government? What were the other causes?

The answers are necessarily complicated, because they can be found only in the interplay between government's subjective appreciations and the objective emergencies. The moving causes appear to arise from chains of diverse circumstances in Britain, Europe, the Mediterranean, Asia and Africa itself, which interlocked in a set of unique relationships. These disparate situations, appraised by the official mind as a connected whole, were the products of different historical evolutions, some arising from national growth or decay, others from European expansion stretching as far back as the Mercantilist era. All of them were changing at different levels at different speeds. But although their paths were separate, they were destined to cross. There were structural changes taking place in European industry cutting down Britain's lead in commerce. The European balance of power was altering. Not only the emergence of Germany, but the alignment of France with Russia, the century-old opponent of British expansion, lessened the margins of imperial safety. National and racial feelings in Europe, in Egypt and south Africa were becoming more heated, and liberalism everywhere was on the decline. All these movements played some part in the African drama. But it seems that they were only brought to the point of imperialist action by the idiosyncratic reactions of British statesmen to internal crises in Africa. Along the Mediterranean shores, Muslim states were breaking down under European penetration. In the south, economic growth and colonial expansion were escaping from imperial control. These processes of growth or decay were moving on time scales different from that of the European expansion which was bringing them about.

By 1882 the Egyptian Khedivate had corroded and cracked after decades of European paramountcy. But economic expansion was certainly not the sufficient cause of the occupation. Hitherto, commerce and investment had gone on without the help of outright political control. The thrusts of the industrial economy into Egypt had come to a stop with Ismail's bankruptcy, and little new enterprise was to accompany British control. Although the expanding economy had helped to make a revolutionary situation in Egypt, it was not the moving interest behind the British invasion. Nor does it seem that Anglo-French rivalry or the state of the European balance precipitated the invasion. It was rather the internal nationalist reaction against a decaying government which split Britain from France and switched European rivalries into Africa.

But the cast of official thinking profoundly influenced the outcome of the emergency. Moving instinctively to protect the Canal, the Liberals intended a Palmerstonian blow to liberate the progressives and chasten the disruptive elements in Egyptian politics. But instead of restoring their influence and then getting out, the need to bottle up anarchy and stave off the French forced them to stay on. This failure to work the mid-Victorian techniques, by coming to terms with the nationalists and finding Egyptian collaborators, meant that Indian solutions had to be applied to Egypt as well. The disenchantment of the 'Guardians' was replacing the liberal faith in voluntary co-operation; and Gladstone's sympathy with oppressed nationalities was hardening into Cromer's distrust of subject races. For similar reasons, official pessimism deepened about the reliability of the Turkish bastion in the Mediterranean; and as the balance tilted against Britain in the inland sea, her rulers realised that they were in Egypt to stay. Weighing the risks of Ottoman decay and the shifts in the European balance, remembering Indian experience and distrusting Egyptian 'fanatics', England's rulers pessimistically extended the search for security up the Nile to Fashoda, and from the Indian Ocean to Uganda and the Bahr-el-Ghazal.

The causes of imperial expansion in southern Africa were altogether different. It was essentially unconnected with the contemporary crisis in Egypt and its consequences in tropical Africa; it moved on a different time-scale, and the impulses behind it were separate. Unlike Egypt and tropical Africa, south Africa was to a great extent insulated from the rivalries of European Powers. Unlike them also, it was being rapidly developed by British commercial interests. The crisis which faced British governments was produced by colonial growth, and not by the decay of a native government. It arose from internal conflicts among the colonists, rather than from rivalries among the Powers. But the south African and Egyptian crises were alike in this: neither was precipitated by drastic changes in the local purposes of British expansion; but in both, the late-Victorians strained to keep up their supreme influence against a nationalist threat, and they were drawn at last into reconquering paramountcy by occupation.

South Africa was a case of colonial society receding beyond imperial control. It was also a case of economic development raising the enemies of the imperial connection to political preponderance over the colonial collaborators. By 1895 the new found commercial supremacy of the Transvaal was sustaining republicanism and threatening to draw the colonies into a United States of South Africa.

Here also the subjective appraisals of the policy-makers combined with objective situations to produce imperial advances. British aims in the south were specifically imperial, as they were not in tropical Africa. For years it had been assumed without question that south Africa must eventually turn into another Canada. But it was not only in London that official thinking was crucial. Their special historiography had taught ministers that with self-governing colonials it was prudent to follow their friends and rash to push or thwart them. As a result throughout the south African crisis, policy had to be warped to the theorems of the British colonial party.

In 1881 Gladstone had hoped to stultify Afrikaner nationalism by conciliation, as he was to try to do in Ireland. He switched policy back to the mid-Victorian technique of resting imperial supremacy upon a responsible ministry at the Cape and indirect influence over the Boer republics. It was assumed until 1895 that British immigrants and business would engulf the republicans and strengthen the natural imperial ties of self-interest and kinship. Nationalism would be killed by kindness. So long as London kept in line with colonial opinion and Britain's collaborators were upheld, south Africa would eventually turn itself into a loyal dominion. In this belief, Colonial Secretaries from Kimberley to Ripon kept intervention to a minimum, so as to avert another war between Boer and Briton and the risk of another Ireland. Hence they went on dismantling the 'Imperial Factor'. But by 1896 this system of imperial influence at second hand seemed to have broken under the strain of internal conflicts. South Africa had outgrown imperial supremacy in any form; it had passed beyond the power of British influence to compose the rivalry of its separate states. As Chamberlain saw it, economic development and political catastrophe had wrecked the imperial position in south Africa. It was the Rhodesians' thesis that the Transvaal must be brought under the control of an English-speaking majority. Fearing to lose their last allies, Chamberlain and Milner became their prisoners and followed them over the edge of war. Drawn on by hopes of re-integrating the empire, hardened by the recalcitrance of Afrikaner, as of Irish nationalists, and haunted by the fear of declining national greatness, the Unionists feared that free association would no longer keep south Africa in the empire. The nostrums of the Durham Report had not worked with the nationalists of the Transvaal, as they had done with those of Quebec. South African pressure drove ministers into action as anomalous as that taken at Fashoda. Admitting that imperial supremacy over white colonies was fast becoming a fiction, they were drawn into trying to restore it in south Africa by compulsion.

There are many evidences that towards the end of the century the wearing out of well-tried devices and the emergence of so many intractable problems shocked ministers out of their self-confidence and turned them to desperate expedients. The beliefs which had inspired earlier expansion were failing. Palmerston's axioms were giving way to Salisbury's reappraisals. Liberal values could not be exported to all with cases of Birmingham hardware. Self-government would not always travel. Some nationalisms could not be killed by kindness. The growth of communities into harmonious commercial and political partnership with Britain was not after all a law of nature. The technique of collaborating classes had not worked everywhere. And as difficulties and doubts mounted, the men presiding over the destinies of the British Empire found themselves surrounded by the Eumenides.

Why were these catastrophes overtaking them? All the processes of British expansion were reaching their peak. The metropolitan society was putting forth its strongest energies. It was at this climactic point that the social changes in its satellites were quickest and most violent. Hence it was at this time that their relations with the metropolis tended to move into crisis. The colonial communities were breaking off toward full independence; while anti-western nationalism and social upheaval Were estranging the non-European partners of British interests. The effects of growth were also coming back to roost at Home. England's rulers were alarmed by the symptoms of disintegration, the demand for collectivism, the decay of the landed inter-

est and the running sore of Ireland. The late-Victorians were confronted with nationalist upsurges in Ireland, Egypt and south Africa, and with their beginnings in India.

They were losing the faith of their fathers in the power of trade and anglicisation to turn nationalists into friends and partners. They were no longer so sure as they had been that revolutionary change worked naturally and inevitably to advance British interests. And so they ceased to foster and encourage change and tended to be content to preserve the *status quo*. They became less concerned to liberate social energies abroad and concentrated on preserving authority instead.

Canning and Palmerston had known that the liberals of the world were on their side. But the late-Victorians had to find their allies more and more among Indian princes, Egyptian pashas or African paramount chiefs. Finding themselves less successful in assimilating nationalists to British purposes, their distrust of them grew. And becoming uncertain of the reliability of mere influence, they turned more often from the technique of informal control to the orthodoxies of the Indian *raj* for dealing with political anomalies and for securing their interests. They were ceasing to be a dynamic force and becoming a static power. They were more and more preoccupied throughout the world to guard what they had won; and they became less able to promote progress, as they lapsed into the cares of consolidation.

Fundamentally, the official calculations of policy behind imperial expansion in Africa were inspired by a hardening of arteries and a hardening of hearts. Over and over again, they show an obsession with security, a fixation on safeguarding the routes to the East. What stands out in that policy is its pessimism. It reflects a traumatic reaction from the hopes of mid-century; a resignation to a bleaker present; a defeatist gloss on the old texts of expansion. Perhaps at the deepest level the causes of the British share in the African partition are not found in strategic imperatives, but in the change from Canning's hopes for liberalism to Salisbury's distrust of nationalism, from Gladstone's old-fashioned concern not to turn south Africa into another Ireland, to Chamberlain's new-fangled resolve to reforge it into another Canada.

The notion that world strategy alone was the sole determinant of British advances is superficial. For strategy is not merely a reflection of the interests which it purports to defend, it is even more the register of the hopes, the memories and neuroses which inform the strategists' picture of the world. This it is which largely decides a government's view about who may be trusted and who must be feared; whether an empire assumes an optimistic or pessimistic posture; and whether the forces of change abroad are to be fostered or opposed. Indeed any theory of imperialiam grounded on the notion of a single decisive cause is too simple for the complicated historical reality of the African partition. No purely economic interpretation is wide enough, because it does not allow for the independent importance of subjective factors. Explanations based entirely on the swings of the European balance are bound to remain incomplete without reference to changes outside Europe.

Both the crises of expansion and the official mind which attempted to control them had their origins in an historical process which had begun to unfold long before the partition of Africa began. That

movement was not the manifestation of some revolutionary urge to empire. Its deeper causes do not lie in the last two decades of the century. The British advance at least, was not an isolated African episode. It was the climax of a longer process of growth and decay in Africa. The new African empire was improvised by the official mind, as events made nonsense of its old historiography and hustled government into strange deviations from old lines of policy. In the widest sense, it was an offshoot of the total processes of British expansion throughout the world and throughout the century.

How large then does the new African empire bulk in this setting? There are good reasons for regarding the mid-Victorian period as the golden age of British expansion, and the late-Victorian as an age which saw the beginnings of contraction and decline. The Palmerstonians were no more 'anti-imperialist' than their successors, though they were more often able to achieve their purposes informally; and the late-Victorians were no more 'imperialist' than their predecessors, though they were driven to extend imperial claims more often. To label them thus is to ignore the fact that whatever their method, they were both of set purpose engineering the expansion of Britain. Both preferred to promote trade and security without the expense of empire; but neither shrank from forward policies wherever they seemed necessary.

But their circumstances were very different. During the first three-quarters of the century, Britain enjoyed an almost effortless supremacy in the world outside Europe, thanks to her sea power and her industrial strength, and because she had little foreign rivalry to face. Thus Canning and Palmerston had a very wide freedom of action. On the one hand, they had little need to bring economically valueless regions such as tropical Africa into their formal empire for the sake of strategic security; and on the other, they were free to extend their influence and power to develop those regions best suited to contribute to Britain's strength. Until the Eighteen eighties, British political expansion had been positive, in the sense that it went on bringing valuable areas into her orbit. That of the late-Victorians in the so-called 'Age of Imperialism' was by comparison negative, both in purpose and achievement. It was largely concerned with defending the maturing inheritance of the mid-Victorian imperialism of free trade, not with opening fresh fields of substantial importance to the economy. Whereas the earlier Victorians could afford to concentrate on the extension of free trade, their successors were compelled to look above all to the preservation of what they held, since they were coming to suspect that Britain's power was not what it once had been. The early Victorians had been playing from strength. The supremacy they had built in the world had been the work of confidence and faith in the future. The African empire of their successors was the product of fear lest this great heritage should be lost in the time of troubles ahead.

Because it went far ahead of commercial expansion and imperial ambition, because its aims were essentially defensive and strategic, the movement into Africa remained superficial. The partition of tropical Africa might seem impressive on the wall maps of the Foreign Office. Yet it was at the time an empty and theoretical expansion. That British governments before 1900 did very little to pacify, administer and develop their spheres of influence and protectorates, shows once again the weakness of any commercial and imperial motives for claiming them. The partition did not accompany, it preceded the invasion of tropical Africa by the trader, the planter and the official. It was the prelude to European occupation; it was not that occupation itself. The sequence illuminates the true nature of the British movement into tropical Africa. So far from commercial expansion requiring the extension of territorial claims, it was the extension of territorial claims which in time required commercial expansion. The arguments of the so-called new imperialism were *ex post facto* justifications of advances, they were not the original reasons for making them. Ministers had publicly justified their improvisations in tropical Africa with appeals to imperial sentiment and promises of African progress. After 1900, something had to be done to fulfil these aspirations, when the spheres allotted on the map had to be made good on the ground. The same fabulous artificers who had galvanised America, Australia and Asia, had come to the last continent.

POSTSCRIPT

Was Economic Motivation the Key Factor Behind Nineteenth-Century Imperialism?

Hobson concludes, "Thus we reach the conclusion that Imperialism is the endeavor of the great controllers of industry to broaden the channel for the flow of their surplus wealth by seeking foreign markets and foreign investments to take off the goods and capital they cannot sell or use at home." For Hobson—who, at the time he wrote these words, was chiefly concerned with ameliorating the condition of the working class in his home country—the evil of imperialism lay behind the decisions of the "captains of industry," who were able to manipulate governments into forcing open foreign markets, either diplomatically or at gunpoint. To him, the answer to the question of how to dispose of surplus capital was not to impose it on unwilling and undeserving overseas nations but to stimulate and facilitate the consuming ability of the average laborer on the home front. By doing so domestic social problems would be resolved and the engagement of Western nations in overseas adventures that cost working-class lives would be over.

Robinson, Gallagher, and Denny, however, pose the chicken-and-egg question: Did the industrialists and capitalists maneuver the home governments into aggressive foreign policies, or did the bureaucrats of the Foreign Office manipulate industry and finance to support the governments' policy aims of international stability and military security? Robinson et al. reply, "At the first level of analysis, the decisive motive behind late-Victorian strategy in Africa was to protect the all-important stakes in India and the East." For these authors, the reason for the "New Imperialism" was simply to protect the gains of the "Old Imperialism."

Robinson et al.'s attack on Hobson's thesis of imperialism inspired a series of new viewpoints and studies on the causes of European expansion in the late nineteenth century. Lance E. Davis and Robert A. Huttenback explore whether or not the British Empire was profitable in *Mammon and the Pursuit of Empire: The Economics of British Imperialism* (Cambridge University Press, 1987). Daniel R. Headrick's *Tools of Empire: Technology and European Imperialism in the Nineteenth Century* (Oxford University Press, 1981) is a must read for anyone interested in exploration, imperialism, and technology. In addition, John M. Mackenzie's edited work *Imperialism and Popular Culture* (St. Martin's Press, 1989) demonstrates the widespread popularity of empire among all the classes of the nineteenth century.

For a particularly interesting study on the effect that imperialism had on shaping erroneous attitudes held by the West toward Asians, which in turn encouraged colonialism, read Edward W. Said's *Orientalism* (Random House, 1979).

On the Internet . . .

Center for Strategic and International Studies

The Center for Strategic and International Studies is a public policy institution dedicated to analysis and policy impact. This site includes links for international news updates.
http://www.csis.org/

Eliot Elisofon Photographic Archives at the National Museum of African Art

This is a research and reference center for visual material. It is devoted to the collection, preservation, and dissemination of visual resources that encourage and support the study of the arts, peoples, and history of Africa.
http://www.si.edu/organiza/museums/africart/elisofon.htm

Russia on the Web

In addition to the many other links at this comprehensive site, click on "History" for a virtual tour of the palace where Nicholas II and Alexandra lived, Mikhail Gorbachev's home page, and Russian Studies on the Internet, which is a listing of sites related to Russian history and culture.
http://www.valley.net/~transnat/

U.S. Holocaust Memorial Museum

From this site you can access the official trial records as well as photographs of the Nuremberg trials, along with extensive information about the Holocaust.
http://www.ushmm.org/

World War I (1914–1918)

This page is dedicated to World War I and features links to many related subjects, including trench warfare, the Versailles Treaty, individual countries' participation, and lost poets of the war.
http://www.cfcsc.dnd.ca/links/milhist/wwi.html/

World War II on the Web

From this page you can explore over 400 links to World War II material, including Pacific War chronology, women at war, rescuers during the Holocaust, and the rise of Adolf Hitler.
http://www.bunt.com/~mconrad/

PART 2

The Modern World

Starting with the twentieth century, this section covers the problems and promises that the technologically minded modern world has bestowed upon the present generation. The triumphs can be a positive sign for the future of humankind, while the continuous presence of the same problems that have plagued civilizations since their inception stands as a stark warning that humankind is still not free of folly.

■ Was German Militarism and Diplomacy Responsible for World War I?

■ Did the Bolshevik Revolution Improve the Lives of Soviet Women?

■ Was the German National Spirit of the 1930s Responsible for the Holocaust?

■ Did the Soviet Union Provoke the Cold War?

■ Does Islamic Revivalism Threaten a Secular World Order?

■ Will History Look Favorably Upon Mikhail Gorbachev?

■ Should Africa's Leaders Be Blamed for the Continent's Current Problems?

■ Has the United Nations Outlived Its Usefulness?

■ Is Western Civilization in a State of Decline?

ISSUE 9

Was German Militarism and Diplomacy Responsible for World War I?

YES: Hartmut Pogge von Strandmann, from "Germany and the Coming of War," in R. J. W. Evans and Hartmut Pogge von Strandmann, eds., *The Coming of the First World War* (Clarendon Press, 1988)

NO: Sidney Bradshaw Fay, from *After Sarajevo: The Origins of the World War*, *vol. 2*, 2d rev. ed. (Free Press, 1966)

ISSUE SUMMARY

YES: University College curator Hartmut Pogge von Strandmann contends that the German government launched a war of conquest against France and Russia in August 1914.

NO: Historian Sidney Bradshaw Fay argues that every European nation that was involved in World War I bore a measure of responsibility for the outbreak of war.

Without question, World War I was one of the most cataclysmic events in history. Between August 1914 and November 1918, 11 million combatants lost their lives, and much of Europe was physically devastated. In a very real sense, the war marked the turning point between the nineteenth and twentieth centuries. By the time the armistice was signed, four empires had vanished—the Austro-Hungarian Empire, the Second Reich, the Russian Empire, and the Ottoman Empire. Gone also were the sense of optimism and the faith in progress that had marked the late Victorian period.

The debate over the causes of the war began even before the fighting ended. Each of the combatants blamed the enemy for starting the war; these claims were reiterated repeatedly on all sides through government propaganda. At the Paris Peace Conference of 1918–1919, however, the victorious Allies wrote into the peace treaty a "war guilt" clause, stating that Germany bore sole responsibility for starting the war. Since Germany had, in fact, invaded neutral Belgium before any other nation had attacked another, the clause appeared to have an obvious measure of validity. Nevertheless, the war guilt clause infuriated the German delegation to the conference, and it continued to rankle the German population during the interwar years.

Almost immediately after the armistice was signed in June 1919, revisionist historians began advancing alternative theories of the war's origins. While some historians pointed the finger at other specific nations—including Russia, which had been the first country to mobilize, and Serbia, which had refused to accede to Austria-Hungary's demands—most scholars chose to emphasize the long-term causes of the conflict. Foremost among these were the competition among the major European powers for military and naval supremacy that began in the late nineteenth century; the scramble for colonies; and the alliance system, which turned a local conflict in the Balkans into a general European conflagration. In short, these scholars believe that a world war was virtually inevitable, given the pressures that were building up in early-twentieth-century Europe.

Still, many historians continue to hold Germany primarily responsible for the conflict. In the following selection, Hartmut Pogge von Strandmann asserts that scholars of World War I need to determine why war erupted in August 1914 and not a year or two earlier or later. For von Strandmann, the answer lies in the expansionist policies of the imperial German government, which he believes cleverly contrived and then took advantage of a series of circumstances that masked its aggressive intentions. According to von Strandmann, the French and Russian mobilizations of July and August 1914 were primarily defensive in nature; neither nation actually would have attacked Germany at that time. Nor was Germany justified in seeking new territory by valid internal imperatives. The war, he concludes, began as a German quest for markets, profits, prestige, and international influence.

Sidney Bradshaw Fay provides a classic rejoinder to the German "war guilt" thesis: he apportions blame among all the major European powers. Austria-Hungary, for instance, maintained an aggressive posture because any sign of weakness might have encouraged the separatist tendencies that were already tearing the empire apart. For its part, Russia was the first major power to mobilize, and it continued to prepare for war even while it carried on diplomatic negotiations for a peaceful settlement of the crisis. Faced with Russian mobilization and the threat of a two-front war, Germany had little choice but to initiate an attack upon France in self-defense. Instead of blaming any individual nation for the war, Fay prefers to focus on economic rivalry, nationalist ambitions, popular emotions whipped up by the press, and the ill-fated alliance system.

YES Hartmut Pogge von Strandmann

GERMANY AND THE COMING OF WAR

In the present state of research, the evidence that Germany and Austria started the war and dragged the rest of the powers into it is even stronger than in the early 1960s when Fritz Fischer published his analysis of German war aims policies. Now the demands of the 1960s for detailed analyses of the war aims of the other states have been largely fulfilled. Thorough studies for all the major European powers have been undertaken which are based on the extensive use of unpublished material. The evidence gathered makes the view that Germany fought a defensive war untenable and the interpretation that all nations 'slithered over the brink into... war' unconvincing. It is clear that there was no general drift into war.

In the literature other general reasons for the inevitability of the war have been put forward. But the assumption that a general European war must have general European causes is not borne out by the evidence. The alliance system, the arms race, the highest stage of capitalism, the Anglo-German trade rivalry, the supposedly age-old clash between Teuton and Slav, or colonial rivalry, or the assumed hereditary animosity between France and Germany: all have been referred to in order to make the war appear as an event from which there was no escape. The analogy with the weather has been used by some authors to illustrate the inevitability of war and make its central outbreak seem like the workings of a fate beyond human control. Expressions like 'the darkening of the horizon', 'the gathering of clouds', 'the stifling atmosphere', 'the distant thunder', 'the first lightning', and finally 'the breaking of the storm' have been used to provide explanatory images for the outbreak of war in 1914. But the war was not a natural catastrophe.

If one were to follow some populist literature, general political analyses, and the press, the political climate would appear to have been laden with animosities which did not improve relations in Europe. However useful general atmospheric studies might be, they are no substitute for the search to find out which of the European states intended to pull the trigger first. Otherwise it remains unclear why the war broke out in August 1914 and not in 1915–16 or, for that matter earlier, in 1913. What is more, the emphasis on very general causes for the war tends to make the intention to start a war seem irrelevant.

The stress A. J. P. Taylor has laid on 'war by timetable' makes the outbreak of war appear to be automatic. However, what the mobilization demonstrated is how well prepared the military plans were and how quickly military actions could be started. But the historian who is interested in the question of why wars break out in particular situations has to go further and analyse the links between causes, motivations, aims, reasons, and actions.

The attraction of automatic causes of the war is also shown by the work of American scholars who tried to make use of the quantitative method. They went through the great documentary editions which appeared after the First World War and through which each country tried to prove that it had not caused the war, and quantified certain terms and certain reactions. To their surprise the term 'war' was increasingly used during the crisis of July and to top it all even more in August 1914. Whatever the merits of the quantitative methodology, it does not seem sufficiently convincing in this context to be useful for historical analysis. Thus a survey of general causes may show why war was possible and even likely, but not why it broke out in the summer of 1914.

The First World War was, like any other war, the result of political and military decisions which exploited international constellations and in turn realized political aims and concepts. Obviously the decisions leading to war in 1914 were not taken in a vacuum, remote from public opinion, economic concerns, and domestic pressures. The interplay between the public at large and the political and military leadership was crucial for the years before the outbreak of war and the actual crisis in July 1914, regardless of whether

we look at the different political systems of France, Britain, Germany, or Russia. Of course, it remains difficult to establish a direct link between public pressures and political actions, especially as the political and military leaders cannot be separated from the public at large. How strongly both sides were similarly affected can be seen in the mounting international crises in the first years of the century. The prospect of war escalating from crisis to crisis may have heightened the expectation of war, but it also had a numbing effect and the public in the European states became used to the fact that international crises did not result in the major war so often forecast. But while public opinion soon forgot the latest crisis, the political and military leaders often prepared new initiatives to cope with the effects that crisis had had on the international, domestic, and military scene. In this way Germany and Austria edged closer to war after 1912. The political and military leadership grew increasingly familiar with the idea that a major war was coming without knowing exactly when. Politicians and generals did not talk each other into war; they expected a major war to happen, although few had any clear vision of who would start it and when. In any case international crises were not good opportunities for starting a war because none of the major powers was sufficiently prepared, from a military point of view, to spring a surprise upon the enemy in such a crisis. . . .

When mobilization was declared on 1 August Frenchmen rallied to the cause of national defence in the face of German aggression. It was widely accepted that the French government had no hand in unleashing the war. In any case, [French president] Poincaré favoured a firm stand against Germany, but not a war. Recent research has established him as a politician who was keen on finding a *modus vivendi* with Germany rather than as a warmonger whose main aim in life was to regain the provinces of Alsace and Lorraine. The *Kölnische Zeitung*, a mouthpiece of the German Foreign Office, confirmed the generally peaceful attitude prevalent in France. On 1 August the Paris correspondent of the paper noticed that there was no enthusiasm for war or revanchism to be found. He even noted that some people in France regretted that there was no alliance with Germany, because then the world would be safe. To them Germany was closer and meant more than Russia. And the London correspondent of the same paper reported that a general animosity against Germany was missing in England too. However, the mood in London and Paris changed rapidly as the likelihood of war increased. In Britain it was hoped that war could be avoided, and some efforts at mediation were made which Germany turned down on 27 July. But Britain was deeply involved with the Irish situation and worried about a possible confrontation with Russia in Persia. Thus the Austro-Serbian clash was, to begin with, not of the greatest concern for British politicians. But once the prospect of a European conflagration began to loom, those groups which regarded India as the most important British preoccupation were not all that unhappy about a war between Germany and Russia, because a serious weakening of the latter would reduce, for some time, the potential for Anglo-Russian conflicts in Asia, even if Russia belonged to the ultimate victors. Britain's multi-dimensional concerns in foreign policy do not make it easy to detect consistency in her political line or to identify the

dominant groups which influenced the politicians. Nevertheless the majority of the Liberal Cabinet followed a consistent line in its foreign policy when it decided to defend France against a German invasion.

In comparison with the two Western powers Russia had gone a step further. The situation in Belgrade and Vienna was being closely watched. On the day after the delivery of the Austrian ultimatum to Serbia it was decided at a meeting of the Russian Council of Ministers to make a stand against the diplomatic pressure from Austria and Germany. It was held that 'firmness rather than conciliation was likely to secure peace'. Russia did not want to repeat her experience in the Bosnian crisis and preferred to present a much more resolute image. Her firmness was not solely dictated by her concern for Serbia. The forthcoming trade negotiations with Germany cast their shadow. The signal was that Germany should expect a much tougher Russian stance at the negotiating table when the trade treaty and the tariffs were at issue. Russia resented being at the mercy of Germany's industrial power.

At the meeting of ministers it was also resolved to prepare for partial mobilization of some military districts, against Austria, should events require it. This would be in reaction to Austria's moves if she decided to escalate the crisis. But neither the anticipation of mobilization nor the possibility of ordering it was equated with causing the war.... Only when Austria had rejected Serbia's reply and when she finally declared war against Serbia on 28 July, did Russia order partial mobilization. Even then Russia did not want to fight a war. But as Austria was unwilling to guarantee Serbia's political integrity despite the general acceptance of some punitive measure, Russia was left with little choice.

At this stage a new situation emerged as Berlin tried to put pressure on Russia to stop her military preparations in the hope that Russia would refuse to comply with the German *démarche*. Berlin calculated correctly that St Petersburg would be unwilling to repeat the process of backing down as in 1909. As the Russian conviction grew that the Central Powers were bent on war, the Tsar ordered full mobilization on 29 July, after Austrian artillery had begun to shell Belgrade, the Serbian capital. However, the order for full mobilization was rescinded in response to a telegram from the Kaiser to the Tsar on that same day. This created a hopeless situation, and under pressure from his Foreign Minister and his Chief of Staff the Tsar was persuaded on 30 July of the need for general mobilization. It was argued that delay would destroy Russia's chances in any conflict before it had even begun. General mobilization was part of Russia's new firmness, but was not intended to mean war, although the Russian Foreign Minister, Sazonov, believed that Germany wanted it. The Chief of Staff, Yanushkevich, also had military reasons for ordering general mobilization. Partial mobilization against Austria was proving unworkable. The French warning against Russian mobilization came too late. The French government feared that it would provide Germany with the pretext for mobilizing herself. In the event the French government proved to be right.

The German response to the Russian threat was swift, first by mobilization and then by her declaration of war against Russia on 1 August, whilst the Austrians followed suit only five days later. It has often been pointed out that Russia's mobilization made a European conflict likely. Even Fritz Fischer has argued that Russia has to share some responsibility for the outbreak of the war because she was determined to defend the status quo in the Balkans against any Austrian expansion. That is the reason, it is said, why she was the first power to order a general mobilization. However, this argument overlooks the fact that the German leadership was waiting for just this move. Before the Russian order for mobilization appeared, the Prussian War Minister had tried to declare 'the state of imminent danger of war', but was held back by Bethmann Hollweg and Moltke, the Chief of Staff. The Chancellor resisted military pressure for action because he believed it was essential to wait until he could accuse Russia of being the aggressor and of having started the war. The evidence for his insistence on this sequence of events is overwhelming. Once Russian mobilization had been proclaimed it would be possible to issue a call to arms to defend the fatherland. This move was vital to enable the Social Democrats to join the war effort and so unite the German people.

The German press in July 1914 indicated clearly that Russia would be held responsible if war broke out. The officially inspired tenor was therefore anti-Russian and most papers accepted this line. Even before the Russian order for mobilization became known the German war mood was noticeable. The news from Russia fell on prepared ground. Thus we cannot avoid the impression that, by means of the Austrian action, a trap was laid for Russia into which she fell when she declared her mobilization. However, there is another argument as to why it is difficult to deduce from Russian actions in July any intention to start a war.

A qualitative and technical difference existed between the Russian and the German mobilization. The former was intended to prepare the Russian army for war and then to wait for the formal declaration of hostilities. It was still hoped in St Petersburg that war would be prevented and that Russia's firmness would stop the Austrians from crushing Serbia. German mobilization, on the other hand, meant the beginning of the planned military offensive into Belgium and France.

How was it possible that the term 'preventive war' came into use in order to describe the German actions? The term was necessary to substantiate the German claim that she was fighting a defensive war when she was launching a massive offensive in the west and not in the east. This leads to another, yet related question. Why did Germany declare war against Russia when mobilization had been ordered only two hours before and when the German army was not ready to strike at the Russian forces? The reason was France. France was obliged to come to Russia's aid once war had been declared upon Russia. But she could only help militarily if she launched an offensive herself against Germany. This the German army tried to prevent by speedy mobilization and an immediate offensive in the west. In this narrow technical sense it seems possible to use the term 'preventive war' for the planned early operations in the west, but if the war on the whole is meant then the term is misused. The German General Staff had already used the term years before when it was demanding another war against France after 1871 because it was feared that otherwise France would start a war against her eastern neighbour. However, France was never in a position to attack Germany and it is very doubtful whether she ever would have been. Some historians and a few politicians of the time emphasized the politically negative effects which increased Russian and French military strength would have on Germany in the future. In this situation when spending on armaments was growing the term 'preventive war' loses its precise meaning because it comes to be burdened with too many imponderable factors and as yet unknown developments. Bethmann Hollweg used the term in 1917 in an apologetic sense, although admitting that the initiative for war had come from Germany. Some historians have accepted this interpretation in order to render the German action understandable and to hold the other powers responsible for their own development of military potential. What is the upshot of analysing the use of the term 'preventive war'? It makes it clear why Germany had to let Russia appear as the aggressor and why it wanted to exploit the Franco-Russian alliance in order to start a 'preventive war' against France. The obvious deduction from these German intentions and calculations is that it was Germany which pushed for the war....

All the available evidence suggests that it was mainly Germany which pushed for war and that without the German drive to extend her hegemony a major war would not have started in Europe in 1914. However, it must be stated that German aspirations had existed for some time without resulting in war. If it had not been for the Austrian initiative in early July and the Russian decision to remain firm and call what was perceived as an Austrian bluff at the end of July, Berlin would have found it difficult to push for war in the summer of 1914. Yet Berlin

had, before Hoyos's visit,* anticipated the
Austrian move. 'The military keep on
urging for a war now while Russia is
not yet ready', reported the Saxon envoy,
and the Saxon military attaché wrote a
day later: 'The General Staff thought that
it would not be too bad if there was
a war now.' So Austrian determination
and Russian firmness suited German
intentions.

But why were Germany's rulers so
keen on war? Did they leap forward
into the dark as some historians would
make us believe? Did the German policy-
makers really see no way out, but to
engage in a *Flucht nach vorn*? What gains
would Germany make which she did
not already have? Was Germany not the
biggest power on the Continent? Was
her economy not expanding? Germany
regarded herself as bursting at the seams.
There was a consensus among the non-
Socialist parties, the military, and the
business men that Germany needed to
be a larger empire on the Continent as
well as overseas. But this expansion was
not intended to divert attention from a
growing domestic crisis, though much
depends on the definition of a crisis.
None of the indicators pointed to a crisis
situation. The economy was booming. A
brief recession in 1913 had by the spring
of 1914 come to an end. In the large
business concerns there was little fear
of trade-union power despite the recent
wave of strikes. The Social Democrats
were divided and had recently voted
in favour of the taxes with which the
army bill of 1913 was to be financed.
In this situation the Conservatives found

*[In early July 1914, Count Hoyos, who belonged
to the hawks in the Austrian Foreign Ministry,
volunteered to go to Berlin and gain the assurances
needed for Austria to attack Serbia.—Eds.]

themselves isolated, threatened more by
the rising power of the Reichstag than
the Social Democrats on the one side and
by nationalist populism on the other. The
rallying of right-wing pressure groups
in 1913 indicated a regrouping on the
Right rather than an initiative to check
a growing political crisis.

Similar developments took place on the
military side. A growing 'militarism from
below' put pressure on the older type
of 'militarism from above'. The demand
for a larger army which had gained
ground through the foundation of the
Wehrverein (Defence League) aimed at
eliminating the privileges of those who
were able to opt out of the principle of
equal conscription for all. In the wake
of the two army bills, the purpose of the
enlarged army, the politics of militarism,
and nationalist themes were much more
widely discussed than ever before. In
this climate the shift of the General Staff
towards war as a method of advancing
Germany's expansionism seems crucial.
If the international constellation were
right, then the army would become the
most consistent factor in pressing for war.
This is not to say that sole responsibility
for the war rested with the General Staff.
In his recent article, David Kaiser, the
American historian, followed Fischer's
line of argument that it was Bethmann
Hollweg who influenced the decision for
war because of his belief in the need for
German expansion. The success of such a
policy was ultimately based on military
supremacy established by war against
France and Russia. So the Chancellor,
Kaiser argues, made the decision for
war in conjunction with the military
even though he was later to blame 'the
generals' for plunging Germany into
war. A division between military and
civilian leaders in this respect did not

exist. Even if it had been the other way round and it had been the political leaders who had pushed for war, it would not have made much difference to the exploitation of the situation in 1914. The strength of the Chancellor's position is also demonstrated by the fact that he was even able to influence some military decisions by delaying the proclamation of the 'state of imminent danger of war' in certain areas.

Although there was widespread support for the line the government took, some industrialists like Stinnes and Rathenau were convinced that Germany would achieve its economic predominance in Europe without a war. However strongly the political and military leadership was influenced by the public and its political debates, the war was not started for domestic reasons nor to defend a social status quo. The concept of expansion based on a military victory found enough support to command a consensus among the military, political, and business leaders of Wilhelmine Germany. The drive to the east and to the west was underpinned by an imperialist culture which spread the virtues of Social Darwinism, the conquest of markets, the penetration of spheres of influence, competition between capitalist partners, the winning of living-space, and the rising power of the state. Buoyed up by an assumed military superiority, general economic strength and particular industrial vigour, widespread optimism and a mood of belligerence, the military and political leaders found, when they made the decision to push for war, that this was an acceptable option to many Germans, possibly even to the majority. The notion of 'cultural despair' is of limited value. There were no signs of panic and no indications that Wilhelmine Germany could not continue to muddle through politically for years to come. Confidence, determination, and the belief in victory were the ingredients of a willingness to fight an expansionist war, disguised as a defensive or preventive action, which was widely shared by political and military leaders, political groupings, as well as large sectors of the population. This consensus enabled Germany to sustain the war effort until the military defeats of August and September 1918.

NO

Sidney Bradshaw Fay

AFTER SARAJEVO: THE ORIGINS OF THE WORLD WAR

None of the Powers wanted a European War. Their governing rulers and ministers, with very few exceptions, all foresaw that it must be a frightful struggle, in which the political results were not absolutely certain, but in which the loss of life, suffering, and economic consequences were bound to be terrible. This is true, in a greater or less degree, of Pashitch, Berchtold, Bethmann, Sazonov, Poincaré, San Giuliano and Sir Edward Grey. Yet none of them, not even Sir Edward Grey, could have foreseen that the political results were to be so stupendous, and the other consequences so terrible, as was actually the case.

For many of the Powers, to be sure, a European War might seem to hold out the possibility of achieving various desired advantages: for Serbia, the achievement of national unity for all Serbs; for Austria, the revival of her waning prestige as a Great Power, and the checking of nationalistic tendencies which threatened her very existence; for Russia, the accomplishment of her historic mission of controlling Constantinople and the Straits; for Germany, new economic advantages and the restoration of the European balance which had changed with the weakening of the Triple Alliance [Germany, Austria, and Italy] and the tightening of the Triple Entente [Great Britain, France, and Russia]; for France, the recovery of Alsace-Lorraine and the ending of the German menace; and for England, the destruction of the German naval danger and of Prussian militarism. All these advantages, and many others, were feverishly striven and intrigued for, on all sides, the moment the War actually broke out, but this is no good proof that any of the statesmen mentioned deliberately aimed to bring about a war to secure these advantages. One cannot judge the motives which actuated men before the War, by what they did in an absolutely new situation which arose as soon as they were overtaken by a conflagration they had sought to avert. And in fact, in the case of the two Powers between whom the immediate conflict arose, the postponement or avoidance of a European War would have facilitated the accomplishment of the ultimate advantages aimed at: Pashitch knew that there was a better chance for Serbian national unity after he had consolidated Serbian gains

From Sidney Bradshaw Fay, *After Sarajevo: The Origins of the World War*, vol. 2, 2d rev. ed. (Free Press, 1966). Copyright © 1928, 1930 by Macmillan Publishing Company; copyright renewed 1956, 1958 by Sidney Bradshaw Fay. Reprinted by permission of Simon & Schuster, Inc.

in the Balkan Wars, and after Russia had completed her military and naval armaments as planned for 1917; and Berchtold knew that he had a better chance of crushing the Greater Serbia danger and strengthening Austria, if he could avoid Russian intervention and a general European War.

It is also true, likewise, that the moment war was declared, it was hailed with varying demonstrations of enthusiasm on the part of the people in every country—with considerable in Serbia, Austria, Russia and Germany, with less in France, and with almost none in England. But this does not mean that the peoples wanted war or exerted a decisive influence to bring it about. It is a curious psychological phenomenon that as soon as a country engages in war, there develops or is created among the masses a frenzy of patriotic excitement which is no index of their pre-war desires. And in the countries where the demonstrations of enthusiasm were greatest, the political influence of the people on the Government was least.

Nevertheless, a European War broke out. Why? Because in each country political and military leaders did certain things, which led to mobilizations and declarations of war, or failed to do certain things which might have prevented them. In this sense, all the European countries, in a greater or less degree, were responsible. One must abandon the dictum of the Versailles Treaty that Germany and her allies were solely responsible. It was a dictum exacted by victors from vanquished, under the influence of the blindness, ignorance, hatred, and the propagandist misconceptions to which war had given rise. It was based on evidence which was incomplete and not always sound.[1] It is generally recognized by the best historical scholars in all countries to be no longer tenable or defensible. They are agreed that the responsibility for the War is a divided responsibility. But they still disagree very much as to the relative part of this responsibility that falls on each country and on each individual political or military leader.

Some writers like to fix positively in some precise mathematical fashion the exact responsibility for the war. This was done in one way by the framers of Article 231 of the Treaty of Versailles. It has been done in other ways by those who would fix the responsibility in some relative fashion, as, for instance, Austria first, then Russia, France and Germany and England. But the present writer deprecates such efforts to assess by a precise formula a very complicated question, which is after all more a matter of delicate shading than of definite white and black. Oversimplification, as Napoleon once said in framing his Code, is the enemy of precision. Moreover, even supposing that a general consensus of opinion might be reached as to the relative responsibility of any individual country or man for immediate causes connected with the July crisis of 1914, it is by no means necessarily true that the same relative responsibility would hold for the underlying causes, which for years had been tending toward the creation of a dangerous situation.

One may, however, sum up very briefly the most salient facts in regard to each country.

Serbia felt a natural and justifiable impulse to do what so many other countries had done in the nineteenth century—to bring under one national Government all the discontented Serb people. She had liberated those under Turkish rule; the next step was to liberate those under Haps-

NO Sidney Bradshaw Fay / 171

burg rule. She looked to Russia for assistance, and had been encouraged to expect that she would receive it. After the assassination, Mr. Pashitch took no steps to discover and bring to justice Serbians in Belgrade who had been implicated in the plot. One of them, Ciganovitch, was even assisted to disappear. Mr. Pashitch waited to see what evidence the Austrian authorities could find. When Austria demanded coöperation of Austrian officials in discovering, though not in trying, implicated Serbians, the Serbian Government made a very conciliatory but negative reply. They expected that the reply would not be regarded as satisfactory, and, even before it was given, ordered the mobilization of the Serbian army. Serbia did not want war, but believed it would be forced upon her. That Mr. Pashitch was aware of the plot three weeks before it was executed, failed to take effective steps to prevent the assassins from crossing over from Serbia to Bosnia, and then failed to give Austria any warning or information which might have averted the fatal crime, were facts unknown to Austria in July, 1914; they cannot therefore be regarded as in any way justifying Austria's conduct; but they are part of Serbia's responsibility, and a very serious part.

Austria was more responsible for the immediate origin of the war than any other Power. Yet from her own point of view she was acting in self-defence— not against an immediate military attack, but against the corroding Greater Serbia and Jugoslav agitation which her leaders believed threatened her very existence. No State can be expected to sit with folded arms and await dismemberment at the hands of its neighbors. Russia was believed to be intriguing with Serbia and Rumania against the Dual Monarchy. The assassination of the heir to the throne, as a result of a plot prepared in Belgrade, demanded severe retribution; otherwise Austria would be regarded as incapable of action, "worm-eaten" as the Serbian Press expressed it, would sink in prestige, and hasten her own downfall. To avert this Berchtold determined to crush Serbia with war. He deliberately framed the ultimatum with the expectation and hope that it would be rejected. He hurriedly declared war against Serbia in order to forestall all efforts at mediation. He refused even to answer his own ally's urgent requests to come to an understanding with Russia, on the basis of a military occupation of Belgrade as a pledge that Serbia would carry out the promises in her reply to the ultimatum. Berchtold gambled on a "local" war with Serbia only, believing that he could rattle the German sword; but rather than abandon his war with Serbia, he was ready to drag the rest of Europe into war.

It is very questionable whether Berchtold's obstinate determination to diminish Serbia and destroy her as a Balkan factor was, after all, the right method, even if he had succeeded in keeping the war "localized" and in temporarily strengthening the Dual Monarchy. Supposing that Russia in 1914, because of military unpreparedness or lack of support, had been ready to tolerate the execution of Berchtold's designs, it is quite certain that she would have aimed within the next two or three years at wiping out this second humiliation, which was so much more damaging to her prestige than that of 1908–09. In two or three years, when her great program of military reform was finally completed, Russia would certainly have found a pretext to reverse the balance in the Balkans in her own favor again. A further consequence of Berchtold's policy, even if successful, would have been the still closer consolidation of the Triple Entente, with the possible addition of Italy. And, finally, a partially dismembered Serbia would have become a still greater source of unrest and danger to the peace of Europe than heretofore. Serbian nationalism, like Polish nationalism, would have been intensified by partition. Austrian power and prestige would not have been so greatly increased as to be able to meet these new dangers. Berchtold's plan was a mere temporary improvement, but could not be a final solution of the Austro-Serbian antagonism. Franz Ferdinand and many others recognized this, and so long as he lived, no step in this fatal direction had been taken. It was the tragic fate of Austria that the only man who might have had the power and ability to develop Austria along sound lines became the innocent victim of the crime which was the occasion of the World War and so of her ultimate disruption.

Germany did not plot a European War, did not want one, and made genuine, though too belated efforts, to avert one. She was the victim of her alliance with Austria and of her own folly. Austria was her only dependable ally, Italy and Rumania having become nothing but allies in name. She could not throw her over, as otherwise she would stand isolated between Russia, where Panslavism and armaments were growing stronger every year, and France, where Alsace-Lorraine, Delcassé's fall, and Agadir were not forgotten. Therefore, Bethmann felt bound to accede to Berchtold's request for support and gave him a free hand to deal with Serbia; he also hoped and expected to "localize" the Austro-Serbian conflict. Germany then gave grounds to the Entente for suspecting the sincerity of her peaceful intentions by her denial of any

foreknowledge of the ultimatum, by her support and justification of it when it was published, and by her refusal of Sir Edward Grey's conference proposal. However, Germany by no means had Austria so completely under her thumb as the Entente Powers and many writers have assumed. It is true that Berchtold would hardly have embarked on his gambler's policy unless he had been assured that Germany would fulfil the obligations of the alliance, and to this extent Germany must share the great responsibility of Austria. But when Bethmann realized that Russia was likely to intervene, that England might not remain neutral, and that there was danger of a world war of which Germany and Austria would appear to be the instigators, he tried to call a halt on Austria, but it was too late. He pressed mediation proposals on Vienna, but Berchtold was insensible to the pressure, and the Entente Powers did not believe in the sincerity of his pressure, especially as they produced no results.

Germany's geographical position between France and Russia, and her inferiority in number of troops, had made necessary the plan of crushing the French army quickly at first and then turning against Russia. This was only possible, in the opinion of her strategists, by marching through Belgium, as it was generally anticipated by military men that she would do in case of a European War. On July 29, after Austria had declared war on Serbia, and after the Tsar had assented to general mobilization in Russia (though this was not known in Berlin and was later postponed for a day owing to the Kaiser's telegram to the Tsar), Bethmann took the precaution of sending to the German Minister in Brussels a sealed envelope. The Minister was not to open it except on further instructions. It contained the later demand for the passage of the German army through Belgium. This does not mean, however, that Germany had decided for war. In fact, Bethmann was one of the last of the statesmen to abandon hope of peace and to consent to the mobilization of his country's army. General mobilization of the continental armies took place in the following order: Serbia, Russia, Austria, France and Germany. General mobilization by a Great Power was commonly interpreted by military men in every country, though perhaps not by Sir Edward Grey, the Tsar, and some civilian officials, as meaning that the country was on the point of making war,—that the military machine had begun to move and would not be stopped. Hence, when Germany learned of the Russian general mobilization, she sent ultimatums to St. Petersburg and Paris, warning that German mobilization would follow unless Russia suspended hers within twelve hours, and asking what would be the attitude of France. The answers being unsatisfactory, Germany then mobilized and declared war. It was the hasty Russian general mobilization, assented to on July 29 and ordered on July 30, while Germany was still trying to bring Austria to accept mediation proposals, which finally rendered the European War inevitable.

Russia was partly responsible for the Austro-Serbian conflict because of the frequent encouragement which she had given at Belgrade—that Serbian national unity would be ultimately achieved with Russian assistance at Austrian expense. This had led the Belgrade Cabinet to hope for Russian support in case of a war with Austria, and the hope did not prove vain in July, 1914. Before this, to be sure, in the Bosnian Crisis and during the Balkan Wars, Russia had put restraint upon Serbia, because Russia, exhausted by the effects of the Russo-Japanese War, was not yet ready for a European struggle with the Teutonic Powers. But in 1914 her armaments, though not yet completed, had made such progress that the militarists were confident of success, if they had French and British support. In the spring of 1914, the Minister of War, Sukhomlinov, had published an article in a Russian newspaper, though without signing his name, to the effect, "Russia is ready, France must be ready also." Austria was convinced that Russia would ultimately aid Serbia, unless the Serbian danger were dealt with energetically after the Archduke's murder; she knew that Russia was growing stronger every year; but she doubted whether the Tsar's armaments had yet reached the point at which Russia would dare to intervene; she would therefore run less risk of Russian intervention and a European War if she used the Archduke's assassination as an excuse for weakening Serbia, than if she should postpone action until the future.

Russia's responsibility lay also in the secret preparatory military measures which she was making at the same time that she was carrying on diplomatic negotiations. These alarmed Germany and Austria. But it was primarily Russia's general mobilization, made when Germany was trying to bring Austria to a settlement, which precipitated the final catastrophe, causing Germany to mobilize and declare war.

The part of France is less clear than that of the other Great Powers, because she has not yet made a full publication of her documents. To be sure, M. Poincaré, in the fourth volume of his memoirs, has made a skillful and elaborate plea, to prove "*La France innocente.*" But he is not convincing. It is quite clear that on his visit to Russia he assured the Tsar's Government that France would support her as an ally in preventing Austria from humiliating or crushing Serbia. Paléologue renewed these assurances in a way to encourage Russia to take a strong hand. He did not attempt to restrain Russia from military measures which he knew would call forth German counter-measures and cause war. Nor did he keep his Government promptly and fully informed of the military steps which were being taken at St. Petersburg. President Poincaré, upon his return to France, made efforts for peace, but his great preoccupation was to minimize French and Russian preparatory measures and emphasize those of Germany, in order to secure the certainty of British support in a struggle which he now regarded as inevitable.

Sir Edward Grey made many sincere proposals for preserving peace; they all failed owing partly, but not exclusively, to Germany's attitude. Sir Edward could probably have prevented war if he had done either of two things. If, early in the crisis, he had acceded to the urging of France and Russia and given a strong warning to Germany that, in a European War, England would take the side of the Franco-Russian Alliance, this would probably have led Bethmann to exert an earlier and more effective pressure on Austria; and it would perhaps thereby have prevented the Austrian declaration of war on Serbia, and brought to a successful issue the "direct conversations" between Vienna and St. Petersburg. Or, if Sir Edward Grey had listened to German urging, and warned France and Russia early in the crisis, that if they became involved in war, England would remain neutral, probably Russia would have hesitated with her mobilizations, and France

would probably have exerted a restraining influence at St. Petersburg. But Sir Edward Grey could not say that England would take the side of France and Russia, because he had a Cabinet nearly evenly divided, and he was not sure, early in the crisis, that public onion in England would back him up in war against Germany. He could resign, and he says in his memoirs that he would have resigned, but that would have been no comfort or aid to France, who had come confidently to count upon British support. He was determined to say and do nothing which might encourage her with a hope which he could not fulfil. Therefore, in spite of the pleadings of the French, he refused to give them definite assurances until the probable German determination to go through Belgium made it clear that the Cabinet, and Parliament, and British public opinion would follow his lead in war on Germany. On the other hand, he was unwilling to heed the German pleadings that he exercise restraint at Paris and St. Petersburg, because he did not wish to endanger the Anglo-Russian Entente and the solidarity of the Triple Entente, because he felt a moral obligation to France, growing out of the Anglo-French military and naval conversations of the past years, and because he suspected that Germany was backing Austria up in an unjustifiable course and that Prussian militarists had taken the direction of affairs at Berlin out of the hands of Herr von Bethmann-Hollweg and the civilian authorities.

Italy exerted relatively little influence on the crisis in either direction.

Belgium had done nothing in any way to justify the demand which Germany made upon her. With commendable prudence, at the very first news of the ominous Austrian ultimatum, she had foreseen the danger to which she might be exposed. She had accordingly instructed her representatives abroad as to the statements which they were to make in case Belgium should decide very suddenly to mobilize to protect her neutrality. On July 29, she placed her army upon "a strengthened war footing," but did not order complete mobilization until two days later, when Austria, Russia, and Germany had already done so, and war appeared inevitable. Even after being confronted with the terrible German ultimatum, at 7 P.M. on August 2, she did not at once invite the assistance of English and French troops to aid her in the defense of her soil and her neutrality against a certain German assault; it was not until German troops had actually violated her territory, on August 4, that she appealed for the assistance of the Powers which had guaranteed her neutrality. Belgium was the innocent victim of German strategic necessity. Though the German violation of Belgium was of enormous influence in forming public opinion as to the responsibility for the War after hostilities began, it was not a cause of the War, except in so far as it made it easier for Sir Edward Grey to bring England into it.

In the forty years following the Franco-Prussian War, as we have seen, there developed a system of alliances which divided Europe into two hostile groups. This hostility was accentuated by the increase of armaments, economic rivalry, nationalist ambitions and antagonisms, and newspaper incitement. But it is very doubtful whether all these dangerous tendencies would have actually led to war, had it not been for the assassination of Franz Ferdinand. That was the factor which consolidated the elements of hostility and started the rapid and complicated succession of events which culminated in a World War, and for that factor Serbian nationalism was primarily responsible.

But the verdict of the Versailles Treaty that Germany and her allies were responsible for the War, in view of the evidence now available, is historically unsound. It should therefore be revised. However, because of the popular feeling widespread in some of the Entente countries, it is doubtful whether a formal and legal revision is as yet practicable. There must first come a further revision by historical scholars, and through them of public opinion.

NOTES

1. For a recent analysis of the evidence laid before the Commission on Responsibility for the War at the Paris Peace Conference, and the Untenability of the conclusions based upon it, see A. von Wegerer, "Die Wiederlegung der Versailles Kriesgsschuldthese," in *Die Kriegsschuldfrage*, VI, 1-77, Jan., 1928; also his article, with replies to it, in *Current History*, Aug., 1928, pp. 810–828.

POSTSCRIPT

Was German Militarism and Diplomacy Responsible for World War I?

Contemporary political developments have always had a powerful effect on the historiographical debate over the causes of World War I, and occasionally vice versa. The wave of revisionism that swept across Western Europe in the 1920s and 1930s—fueled in part by disillusionment over the terms and consequences of the Versailles peace treaty—made the British and French governments less willing to enforce the treaty's terms when the Nazi German regime commenced its program of rearmament and expansion. Ultimately, this reluctance culminated in British prime minister Neville Chamberlain's surrender of the Sudentenland at Munich in 1938. And after World War II, the outbreak of the cold war suddenly led Western historians to reexamine the role of Russia—now an international villain—in starting World War I.

Nevertheless, the recent debate over the causes of World War I continues to center around the culpability of Germany. Perhaps the classic scholarly interpretation of Germany as the aggressor in 1914 is Fritz Fischer's *Germany's Aims in the First World War* (W. W. Norton, 1967). An elaborate rejoinder may be found in *The Fateful Alliance: France, Russia, and the Coming of the First World War* by historian and diplomat George F. Kennan (Pantheon Books, 1984), which traces the causes of the war back to the formation of the Franco-Russian rapprochement in the 1890s. James Joll provides a more balanced overview of the war's causes in *The Origins of the First World War* (Longman, 1984). Finally, few studies have ever surpassed Barbara Wertheim Tuchmann's *Guns of August* (Macmillan, 1962) for sheer narrative power and drama.

ISSUE 10

Did the Bolshevik Revolution Improve the Lives of Soviet Women?

YES: Richard Stites, from *The Women's Liberation Movement in Russia: Feminism, Nihilism, and Bolshevism, 1860–1930* (Princeton University Press, 1978)

NO: Françoise Navailh, from "The Soviet Model," in Françoise Thébaud, ed., *A History of Women in the West, vol. 5: Toward a Cultural Identity in the Twentieth Century* (Belknap Press, 1994)

ISSUE SUMMARY

YES: History professor Richard Stites argues that in the early years of the Bolshevik Revolution, the Zhenotdel, or Women's Department, helped many working women take the first steps toward emancipation.

NO: Film historian Françoise Navailh contends that the Zhenotdel had limited political influence and could do little to improve the lives of Soviet women in the unstable period following the revolution.

Compared with life under the czars, life for women after the Bolshevik Revolution was characterized by greater variety and freedom. The Romanov dynasty had ruled Russia for 300 years, and the Orthodox Church had ruled for a much longer period. Both had reinforced a world of patriarchal authority, class structure, and patterns of deference. Although the revolution overthrew the power of both church and monarch, the new communist state had a power and authority of its own. Between 1917 and 1920 Soviet women received equal rights in education and marriage, including the choice to change or keep their own names and the opportunity to own property; the rights to vote and to hold public office; access to no-fault divorce, common-law marriage, and maternity benefits; workplace protection; and access to unrestricted abortion. They were the first women to gain these rights—ahead of women in France, England, and the United States—but the question is whether or not these legal rights translated into improvements in their day-to-day lives.

A feminist movement had developed in urban areas as early as the 1905 workers' revolution, and women joined men in leading strikes and protest demonstrations. By the time of the Bolshevik Revolution in 1917, however, the goals of the leadership were primarily economic, and feminism was dismissed as bourgeois or middle class. In a workers' revolution, women and men were to be equal. Housework and child care were to be provided collectively, and the family, like the monarchy, was to be replaced with something new. Women gained access to economic independence by becoming workers, which was supposed to provide them with the basis for equality within marriage.

The German philosopher Karl Marx had argued that the family reflects the economic system in society. Under capitalism, the bourgeois family exists to reproduce workers and consumers; it exploits women by unfairly burdening them with full responsibility for housework and child care. If similarly exploited workers—what Marx called the proletariat—overthrew the capitalist system that allowed factory owners to grow rich from their workers' labor, Marx believed that the family would undergo an equally dramatic transformation. In this scenario, no one would be "owned" by anyone else. Prostitution would disappear, and, as the state took responsibility for childrearing and education, women would be free to work and become economically self-sufficient. People would then be free to marry for love or sexual attraction rather than for economic considerations.

V. I. Lenin, who emerged as the leader and architect of the new order, was committed to women's rights. First and foremost, however, he was committed to a socialist revolution. When the struggle to make legal changes that would be felt in women's lives came into conflict with the goals of the revolution, there was no question in Lenin's mind about which would have to be sacrificed. In this early period, a fascinating group of women briefly held highly visible leadership positions and had the chance to put their ideas into practice, at least during the first decade. Alexandra Kollontai was one of the most articulate and effective leaders of the Zhenotdel, or Women's Department of the Communist Party, whose purpose between 1919 and 1930 was to educate and mobilize the women of the Soviet state to participate fully in the revolution.

In the following selections, Richard Stites focuses on the work of the Zhenotdel in reaching out to the Jewish, Christian, Muslim, and Buddhist women of the East whose lives in the Caucasus, Volga, and Central Asia were the most severely restricted. Raising the consciousness of these women in the face of brutal male opposition contributed significantly to women's liberation and the development of the socialist state, Stites concludes.

Françoise Navailh, in contrast, maintains that although Soviet women were granted unprecedented legal rights, almost without a struggle, the real task of Zhenotdel was to translate these rights into a new way of life. Navailh judges it to have failed in significantly improving the lives of Soviet women.

YES

Richard Stites

BOLSHEVIK LIBERATION

"Don't make an issue of my womanhood."

—*Ninotchka* (1939)
C. Brackett, B. Wilder, *and* W. Reisch

THE LIMITS OF EQUALITY

"The future historian," said Kollontai after the Civil War, "will undoubtedly note that one of the characteristics of our revolution was that women workers and peasants played not—as in the French Revolution—a passive role, but an active important role." The following paragraphs may serve as a gloss on this remark. Though there was a good deal of spontaneous activity among the women of the Red side, Bolshevik women organizers—Kollontai foremost among them—did not leave much to chance. In a propaganda pamphlet of 1920 addressed to women, Kollontai directly invited working and peasant women to support the Red Front in every possible way including combat. Conscious of her own former anti-war propaganda, she was careful to point out the difference between the exploitative character of the Great War and the liberating and defensive nature of the present one, tying together the thesis of women's capacity to fight with the need to defend the equality that they had won in the Revolution. The Soviet publicist, V. Bystryansky, began his argument in *Revolution and Woman* (1920) with a reference to Fourier's statement about measuring a society's level of progress by examining the level of women's emancipation in that society, and made flattering comments about the military potential of women. Variations of these themes were the stock in trade of propagandists such as Krupskaya, Balabanova, and other Bolshevik women who held important propaganda posts during the Civil War.

What is striking about Russian women's participation in this War is the variety and novelty of the functions that they performed. As in the past, women carried out every conceivable support task on the home front, ranging from feeding and sanitary operations to building fortifications and digging trenches in beleaguered cities. As in World War I, women served in medical

From Richard Stites, *The Women's Liberation Movement in Russia: Feminism, Nihilism, and Bolshevism, 1860–1930* (Princeton University Press, 1978). Copyright © 1978 by Princeton University Press. Reprinted by permission. Notes omitted.

and combat capacities, but on a broader scale and in a much more organized context. Propaganda, psychological warfare, espionage, and police work—known previously to only a few exceptional women —now recruited large numbers of them. Women's participation was erratic and tentative during the first year of the War. In October 1919, the Zhenotdel gave greater definition to the functions of women and set up the machinery for large-scale and orderly recruitment. By the end of the war in 1920, conscription of young women for non-combatant service had begun, and high-ranking posts in Military Revolutionary Committees and Political Departments of the Red Army were occupied by women....

The role of women in the political life of the country in the generation following the Revolution may be seen in two fairly distinct stages. In the first, roughly 1917–1923, a small but visible group of women held responsible positions during and immediately after the Civil War. After 1923–1925, when there were no more prominent individual Bolshevik women even close to the seats of power, a second stage began. Women were then and for the future absent both from positions of power and prestige and largely from public prominence; but at the same time, the lowest strata of women had begun to stir and to participate in a limited but real way in the political process, such as it was. And a modest number of women were permanently lodged in the middle range of political and administrative authority. The "major" women Bolsheviks as a group were clearly less eminent than the men on any reasonable list of leading Bolsheviks. There are, however, a few who, in terms of political work, public image, or both, may be set off from other Bolshevik women: Stasova, Armand, Bal-

abanova, Kollontai, and Krupskaya, all born between 1869 and 1878, and all possessing revolutionary credentials dating from the turn of the century or earlier (though only Krupskaya and Stasova could claim to be Old Bolsheviks).

Elena Stasova was at the very center of events in 1917, serving as the functioning Secretary of the Party during and immediately after the Revolution. Her reputation as storehouse of the Party's traditions had made her the logical candidate for the job. When the government moved to Moscow, however, Stasova remained behind; Lenin had found a more effective administrator in Yakov Sverdlov who had a talent for making policy as well. When Sverdlov died in 1919, Stasova resumed her work in the Secretariat under the tripartite management of Krestinsky, Preobrazhensky, and Serebryakov. But in 1920, when the staff was reorganized, Stasova resigned and requested a chancery position in one of the higher Party organizations. Krestinsky suggested instead that she go to work in Zhenotdel—a suggestion that Stasova immediately declined. Having worked at the center of political life, she perhaps resented being shunted off to what might have seemed mere auxiliary work. Stasova eventually found a congenial assignment as leader of the International Red Aid (MOPR)—a Comintern version of the old political Red Cross. From 1920 onward, she had no impact on the Soviet political scene. Here is a clear case of a woman who, in spite of certain administrative talents, was by her own admission always hazy on matters of theory and thus ultimately unsuited for top leadership in a Party which was still composed largely of intellectuals.

Inessa Armand died of cholera in 1920. She had been second only to Kollontai in energy and range of political work. In addition to founding and directing Zhenotdel, Inessa held important posts in the highest Party, Soviet, and economic agencies of Moscow Province; and she helped shape the international communist movement by organizing foreigners of Bolshevik sympathies into the Club of the Third International. Her political prominence was clearly enhanced by her exceptionally close relationship with Lenin (and Krupskaya). The notion, however, that Inessa had been Lenin's mistress—though gaining acceptance among a number of Western student—has no relevance to the question of her political importance, and the evidence is flimsy and unconvincing.

Angelica Balabanova (Balabanoff)... was an almost archetypical radical Russian woman. Brought up amid the luxury of a large Ukrainian manor house, she had felt the stirrings of revolutionary consciousness early, perceiving, as she says, the "difference between those who could *give* and those who had to *receive*." "My ardent desire," she recalled, "was to escape my conventional and egoistic milieu in order to devote myself fully to a cause from which I could live and die. This was not self-abnegation, but a wish to live a life which would make me *useful* to the suffering masses." The route of her "escape" took her to Brussels and then to Italy where she became a key figure in the socialist movement, acting for a time as Mussolini's secretary. After 1917, she came back to Russia and served in a number of posts including Foreign Minister of the Ukraine and Secretary of the Comintern. But her ardent service to the Bolshevik regime did not prevent her from repudiating it when it failed to meet her expectations. "The deformation of the October Revolution," she wrote, "progressed at the same rate at which the individual replaced the masses. This substitution, which was made at the outset in good faith, was bound to degenerate in time." In 1921, she resigned her positions and left Soviet Russia forever.

Kollontai was by far the most active and versatile of the Bolshevik women of this era. A member of the tiny Central Committee at the time of the overthrow, she was soon appointed Commissar of Public Welfare. During her brief tenure as Commissar, Kollontai betrayed some administrative vacillation. At first she was reluctant to use force in dealing with left-over recalcitrant civil servants of the tsarist days. Lenin chided her by asking if she thought a revolution could be made with white gloves. But when she took some rather strong public measures against the Orthodox Church, he warned her to exercise tact when dealing with religious sensibilities. But it was her marriage to the younger revolutionary sailor, Pavel Dybenko, ... that undercut the confidence that the Party leaders had briefly shown in her. Her association with him and his reckless and erratic behavior brought no credit upon her political reputation. "I will not vouch for the reliability or the endurance" said Lenin a few years later "of women whose love affair is intertwined with politics." Not that her revolutionary career was over by any means. She served as Commissar for Propaganda in the Ukraine, toured the front with Dybenko on an agit-train, and headed Zhenotdel.

Kollontai's exit from Soviet politics came in 1922, in connection with her role in the dissenting Workers' Opposition Group whose leader, Shlyapnikov, was her former lover. Kollontai herself drafted the program and distributed it to Party members in 1921. It was as much a product of her longstanding faith in the creative powers of the proletariat, first enunciated in *Social Bases,* as it was a tract for the times. Against the increasing centralism, authoritarianism, and bureaucratism which had overtaken the Party during the Civil War, she proposed "the collective, creative effort of the workers themselves." Her most suggestive theme was that collective, interpersonal relations among the producers generated great productivity, and that this productivity was diminished by the alienating presence of authoritarian officials—"the bosses and the bureaucrats." Kollontai's form of syndicalism, shared by many in the Russian labor movement, was seen by Lenin and others as a menace to unity and discipline in the Party. Lenin displayed his fury at the fateful Tenth Party Congress; when Kollontai persisted in her efforts to disseminate her ideas, she was removed from her posts and sent off to Norway on a minor diplomatic mission. She was eventually promoted to Soviet ambassador to Sweden; but her career as a Bolshevik political figure was over.

As Lenin's wife, Krupskaya had been a key organizational figure of the early Bolshevik movement in emigration because of her network of correspondence with agents in Russia. But after Lenin and Krupskaya arrived in revolutionary Russia, Stasova, not she, was appointed to head up the Secretariat of the Party in the Kseshinskya Palace. Krupskaya's main work and her abiding concern both before and after Lenin's death was propaganda and education. By her own admission, high politics held little interest for her, and she was almost reprimanded by the Central Committee for failing to attend Party meetings regularly. On the other hand, she was certainly a good deal

more than "first lady of the great Russian state" (Zetkin's pious phrase). Her pedagogical and journalistic activities contributed much to the training and liberation of women. After her well-known clash with Stalin during Lenin's illness, she did emerge as a potential rallying point for oppositional elements; but by 1925, this was all over, and she had come to realize that she was far from being a political match for the wily Stalin....

ZHENOTDEL

Whenever a revolution has been preceded by a long established underground movement, the structure of that movement—just as much as its leadership and its ideology—super-imposes itself on the political life of the new society. This is why Bolshevik Russia became a land of committees, commissions, congresses, and cells. Before 1917, the Bolshevik Party had been a congeries of local committees directed from the center by a small group that communicated with its branches by means of a newspaper (for general ideas) and peripatetic agents (for specific instructions); feedback to the center came through correspondence and rare congresses and conferences. After 1917, the Bolsheviks used these devices (now amplified by railroad, telegraphy, and wireless) of political organization and communication for social mobilization of the country in the same way that they had used them to destroy its former regimes. The "novel" methods of social communication all had their counterparts in the history of the revolutionary underground. The techniques of Zhenotdel— the post-revolutionary organ responsible for women's liberation in Soviet Russia —were no exception. They were summarized long before Zhenotdel came into existence in a list of instructions given by Klavdiya Nikolaeva to women workers in May 1917: Organize Social Democratic groups in your factory; appoint a liaison to *Rabotnitsa;* arrange meetings. It was all there—organization, filtering down of leaders, responsibility to the center (an editorial board), communication back to the rank and file through liaison and newspaper, and processing the instructions at local meetings. And it had been there, in embryo, for a generation.

But would the machinery be used? And to what end? That the "proletarian women's movement" would continue after the Revolution was a tacit assumption of its leaders and was inherent in the revolutionary movement itself. Kollontai, in 1921, spoke in retrospect of the hostility to the regime nourished by the vast majority of women and of their fears that it would uproot the family, decree the "heartless" separation of children from parents, and destroy the church. In 1918, she was already aware of the danger of disillusionment among the masses of women and of the need for long-range and patient work among them. Lenin, though he had little time to voice his opinion on the matter in the first years of Soviet power, was in full agreement with Kollontai, Inessa, and the others on the need for active liberation of Russian women—in life as well as in law. Thus the formal, legislative program of emancipation (the only one usually noted by historians) had to be given meaning in a social revolution from below. This is the true historical context of the Zhenotdel....

During the Civil War, Inessa used the Zhenotdel to mobilize women in support of the Red Army and the new regime. Propaganda teams, like the ones headed by Krupskaya and Kollontai, threaded their way on agit-trains and boats through the Red areas, stopping at remote villages to regale the population with poster art, song-and-dance groups, and speeches. The popular "Natasha" (K. I. Samoilova), known affectionately among Russian women as "our own mother," sailed up and down the Volga with a plea for support and a promise of liberation which she proclaimed from the decks of the *Red Star.* She died of cholera during one of her cruises. At the local level, "volunteer Saturdays" (*subbotniki*) and "days of wounded Red Army Men" were launched to recruit previously inactive women in jobs like sewing underwear, bathing soldiers, and bandaging wounds. Recruiting work grew very slowly; and the Party sometimes tended to use Zhenotdel workers exclusively in such endeavors as food distribution, child and orphan care, and the struggle against illiteracy and superstition—areas of activity that, in the context, were really the Soviet equivalents of *Küche, Kinder,* and *Kirche.* Inessa Armand drove herself to exhaustion working fourteen to sixteen hours a day. By a stroke of fate, she was ordered by the Party to the Caucasus for a rest. There, in the fall of 1920, she took cholera and died.

Kollontai was chosen to succeed her. If she had been bypassed in 1918, it was probably only because of the Party's, especially Lenin's, greater confidence in Armand's reliability and obedience. Kollontai and Inessa had helped forge the women's movement, separately before the Revolution and together after it; and they shared the same philosophy of women's liberation. Kollontai held no brief for a "feminist" movement separate from or outside the Party; she even hoped to dissolve some of the purely "female" features of Zhenotdel work (such as the "women's pages" in Party newspapers). But she was equally firm in resisting any suggestions of liquidating the Zhenotdel itself. Passivity and lack of consciousness were the hallmarks of Russian women. She told Emma Goldman (who refused her invitation to work in Zhenotdel) that women "were ignorant of the simplest principles of life, physical and otherwise, ignorant of their own functions as mothers and citizens." It was imperative, then, to raise the consciousness of these women and to deal with specifically woman-related problems, such as maternity care, in their own special way. This, she said, was not feminism.

Kollontai was right. It was not feminism, at least as the word was then understood. The feminist movement in Western Europe and America, from 1848 to 1920, had ultimately settled on the vote as the capstone of emancipation. After acquiring it, no feminist movement in the West, until recent years, made many further steps toward realizing economic or sexual liberation; even less did it engage in any mass movement for the liberation of women of the working class or minorities. Bolshevik "feminism" reversed the social timetable of Western feminism. For the latter, political emancipation was the goal; for the former, it was only the beginning.

During her manifold assignments of the Civil War period, Kollontai had always (except during a serious illness) kept in touch with Zhenotdel activities. After her appointment, she led Zhenotdel with the abundant optimism, energy, and talent which she had displayed in other realms of revolutionary work. Her two year tenure as its leader (1920–1922) also happened to be a period of deep emotional and political tribulation for

her. Kollontai's most important practical accomplishment was to turn Zhenotdel's energy away from wartime auxiliary work (the War ended in 1920) toward the subtler tasks of psychological and social demobilization. More spectacular and in the long run just as important was initiating the liberation of the so-called women of the East—the Muslim, Christian, Jewish, and Buddhist women of the non-western borderlands of Caucasia, the Volga, and Central Asia who were subjected to codes of sexual behavior unknown in the rest of Russia. The most severe of these was the Muslim şeriat that in practice gave women no status and no purpose other than as pleasure-giver, servant, housekeeper, and childbearer. Their isolation and untouchability was symbolized by "the veil" in all its varieties, the most severe of which was the paranja, a heavy horsehair garment that hung from the nose to the floor. Aside from serious organizational work among these women, Kollontai also brought some of them to Moscow for congresses where the exotic guests would tear off their face coverings before a startled audience. Criticized by some for excessive theatricality, Kollontai told Louise Bryant that "all pioneering work is theatrical." It was not the last time that an article of women's clothing would be seen as an enslaving, sexist fetish; and the doffing of the veil became the favorite gesture of baptism into free womanhood in the Soviet East. . . .

Provincial Zhenotdels were assigned only eight full-time people in the organizational setup. Since five of them sat in the center, this meant only one instructor or zhenorg for every three districts of a province. Furthermore, [Bette] Stavrakis' study indicates that Zhenotdel, like most analogous Party organizations, suffered from personnel deficiency, shortage of funds, jurisdictional overlap, and superficiality at the grass roots level. The areas of greatest resistance to its efforts were the villages and the non-Slavic borderlands. The Ukrainian organizer, Kiselëva, walked miles from *raikom* headquarters to the little village of Sripal to gather the women into a reading cabin in order to organize them. The menfolk surrounded the cabin and shouted, "We'll beat you up if you touch our wives." In Chigirin district, three Zhenotdel workers were killed in one year by "bandits." At the beginning of collectivization, women organizers in the Ukraine had to dispel the rumors which said that in the new kolkhozes the young women would he "shared" by the men and the old ones boiled down for soap. Everywhere, men (invariably called "kulaks" in the literature) fought efforts of the Zhenotdel to organize and politicize their wives.

Of vastly greater difficulty was Zhenotdel work among "eastern" women. Kollontai's congresses were only the beginning. These women could barely hint, and only after patient prying, at the kind of life they had had under the traditional order. "We were silent slaves," said one. "We had to hide in our rooms and cringe before our husbands, who were our lords." Another recalled: "Our fathers sold us at the age of ten, even younger. Our husband would beat us with a stick and whip us when he felt like it. If he wanted to freeze us, we froze. Our daughters, a joy to us and a help around the house, he sold just as we had been sold." These words were spoken to Clara Zetkin who inspected the Zhenotdel operations in the Caucasus during her recuperation there in the early 1920's. Lacking in native Bolshevik cadres, Zhenotdel sent out Russian revolutionaries and educators to take up

the work. Typical of these was Nadezhda Kolesnikova, veteran propagandist and wife of one of the fabled Twenty-Six Commissars. Another was Olga Chulkova, a librarian-teacher and Bestuzhev graduate, who worked from her Zhenotdel base in Sukhumi to organize the women of Abkhaziya. Teams were sent out into the mountain villages and women who had never left their native settlements before were brought down to Sukhumi. Some were shuttled off to Moscow to study; the rest went back to the mountains to organize day nurseries.

As Bette Stavrakis has observed, the lack of native Bolsheviks, the difficulties of language, the size of the territory, the prevalence of illiteracy, the varieties of religion, the tenuous communist control of some areas, and, most important, the ferocious hostility of the males, led the Zhenotdel leaders to adopt methods in accordance with the local situation. These included secret visits, rendezvous in bath-houses, and small groups or *artels* in the initial stages, and the "women's clubs"—social covers for political consciousness raising. In Batumi, the woman's club used male speakers at first until the first shrouded woman stood up and tore off her veil; in Baku it had thousands of members and became the school, church, and social center for women, replacing the gossipy bazaar. Zhenotdel workers appeared in places where a city person had never been seen before; in Central Asia they wandered over the steppe in makeshift transport, stopping at camp, *aul*, and oasis to lecture with the magic lantern (as the Sunday School teachers of Petersburg had done in the 1890's) or to show a motion picture featuring a Muslim heroine who refused to marry the old man who had bought her.

Men reacted to all this with savage violence. Women coming out of the club at Baku were assaulted by men with wild dogs and boiling water. A twenty-year-old Muslim girl who flaunted her liberation by appearing in a swimsuit was sliced to pieces by her father and brothers because they could not endure the social indignity. An eighteen-year-old Uzbek woman activist was mutilated and thrown into a well. Central Asia witnessed three hundred such murders during one quarter of 1929 alone. The Presidium of the Soviet Central Executive Committee, after consulting with the Zhenotdel, decided to classify such crimes as "counter-revolutionary offences." Yet, in spite of the danger, hundreds of native women volunteered as translators and assistants and eventually worked their way into administrative Zhenotdel positions. And each May Day or International Women's Day, thousands of women would assemble in the market places of "eastern" Soviet lands and defiantly tear off their chadras, paranjas, and veils. If it had accomplished nothing else, Zhenotdel would deserve a place in social history for having brought this about.

The variety of enterprises engaged in by the Zhenotdel was enormous: child and orphan care, school service and inspection, food distribution, housing supervision, preventive medicine and public health, anti-prostitution campaigns, war work, education, legislation, placement, family service, and mass propaganda for every campaign that the Party decided to undertake. Some of this resembled the kind of activity which traditional feminists had busied themselves with. But, as an arm of the Party, Zhenotdel had better resources to help it unlock the energies of the most backward and remote communities of Russia's women.

In doing this, Zhenotdel served not only the cause of women's liberation but also the regime as a whole by helping to create new reserves of skilled and politically conscious labor....

A final word about Zhenotdel. There can be little doubt that it made an enormous impact on Soviet society, particularly in the cities. Its frequent mention in Soviet literature attests to its prominent place in everyday consciousness. Fictional treatment of Zhenotdel varied. Sometimes it was used merely as a backdrop; often it was a cause of domestic friction or an object of ridicule—and just as often as a problem-solver and proper haven for the newly conscious Soviet woman, but always a symbol of newness on the social landscape. The images were never far from the reality; Zhenotdel was an engine of mobilization in an environment of extreme social backwardness. Organizational and communication skills enabled it to go beyond the specific social task—the "small deed" of the nineteenth-century intelligentsia—toward the larger goal of mass socialization. As an arm of the Party, it lacked the independence and perhaps some of the imaginative initiative of prewar feminism; but, in spite of weaknesses noted above, the Zhenotdel surpassed the feminists in power and prestige. Zhenotdel represented a combination of class and sexual struggle and thus was a working out not only of Marxist notions about the female half of the labor movement, not only of the revolutionary Populist tradition of the "common cause," but also, in some ways, of the much more feminist belief, given expression by Lenin in 1919 that "the emancipation of working women is a matter for the working women themselves." The successes registered by Zhenotdel in raising the consciousness of poor and backward women were proof enough that there was something more to female emancipation than winning the suffrage. But its abolition in 1930 was also proof that without political equality, the "common cause" for which women had fought for three generations would always be defined by men.

NO

Françoise Navailh

THE SOVIET MODEL

The Russian Empire that preceded the Soviet Union was an autocracy. Although serfdom was not abolished until 1861 and the first elections were not held until 1906, the opposition quickly grew radical, and the "woman question" was incorporated into a broad revolutionary program. From the beginning large numbers of women joined the revolutionary movement, accounting for between 15 and 20 percent of the active membership of the revolutionary parties. In urban areas an independent feminist movement was especially active between 1905 and 1908. It concentrated its efforts chiefly on obtaining the right to vote, but in vain. On the eve of World War I Russian society consisted of a very small cultivated and westernized elite, a bourgeoisie still in embryo, and a backward peasantry that made up the remaining 80 percent of the population. People belonging to these different strata of society generally kept to themselves and knew little of other groups. This ignorance would prove a major impediment later on.

World War I broke out on August 1, 1914. Between 1914 and 1917 more than ten million men were mobilized, mostly peasants. Conditions in the countryside, already wretched, grew even worse. Many women were pressed into farm work, so many that women ultimately accounted for 72 percent of the rural workforce. They also replaced men in industrial jobs: the proportion of women in the workforce rose from 33 percent in 1914 to nearly 50 percent in 1917. From 1915 on, women found employment in new branches of industry and joined the government bureaucracy in large numbers. Their wages were lower than men's, however, at a time when prices were soaring. After 1916, the effort to keep food flowing to the cities and to the troops collapsed. The war, always unpopular, seemed hopeless, with no end in sight. For more than a year the country had been afflicted with bread riots and hunger strikes in which women played leading roles. Tension mounted. The regime began to crumble. The honor of initiating the revolution fell to women.

On February 23, 1917 (according to the Julian calendar, or March 8, according to our calendar), working women took their children out into the streets of Petrograd and staged a demonstration. Since the socialists had been unable to agree on a theme for the demonstration, the women improvised, calling for

From Françoise Navailh, "The Soviet Model," in Françoise Thébaud, ed., *A History of Women in the West*, vol. 5: *Toward a Cultural Identity in the Twentieth Century* (Belknap Press, 1994). Copyright © 1994 by the President and Fellows of Harvard College. Reprinted by permission of Harvard University Press. Notes omitted.

peace and bread. On the following day their ranks were swelled by an influx of male demonstrators, and the scope of the turmoil grew rapidly. On March 2 the czar abdicated. A provisional government was formed, and on July 20 it granted women the rights to vote and hold office (rights not granted in England until 1918 and the United States until 1920). Feminists, having achieved their goal, disappeared as an autonomous force. Liberal women lost control of events. When the Winter Palace was seized by the Bolsheviks on the night of October 25–26, it was defended by a women's contingent composed of intellectuals along with women of the bourgeoisie, aristocracy, and working class. The revolution now erupted into a bloody civil war whose outcome hung for a long time in the balance.

A DECADE OF CONTRADICTION

Though surrounded by Whites, forces of the Allied powers, and nationalists, the Bolsheviks sallied forth from Moscow and Petrograd (later Leningrad) to regain control of nearly all of the territory that had constituted the old Russian Empire. They lost no time adopting a host of new laws concerning women. A decree of December 19, 1917, stipulated that in case of mutual consent divorce was to be granted automatically by the courts or the Registry offices (ZAGS); the principle according to which one party must be assigned blame was abolished, and the divorce decree no longer had to be publicized. Russia was the first country in the world to adopt such a liberal divorce policy. A decree of December 20, 1917, abolished religious marriage and standardized and simplified the civil marriage procedure.

All children, legitimate or not, enjoyed the same legal rights. These two measures were extended by the Family Code of December 16, 1918—the most liberal in Europe at the time. The ZAGS became the chief agency for dealing with family matters. A man could no longer force his wife to accept his name, residence, or nationality. Husband and wife enjoyed absolute equality even with respect to the children. Maternity leave and workplace protection were guaranteed. The Family Code adopted a narrow definition of the family: direct ancestors and descendants together with brothers and sisters. A spouse enjoyed the same status as kin and collaterals, with no special privileges or prerogatives. The new family proved less stable than the old. Bonds between individuals were loosened: inheritance was outlawed in April 1918 (and only partially restored in 1923). Unrestricted abortion was legalized on November 20, 1920.

The Code of November 19, 1926, confirmed these earlier changes and took yet another step, abolishing all differences between marriages legally recorded by the ZAGS and de facto (common-law) marriages. Divorce could henceforth be obtained on the written request of either party: "postcard divorce" was now legal. Love was freer, but mutual obligations were more onerous owing to new alimony and child support requirements. The new Family Code was intended to liberate men, women, and children from the coercive regulations of another era. The past was to be completely effaced. People were urged to change their family names in March 1918 and their first names in 1924: suggestions for new names included Marlen (short for Marxism-Leninism), Engelsine, and Octobrine. Though intended to be an instrument of liberation, the code was also an instrument of coercion that could be used to strike at conservative segments of the society, particularly peasants and Muslims. In fact, the Communist Party, composed of a handful of urban intellectuals, deliberately ignored the views of those whom it sped along the road to a better tomorrow. Although lawmakers occasionally reversed themselves, their actions were always guided by two principles: to destroy czarism and build socialism....

Kollontai: A Reluctant Feminist

Alexandra Kollontai (1872–1952) was a pivotal figure in debates on women and the family during the first Soviet decade. She epitomizes all the contradictions of the period. Her biography is typical of her generation. Aristocratic by birth, she enjoyed a luxury-filled, dreamy childhood. After marrying at age nineteen to escape her family and milieu, she left her husband at age twenty-six and went to school in Zurich, then a Mecca for Russian intellectuals, where she became involved in politics, took increasingly radical positions, and eventually became a professional revolutionary. Her record was brilliant: as the first woman elected to the Central Committee in 1917, she voted in favor of the October insurrection. She then became the first woman to serve in the government, as people's commissar for health, and took an active part in drafting the Family Code of 1918. As an active member of the Workers' Opposition in 1920–1921, she sought to limit the vast powers of the Communist Party. In 1922 she became the first woman ambassador in the world. Her diplomatic career abroad kept her away from Moscow until 1945, yet her name is inseparable from the controversies of the 1920s, whose

passions she fueled with countless articles, pamphlets, and brochures that were widely criticized, distorted, and even caricatured. She also wrote a number of theoretical tomes (*The Social Bases of the Woman Question*, 1909; *The Family and the Communist State*, 1918; *The New Morality and the Working Class*, 1918), as well as six works of fiction, all published in 1923. Although certain aspects of her work now seem dated, much of it remains remarkably up to date.

Kollontai proposed a synthesis of Marxism with a feminism she never avowed (and in fact always combated). Marxism, combined with a touch of Fourierist utopianism, would facilitate the realization of feminist goals. Like Marx and Engels, Kollontai believed that the bourgeois family had fallen apart and that revolution would lead to the regeneration of family life. She also drew extensively on the work of Bebel, particularly his idea that oppression tends to create unity among women. But she tried to go beyond these general arguments. Aware that the revolution was merely a starting point, she argued that to change the essence of marriage required changing people's attitudes and behavior. Therein lay her originality. She stressed the reifying tendency of the masculine will and noted the alienation of women who prefer any kind of marriage to solitude and are thus driven to wager everything on love. So Kollontai taught that love could be a kind of sport: if tender erotic friendship were based on mutual respect, jealousy and the possessive instinct might be eliminated. The "new woman," one of her recurrent subjects, was energetic and self-assertive. She let men know what she wanted; she refused to be dependent either materially or emotionally; she rebelled against socioeconomic obstacles, hypocritical morals, and "amorous captivity." Autonomous and active, she was free to explore "serial monogamy." In "Make Room for Wingèd Eros," an article published in 1923, Kollontai analyzed love's many facets: friendship, passion, maternal affection, spiritual affinity, habit, and so on. "Wingless Eros," or purely physical attraction, was to make room for "wingèd Eros," wherein physical gratification was combined with a sense of collective duty, that indispensable attribute in the era of transition to socialism. Finally, once socialist society had been established, there would be room for "Eros transfigured," or marriage based on healthy, free, and natural sexual attraction. To allow couples to develop, "kitchens must be separated from homes": in other words, society must build cafeterias, day-care centers, and dispensaries in order to relieve women of certain of their traditional responsibilities. Last but not least, motherhood was cast in a new light: it was "no longer a private affair but a social duty." Women must have children for the sake of the community. Kollontai considered abortion to be a temporary evil, to be tolerated only until the consciousness of working women had been raised to the point where it was no longer necessary. She denounced the refusal to bear children as petty-bourgeois selfishness. Nevertheless, she did not advocate the collectivization of child-rearing: parents should decide whether children were to be raised in a nursery school or at home.

As a spiritual value, however, love in general—and sex—should take precedence over the maternal instinct: "The workers' state needs a new type of relation between the sexes. A mother's narrow, exclusive love for her own child must broaden to embrace all the chil-

dren of the great proletarian family. In the place of indissoluble marriage, based on the servitude of women, we look forward to the birth of free matrimony, an institution made strong by the mutual love and respect of two members of the brotherhood of Labor, equals in rights as well as obligations. In place of the individualistic, egoistic family will arise the great universal family of working people, in which everyone, men and women alike, will be first and foremost brothers and comrades." Kollontai called upon women to defend, propagate, and internalize the idea that they had value as human beings in their own right.

To be sure, Kollontai's argument was framed in terms of classical Marxism, to which the economy is primary, but she also insisted on the qualitative aspect of interpersonal relations: men and women should be attentive to each other's needs and playful toward one another. Ethics mattered to her as much as politics. Well before Wilhelm Reich, she was among the first to link sexuality with class struggle: "Why is it that we are so unforgivably indifferent to one of the essential tasks of the working class? How are we to explain the hypocritical relegation of the sexual problem to the realm of 'family affairs' not requiring collective effort? As if sexual relations and the morals governing them have not been a constant factor in social struggle throughout history."

Few people shared Kollontai's ideas in the Soviet Union of the 1920s. Her comrades looked upon her ideas as frivolous and ill-timed. Her views presupposed a yet-to-be-achieved social and economic infrastructure, and they came in for vehement criticism in a 1923 article by the Bolshevik P. Vinogradskaya, who had worked with Kollontai on Women's Department of the Central Committee Secretariat (*Zhenotdel*) in 1920. Vinogradskaya attacked her opponent for confusing priorities, neglecting the class struggle, and encouraging sexual anarchy in an irresponsible way, since disorder in private life could lead to counterrevolutionary agitation. The task of the moment was to protect wives and children and to champion the cause of women without attacking men. Marx and Engels had already said everything there was to be said on the question, and it was pointless to indulge in "George-Sandism."

Lenin, for his part, related everything to the economy and opted in favor of monogamous marriage, egalitarian, earnest, and devoted to the cause, like his own tranquil union with Nadezhda Krupskaya. When Ines Armand saw poetry in free love, Lenin responded that what she mistook for poetry was nothing but bourgeois immorality. He borrowed his ideal from Nikolai Chernysbevski's austere novel *What Is to Be Done?* (1863), which, as lie said, "bowled him over." Indeed, he thought so highly of the book that he used its title for his own theoretical work of 1902. His conversations with Clara Zetkin, which took place in 1920 but were not published until 1925, after Lenin's death, accurately reflected his rejection of lack of discipline in love and sexual matters. Lenin saw such lack of discipline as a sign of decadence and a danger to young people's health, hence to the revolution itself. He attacked the "anti-Marxist" theory according to which "in Communist society the satisfaction of sexual desires is as simple and soothing as drinking a glass of water." Lenin had nobody particular in mind. He was not attacking Kollontai, for his remarks preceded the polemic of 1923, but later Kollontai's adversaries used his wrath

against her: "Of course thirst must be satisfied! But would a normal man, under normal conditions, prostrate himself in the street to drink from a filthy puddle? Or even from a glass previously soiled by dozens of other lips?" Here, purity is restored as an absolute value, and the underlying idea is that having more than one sexual partner is in itself immoral. Lenin's credo was a negative one: "No to the monk, no to the Don Juan, and no to that supposed happy medium, the German philistine." To be sure, he denounced the slavery of housework: "Woman is stifled, strangled, stupefied, and humiliated by the trivial occupations of domestic life, which chain her to the kitchen and nursery and sap her strength for work that is as unproductive, difficult, and exhausting as one can imagine." But he said nothing about the new family.

For orthodox Marxists, children did not figure in the conjugal scheme. They were to be taken care of either by certain designated women or by all the women of the community collectively—at the outset the choice is not clear. Fathers certainly play no role in the new system of child-rearing. The community supports, envelops, permeates, and transcends the reduced couple, in which man and woman are strict equals. The woman, like her husband, is a worker; traditional femininity is disparaged as a product of old bourgeois social relations. Equality in fact means identity of the sexes. The new industrious humanity consists of male and female twins, identical insofar as both are workers. "Economically and politically, which also means physiologically, the modern proletarian woman can and must become more and more like the modern proletarian man," wrote Marxist psychoneurologist Aaron Zalkind in

1924. Sexual relations, we are told, will not be a matter of great importance for such indistinguishable twins. One can interpret this claim in two ways. If sex is merely a physiological need, then the number of partners is unimportant: this is the attitude of the youth Zhenya in Kollontai's short story, "Three Generations of Love." The other interpretation leads to Leninist asceticism. In either case love must be restrained; it is a disruptive force. All of this was merely speculative, however. During the 1920s the private sphere remained intact, and various norms of sexual behavior coexisted.

A New Russia

In order to enforce the law, achieve economic equality, bring uniformity to a very disparate country, and accelerate the integration of women into the society, the Party in 1919 created the Zhenotdel, or Women's Department of the Central Committee Secretariat, with equivalents at every echelon of the hierarchy. Five women in succession led this Department during its existence, among them Ines Armand in 1919–20 and Alexandra Kollontai from 1920 to 1922. The Zhenotdel offered advice and assistance, settled labor and domestic conflicts, proposed laws and suggested amendments to Central Committee edicts, joined in actions such as the campaigns to eradicate illiteracy and abolish prostitution, coordinated the work of various agencies, oversaw the application of quotas that favored women in hiring and admission to soviets, dealt with problems of supply, housing, and sanitation, and inspected schools and orphanages. In addition to the Zhenotdel there was also a system of female delegates: women workers and peasants elected by their colleagues to participate in year-long training and indoctrination courses, after which they spent two months working with the soviets or the courts before returning to work. This system trained women to become "Soviet citizens." More than ten million of them signed up during the 1920s. Dasha, the heroine of Fedor Gladkov's novel *Cement* (1925), is a perfect example of the liberated woman. A militant delegate, she so completely threw off her old bonds that she sacrificed her marriage, her home, and even her little daughter, who died in an orphanage. There is no doubt that the Zhenotdel, together with the delegate system, had an impact on the consciousness of women. Its political influence remained negligible, however, and all too often it served only to convey the wishes of the hierarchy to the rank and file. In 1923 it was accused of "feminist deviationism," a fatal sin....

Freedom and Disorder

... In one sense, women were granted all they could have hoped for right at the outset, without a struggle. But the most difficult part of the task remained: they had to learn how to make use of their newly won rights to forge a new way of life. But given the sociohistorical context and the gaps in the codes of 1918 and 1926, new freedoms gave rise to unintended consequences.

Two signs of the times were marital instability and a widespread reluctance to have children. The number of abortions rose, the birthrate declined precipitously, and newborn babies were frequently abandoned. Orphanages, overwhelmed by new admissions, became veritable charnel houses. Infanticide and wife-murder increased. In effect, women and children were the first victims of the new order. The condition of women clearly became more dire, especially in the cities.

Men abandoned their families, leaving their wives without resources. The availability of divorce merely on application by either party led to cynical abuses. The government allowed common-law marriages in order to protect women from seduction and abandonment (and also to protect any children that might result from fleeting affairs); men were required to provide for the women they left behind, and thus to assume a burden that the government itself was unable to bear. But women had to prove that an affair had taken place, and the law failed to specify what constituted proof. The courts improvised. Lengthy and often fruitless paternity suits poisoned relations between the sexes and became a recurrent theme of contemporary fiction. The laws governing alimony were just as vague, and the courts were obliged to fix amounts on a case-by-case basis. Often it was set at one-third or one-fourth of the man's monthly wage, which sometimes created insurmountable difficulties. How was a man to survive if ten rubles were deducted from his wage of forty rubles? How was he to support a child born out of wedlock when he already had four "legitimate" children to take care of? Few men earned enough to cover alimony, and many refused to pay up. Rulings of the court went unenforced in more than half the cases.

There were practical problems as well. Allocation of housing was a state monopoly, and waiting lists were extremely long. Divorced couples were therefore obliged in some cases to go on living together. Abram Room's film *Bed and Sofa* (1927) is a marvelous depiction of conditions under the NEP [New Economic Policy]. It offers a new perspective on the eternal triangle, portraying a husband, wife, and lover forced to share a single room. After the seduction, moreover, the two men take a nonchalant attitude toward the situation and join in a macho alliance against the woman, the wife of one and mistress of the other.

Many women who wanted children were nevertheless forced to seek abortions because of the scarcity of housing, low wages, short supplies, and/or lack of a man. In a survey conducted in Moscow in 1927, 71 percent of women seeking abortions cited "living conditions" as the reason and 22 percent mentioned unstable love lives." Only 6 percent rejected motherhood on principle.

Although intellectuals and quasi-intellectuals in the cities went on leading bohemian lives, some segments of the population resisted any change in traditional mores. In 1928, 77.8 percent of the population still consisted of peasants, compared with only 17.6 percent blue- and white-collar workers. The Code of 1926 triggered a huge controversy that illustrates the continuing influence of the peasantry. Since accurate news was hard to come by despite innumerable published articles, brochures, and meetings, peasants were liable to be affected by unsubstantiated rumors, and many were convinced that the new code was going to make the sharing of women compulsory. The most controversial provision of the law concerned the treatment of de facto marriage as completely equivalent to lawful matrimony. The Agrarian Code of 1922 reinforced the communal organization of the village, or *mir*, and retained the undivided family property, or *dvor*. If a couple sharing in the *dvor* divorced and payment "of alimony led to division of the property, the farm might cease to be viable. Wary after years of ceaseless combat (1914–1921), the peasantry, fearful of novelty, drew back and clung to its traditional values.

It was an ambiguous image of woman that emerged from all the articles, brochures, pamphlets, investigations, speeches, novels, and films of the day: sometimes she was portrayed as a member of the vanguard of the working class, wearing an earnest look, work clothes, and a red scarf; at other times she was the backward peasant with her white kerchief pulled down over her eyes; or the mannish girl of the Komsomol (Young Communists), shockingly liberated in her ways; or the pert, flirtatious typist. Woman simultaneously embodied the past and the future. Conviction vied with confusion in the minds of the masses. Novels of the late 1920s are filled with restless, confused, unhappy heroines. Urban immorality and rural conservatism were matters of concern to both rulers and ruled. Women wanted stability, men declined responsibility, and the Party wanted to keep its program on course. By 1926 it was clear that, like it or not, the family would survive. Certain sectors of light industry were sacrificed in the name of economic progress. Home and children once again became the concern of women. The woman question was held to have been resolved once and for all, and in 1929 the Zhenotdel was abolished. ...

A Contestable and Contested Model

By 1923 the die was cast. Although there was progress at the grass roots, there was stalemate at the top. The masses were enlisted in the struggle, but the once competent, combative, and cultivated elite was supplanted by squadrons of colorless yes-men. Strong personalities such as Alexandra Kollontai were removed or liquidated.

In the end Kollontai's fears were justified. Without a redefinition of sex roles economic emancipation proved to be a trap, for women were obliged to conform to a male model without being relieved of their burden as women. It may be that a comparable danger exists in any developing industrial society. A century of European evolution was compressed into two decades in the Soviet Union: the sexual revolution of the 1920s broke down the old family unit, while the Stalinist reaction of the 1930s reshaped the family in order to impose breakneck industrialization on a backward peasant society. The gap between the idealistic slogans and everyday reality was enormous.

The one-party state was not solely responsible for these developments, however. As in other countries, the role of women was ambiguous. Whether responding by instinct to ensure their own survival and that of their children or acting out of alienation, women accepted and internalized the rules of the Soviet game to a greater extent than men—and much to men's annoyance. Sober, long-suffering, conscientious, and disciplined, woman was one of the pillars of the regime: she did the washing, stood in line to buy food, cooked meals, took care of the children, worked in factories and offices and on collective farms, and did whatever she had to do. But to what end? Equality only added to her burden.

POSTSCRIPT

Did the Bolshevik Revolution Improve the Lives of Soviet Women?

It is one of history's ironies that, with the stroke of a pen, Soviet women were granted all the legal and political rights that women in Britain and the United States were struggling to achieve. Having won the rights to vote and hold public office, Soviet women struggled to translate those paper rights into improved lives for themselves and their children. It has been a conviction of Western feminism that legal and political equality pave the way for full emancipation of women. The Soviet case raises interesting questions about the confusion that arises when there are conflicting revolutions. Real political power belongs to those who can ensure that the goals of their revolution receive first priority. It was the socialist revolution, not women's emancipation, that the party leadership worked to achieve.

Popular accounts of the Russian Revolution may be found in John Reed's *Ten Days That Shook the World* (Penguin, 1977) and Louise Bryant's *Mirrors of Moscow* (Hyperion Press, 1973). The story of Reed and Bryant, two Americans who find themselves eyewitnesses to the Bolshevik Revolution, is captured in the film *Reds*. Another film covering the same period is *Doctor Zhivago*, which is based on the book of the same title by Boris Pasternak (1958). For Lenin's views on women, one of the best sources is his book *The Emancipation of Women* (International Publishers, 1972). *The Unknown Lenin: From the Secret Archives* edited by the eminent Russian historian Richard Pipes (Yale University Press, 1996) dips into the secret archives and brands Lenin a ruthless and manipulative leader. Robert McNeal's *Bride of the Revolution* (University of Michigan Press, 1972) focuses on the fascinating marriage and revolutionary relationship between Lenin and Bolshevik propagandist Nadezha Krupskaya. And Sheila Fitzpatrick, in *The Russian Revolution* (Oxford University Press, 1982), surveys the critical 1917–1932 period with special emphasis on the work of Zhenotdel. For essays on the lives of women during this period, students may want to see *Women in Soviet Society* edited by Gail Lapidus (University of California Press, 1978) and *Women in Russia* edited by D. Atkinson, A. Dallin, and G. Lapidus (Stanford University Press, 1977), which grew out of a 1975 conference that was held at Stanford University entitled "Women in Russia." The fascinating character Alexandra Kollontai, who died at 80, may be explored through her own writings in *Selected Writings* (W. W. Norton, 1972), *Red Love* (Hyperion Press, 1990), and *Love of Worker Bees* (Academy of Chicago Press, 1978). Books about Kollontai include *Bolshevik Feminist* by Barbara Clements (Indiana University Press, 1979).

ISSUE 11

Was the German National Spirit of the 1930s Responsible for the Holocaust?

YES: Daniel Jonah Goldhagen, from *Hitler's Willing Executioners: Ordinary Germans and the Holocaust* (Alfred A. Knopf, 1996)

NO: Fritz Stern, from "The Goldhagen Controversy: One Nation, One People, One Theory?" *Foreign Affairs* (November/December 1996)

ISSUE SUMMARY

YES: Professor of government Daniel Jonah Goldhagen states that due to the nature of German society in the twentieth century—with its endemic, virulent anti-Semitism—thousands of ordinary German citizens became willing participants in the implementation of Holocaust horrors.

NO: Professor of history Fritz Stern argues that, in spite of the legitimacy of some of his arguments, Goldhagen's approach to Holocaust causation is deliberately provocative and overly simplistic in its treatment of the subject.

Few historical events engender stronger emotional responses than the Nazi-directed Holocaust of World War II, in which millions of Jews were systematically exterminated as part of a ghastly plan for a diabolical new world order. Since its occurrence, many scholarly works have been written in an attempt to answer the questions that this "crime against humanity" has raised: What historical factors were responsible for it? How did people and nations allow it to roll toward its final destructive consequences? What lessons did it teach us about human nature? Could something like this happen again? Who bears the ultimate responsibility for it?

Much of Holocaust scholarship has concentrated on European anti-Semitism as a major factor in the cause of the event itself and as a major reason why little was done to stop it. Some scholars have emphasized the schizophrenic nature of post–World War I politics, which they say allowed demagogic madmen to weave their magic web around an unsuspecting public. And, of course, the major blame has been placed on Adolf Hitler and his Nazi henchmen for the initiation, design, and implementation of the Holocaust.

But just how unsuspecting was this public? Most people have long dismissed (as did the Nuremberg War Crimes Tribunal) the "I was only following orders" argument that so many who actively participated in the Holocaust have used. Others who were not directly involved have cited hopelessness and fear of reprisal for their actions. But as we have been made witness to countless trials for war crimes in the last 50 years, some have wondered whether or not a larger segment of the population in those Nazi-controlled countries was involved in the Holocaust's worst aspects.

Daniel Jonah Goldhagen was not the first scholar to investigate this question, but his 1996 book *Hitler's Willing Executioners: Ordinary Germans and the Holocaust*, which is excerpted in the following selection, has raised the issue to a new level and has created a maelstrom of controversy within the historical profession. Using recently discovered sources of information and tools of analysis newly available to social scientists, Goldhagen takes a fresh look at why and how the Holocaust occurred through an analysis of three related subjects: "the perpetrators of the Holocaust, German antisemitism, and the nature of German society during the Nazi period." Goldhagen's conclusions are a stinging indictment of large numbers of ordinary Germans, who he claims willingly participated in the Holocaust's worst aspects, including police battalions, work camps, and death marches.

Goldhagen's work has received much praise, including a National Book Critics nomination for nonfiction book of the year. But it has also had its share of critics. Some have found his work to be one-sided, inflammatory, and too narrow in its focus. In the second selection, Fritz Stern states that Goldhagen's study of anti-Semitism fails to account for its presence in other areas of Europe (especially Austria). Stern also maintains that Goldhagen fails to account for the fact that thousands of non-Germans were "willing executioners, willing auxiliaries to the Holocaust." Overall, he sees Goldhagen's work as essentially unhistorical because it attempts to indict an entire nation through a selective use of sources and the drawing of conclusions that are tenuous at best.

A proverbial hornet's nest has been stirred up by *Hitler's Willing Executioners*, and its reverberations are not likely to subside anytime in the near future. Regardless of opinions of the book, any future works on the Holocaust will have to at least consider the questions that it has raised.

YES

Daniel Jonah Goldhagen

RECONCEIVING CENTRAL ASPECTS OF THE HOLOCAUST

During the Holocaust, Germans extinguished the lives of six million Jews and, had Germany not been defeated, would have annihilated millions more. The Holocaust was also the defining feature of German politics and political culture during the Nazi period, the most shocking event of the twentieth century, and the most difficult event to understand in all of German history. The Germans' persecution of the Jews culminating in the Holocaust is thus the central feature of Germany during the Nazi period. It is so not because we are retrospectively shocked by the most shocking event of the century, but because of what it meant to Germans at the time and why so many of them contributed to it. It marked their departure from the community of "civilized peoples." This departure needs to be explained.

Explaining the Holocaust is the central intellectual problem for understanding Germany during the Nazi period. All the other problems combined are comparatively simple. How the Nazis came to power, how they suppressed the left, how they revived the economy, how the state was structured and functioned, how they made and waged war are all more or less ordinary, "normal" events, easily enough understood. But the Holocaust and the change in sensibilities that it involved "defies" explanation. There is no comparable event in the twentieth century, indeed in modern European history. Whatever the remaining debates, every other major event of nineteenth- and twentieth-century German history and political development is, in comparison to the Holocaust, transparently clear in its genesis. Explaining how the Holocaust happened is a daunting task empirically and even more so theoretically, so much so that some have argued, in my view erroneously, that it is "inexplicable." The theoretical difficulty is shown by its utterly new nature, by the inability of social theory (or what passed for common sense) preceding it to provide a hint not only that it would happen but also that it was even possible. Retrospective theory has not done much better, shedding but modest light in the darkness.

... [T]o explain why the Holocaust occurred, to explain how it could occur... depends upon a number of subsidiary tasks, which consist fundamentally of reconceiving three subjects: the perpetrators of the Holocaust, German antisemitism, and the nature of German society during the Nazi period.

* * *

Foremost among the three subjects that must be reconceived are the perpetrators of the Holocaust. Few readers of this book will have failed to give some thought to the question of what impelled the perpetrators of the Holocaust to kill. Few have neglected to provide for themselves an answer to the question, an answer that necessarily derives usually not from any intimate knowledge of the perpetrators and their deeds, but greatly from the individual's conception of human nature and social life. Few would probably disagree with the notion that the perpetrators should be studied.

Yet until now the perpetrators, the most important group of people responsible for the slaughter of European Jewry, excepting the Nazi leadership itself, have received little concerted attention in the literature that describes the events and purports to explain them. Surprisingly, the vast literature on the Holocaust contains little on the people who were its executors. Little is known of who the perpetrators were, the details of their actions, the circumstances of many of their deeds, let alone their motivations. A decent estimate of how many people contributed to the genocide, of how many perpetrators there were, has never been made. Certain institutions of killing and the people who manned them have been hardly treated or not at all. As a consequence of this general lack of knowledge, all kinds of misunderstandings and myths about the perpetrators abound. These misconceptions, moreover, have broader implications for the way in which the Holocaust and Germany during the Nazi period are conceived and understood.

We must therefore refocus our attention, our intellectual energy, which has overwhelmingly been devoted elsewhere, onto the perpetrators, namely the men and women who in some intimate way knowingly contributed to the slaughter of Jews. We must investigate their deeds in detail and explain their actions. It is not sufficient to treat the institutions of killing collectively or singly as internally uncomplicated instruments of the Nazi leadership's will, as well-lubricated machines that the regime activated, as if by the flick of a switch, to do its bidding, whatever it might have been. The study of the men and women who collectively gave life to the inert institutional forms, who peopled the institutions of genocidal killing must be set at the focus of scholarship on the Holocaust and become as central to investigations of the genocide as they were to its commission.

These people were overwhelmingly and most importantly Germans. While members of other national groups aided the Germans in their slaughter of Jews, the commission of the Holocaust was primarily a German undertaking. Non-Germans were not essential to the perpetration of the genocide, and they did not supply the drive and initiative that pushed it forward. To be sure, had the Germans not found European (especially, eastern European) helpers, then the Holocaust would have unfolded somewhat differently, and the Germans would likely not have succeeded in killing as many Jews. Still, this was above all a German enterprise; the decisions, plans, organizational resources, and the majority of its executors were German. Comprehension and explanation of the perpetration of the Holocaust therefore requires an explanation of the Germans' drive to kill Jews. Because what can be said about the Germans cannot be said about any other nationality or about all of the other nationalities combined —namely no Germans, no Holocaust— the focus here is appropriately on the German perpetrators.

The first task in restoring the perpetrators to the center of our understanding of the Holocaust is to restore them their identities, grammatically by using not the passive but the active voice in order to ensure that they, the actors, are not absent from their own deeds (as in, "five hundred Jews were killed in city X on date Y"), and by eschewing convenient, yet often inappropriate and obfuscating labels, like "Nazis" and "SS men," and calling them what they were, "Germans." The most appropriate, indeed the only appropriate *general* proper name for the Germans who perpetrated the Holocaust is "Germans." They were Germans acting in the name of Germany and its highly popular leader, Adolf Hitler. Some were "Nazis," either by reason of Nazi Party membership or according to ideological conviction; some were not. Some were SS men; some were not. The perpetrators killed and made their other genocidal contributions under the auspices of many institutions other than the SS. Their chief common denominator was that they were all Germans pursuing German national political goals—in this case, the genocidal killing of Jews. To be sure, it is sometimes appropriate to use institutional or occupational names or roles and the generic terms "perpetrators" or "killers" to de-

scribe the perpetrators, yet this must be done only in the understood context that these men and women were Germans first, and SS men, policemen, or camp guards second.

A second and related task is to reveal something of the perpetrators' backgrounds, to convey the character and quality of their lives as genocidal killers, to bring to life their *Lebenswelt*. What *exactly* did they do when they were killing? What did they do during their time as members of institutions of killing, while they were not undertaking killing operations? Until a great deal is known about the details of their actions and lives, neither they nor the perpetration of their crimes can be understood. The unearthing of the perpetrators' lives, the presentation of a "thick," rather than the customary paper-thin, description of their actions, as important and necessary as it is for its own sake, lays the foundation for the main task for this... consideration of them, namely to explain their actions.

It is my contention that this cannot be done unless such an analysis is embedded in an understanding of German society before and during its Nazi period, particularly of the political culture that produced the perpetrators and their actions. This has been notably absent from attempts to explain the perpetrators' actions, and has doomed these attempts to providing situational explanations, ones that focus almost exclusively on institutional and immediate social psychological influences, often conceived of as irresistible pressures. The men and women who became the Holocaust's perpetrators were shaped by and operated in a particular social and historical setting. They brought with them prior elaborate conceptions of the world, ones that were common to their society, the investigation of which is necessary for explaining their actions. This entails, most fundamentally, a reexamination of the character and development of antisemitism in Germany during its Nazi period and before, which in turn requires a theoretical reconsideration of the character of antisemitism itself.

Studies of the Holocaust have been marred by a poor understanding and an under-theorizing of antisemitism. Antisemitism is a broad, typically imprecisely used term, encompassing a wide variety of phenomena. This naturally poses enormous obstacles for explaining the perpetration of the Holocaust because a central task of any such attempt is to evaluate whether and how antisemitism produced and influenced its many aspects. In my view, our understanding of antisemitism and of the relationship of antisemitism to the (mal)treatment of Jews is deficient. We must begin considering these subjects anew and develop a conceptual apparatus that is descriptively powerful and analytically useful for addressing the ideational causes of social action....

The study of the perpetrators further demands a reconsideration, indeed a reconceiving, of the character of German society during its Nazi period and before. The Holocaust was the defining aspect of Nazism, but not only of Nazism. It was also the defining feature of German society during its Nazi period. No significant aspect of German society was untouched by anti-Jewish policy; from the economy, to society, to politics, to culture, from cattle farmers, to merchants, to the organization of small towns, to lawyers, doctors, physicists, and professors. No analysis of German society, no understanding of characterization of it, can be made without placing the persecution and exter-

mination of the Jews at its center. The program's first parts, namely the systematic exclusion of Jews from German economic and social life, were carried out in the open, under approving eyes, and with the complicity of virtually all sectors of German society, from the legal, medical, and teaching professions, to the churches, both Catholic and Protestant, to the gamut of economic, social, and cultural groups and associations. Hundreds of thousands of Germans contributed to the genocide and the still larger system of subjugation that was the vast concentration camp system. Despite the regime's half-hearted attempts to keep the genocide beyond the view of most Germans, millions knew of the mass slaughters. Hitler announced many times, emphatically, that the war would end in the extermination of the Jews. The killings met with general understanding, if not approval. No other policy (of similar or greater scope) was carried out with more persistence and zeal, and with fewer difficulties, than the genocide, except perhaps the war itself. The Holocaust defines not only the history of Jews during the middle of the twentieth century but also the history of Germans. While the Holocaust changed Jewry and Jews irrevocably, its commission was possible, I argue, because Germans had *already* been changed. The fate of the Jews may have been a direct, which does not, however, mean an inexorable, outgrowth of a worldview shared by the vast majority of the German people.

Each of these reconceivings—of the perpetrators, of German antisemitism, and of German society during the Nazi period—is complex, requires difficult theoretical work and the marshaling of considerable empirical material, and, ultimately, is deserving of a separate book in its own right. While the undertaking of each one is justifiable on its own theoretical and empirical grounds, each, in my view, is also strengthened by the others, for they are interrelated tasks. Together the three suggest that we must substantially rethink important aspects of German history, the nature of Germany during the Nazi period, and the perpetration of the Holocaust. This rethinking requires, on a number of subjects, the turning of conventional wisdom on its head, and the adoption of a new and substantially different view of essential aspects of this period, aspects which have generally been considered settled. Explaining why the Holocaust occurred requires a radical revision of what has until now been written.....

This revision calls for us to acknowledge what has for so long been generally denied or obscured by academic and nonacademic interpreters alike: Germans' antisemitic beliefs about Jews were the central causal agent of the Holocaust. They were the central causal agent not only of Hitler's decision to annihilate European Jewry (which is accepted by many) but also of the perpetrators' willingness to kill and to brutalize Jews. The conclusion [here] is that antisemitism moved many thousands of "ordinary" Germans—and would have moved millions more, had they been appropriately positioned—to slaughter Jews. Not economic hardship, not the coercive means of a totalitarian state, not social psychological pressure, not invariable psychological propensities, but ideas about Jews that were pervasive in Germany, and had been for decades, induced ordinary Germans to kill unarmed, defenseless Jewish men, women, and children by the thousands, systematically and without pity.

* * *

For what developments would a comprehensive explanation of the Holocaust have to account? For the extermination of the Jews to occur, four principal things were necessary:

1. The Nazis—that is, the leadership, specifically Hitler—had to decide to undertake the extermination.
2. They had to gain control over the Jews, namely over the territory in which they resided.
3. They had to organize the extermination and devote to it sufficient resources.
4. They had to induce a large number of people to carry out the killings.

The vast literature on Nazism and the Holocaust treats in great depth the first three elements, as well as others, such as the origins and character of Hitler's genocidal beliefs, and the Nazis' ascendancy to power. Yet, as I have already indicated, it has treated the last element... perfunctorily and mainly by assumption. It is therefore important to discuss here some analytical and interpretive issues that are central to studying the perpetrators.

Owing to the neglect of the perpetrators in the study of the Holocaust, it is no surprise that the existing interpretations of them have been generally produced in a near empirical vacuum. Until recently, virtually no research has been done on the perpetrators, save on the leaders of the Nazi regime. In the last few years, some publications have appeared that treat one group or another, yet the state of our knowledge about the perpetrators remains deficient. We know little about many of the institutions of killing, little about many aspects of the perpetration of the genocide, and still less about the per-petrators themselves. As a consequence, popular and scholarly myths and misconceptions about the perpetrators abound, including the following. It is commonly believed that the Germans slaughtered Jews by and large in the gas chambers, and that without gas chambers, modern means of transportation, and efficient bureaucracies, the Germans would have been unable to kill millions of Jews. The belief persists that somehow only technology made horror on this scale possible. "Assembly-line killing" is one of the stock phrases in discussions of the event. It is generally believed that gas chambers, because of their efficiency (which is itself greatly overstated), were a necessary instrument for the genocidal slaughter, and that the Germans chose to construct the gas chambers in the first place because they needed more efficient means of killing the Jews. It has been generally believed by scholars (at least until very recently) and non-scholars alike that the perpetrators were primarily, overwhelmingly SS men, the most devoted and brutal Nazis. It has been an unquestioned truism (again until recently) that had a German refused to kill Jews, then he himself would have been killed, sent to a concentration camp, or severely punished. All of these views, views that fundamentally shape people's understanding of the Holocaust, have been held unquestioningly as though they were self-evident truths. They have been virtual articles of faith (derived from sources other than historical inquiry), have substituted for knowledge, and have distorted the way in which this period is understood.

The absence of attention devoted to the perpetrators is surprising for a host of reasons, only one of which is the existence of a now over-ten-year-long debate

about the genesis of the *initiation* of the Holocaust, which has come to be called by the misnomer the "intentionalist-functionalist" debate. For better or worse, this debate has become the organizing debate for much of the scholarship on the Holocaust. Although it has improved our understanding of the exact chronology of the Germans' persecution and mass murder of the Jews, it has also, because of the terms in which it has been cast, confused the analysis of the causes of the Germans' policies, . . . and it has done next to nothing to increase our knowledge of the perpetrators. Of those who defined this debate and made its central early contributions, only one saw fit to ask the question, Why, once the killing began (however it did), did those receiving the orders to kill do so? It appears that for one reason or another, all the participants in the debate assumed that executing such orders was unproblematic for the actors, and unproblematic for historians and social scientists. The limited character of our knowledge, and therefore our understanding, of this period is highlighted by the simple fact that (however the category of "perpetrator" is defined) the number of people who were perpetrators is unknown. No good estimate, virtually no estimate of any kind, exists of the number of people who knowingly contributed to the genocidal killing in some intimate way. Scholars who discuss them, inexplicably, neither attempt such an estimate nor point out that this, a topic of such great significance, is an important gap in our knowledge. If ten thousand Germans were perpetrators, then the perpetration of the Holocaust, perhaps the Holocaust itself, is a phenomenon of one kind, perhaps the deed of a select, unrepresentative group. If five hundred thousand or one million Germans were perpetrators, then it is a phenomenon of another kind, perhaps best conceived as a German national project. Depending on the number and identity of the Germans who contributed to the genocidal slaughter, different sorts of questions, inquiries, and bodies of theory might be appropriate or necessary in order to explain it.

This dearth of knowledge, not only about the perpetrators but also about the functioning of their host institutions has not stopped some interpreters from making assertions about them—although the most striking fact remains how few even bother to address the subject, let alone take it up at length. Still, from the literature a number of conjectured explanations can be distilled, even if they are not always clearly specified or elaborated upon in a sustained manner. (In fact, strands of different explanations are frequently intermingled without great coherence.) Some of them have been proposed to explain the actions of the German people generally and, by extension, they would apply to the perpetrators as well. Rather than laying out what each interpreter has posited about the perpetrators, an analytical account is provided here of the major arguments, with references to leading exemplars of each one. The most important of them can be classified into five categories:

One explanation argues for external compulsion: the perpetrators were coerced. They were left, by the threat of punishment, with no choice but to follow orders. After all, they were part of military or police-like institutions, institutions with a strict chain of command, demanding subordinate compliance to orders, which should have punished insubordination severely, perhaps with death. Put a gun to anyone's head,

so goes the thinking, and he will shoot others to save himself.

A second explanation conceives of the perpetrators as having been blind followers of orders. A number of proposals have been made for the source or sources of this alleged propensity to obey: Hitler's charisma (the perpetrators were, so to speak, caught in his spell), a general human tendency to obey authority, a peculiarly German reverence for and propensity to obey authority, or a totalitarian society's blunting of the individual's moral sense and its conditioning of him or her to accept all tasks as necessary. So a common proposition exists, namely that people obey authority, with a variety of accounts of why this is so. Obviously, the notion that authority, particularly state authority, tends to elicit obedience merits consideration.

A third explanation holds the perpetrators to have been subject to tremendous social psychological pressure, placed upon each one by his comrades and/or by the expectations that accompany the institutional roles that individuals occupy. It is, so goes the argument, extremely difficult for individuals to resist pressures to conform, pressures which can lead individuals to participate in acts which they on their own would not do, indeed would abhor. And a variety of psychological mechanisms are available for such people to rationalize their actions.

A fourth explanation sees the perpetrators as having been petty bureaucrats, or soulless technocrats, who pursued their self-interest or their technocratic goals and tasks with callous disregard for the victims. It can hold for administrators in Berlin as well as for concentration camp personnel. They all had careers to make, and because of the psychological propensity among those who are but cogs in a machine to attribute responsibility to others for overall policy, they could callously pursue their own careers or their own institutional or material interests. The deadening effects of institutions upon the sense of individual responsibility, on the one hand, and the frequent willingness of people to put their interests before those of others, on the other, need hardly to be belabored.

A fifth explanation asserts that because tasks were so fragmented, the perpetrators could not understand what the real nature of their actions was; they could not comprehend that their small assignments were actually part of a global extermination program. To the extent that they could, this line of thinking continues, the fragmentation of tasks allowed them to deny the importance of their own contributions and to displace responsibility for them onto others. When engaged in unpleasant or morally dubious tasks, it is well known that people have a tendency to shift blame to others.

The explanations can be reconceptualized in terms of their accounts of the actors' capacity for volition: The first explanation (namely coercion) says that the killers could not say "no." The second explanation (obedience) and the third (situational pressure) maintain that Germans were psychologically incapable of saying "no." The fourth explanation (self-interest) contends that Germans had sufficient personal incentives to kill in order not to want to say "no." The fifth explanation (bureaucratic myopia) claims that it never even occurred to the perpetrators that they were engaged in an activity that might make them responsible for saying "no."

Each of these conventional explanations may sound plausible, and some of them obviously contain some truth, so what is wrong with them? While each suffers from particular defects,... they share a number of dubious *common* assumptions and features worth mentioning here.

The conventional explanations *assume* a neutral or condemnatory attitude on the part of the perpetrators towards their actions. They therefore premise their interpretations on the assumption that it must be shown how people can be brought to commit acts to which they would not inwardly assent, acts which they would not agree are necessary or just. They either ignore, deny, or radically minimize the importance of Nazi and perhaps the perpetrators' ideology, moral values, and conception of the victims, for engendering the perpetrators' willingness to kill. Some of these conventional explanations also caricature the perpetrators, and Germans in general. The explanations treat them as if they had been people lacking a moral sense, lacking the ability to make decisions and take stances. They do not conceive of the actors as human agents, as people with wills, but as beings moved solely by external forces or by transhistorical and invariant psychological propensities, such as the slavish following of narrow "self-interest." The conventional explanations suffer from two other major conceptual failings. They do not sufficiently recognize the extraordinary nature of the deed: the mass killing of people. They *assume* and imply that inducing people to kill human beings is fundamentally no different from getting them to do any other unwanted or distasteful task. Also, none of the conventional explanations deems the *identity* of the victims to have mattered. The conventional explanations imply that he perpetrators would have treated any other group of intended victims in exactly the same way. That the victims were Jews—according to the logic of these explanations—is irrelevant.

I maintain that any explanation that fails to acknowledge the actors' capacity to know and to judge, namely to understand and to have views about the significance and the morality of their actions, that fails to hold the actors' beliefs and values as central, that fails to emphasize the autonomous motivating force of Nazi ideology, particularly its central component of antisemitism, cannot possibly succeed in telling us much about why the perpetrators acted as they did. Any explanation that ignores either the particular nature of the perpetrators' actions—the systematic, large-scale killing and brutalizing of people—or the identity of the victims is inadequate for a host of reasons. All explanations that adopt these positions, as do the conventional explanations, suffer a mirrored, double failure of recognition of the human aspect of the Holocaust: the humanity of the perpetrators, namely their capacity to judge and to choose to act inhumanely, and the humanity of the victims, that what the perpetrators did, they did to these people with their specific identities, and not to animals or things.

My explanation—which is new to the scholarly literature on the perpetrators—is that the perpetrators, "ordinary Germans," were animated by antisemitism, by a particular *type* of antisemitism that led them to conclude that the Jews *ought to die*. The perpetrators' beliefs, their particular brand of antisemitism, though obviously not the sole source, was, I maintain, a most significant and indispensable source of the perpetrators' actions and must be at the center of any explanation of them. Simply put, the perpetrators, having consulted their own convictions and morality and having judged the mass annihilation of Jews to be right, did not *want* to say "no." ...

The perpetrators were working within institutions that prescribed roles for them and assigned them specific tasks, yet they individually and collectively had latitude to make choices regarding their actions. Adopting a perspective which acknowledges this require that their choices, especially the patterns of their choices, be discerned, analyzed, and incorporated into any overall explanation or interpretation. Ideal data would answer the following questions:

- What did the perpetrators actually do?
- What did they do in excess of what was "necessary"?
- What did they refuse to do?
- What could they have refused to do?
- What would they not have done?
- What was the manner in which they carried out their tasks?
- How smoothly did the overall operations proceed?

In examining the pattern of the perpetrators' actions in light of the institutional role requirements and incentive structure, two directions beyond the simple act of killing must be explored. First, in their treatment of Jews (and other victims), the Germans subjected them to a wide range of acts other than the lethal blow. It is important to understand the *gamut* of their actions towards Jews, if the genocidal slaughter is to be explicated. This is discussed in more detail presently. Second, the perpetrators' actions when they were *not* engaged in genocidal activities also shed light on the killing; the insights that an analysis of their non-killing activities offers into their general character and disposition to action, as well as the general social psychological milieu in which they lived might be crucial for understanding the patterns of their genocidal actions.

All of this points to a fundamental question: Which of the gamut of perpetrators' acts constitute the universe of the perpetrators' actions that need to be explained? Typically, the interpreters of the perpetrators have focused on one facet of the Germans' actions: the killing. This tunnel-vision perspective must be broadened. Imagine that the Germans had not undertaken to exterminate the Jews but had still mistreated them in all the other ways that they did, in concentration camps, in ghettos, as slaves. Imagine if, in our society today, people perpetrated against Jews or Christians, Whites or Blacks anything approaching one one-hundredth of the brutality and cruelty that Germans, independent of the killing, inflicted on Jews. Everyone would recognize the need for an explanation. Had the Germans not perpetrated a genocide, then the degree of privation and cruelty to which the Germans subjected Jews would in itself have come into focus and have been deemed a historic outrage, aberration, perversion that requires explanation. Yet these same actions have been lost in the genocide's shadow and neglected by previous attempts to explain the significant aspects of this event.

The fixation on the mass killing to the exclusion of the other related actions of the perpetrators has led to a radical misspecification of the explanatory task. The killing should be, for all the obvious reasons, at the center of scholarly attention. Yet it is not the only aspect of the Germans' treatment of the Jews that demands systematic scrutiny and explication. Not only the killing but also *how* the Germans killed must be explained. The

"how" frequently provides great insight into the "why." A killer can endeavor to render the deaths of others—whether he thinks the killing is just or unjust—more or less painful, both physically and emotionally. The ways in which Germans, collectively and individually, sought in their actions, or merely considered, to alleviate or intensify their victims' suffering must be accounted for in any explanation. An explanation that can seemingly make sense of Germans putting Jews to death, but not of the manner in which they did it, is a faulty explanation....

* * *

... Previous studies, and almost all previous explanations of the perpetrators' actions, have been generated either in the laboratory, have been deduced purely from some philosophical or theoretical system, or have transferred conclusions (which themselves are often erroneous) from the societal or institutional levels of analysis to the individual. As such, they underdetermine the sources of the perpetrators' actions, and they fail to account for, or even to specify, the varieties and variations of those actions. This is particularly the case with all non-cognitive "structural" explanations. Few interpreters have concerned themselves with the microphysics of the Holocaust's perpetration, which is where the investigation of the perpetrators' actions must begin....

People must be motivated to kill others, or else they would not do so. What conditions of cognition and value made genocidal motivations plausible in this period of German history? What was the structure of beliefs and values that made a genocidal onslaught against Jews intelligible and sensible to the ordinary Germans who became perpetrators? Since any explanation must account for the actions of tens of thousands of Germans of a wide variety of backgrounds working in different types of institutions, and must also account for a wide range of actions (and not merely the killing itself), a structure common to them must be found which is adequate to explaining the compass of their actions. This structure of cognition and value was located in and integral to German culture.

NO

Fritz Stern

THE GOLDHAGEN CONTROVERSY: ONE NATION, ONE PEOPLE, ONE THEORY?

Holocaust literature abounds, as survivors seek to bear witness and historians try to understand. So far the very magnitude of the satanic murder has inspired a kind of awed reticence about pronouncing overarching explanations. Now a 37-year-old political scientist from Harvard claims: "Explaining why the Holocaust occurred requires a radical revision of what has until now been written. This book is that revision." *Hitler's Willing Executioners: Ordinary Germans and the Holocaust,* published in this country in April and in Germany in early August, has become an international sensation, a bestseller on both sides of the Atlantic.

The book is a deliberate provocation—I consider this a neutral judgment. Provocations can shock people out of their settled, comfortable views; they can also be self-promoting attacks on earlier work and professional standards. Goldhagen's title is provocative and delivers his thesis: the executioners of Jews were willing murderers, who willingly chose to torment and kill their victims; they were ordinary Germans, not Nazi monsters, not specially trained or indoctrinated by party membership or ideology, but simply acting out of what Goldhagen calls the common German "eliminationist mind-set." And being "ordinary" Germans responding to a common "cognitive model" about Jews, their places could have been taken by millions of other ordinary Germans.

Goldhagen's book comes in two related parts: the explanatory model, or "the analytical framework," as he also calls it, and the empirical evidence. The parts are joined by a single intent: the indictment of a people. The duality of presentation marks the style as well. Goldhagen depicts horror and renders judgment in evocative and compelling phrases. He bolsters polemical certainty with concepts drawn from the social sciences, relying on the vaporous, dreary jargon of the worst of academic "discourse." Unintelligible diagrams distract, even as horrendous photographs confirm. "The book's intent is primarily explanatory and theoretical," he notes. Theory explains and, as there

From Fritz Stern, "The Goldhagen Controversy: One Nation, One People, One Theory?" *Foreign Affairs* (November/December 1996). Copyright © 1996 by The Council on Foreign Relations, Inc. Reprinted by permission. Notes omitted.

is a persistent mismatch between the powerful, unsparing description of Holocaust bestiality and simplistic theoretical explanation, theory triumphs. Astoundingly repetitive, the book has 125 pages of notes but, regrettably, no bibliography.

To say it at once: the book has some merit, especially in the middle section, which depicts three specific aspects of the Holocaust, and it has one overriding defect: it is in its essence unhistorical. It is unhistorical in positing that one (simplistically depicted) strain of the past, German antisemitism, explains processes that the author strips of their proper historical context; it is unhistorical in over and over again presenting suppositions as "incontestable" certainty. Sir Lewis Namier, a great English historian, once remarked that " ... the historical approach is intellectually humble; the aim is to comprehend situations, to study trends, to discover how things work: and the crowning attainment of historical study is a historical sense—an intuitive understanding of how things do not happen. ..." Goldhagen's tone mocks humility, and he seems to lack any sense "of how things do not happen," of how complex human conduct and historical change really are.

THE GERMAN IDEOLOGY

Goldhagen begins with a disquisition of some hundred pages on what he believes is the peculiar character of German antisemitism, emphasizing medieval Christian hostility to Jews and concluding that in the largely secularized Germany of the nineteenth century this doctrinal hostility sharpened into a racial one, demonizing Jews as alien, as the enemy that needed to be eliminated. This version is of course dangerously close to the old cliché that a clear line of authoritarian, antisemitic thought runs from Luther to Hitler and was largely responsible for the triumph of Nazism.

Goldhagen draws on the rich literature about German antisemitism even as he dismisses it, distills what is useful for his thesis while ignoring whatever might contradict or complicate it, and then celebrates the originality of his own version. The result is a potpourri of half-truths and assertions, all meant to support his claim that German antisemitism was unique in its abiding wish to eliminate Jews, its "eliminationist mind-set." He suggests that one needs to look at Germans as anthropologists look at preliterate societies; they are not like "us," meaning Americans or Western Europeans.

He considers but dismisses the need to compare German antisemitism to other varieties, although we know that antisemitism was endemic in the Western world. Some scholars, including George L. Mosse and Zeev Steinhell, have plausibly argued that before 1914 French antisemitism was more pervasive and more aggressive than German antisemitism (on the other hand, French defense of Jews was more vigorous than similar efforts in Germany). Or take a perhaps even more revealing comparison: a leading historian of Germany, James J. Sheehan, wrote in 1992 that "animosity towards Jews [in the pre-1914 era] was substantially stronger in Austria than in Germany," and estimated "that whereas Austrians made up less than 10 per cent of the population of Hitler's Reich, they were involved in half the crimes associated with the Holocaust." Goldhagen certainly knows that thousands of non-Germans were willing executioners, willing auxiliaries to the Holocaust. But their motivation or, indeed, their historical role, is of no interest to him.

Even in his discussion of German antisemitism he fails to make the necessary distinctions. There was a wide range of attitudes toward Jews, from those few who did indeed see them as the enemy and chief corrupters of their society—as "vermin" to be exterminated—to those men and women who welcomed Jews but regretted what they saw as Jewish "pushiness" or preeminence in some realms. Goldhagen takes remarks out of context and treats almost equally the ranting of the rabble-rouser and the private musings confined to a writer's diary. Everything is grist for his mill.

A Goldhagen version of antisemitism in twentieth-century America might lump Eleanor Roosevelt's early remarks about "Jew-boys" in Franklin's law school class with Henry Ford's championing of the *Protocols of the Elders of Zion* or Father Coughlin's tirades. Only by summary judgment and indifference to nuance can Goldhagen contend that in the nineteenth century "German society ... was *axiomatically* antisemitic." And hence, "It is thus *incontestable* that the fundamentals of Nazi antisemitism ... had deep roots in Germany, was part of the cultural cognitive model of German society, and was integral to German political culture. ... It is *incontestable* that this racial antisemitism which held the Jews to pose a mortal threat to Germany was pregnant with murder" (my italics). Incontestable? I would say unprovable and implausible.

GERMAN JEWS

The very Germany Goldhagen discusses was the country in which Jews had made the most extraordinary leaps to cultural and economic prominence. But

Goldhagen omits this integral element of history. After emancipation and after legal equality was decreed in 1869, German Jews began their astounding ascendancy. Their achievements were the envy of Jews elsewhere. It is perfectly true that any hope they had for complete acceptance remained unfulfilled. They knew that they were being treated as second-class citizens, and their very successes heightened their vulnerability. But this was a society at once dynamically expanding and severely weakened by internal strains; it seems odd to single out "eliminationist antisemitism" as the key social dynamic and say nothing of the still sharp antagonisms between Protestants and Catholics, or the intense class conflict that Germans called "the social question" and that weighed on them far more than "the Jewish question" did.

The salience of German antisemitism varied with the mood and condition of German politics. During the Great War these politics became radicalized, and by 1917, when hope for total victory turned to apprehension of defeat, an enraged right wing fastened on violent, chauvinist, antisemitic beliefs; but for many other Germans defeat was the result of internal enemies, the Weimar Republic was a Jewish excrescence in German politics, and both Marxism and Bolshevism were Jewish machinations. Men and women on the left or liberal end of the German political spectrum rejected these delusions and defended the Republic, in which Jews had achieved a certain political prominence. Of all this Goldhagen says very little; the Great War, during which both Jewish patriotism and German antisemitism flourished as never before, is mentioned in only one paragraph. This distorted view of

German political culture is unconvincing in its simplicity.

HITLER AND ANTISEMITISM

Scholars have long debated whether Hitler's antisemitism was central to his electoral victories at the end of the Weimar years. It is generally accepted that the more the National Socialists tried to widen their appeal, the more they muted their antisemitic theme. In one of Hitler's key addresses in 1932, for example, he hardly alluded to Jews at all. Yet Goldhagen insists: "The centrality of antisemitism in the Party's world, program and rhetoric— if in a more avowedly elaborated and violent form—mirrored the sentiments of German culture." Actually, it exposed the sentiments of only *some* Germans. In the last free elections in 1932, some 67 percent of the German electorate did not vote for Hitler, although no doubt even among these there were groups that harbored suspicion and dislike of Jews. Perhaps many Germans had some measure of antisemitism in them but lacked the murderous intent that Goldhagen ascribes to National Socialism. Put bluntly: for Goldhagen, as for the National Socialists, *Hitler was Germany.*

But was antisemitism the sole or even the most important bond between Hitler and the Germans? Was it responsible for the failure of Germans to protest the first terrorist measures of the regime, the suppression of civil rights, the establishment of concentration camps in March 1933? The existence of the camps was made public specifically because they were intended to destroy political enemies and to intimidate potential opposition. From the very beginning the Nazis used every vicious means of humiliation and terror— in public sometimes, within the insulated realm of the camps always—against all opponents, real and imagined, German or German Jew, man or woman. They unleashed their pent-up savagery on Socialists and Communists (with the greatest brutality if they happened to be Jews as well). Men were beaten in these camps, and murdered—yet silence was pervasive among the Germans, who had begun to exult in their society's outward order and slowly returning prosperity and power. Would Goldhagen not acknowledge the likelihood of some link between Germans so sadistically falling upon their fellow Germans and their treatment of people whom they came to demonize— Jews and Slavs in particular?

The silence, and in some cases the easy acquiescence of the German elites, including those in churches, universities, and the civil service, had long been considered moral and civic failures of portentous importance. They saw their own freedoms threatened, their own principles violated; yet they showed, in Norbert Elias's phrase, "a lust for submission." They met with silence the first extrusionary acts against Jews; only very few protested when colleagues were removed from their posts or lost their jobs, when friends were ostracized, when all Jews were made the target of steady abuse. One must remember that active protest against the National Socialist regime in the spring of 1933 would not have demanded martyrdom—far from it. The price for the exercise of decency rose only when the regime became stronger.

Goldhagen argues that the road to Auschwitz was straight, and he pays little heed to the improvisations and uncertainties of the regime's first five years. Yet policies during that period aimed at the extrusion, not the extermination, of Jews, at their isolation and impoverishment, so as to drive them out of the country. Goldhagen rightly emphasizes both the antisemitic propaganda of the time and the way Jews were already to some degree "fair game"; yet in Germany there were few acts of spontaneous violence against them, as compared to the explosion of sadistic antisemitism in Austria immediately following the Anschluss. Nevertheless, for Goldhagen it is in Germany that the "eliminationist" mindset was most virulent.

Goldhagen rightly ponders the Germans' responses to the Reich pogrom in November 1938 known as Kristallnacht, with its burning of synagogues, smashing of Jewish property, and public arrest of some 30,000 male Jews who were then herded into concentration camps. He notes that "the world reacted with moral revulsion and outrage, the German people failed to exhibit equivalent revulsion and outrage—and principled dissent from the antisemitic model that underlay the night's depredation—even though what had occurred was done in their name, in their midst, to defenseless people, and to *their* countrymen" (Goldhagen's italics). But Goldhagen has been at pains to demonstrate that Germans had never regarded Jews as their countrymen. He continues: "This, perhaps the most revealing day of the entire Nazi era, the day on which an opportunity presented itself for the German people to rise up in solidarity with their fellow citizens, was the day on which the German people sealed the fate of the Jews by letting the authorities know that they concurred in the unfolding eliminationist enterprise, even if they objected, sometimes vociferously, to some of its measures." What a historical aberration! What chance was there for a people "to rise up" against a firmly entrenched terrorist regime that, moreover, had just scored the most extraordinary peaceful triumphs of incorporating Austria and emasculating Czechoslovakia—and all this with the passive or even active support of the western democracies. The November horror occurred six weeks after the Munich Conference and a month before the signing of a special Franco-German friendship treaty. If Germans "concurred in the unfolding eliminationist enterprise," why did the National Socialist regime make such strenuous efforts to hide its later crimes from them, to carry them out, as the famous phrase put it, "in night and fog," to place the early extermination camps outside the borders of the Reich? Was it afraid of phantoms?

Moreover, Goldhagen slights the acts of decency that did occur, every act at the risk of horrible retribution. (In general, these acts of decency and defiance have received too little attention, especially in Germany itself.)

American readers will soon be able to read German works in translation that either supplement or balance Goldhagen's version of events. The diaries of Victor Klemperer, kept in secret from 1933 to 1945 and only now published, have been a bestseller in Germany. They record the sentiments and sufferings of a Jewish professor married to a Christian; they offer a nuanced picture of both the Germans' brutality and callousness toward Jews and their moments of decency and quiet help. Wolfgang Sofsky's *The Order of Terror: The Concentration Camp*, appearing in the United States, … is a major study that characterizes the camp as the emblematic institution of the Nazi regime and insists "that the universe of the concentration camp is unprecedented in its torture and destruction," in its organized effort at degradation and murder. Goldhagen's one-sided remarks about the antisemitic attitudes and even murderous complicity with the regime of some of the heroic men who tried to kill Hitler in July 1944 receives more thorough and balanced attention in Joachim Fest's *Plotting Hitler's Death: The Story of the German Resistance.*

FOLLOWING ORDERS?

Less than half of this irksomely repetitive book deals with Goldhagen's own research into three specific aspects of the Holocaust: the murderous conduct of police battalions (the ordinary men of the title), the misnamed work camps that were way stations on the road to death, and the death marches at the end of the war. Goldhagen focuses on the perpetrators, particularly on their putative motives, and gives most terrifying, memorable accounts of their wanton cruelty. He reminds us that a very large number of Jews perished not in the gas chambers but by means of executions, planned starvation, and induced disease, always amidst unspeakable bestiality.

Goldhagen examines the lives and cruelties of the men of the 101st Police Battalion—a reconstruction made possible by the thorough record of a German prosecutorial investigation conducted after 1945. These men, most of them from the lower or lower-middle class in Hamburg, tended to be older than soldiers; most of them were family men and only a few of them were members of any Nazi organization. In 1992, Christopher R. Browning published *Ordinary Men: Reserve Police Battalion 101 and the Final Solution in Poland,* a meticulous study of precisely this same police battalion of 500 men, in which he examined their

backgrounds and vicious deeds, their massacres of Jews—men, women, and children in Poland—just because they were Jews. The commander offered his men nonpunitive exemption from such horror as killing mothers and babies but most men participated (as happened elsewhere), some with apparent sadistic satisfaction, some even though they had wives with them in Poland who knew and on occasion saw what their husbands did.

Goldhagen analyzes much of the same material but fiercely rejects Browning's account of the murderers' motives. Browning acknowledges the effect of the relentless Nazi propaganda against the Jews but wisely considers what other factors may have been responsible, including the fear of breaking ranks, acknowledging "weakness," and, in a few cases, considerations of career advancement. Goldhagen will have none of this. He insists on a monocausal explanation: antisemitic beliefs alone accounted for this behavior. Browning thinks that "the historian who attempts to 'explain' [this behavior] is indulging in a certain arrogance." True.

Next Goldhagen analyzes some of the so-called work camps, in which Jews were treated as worse than slaves, whipped to perform such senseless tasks as carrying rocks from one end of the camp to the other and back again. They were meant to die at hard, purposeless labor; they were starved, beaten, and killed, caught in a hell ruled by dogs and the whims of all-powerful sadist-guards (not all of them German). Jews were destined for extermination in these work camps, even as the Reich suffered from a labor shortage that led it to exploit more than seven million foreign slave laborers. Goldhagen emphasizes the economic irrationality of this strategy, citing it as proof once again of the primacy of the German drive to exterminate Jews. True, but there were many other instances of both economic irrationality and cruelty to *non*-Jews that were just as injurious to German interests.

The book's most gripping chapter concerns the death marches that began in the winter of 1944 and spring of 1945, when Jews, separated from non-Jewish fellow prisoners, were hounded from camp to camp as the Allied armies closed in on Germany. Goldhagen concentrates on one hellish march in particular, the 22-day trek from the Helmbrechts camp in Franconia to a place some 120 miles away, across the Czech border. The march "began and ended in slaughter." From the first, Jews were beaten, killed, or left to freeze, starve, and die under conditions far worse than the abominations that non-Jews suffered. All this in spite of the fact that Himmler had given orders—for his own opportunistic reasons—to cease killing Jews. The guards on this march disregarded the orally transmitted order and indulged in crazed sadism, women guards showing special cruelty. (A few Germans tried to throw the prisoners scraps of bread, but the guards brutally prevented such succor.) Goldhagen's passion finds its best expression in this and other accounts of harrowing horror. He recounts these scenes of utter inhumanity with admirable fortitude. But the ever-repeated judgment is of course less compelling: "These Germans... were voluntaristic actors... Their trueness to meting out suffering and death was not an imposed behavior; it came from within, an expression of their innermost selves."

Reviewers have commented on the originality of his treatment of the death

marches. Actually, Martin Gilbert's *Holocaust*—a book Goldhagen does not mention—gives an overview of the marches from accounts of the few survivors, focusing on the victims and not on the few known perpetrators.

All these acts of barbarism, these human enactments of the worst of Hieronymous Bosch's nightmares, were committed by Germans (and, Goldhagen notwithstanding, by non-Germans) who, according to Goldhagen, felt neither shame nor compunction. The Jew was the enemy, at once all-powerful and subhuman; the demonization had struck roots. Goldhagen wants to correct a perspective that focuses on "the desk murderers." The Holocaust was more than a bureaucratic operation; it was not the work of so many banal cogs in the wheels of evil. But while he rightly points to the thousands of individual tormentors and murderers, Goldhagen tends to underplay the powerful role of the state apparatus that gave those murderers license, one that involved the collaborative efforts of the rulers of the Reich and their servants, officials in multiple ministries, party desk officers, the government, the army, the judiciary, and the medical establishment.

Goldhagen singles out those murderers who were "ordinary Germans" and who, he insists, were motivated solely by their "cognitive model" of the Jew. He then moves from specific and harrowing examples to a grotesque extrapolation: having examined the acts of some hundreds or perhaps even thousands of people, he insists that almost all Germans were moved by the same hatred, approved the killing, would have acted in like fashion if chance had so decreed. As he writes, "... the institutions treated here... should permit the motivations of the perpetrators in those particular institutions to be uncovered, and also allow for generalizing both to the perpetrators as a group and to the second target group of this study, the German people." The leap from individual cases to the German people at large is unpersuasive, but necessary for his indictment of his "second target group."

Some 50 years ago, at the end of the war, this view of the uniqueness of German criminality was commonly held. It was once a comforting certainty that Germans and only Germans were capable of such organized atrocities—for which Goldhagen is the first to assign a single motive. But in time the interpretation of the Holocaust became more differentiated, less self-exculpatory; we also know more about atrocities today, whether in Cambodia, Biafra, or Bosnia.

Can one even try to explain the Holocaust (the horror of which for many, myself included, somehow eludes understanding) without regard to its historical context? Should one? The Inferno occurred at a given historical moment, at a time of mounting barbarism and moral indifference, which had returned to Europe in unimaginable force during the Great War, barely diminished in the interwar years, and reached an apogee during this second world war. National Socialism, we know, was at once Germany's most criminal and most popular regime, Hitler the century's most charismatic leader. The terror that he launched in Germany spread to conquered Europe: German troops of various formations extended the terror to Poland, Russia, Greece, everywhere. Thus villages were burned, hostages shot, and men, women, and children hounded, starved, separated, and killed—all that and everywhere. There were thousands of massacres in Poland, and 2.5 million Russian prisoners of war were deliberately starved to death. The links that connect this pervasive brutality to the systematic extermination of European Jewry cannot be found in specific documents or individual decisions, but can those links be doubted? Furthermore, scholars have now established that both Germans and non-Germans knew far more far earlier about the Holocaust and the atrocities in the east than was once assumed. But most of these people worried about their own predicaments and tried to preserve their complacent self-regard, their moral self-esteem, by choosing not to know or believe—a denial that has marked much of the world in our century. In brief: the Holocaust took place in the long night of organized bestiality. That is its context.

THE CONTROVERSY

Hitler's Willing Executioners and its reception in this country aroused instant concern in Germany. As early as April [1996], the German media organized extensive discussions on the book; some of the talk was favorable, as were the first reviews in America, but much of it was critical, sometimes in an ad hominem way. In early August, just before the German translation was published, *Die Zeit,* Germany's celebrated weekly, which had already given uncommon, perhaps unwarranted, attention to the book, allotted Goldhagen exceptional space to respond to what he called "The Failure of the Critics." In his response, Goldhagen attacked all his critics and rejected all their arguments—with dazzling arrogance. He accused them not only of failing to answer central questions, but even of failing to ask them: "If then they are confronted with a book that delivers precisely these answers, then they react in a rage that makes one think of people who want to silence someone because he touches on a long-preserved taboo." But these scholarly critics include precisely those liberal German historians who for decades have done the most to analyze and document the nature and atrocities of the Third Reich, who by meticulous research have established the complicity of so many German individuals and institutions, including the churches and the Wehrmacht. Goldhagen nowhere acknowledges the immense, courageous labors of these German historians and writers, who have presented their people with as stark and honest a portrait of their past as is possible—and have done so to the irritation of many "ordinary Germans" who would prefer not to be reminded of the uniqueness of that past.

Der Spiegel, which also has extensively covered the sensation that is Goldhagen, reports that the German translation (which I have not seen), with a new introduction by the author, modifies or mutes some of his more sweeping allegations. In his many interviews he has taken pains to highlight the exculpation that appears in a mere note at the end of the American edition, where he writes that he did not mean "to imply that a timeless German character exists. The character structure and the common cognitive models of Germans have developed and evolved historically and, especially since the loss of the Second World War, have changed dramatically." In his appearances in September [1996] before German audiences, Goldhagen denied ever having had the notion of collective guilt and seemed eager to attenuate such sentences in the book as "Germany during the Nazi period was inhabited by a people animated by beliefs about Jews that made them willing to become consenting mass murderers." His subject of course touched the deepest German questions of guilt and individual responsibility, and did so, apparently, in a fashion different from the book. It would seem that he tried to please his German audiences.

Hitler's Willing Executioners was a bestseller in this country, and it sold 80,000 copies in the first four weeks after its publication in Germany. Some Germans have remarked to me that whatever the book's flaws, it should be welcomed because it will reinvigorate the debate and stimulate new scholarship. *Der Spiegel* has made this same point, as has the distinguished American historian Gordon Craig. But the book also reinforces and reignites earlier prejudices: latent anti-German sentiment among Americans, especially News, and a sense among Germans that Jews have a special stake in commemorating the Holocaust, thereby keeping Germany a prisoner of its past. The book is now a major datum in German-American relations. Perhaps it could be viewed as an academic equivalent of the simplistic television series "Holocaust," which also had an enormous impact.

The astounding reception of so polemical and pretentious a book can hardly be attributed solely to its topic or thesis. Shrill and simplistic explanations of monstrous crimes obviously command attention. But there is more at work here: the author's ceaseless boast of radical originality was endorsed on the book's jacket by two well-known scholars, both distinguished in fields other than German history—and between them praising Goldhagen's work as "phenomenal scholarship and absolute integrity... impeccable scholarship, a profound understanding of modern German history...

obligatory reading." The American and German publishers touted the book with all the great promotional power at their command. Perhaps Goldhagen's manipulated, public-relations-orchestrated success tells us more about the culture of the present than the book's substance tells us about the horrors of the past.

POSTSCRIPT

Was the German National Spirit of the 1930s Responsible for the Holocaust?

The publicity engendered by Goldhagen's book has been overwhelming, both in the United States and Germany. Criticism has been strong and so have Goldhagen's rebuttals to his critics in general (see *The New Republic*, December 23, 1996) and to Stern in particular (see *Foreign Affairs*, January/February 1997). Reading these two pieces would provide an interesting and informative conclusion to the issue.

Needless to say, there have been many books written about the Holocaust. A few general sources that should be consulted are Raul Hilberg, *The Destruction of the European Jews* (Holmes & Meier, 1985); Yehuda Bauer, *A History of the Holocaust* (Franklin Watts, 1982); Martin Gilbert, *The Holocaust: A History of the Jews of Europe During the Second World War* (Holt, Rinehart & Winston, 1986); Michael Robert Marrus, *The Holocaust in History* (University Press of New England, 1987); and Arno Mayer, *Why Did the Heavens Not Darken? The "Final Solution" in History* (Pantheon Books, 1988), a fine book with a most appropriate title. Christopher R. Browning, in *Ordinary Men: Reserve Police Battalion 101 and the Final Solution in Poland* (HarperCollins, 1992), concentrates on one of the same police units as Goldhagen does and concludes that peer pressure and fear of "breaking ranks" were important factors in encouraging participation in the Holocaust by "ordinary Germans."

A recent work dealing with this issue is Saul Friedlander, *Nazi Germany and the Jews* (HarperCollins, 1997). In a chapter entitled "An Austrian Model?" the author states, "The persecution in Austria, particularly in Vienna, outpaced that in the Reich." This lends credibility to Stern's claim that virulent anti-Semitism was not uniquely a German problem, and the chapter title itself suggests that the Austrian example in dealing with its Jewish citizens may have provided a model for Hitler's future plans.

Lastly, in a book entitled *Hyping the Holocaust: Scholars Answer Goldhagen* (Cummings & Hathaway, 1997), 12 international scholars offer their criticisms of *Hitler's Willing Executioners*. In it, Goldhagen is rebuked for everything from intentional sensationalism and selective use of sources to faulty methodology and stereotyping at its worst.

ISSUE 12

Did the Soviet Union Provoke the Cold War?

YES: X, from "The Sources of Soviet Conduct," *Foreign Affairs* (July 1947)

NO: Gar Alperovitz, from *Atomic Diplomacy: Hiroshima and Potsdam: The Use of the Atomic Bomb and the American Confrontation With Soviet Power* (Pluto Press, 1994)

ISSUE SUMMARY

YES: George F. Kennan, a former high-ranking official in the U.S. Department of State, under the pseudonym "X," argues that the Soviet Union started the cold war by adopting an expansionist policy in post–World War II Europe.

NO: Gar Alperovitz, president of the National Center for Economic and Security Alternatives, contends that American policymakers acted aggressively toward the Soviet Union in 1945, secure in the knowledge that the United States had the atomic bomb and the Soviets did not.

It is difficult to say precisely when the cold war began. Certainly strains in the wartime alliance between the United States and the Soviet Union had begun to appear as early as February 1945, when President Franklin Delano Roosevelt and Soviet dictator Joseph Stalin met at Yalta to discuss the fate of postwar Europe. In April 1945 Roosevelt—who had enjoyed a relatively amicable working relationship with Stalin—suddenly died, and Harry S. Truman succeeded to the presidency. One month later, Germany surrendered, removing the primary motive for cooperation between the United States and the Soviet Union. Meanwhile, Soviet troops occupied much of central and eastern Europe, filling the vacuum left by the retreating German armies.

At the Potsdam Conference in the summer of 1945, Truman and his advisers confronted the Soviets over the future of Germany and eastern Europe. By the end of the year, relations between the United States and the Soviet Union were badly frayed. Given the losses that the Soviet Union had suffered during World War II—estimates ranged as high as 22 million casualties —Stalin seemed determined to preserve a buffer zone of friendly eastern European governments to prevent another invasion from the West. For his part, Truman wished to prevent the further spread of communism in Europe, and he pledged to send economic and military assistance to any European nation threatened by "armed minorities" (i.e., communist rebels) seeking to overthrow democratic governments. As 1947 came to a close, the cold war clearly had commenced.

In 1947 George F. Kennan was one of the Truman administration's foremost experts on the Soviet Union. He put forth his theory about Soviet conduct in an anonymous article—he identified himself only as "X" so that no one would think that the article represented an official administrative pronouncement —published in *Foreign Affairs* in July 1947. Kennan's article remains one of the clearest statements of Soviet responsibility for the start of the cold war. In the following excerpt from that article, Kennan asserts that the Soviet leaders operated under the assumption that the rest of the world was innately and implacably hostile to the Soviet Union and its communist ideology. Feeling itself constantly under attack, the Soviet Union persistently sought to extend its boundaries, to probe the Western defenses for weak points, and to expand its influence whenever and wherever possible. It was this relentlessly aggressive policy, Kennan believes, that forced the United States to respond with such measures as the Truman Doctrine and the formation of the North Atlantic Treaty Organization (NATO). Hence, the Soviet Union actually began the cold war, while the United States and its allies were simply reacting to Soviet aggression.

In the second selection, Gar Alperovitz focuses upon American policy during the summer of 1945. According to Alperovitz, Truman and his secretary of state, James F. Byrnes, were far more willing to pursue a confrontational policy than Roosevelt had been. For Alperovitz, the key to Truman's aggressiveness at the Potsdam Conference lay in his knowledge that the United States had sole possession of the atomic bomb. Until that point, Stalin seemed flexible in his policy toward eastern Europe, but Alperovitz claims that Byrnes was willing to threaten the Soviets with atomic destruction to force them to withdraw their troops from that region. Ultimately, Alperovitz sees the use of the atomic bomb at Hiroshima as directed as much against the Soviet Union as against Japan.

YES   X

THE SOURCES OF SOVIET CONDUCT

Now the outstanding circumstance concerning the Soviet régime is that down to the present day [the] process of political consolidation has never been completed and the men in the Kremlin have continued to be predominantly absorbed with the struggle to secure and make absolute the power which they seized in November 1917. They have endeavored to secure it primarily against forces at home, within Soviet society itself. But they have also endeavored to secure it against the outside world. For ideology, as we have seen, taught them that the outside world was hostile and that it was their duty eventually to overthrow the political forces beyond their borders. The powerful hands of Russian history and tradition reached up to sustain them in this feeling. Finally,their own aggressive intransigence with respect to the outside world began to find its own reaction; and they were soon forced, to us [a] Gibbonesque phrase, "to chastice the contumacy" which they themselves had provoked. It is an undeniable privilege of every man to prove himself right in the thesis that the world is his enemy; for if he reiterates it frequently enough and makes it the background of his conduct he is bound eventually to be right.

Now it lies in the nature of the mental world of the Soviet leaders, as well as in the character of their ideology, that no opposition to them can be officially recognized as having any merit or justification whatsoever. Such opposition can flow, in theory, only from the hostile and incorrigible forces of dying capitalism. As long as remnants of capitalism were officially recognized as existing in Russia, it was possible to place on them, as an internal element, part of the blame for the maintenance of a dictatorial form of society. But as these remnants were liquidated, little by little, this justification fell away; and when it was indicated officially that they had been finally destroyed, it disappeared altogether. And this fact created one of the most basic of the compulsions which came to act upon the Soviet régime: since capitalism no longer existed in Russia and since it could not be admitted that there could be serious or widespread opposition to the Kremlin springing spontaneously from the liberated masses under its authority, it became necessary to justify the retention of the dictatorship by stressing the menace of capitalism abroad.

This began at any early date. In 1924 Stalin specifically defended the retention of the "organs of suppression," meaning, among others, the army and the secret police, on the ground that "as long as there is a capitalist encirclement there will be danger of intervention with all the consequences that flow from that danger." In accordance with that theory, and from that time on, all internal opposition forces in Russia have consistently been portrayed as the agents of foreign forces of reaction antagonistic to Soviet power.

By the same token, tremendous emphasis has been placed on the original Communist thesis of a basic antagonism between the capitalist and Socialist worlds. It is clear, from many indications, that this emphasis is not founded in reality. The real facts concerning it have been confused by the existence abroad of genuine resentment provoked by Soviet philosophy and tactics and occasionally by the existence of great centers of military power, notably the Nazi régime in Germany and the Japanese Government of the late 1930's, which did indeed have aggressive designs against the Soviet Union. But there is ample evidence that the stress laid in Moscow on the menace confronting Soviet society from the world outside its borders is founded not in the realities of foreign antagonism but in the necessity of explaining away the maintenance of dictatorial authority at home.

Now the maintenance of this pattern of Soviet Power, namely, the pursuit of unlimited authority domestically, accompanied by the cultivation of the semi-myth of implacable foreign hostility, has gone far to shape the actual machinery of Soviet power as we know it today. Internal organs of administration which did not serve this purpose withered on the vine. Organs which did serve this purpose became vastly swollen. The security of Soviet power came to rest on the iron discipline of the Party, on the severity and ubiquity of the secret police, and on the uncompromising economic monopolism of the state. The "organs of suppression," in which the Soviet leaders had sought security from rival forces, became in large measure the masters of those whom they were designed to serve. Today the major part of the structure of Soviet power is committed to the perfection of the dictatorship and to the maintenance of the concept of Russia as in a state of siege, with the enemy lowering beyond the walls. And the millions of human beings who form that part of the structure of power must defend at all costs this concept of Russia's position, for without it they are themselves superfluous.

As things stand today, the rulers can no longer dream of parting with these organs of suppression. The quest for absolute power, pursued now ... with a ruthlessness unparalleled (in scope at least) in modern times, has again produced internally, as it did externally, its own reaction. The excesses of the police apparatus have fanned the potential opposition to the régime into something far greater and more dangerous than it could have been before those excesses began.

But least of all can the rulers dispense with the fiction by which the maintenance of dictatorial power has been defended. For this fiction has been canonized in Soviet philosophy by the excesses already committed in its name; and it is now anchored in the Soviet structure of thought by bonds far greater than those of mere ideology.

* * *

So much for the historical background. What does it spell in terms of the political personality of Soviet power as we know it today?

Of the original ideology, nothing has been officially junked. Belief is maintained in the basic badness of capitalism, in the inevitability of its destruction, in the obligation of the proletariat to assist in that destruction and to take power into its own hands. But stress has come to be laid primarily on those concepts which relate most specifically to the Soviet régime itself: to its position as the sole truly Socialist régime in a dark and misguided world, and to the relationships of power within it.

The first of these concepts is that of the innate antagonism between capitalism and Socialism. We have seen how deeply that concept has become imbedded in foundations of Soviet power. It has profound implications for Russia's conduct as a member of international society. It means that there can never be on Moscow's side any sincere assumption of a community of aims between the Soviet Union and powers which are regarded as capitalist. It must invariably be assumed in Moscow that the aims of the capitalist world are antagonistic to the Soviet régime, and therefore to the interests of the peoples it controls. If the Soviet Government occasionally sets its signature to documents which would indicate the contrary, this is to be regarded as a tactical manoeuvre permissible in dealing with the enemy (who is without honor) and should be taken in the spirit of *caveat emptor*. Basically, the antagonsim remains. It is postulated. And from it flow many of the phenomena which we find disturbing in the Kremlin's conduct of foreign policy: the secretiveness, the lack of frankness, the duplicity, the wary suspiciousness, and the basic unfriendliness of purpose. These phenomena are there to stay, for the forseeable future. There can be variations of degree and of emphasis. When there is something the Russians want from us, one or the other of these features of their policy may be thrust temporarily into the background; and when that happens there will always be Americans who will leap forward with gleeful announcements that "the Russians have changed," and some who will even try to take credit for having brought about such "changes." But we should not be misled by tactical manoeuvres. These characteristics of Soviet policy, like the postulate from which they flow, are basic to the internal nature of Soviet power, and will be with us, whether in the foreground or the background, until the internal nature of Soviet power is changed.

This means that we are going to continue for a long time to find the Russians difficult to deal with. It does not mean that they should be considered as embarked upon a do-or-die program to overthrow our society by a given date. The theory of the inevitability of the eventual fall of capitalism has the fortunate connotation that there is no hurry about it. The forces of progress can take their time in preparing the final *coup de grâce*. Meanwhile, what is vital is that the "Socialist fatherland"— that oasis of power which has been already won for Socialism in the person of the Soviet Union—should be cherished and defended by all good Communists at home and abroad, its fortunes promoted, its enemies badgered and confounded. The promotion of premature, "adventuristic" revolutionary projects abroad which might embarrass Soviet power in any way would be an inexcusable, even a counter-revolutionary act. The cause of Socialism is the support and promotion of Soviet power, as defined in Moscow.

This brings us to the second of the concepts important to contemporary Soviet outlook. That is the infallibility of the Kremlin. The Soviet concept of power, which permits no focal points of organization outside the Party itself, requires that the Party leadership remain in theory the sole repository of truth. For if truth were to be found elsewhere, there would be justification for its expression in organized activity. But it is precisely that which the Kremlin cannot and will not permit.

The leadership of the Communist Party is therefore always right, and has been always right ever since in 1929 Stalin formalized his personal power by announcing that decisions of the Politburo were being taken unanimously.

On the principle of infallibility there rests the iron discipline of the Communist Party. In fact, the two concepts are mutually self-supporting. Perfect discipline requires recognition of infallibility. Infallibility requires the observance of discipline. And the two together go far to determine the behaviorism of the entire Soviet apparatus of power. But their effect cannot be understood unless a third factor be taken into account: namely, the fact that the leadership is at liberty to put forward for tactical purposes any particular thesis which it finds useful to the cause at any particular moment and to require the faithful and unquestioning acceptance of that thesis by the members of the movement as a whole. This means that truth is not a constant but is actually created, for all intents and purposes, by the Soviet leaders themselves. It may vary from week to week, from month to month.

It is nothing absolute and immutable—nothing which flows from objective reality. It is only the most recent manifestation of the wisdom of those in whom the ultimate wisdom is supposed to reside, because they represent the logic of history. The accumulative effect of these factors is to give to the whole subordinate apparatus of Soviet power an unshakable stubbornness and steadfastness in its orientation. This orientation can be changed at will by the Kremlin but by no other power. Once a given party line has been laid down on a given issue of current policy, the whole Soviet governmental machine, including the mechanism of diplomacy, moves inexorably along the prescribed path, like a persistent toy automobile wound up and headed in a given direction, stopping only when it meets with some unanswerable force. The individuals who are the components of this machine are unamenable to argument or reason which comes to them from outside sources. Their whole training has taught them to mistrust and discount the glib persuasiveness of the outside world. Like the white dog before the phonograph, they hear only the "master's voice." And if they are to be called off from the purposes last dictated to them, it is the master who must call them off. Thus the foreign representative cannot hope that his words will make any impression on them. The most that he can hope is that they will be transmitted to those at the top, who are capable of changing the party line. But even those are not likely to be swayed by any normal logic in the words of the bourgeois representative. Since there can be no appeal to common purposes, there can be no appeal to common mental approaches. For this reason, facts speak louder than words to the ears of the Kremlin; and words carry the greatest weight when they have the ring of reflecting, or being backed up by, facts of unchallengeable validity.

But we have seen that the Kremlin is under no ideological compulsion to accomplish its purposes in a hurry. Like the Church, it is dealing in ideological concepts which are of long-term validity, and it can afford to be patient. It has no right to risk the existing achievements of the revolution for the sake of vain baubles of the future. The very teachings of Lenin himself require great caution and flexibility in the pursuit of Communist purposes. Again, these precepts are fortified by the lessons of Russian history: of centuries of obscure battles between nomadic forces over the stretches of a vast unfortified plain. Here caution, circumspection, flexibility and deception are the valuable qualities; and their value finds natural appreciation in the Russian or the oriental mind. Thus the Kremlin has no compunction about retreating in the face of superior force. And being under the compulsion of no timetable, it does not get panicky under the necessity for such retreat. Its political action is a fluid stream which moves constantly, wherever it is permitted to move, toward a given goal. Its main concern is to make sure that it has filled every nook and cranny available to it in the basin of world power. But if it finds unassailable barriers in its path, it accepts these philosophically and accommodates itself to them. The main thing is that there should always be pressure, unceasing constant pressure, toward the desired goal. There is no trace of any feeling in Soviet psychology that that goal must be reached at any given time.

These considerations make Soviet diplomacy at once easier and more difficult to deal with than the diplomacy of individual aggressive leaders like Napoleon and Hitler. On the one hand it is more sensitive to contrary force, more ready to yield on individual sectors of the diplomatic front when that force is felt to be too strong, and thus more rational in the logic and rhetoric of power. On the other hand it cannot be easily defeated or discouraged by a single victory on the part of its opponents. And the patient persistence by which it is animated means that it can be effectively countered not by sporadic acts which represent the momentary whims of democratic opinion but only by intelligent long-range policies on the part of Russia's adversaries— policies no less steady in their purpose, and no less variegated and resourceful in their application, than those of the Soviet Union itself.

In these circumstances it is clear that the main element of any United States policy toward the Soviet Union must be that of a long-term, patent but firm and vigilant containment of Russian expansive tendencies. It is important to note, however, that such a policy has nothing to do with outward histrionics: with threats or blustering or superfluous gestures of outward "toughness." While the Kremlin is basically flexible in its reaction to political realities, it is by no means unamenable to considerations of prestige. Like almost any other government, it can be placed by tactless and threatening gestures in a position where it cannot afford to yield even though this might be dictated by its sense of realism. The Russian leaders are keen judges of human psychology, and as such they are highly conscious that loss of temper and of self-control is never a source of strength in political affairs. They are quick to exploit such evidences of weakness. For these reasons, it is a *sine qua non* of successful dealing with Russia that the foreign government in question should remain at all times cool and collected and that its demands on Russian policy should be put forward in such a manner as to leave the way open for a compliance not too detrimental to Russian prestige....

* * *

It is clear that the United States cannot expect in the foreseeable future to enjoy political intimacy with the Soviet régime. It must continue to regard the Soviet Union as a rival, not a partner, in the political arena. It must continue to expect that Soviet policies will reflect no abstract love of peace and stability, no real faith in the possibility of a permanent happy coexistence of the Socialist and capitalist worlds, but rather a cautious, persistent pressure toward the disruption and weakening of all rival influence and rival power.

Balanced against this are the facts that Russia, as opposed to the western world in general, is still by far the weaker party, that Soviet policy is highly flexible, and that Soviet society may well contain deficiencies which will eventually weaken its own total potential. This would of itself warrant the United States entering with a reasonable confidence upon a policy of firm containment, designed to confront the Russians with unalterable counterforce at every point where they show signs of encroaching upon the interests of a peaceful and stable world.

But in actuality the possibilities for America policy are by no means limited to holding the line and hoping for the best. It is entirely possible for the United States to influence by its actions the internal developments, both within Russia and throughout the international Communist movement, by which Russian policy is largely determined. This is not only a question of the modest measure of informational activity which this government can conduct in the Soviet Union and elsewhere, although that, too, is important. It is rather a question of the degree to which the United States can create among the peoples of the world generally the impression of a country which knows what it wants, which is coping successfully with the problems of its internal life and with the responsibilities of a World Power, and which has a spiritual vitality capable of holding its own among the major ideological currents of time. To the extend that such an impression can be created and maintained, the aims of Russian Communism must appear sterile and quixotic, the hopes and enthusiasm of Moscow's supporters must wane, and added strain must be imposed on the Kremlin's foreign policies.

NO

Gar Alperovitz

ATOMIC DIPLOMACY: HIROSHIMA AND POTSDAM

BEGINNING OF THE COLD WAR

Let there be no mistake: We still do not have all the facts about the atomic bomb story; there is plenty of digging for young historians to do. However, the focal point for further research is clear, and perhaps future scholarship will give greater precision to what we know about the relationship of the destruction of Hiroshima and Nagasaki to the views top American leaders held about the weapon and diplomacy toward the Soviet Union.

Space does not permit a full treatment of the final question posed by *Atomic Diplomacy*—the role the atomic bomb played in initiating the Cold War. The book was in fact only one of a number which raised serious questions about this period, and despite continuing scholarship by many authors, many issues remain unresolved. A vast literature on the Cold War has been produced in the last two decades, and many revisionists and nonrevisionists have contributed to it.

Nor did the original book do more than suggest a point of departure for inquiry into the overall problem. Nonetheless, the fact that the major questions in dispute primarily concerned *Eastern and Central Europe* in 1945 —and not Russian expansion threatening *Western Europe* in 1947—obviously suggested a reconsideration of the dynamics of the very earliest Cold War years. Let me make only one or two observations about such issues at this point.

First, recent research on U.S. diplomacy during the early fall of 1945 has confirmed and reinforced *Atomic Diplomacy*'s argument that after the demonstration of the new weapon at Hiroshima and Nagasaki a diplomatic offensive was launched to reduce Soviet influence in Eastern Europe—and that confidence to undertake so difficult a task did in fact derive in large part from the atomic bomb. [There are Secretary of War Henry L.] Stimson diary references to [Secretary of State James F.] Byrne's desire to have the bomb "in his pocket" to back up demands for changes in Bulgaria and Rumania at the September 1945 London Council of Foreign Ministers. The work of historians

Gregg Herken and Robert Messer has provided additional documentation of the very clear linkage in Byrne's strategy between the bomb and his approach to Eastern Europe at his first post-Hiroshima encounter with the Russians.

Second, one source of confusion about this period stems from the fact that Byrne's policy failed miserably. Some writers have pointed out that no significant change was achieved—and then attempted to argue *as if this were evidence that U.S. policy did not have major change as its objective.* Others have noted that there were twists and turns in U.S. policy both during and after the period covered by *Atomic Diplomacy.* But the fact is (failure or not, and with all its convolutions, in part the result of Byrne's political problems), one of the Secretary of State's most important objectives nonetheless remained forcing the Russians to reduce their hold on Eastern Europe. Moreover, Byrnes continued to believe the atomic bomb would ultimately give the United States sufficient power to accomplish this objective: He left office complaining the Russians "don't scare"—and went on to write a book urging that the U.S. *demand* that the Soviet Union sign a German peace treaty and withdraw from Central and Eastern Europe. " . . . I do not believe it is wise to suggest a course of action unless one is willing to carry it through . . . ," Byrnes observed. "We should not start something we are not prepared to finish." If the Russians refused to cooperate with his approach, Byrnes proposed the United States should then use "measures of the last resort" to compel them to comply. It is often forgotten that James F. Byrnes was one of the most highly placed of those who recommended a "preventive war" during the period when the United States had a nuclear monopoly if

this were the only way to achieve diplomatic objectives it deemed important.

But this takes us well beyond September 1945, the point at which *Atomic Diplomacy* ends. Nevertheless, in a very fundamental sense, the impact of the basic conceptions which informed policy in the early postwar months did not disappear. As Walter Lippmann observed in 1947, U.S. diplomacy "became confused, lost sight of the primary and essential objective" when it "became entangled in all manner of secondary issues and disputes in the Russian borderlands."

Lippmann's early postwar analysis (published initially as articles responding to the famous "Mr X" containment thesis) still offers a fruitful way to approach a number of problems which have their origins in the early 1945 period. Lippmann's overall argument did not concern malevolence or evil intention. It focused instead on the *situational logic* of American-Soviet relations in Europe. One of Lippmann's fundamental criticisms of U.S. policy was that in 1945 and 1946 it attempted to force the Soviets to relax their grip on Easter Europe *before there was agreement on what to do about postwar Germany.* To the degree the United States tried to resolve Eastern European matters while fears about Germany were still unsettled, Lippmann suggested, the Russians were bound to tighten their hold. Conversely, if there was ever to be a chance of gaining a more flexible Soviet policy in Eastern Europe, the German question had to be resolved first.

I believe the most important effect of the atomic bomb on major European issues was that *from the very start* it altered four aspects of American diplomatic-strategic thinking:

First, the new weapon gave U.S. policy makers confidence that the United States alone had full power to handle postwar Germany: *From the American point of view*, Germany seemed unlikely ever again to be a threat. Instantaneously, the Russians were no longer required to deal with what had until then been the single most important problem worrying American policy makers. As Joseph Davies noted at Potsdam, "because of the New Mexico development [Byrnes] felt secure anyway."

This is perhaps the least recognized shift in strategy brought about by the new technology. Perhaps it is understandable: Things changed so quickly!

American leaders had anticipated the public would likely require the withdrawal of most U.S. troops from the Continent after the war—and until the atomic bomb was proved, the Russians were needed, for better or worse, to a greater or lesser extent to jointly insure against a renewed German threat. Policy makers *may have wanted to* challenge the understandings which Roosevelt had reached with Stalin, but there were limits to the extent to which this could be done.

From the Russian point of view, if the potential German threat were resolved in cooperation with the United States, as Lippmann believed (correctly in my judgment), there were reasons, including possible postwar assistance, for them to try to work out the difficulties which existed. This is not to say there would not have been difficulties with the Soviet Union, or that everything would have worked out well. But it is also not reasonable to assume that the sterility of the Cold War as we know it was an absolute historical inevitability. Austria and Finland, in different ways,

offer suggestive illustrations of other possibilities.

Second, from the American point of view, Germany could even be built up, partly to solve obvious economic problems, partly as a counterweight to the Soviets. There simply was no need to worry. Slowly at first, then faster, U.S. policy rebuilt the economic and then the military power of Germany—a move which, whatever its motivations, nonetheless threatened the Russians, who did not have atomic weapons to protect them.

Third, as we have seen, the atomic bomb gave American policy makers confidence they had sufficient power to attempt to undo the Yalta understandings. Byrnes was quite aware that Roosevelt had conceded substantial control of Eastern Europe to the Soviets, whatever some U.S. policy makers might have wished. Nevertheless, Byrne's strategy was to press for implementation of the vague Declaration on Liberated Europe, which generally promised democratic elections, *even though he understood this to be a contravention of the more specific understandings.* In so doing, U.S. policy created fears that the Soviet Union would be weakened in an area vital to its security at the same time it simultaneously began to rebuild Germany.

Finally, of course, the bomb itself was a threat. Immediately after the failure of Byrne's policy at the London Council of Foreign Ministers, Truman announced that the United States was not interested in serious efforts to achieve international control of nuclear weapons. At Reelfoot Lake in Tennessee the President called a press conference just after the meeting's close to state pointedly that if other nations were to "catch up" with the

United States, "they [would] have to do it on their own hook, just as we did." A few days later in a private conversation with a lifelong Missouri friend, Truman acknowledged full awareness of the implications of his decision. He agreed, he said, with his friend's comment: "Then Mister President, what it amounts to is this. That the armaments race is on...."

Any serious analysis of the beginnings of the Cold War, I believe, requires an assessment of these factors—none of which is comprehensible without recognition of the dramatic impact the atomic bomb had on American policy makers....

[My analysis] begins in the spring of 1945, a time when postwar problems unfolded as rapidly as the Allied armies converged in Central Europe. During the fighting which preceded Nazi surrender the Red Army conquered a great belt of territory bordering the Soviet Union. Debating the consequences of this fact, American policy makers defined a series of interrelated problems: What political and economic pattern was likely to emerge in Eastern and Central Europe? Would Soviet influence predominate? Most important, what power—if any— did the United States have to effect the ultimate settlement on the very borders of Russia?

Roosevelt, Churchill, and Stalin had attempted to resolve these issues of East-West influence at the February 1945 Yalta Conference. With the Red Army clearly in control, the West was in a weak bargaining position. It was important to reach an understanding with Stalin before American troops began their planned withdrawal from the Continent, Poland, the first major country intensely discussed by the Big Three, took on unusual significance; the balance of

influence struck between Soviet-oriented and Western-oriented politicians in the government of this one country could set a pattern for big-power relationships in the rest of Eastern Europe.

Although the Yalta Conference ended with a signed accord covering Poland, within a few weeks it was clear that Allied understanding was more apparent than real. None of the heads of government interpreted the somewhat vague agreement in the same way. Churchill began to press for more Western influence; Stalin urged less. True to his well-known policy of cooperation and conciliation, Roosevelt attempted to achieve a more definite understanding for Poland and a pattern for East-West relations in Europe. Caught for much of the last of his life between the determination of Churchill and the stubbornness of Stalin, Roosevelt at times fired off angry cables to Moscow, and at others warned London against an "attempt to evade the fact that we placed, as clearly shown in the agreement, somewhat more emphasis... [on Soviet-oriented Polish politicians in the government]."

Roosevelt died on April 12, 1945, only two months after Yalta. When Truman met with Secretary Stimson to discuss the "bearing" of the atomic bomb upon foreign relations, the powers were deeply ensnarled in a tense public struggle over the meaning of the Yalta agreement. Poland had come to symbolize all East-West relations. Truman was forced to pick up the tangled threads of policy with little knowledge of the broader, more complex issues involved....

Herbert Feis, a noted expert on the period, has written that "Truman made up his mind that he would not depart from Roosevelt's course or renounce his ways." Others have argued that "we tried to work out the problems of the peace in close cooperation with the Russians." It is often believed that American policy followed a conciliatory course, changing—in reaction to Soviet intransigence—only in 1947 with the Truman Doctrine and the Marshall Plan. My own belief is somewhat different. It derives from the comment of Truman's Secretary of State that by early autumn of 1945 it was "understandable" that Soviet leaders should feel American policy had shifted radically after Roosevelt's death: It is now evident that, far from following his predecessor's policy of cooperation, shortly after taking office Truman launched a powerful foreign policy initiative aimed at reducing or eliminating Soviet influence from Europe. . . .

The ultimate point of this study is now, however, that America's approach to Russia changed after Roosevelt. Rather it is that the atomic bomb played a role in the formulation of policy, particularly in connection with Truman's only meeting with Stalin, the Potsdam Conference of late July and early August 1945. Again, my judgment differs from Feis's conclusion that "the light of the explosion 'brighter than a thousand suns' filtered into the conference rooms at Potsdam only as a distant gleam." I believe new evidence proves not only that the atomic bomb influenced diplomacy, but that it determined much of Truman's shift to a tough policy aimed at forcing Soviet acquiescence to American plans for Eastern and Central Europe. The weapon "gave him an entirely new feeling of confidence," the President told his Secretary of War. By the time of Potsdam Truman had been advised on the role of the atomic bomb by both Secretary Stimson and Secretary of State

Byrnes. Though the two men differed as to tactics, each urged a tough line. . . .

A study of American policy in the very early days of the Cold War must inevitably deal with Soviet actions and reactions. . . . Stalin's approach seems to have been cautiously moderate during the brief few months here described. It is perhaps symbolized by the Soviet-sponsored free elections which routed the Communist Party in Hungary in the autumn of 1945. . . .

The judgment that Truman radically altered Roosevelt's policy in mid-1945 nevertheless obviously suggests a new point of departure for interpretations of the Cold War. In late 1945 General Eisenhower observed in Moscow that "before the atom bomb was used, I would have said, yes, I was sure we could keep the peace with Russia. Now I don't know . . . People are frightened and disturbed all over. Everyone feels insecure again." To what extend did postwar Soviet policies derive from insecurity based upon a fear of America's atom bomb and changed policy? [F]urther research is needed to test Secretary Stimson's judgment that "the problem of our satisfactory relations with Russia [was] not merely connected with but [was] virtually dominated by the problem of the atomic bomb . . ."

Byrnes Firmly pressed his demand that the Bulgarian and Rumanian governments be changed, but when Molotov refused to yield at London, the first peacetime meeting of foreign ministers broke down completely—it was impossible even to agree upon a joint protocol recording the failure. The initial climax of the post-Hiroshima struggle was a continued and open deadlock. "We had come to the cossroads," Byrnes recalls. In forcing a public break over the issue, the Secretary of State's action was intended to be symbolic. As in the Polish dispute in April, American policy aimed not only at a favorable resolution of the specific points at issue, but at a reconsideration of fundamental political and economic arrangements throughout the Soviet-controlled zone of Europe—"Only by refusing to bow to Soviet domination could we establish sound relations for the future."

Byrnes has written that "our attitude was a shock to them," and it is certain, as both he and John Foster Dulles (who assisted the Secretary of State at London) have emphasized, that postwar Soviet-American tension must be dated from the London Conference. It is also undoubtedly true that the atomic bomb not only influenced the attitude American policy makers took in their approach to the confrontation, but also, as Prime Minister Attlee cabled to President Truman at the time, the weapon completely overshadowed the discussions....

The most important point is the most general: Contrary to a commonly held view, it is abundantly clear that the atomic bomb profoundly influenced the way American policy makers viewed political problems. Or, as Admiral [William D.] Leahy has neatly summarized the point, "One factor that was to change a lot of ideas, including my own, was the atom bomb..." The change caused by the new weapon was quite specific. It did not produce American opposition to Soviet policies in Eastern Europe and Manchuria. Rather, since a consensus had already been reached on the need to take a firm stand against the Soviet Union in both areas, the atomic bomb *confirmed* American leaders in their judgment that they had sufficient power to affect developments in the border regions of the Soviet Union. There is both truth and precision

in Truman's statement to Stimson that the weapon "gave him an entirely new feeling of confidence."

This effect was a profoundly important one. Before the atomic bomb was tested, despite their desire to oppose Soviet policies, Western policy makers harbored very grave doubts that Britain and America could challenge Soviet predominance in Eastern Europe. Neither Roosevelt nor Truman could have confidence that the American public would permit the retention of large numbers of conventional troops in Europe after the war. (And Congressional rejection of Truman's military-training program later confirmed the pessimistic wartime predictions.) Thus, at the time of the Yalta Conference, as Assistant Secretary of State William L. Clayton advised Secretary Stettinius, "a large credit... appear[ed] to be the only concrete bargaining lever for use in connection with the many other political and economic problems which will arise between our two countries."

That this lever of diplomacy was not sufficiently powerful to force Soviet acceptance of American proposals was amply demonstrated during the late-April and early-May crisis over Poland. Despite Truman's judgment that "the Russians needed us more than we needed them," Stalin did not yield to the firm approach. Hence, without the atomic bomb it seemed exceedingly doubtful that American policy makers would be able substantially to affect events within the Soviet-occupied zone of Europe. It may well be that, had there been no atomic bomb, Truman would have been forced to reconsider the basic direction of his policy as Churchill had done some months earlier.

Indeed, Churchill's 1944 estimate of the power realities usefully illuminates the problems faced by Western policy makers as they attempted to judge their relative strength vis-à-vis the Soviet Union. As soon as Roosevelt rejected Churchill's desperate pleas for an invasion through the Balkans, the Prime Minister understood that he would have little power in Southeastern Europe, and that, indeed, the British position in Greece was seriously threatened. As he told Roosevelt, "the only way I can prevent [utter anarchy] is by persuading the Russians to quit boosting [the Communist-oriented] E. A. M." Again, there was overwhelming logic in his parallel 1944 argument: "It seems to me, considering the Russians are about to invade Rumania in great force ... it would be a good thing to follow the Soviet leadership, considering that neither you nor we have any troops there at all and that they will probably do what they like anyhow." As he later recalled, before the atomic test, "the arrangements made about the Balkans were, I was sure, the best possible."

As I have attempted to show, by the time of the Yalta Conference, somewhat reluctantly, and against the wishes of the State Department, Roosevelt came to the same conclusion. Even the State Department was forced to adopt the official view that "this Government probably would not oppose predominant Soviet influence in [Poland and the Balkans]." And one high-ranking official went beyond this judgment; substituting this concern for Western Europe for the Prime Minister's specific fears about Greece, he stated: "I am willing to sponsor and support the Soviet arguments if it will save ... the rest of Europe from the diplomacy of the jungle which is almost certain to ensue otherwise." As Truman's Balkan representative recalled the Yalta Conference, it was "fateful that these discussions should have been held at a time when Soviet bargaining power in eastern Europe was so much stronger than that of the western allies." But it remained for Byrnes to summarize the early-1945 relative strengths of the powers: "It was not a question of what we would *let* the Russians do, but what we could *get* them to do."

As I have shown, this appraisal was radically changed by the summer of 1945. Since Byrnes advised Truman on both the atomic bomb and the need for strong opposition to the Russians in Eastern Europe before the President's first confrontation with Molotov, the new weapon's first impact possibly can be seen as early as the April showdown. However, no final judgment can be rendered on this point, using the evidence presently available. But there is no question that by the middle of July leading American policy makers were convinced that the atomic bomb would permit the United States to take a "firm" stand in subsequent negotiations. In fact, American leaders felt able to demand *more* at Potsdam that they had asked at Yalta. Again, Churchill's post-atomic appraisal is in striking contrast to his view of the pre-atomic realities: "We now had something in our hands which would redress the balance with the Russians." And Byrne's new advice to Truman was quite straightforward: "The bomb might well put us in a position to dictate our own terms...."

Once the profound impact of the atomic bomb upon American judgments is recognized, considerable light is cast upon the complicated events of the summer of 1945. The curious reversals in American Polish policy and the Hopkins mission [in which Truman sent emissary Harry Hopkins to Moscow to work out the details for the Potsdam Conference] both become understandable. The period is one in which two groups of officials debated strategy. Although there were differences of emphasis, since all agreed on the broad objective of attempting to force the Soviet Union into cooperative relationships in Eastern and Central Europe, the real struggle was over timing. Those outside the War Department who had little knowledge or little faith in the as yet untested atomic weapon argued that an immediate showdown was necessary. In this their views paralleled Churchill's, who, having come to terms on the Balkans, feared a further weakening of Western determination, combined with a withdrawal of American troops, would convince Stalin time was on his side if he dug in while the West melted away.

Secretary Stimson, however, was able to counter this argument in two ways: He was able to show that conventional strength on the Continent would not be substantially reduced during the two months' delay until the atomic test; and he wa able to promise that if a confrontation could be postponed the United States would soon be possessed of "decisive" powers. After forcing a premature showdown on the symbolic Polish issue, Truman reversed himself and accepted Stimson's broad strategy. The price he paid for delay was not high; he was forced to yield the substance of the point at issue in the Polish controversy, and he had to withdraw American troops to the agreed zonal positions in Germany. Significantly, he later characterized his first attempt to utilize economic bargaining strength through the Lend-Lease cutoff as a "mistake." From Truman's point of view,

not only was the first showdown badly timed, but the need to reverse his public position and to send Hopkins on a mission of conciliation must have been a great personal embarrassment.

However, it is vital to recognize that Truman's conciliatory actions during late May, June, and early July did not represent his basic policy. He had demonstrated in the April showdown and in the decision to maintain American troop positions in Germany that his view of how to treat with Russia was far different from Roosevelt's. His decision abruptly to cut off Lend-Lease, his show of force over the Trieste dispute, his reconsideration of Roosevelt's Far Eastern agreement, his breach of the Balkans understandings, his refusal to adhere to the Yalta reparations accord —all these acts testify to the great gulf between his view and the view of his predecessor.

Those who argue that "Mr. Truman intended to continue the policy laid down by President Roosevelt" have focused attention on an extremely brief period when Truman did indeed adopt a more moderate approach. But his actions during this period—symbolized by his attempt to avoid the appearance of "ganging up" with Britain against the Soviet Union—were only a manifestation of his tactical retreat. In a fundamental sense, even the conciliatory period can only be explained by recognizing that its primary purpose was not to continue Roosevelt's policy, but to facilitate a far different policy based upon the overwhelming power soon to be available. Truman replaced the symbolic April showdown over Poland with a parallel August and September effort in the Balkans. Both before and after the brief conciliatory period, the President's attitude is best summed up on the statement he made eight days after Roosevelt's death: He "intended to be firm with the Russians and make no concessions." And both before and after the temporary period of no "ganging up," Truman's effort to coordinate policy with Britain was a hallmark of his approach. As Byrnes has written, Molotov's conclusion that American policy had changed after Roosevelt's death was "understandable."

POSTSCRIPT

Did the Soviet Union Provoke the Cold War?

The cold war and the subsequent rise of anticommunist hysteria in the United States dominated American politics for several decades. Confronted by an enemy that represented both a strategic and an ideological threat, the American people quickly developed a deep and pervasive sense of insecurity. A series of events in 1949–1950—the victory of Mao Zedong's communist forces in China, the Soviet Union's explosion of its first nuclear test device, and the outbreak of the Korean War—deepened American fears. The result was the age of "McCarthyism," when anticommunist politicians, led by Republican senator Joseph McCarthy of Wisconsin, sought to rid the United States of left-wing influences.

A large measure of this anticommunist crusade was motivated by a desire to advance the fortunes of the Republican Party. Indeed, Democratic Party officials were so scarred by the events of the early cold war period that they felt a persistent need to prove that they, too, could be tough on communism. Hence, the Democratic administrations of John F. Kennedy and Lyndon B. Johnson led the United States into a deep and disastrous military involvement in Vietnam to avoid any charges that they had allowed another Asian nation to succumb to communism. And not until Richard Nixon—a Republican with sterling anticommunist credentials—succeeded to the presidency did the United States deign to recognize the communist government of the People's Republic of China.

The collapse of the Soviet Empire (and the Soviet Union itself) in 1989–1991 brought an end to the cold war, but the historical debate over the origins of the conflict continue. Two of the best recent studies are Melvyn P. Leffler's *Preponderance of Power: National Security, the Truman Administration, and the Cold War* (Stanford University Press, 1992) and *The United States and the End of the Cold War* by John Lewis Gaddis (Oxford University Press, 1992). In *The Winning Weapon: The Atomic Bomb in the Cold War, 1945–1950* (Alfred A. Knopf, 1980), Gregg Herken expands upon Alperovitz's thesis. An excellent summary is Thomas G. Paterson's *On Every Front: The Making of the Cold War* (W. W. Norton, 1979).

ISSUE 13

Does Islamic Revivalism Threaten a Secular World Order?

YES: John L. Esposito, from *The Islamic Threat: Myth or Reality?* 2d ed. (Oxford University Press, 1995)

NO: Albert Hourani, from *A History of the Arab Peoples* (Belknap Press, 1991)

ISSUE SUMMARY

YES: Professor of Middle East studies John L. Esposito sees the Iranian Revolution against Western-inspired modernization and Egypt's "holy war" against Israel as examples of the Islamic quest for a more authentic society and culture, which challenges a stable world order.

NO: Albert Hourani, an emeritus fellow of St. Antony's College, Oxford, finds hope for a stable world order in modern Islam's moderate position, which blends the traditional religious commitment to social justice with a more secular strain of morality and law.

For many Westerners the adjective *Islamic* seems to be linked inexorably with either *fundamentalist* or *terrorist*. Particularly since the Islamic revolution of 1978–1979 in Iran, images of Western hostages and calls for a *jihad*, or holy war, have created a climate of fear and mistrust between the West and Islam. Are the two on a collision course, rooted in history and driven by an absolute incompatibility of beliefs and lifestyles? Or can Islam play a role in a stable world order that affirms Islam's own tradition while accommodating secularism and pluralism?

Because Islam sees itself as the fulfillment of both Judaism and Christianity —as the final word of God for human beings—it has from the beginning sought to spread its truth throughout the world. In the tradition of jihad, those who died in the attempt to bring Islam to nonbelievers were ensured a place in paradise. Early successes came during Europe's Dark Ages. Muslim learning and culture were more advanced, and it was only natural for conquering armies to assume that their religion enjoyed a comparable superiority. Unlike Christianity, Islam gained secular power within the founder Muhammad's lifetime (c. 570–632), and the rulers that followed him, known as caliphs, combined secular and religious power. There could be no conflict between church and state because the church and the state were one.

For many Muslims in the modern world, the political and military domination of the West has brought a secularism that is repugnant to all they hold sacred. They fear that Westerners—with their lack of respect for traditional authority, their emancipated and exploited women, and their shallow and materialistic values—appear to have won. Becoming modern is generally equated with embracing the consumer culture and values of the West. When the Shah of Iran Muhammad Reza Pahlavi imposed a Western revolution on his country in the 1970s, he disregarded Muslim leaders and repressed all resistance. The result was an Islamic backlash that deposed the Shah and installed in his place the Ayatollah Ruholla Khomeini, a rigid religious authority figure who demanded obedience to the teachings of the prophet Muhammad. The question seems to be whether or not Islamic countries can modernize without giving up their core values and embracing those of the West.

In the following selection, historian John L. Esposito notes that the clout provided by oil has brought the Islamic Middle East into the world economy and given it the power to be a significant player in either supporting or destabilizing a peaceful world order. However, the Western concept of religion as a system of belief and worship that remains separate from most of the rest of secular life is incomprehensible to traditional Muslims. Believing that Islam has superseded both Judaism and Christianity calls Muslims to impose the law of God on all the world. In the search for an authentic Islamic culture, Esposito concludes, Muslims present a strong challenge to the political and cultural values of the West.

In the second selection, Albert Hourani contends that between a total rejection of Islam in fashioning a modern state and the belief that Islamic heritage is uniquely qualified to provide the basis lies a third alternative: accepting that the prophet Muhammad received his revelation during a particular historical context might enable modern Islamic scholars to adapt religious truth to the demands of modern life. In a continuing dialogue between past and present, the Qur'an might speak to the modern world. It is this moderate position, asserts Hourani, that offers a role for Islam in a stable world order.

YES

John L. Esposito

THE ISLAMIC THREAT: MYTH OR REALITY?

Are Islam and the West on an inevitable collision course? Are Islamic fundamentalists medieval fanatics? Are Islam and democracy incompatible? Is Islamic fundamentalism a threat to stability in the Muslim world and to American interests in the region? These are critical questions for our times that come from a history of mutual distrust and condemnation.

From the Ayatollah Khomeini to Saddam Hussein, for more than a decade the vision of Islamic fundamentalism or militant Islam as a threat to the West has gripped the imaginations of Western governments and the media. Khomeini's denunciation of America as the "Great Satan," chants of "Death to America," the condemnation of Salman Rushdie and his *Satanic Verses*, and Saddam Hussein's call for a jihad against foreign infidels have reinforced images of Islam as a militant, expansionist religion, rabidly anti-American and intent upon war with the West.

Despite many common theological roots and beliefs, throughout history Muslim-Christian relations have often been overshadowed by conflict as the armies and missionaries of Islam and Christendom have struggled for power and for souls. This confrontation has involved such events as the defeat of the early Byzantine (eastern Roman) empire by Islam in the seventh century; the fierce battles and polemics of the Crusades during the eleventh and twelfth centuries; the expulsion of the Moors from Spain and the Inquisition; the Ottoman threat to Europe; European (Christian) colonial expansion and domination in the eighteenth and nineteenth centuries; the political and cultural challenge of the superpowers (America and the Soviet Union) in the latter half of the twentieth century; the creation of the state of Israel; the competition of Christian and Muslim missionaries for converts in Africa today; and the contemporary reassertion of Islam in politics.

"Islamic fundamentalism" has often been regarded as a major threat to the regional stability of the Middle East and to Western interests in the broader Muslim world. The Iranian Revolution, attacks on Western embassies, hijackings and hostage taking, and violent acts by groups with names like the Army of God (Jund Allah), Holy War (al-Jihad), the Party of God (Hizbullah), and

From *The Islamic Threat: Myth or Reality?* second edition by John L. Esposito. Copyright © 1992, 1995 by John L. Esposito. Used by permission of Oxford University Press, Inc. Notes omitted.

Salvation from Hell have all signaled a militant Islam on a collision course with the West. Uprisings in the Muslim republics of the Soviet Union, in Kosovo in Yugoslavia, in Indian Kashmir, in Sinkiang in China, and on the West Bank and in Gaza, and more recently, Saddam Hussein's attempted annexation of Kuwait, have reinforced images of an expansive and potentially explosive Islam in global politics.

With the triumph of the democratization movement in Eastern Europe and the breakup of the Soviet empire, Islam constitutes the most pervasive and powerful transnational force in the world, with one billion adherents spread out across the globe. Muslims are a majority in some forty-five countries ranging from Africa to Southeast Asia, and they exist in growing and significant numbers in the United States, the Soviet Union, and Europe. For a Western world long accustomed to a global vision and foreign policy predicated upon superpower rivalry for global influence if not dominance—a U.S.–Soviet conflict often portrayed as a struggle between good and evil, capitalism and communism—it is all too tempting to identify another global ideological menace to fill the "threat vacuum" created by the demise of communism.

However diverse in reality, the existence of Islam as a worldwide religion and ideological force embracing one fifth of the world's population, and its continued vitality and power in a Muslim world stretching from Africa to Southeast Asia, will continue to raise the specter of an Islamic threat....

As Western leaders attempt to forge the New World Order, transnational Islam may increasingly come to be regarded as the new global monolithic enemy of the West: "To some Americans, searching

for a new enemy against whom to test our mettle and power, after the death of communism, Islam is the preferred antagonist. But, to declare Islam an enemy of the United States is to declare a second Cold War that is unlikely to end in the same resounding victory as the first." Fear of the Green Menace (green being the color of Islam) may well replace that of the Red Menace of world communism.

Islam and Islamic movements constitute a religious and ideological alternative or challenge and in some instances a potential danger to Christianity and the West. However, distinguishing between a religious or ideological alternative or challenge and a direct political threat requires walking the fine line between myth and reality, between the unity of Islam and the diversity of its multiple and complex manifestations in the world today, between the violent actions of the few and the legitimate aspirations and policies of the many. Unfortunately, American policymakers, like the media, have too often proved surprisingly myopic, viewing the Muslim world and Islamic movements as a monolith and seeing them solely in terms of extremism and terrorism. While this is understandable in light of events in Iran and Lebanon and the Gulf crisis of 1990–91, it fails to do justice to the complex realities of the Muslim world and can undermine relations between the West and Islam....

THE ISLAMIC RESURGENCE

Islam reemerged as a potent global force in Muslim politics during the 1970s and 1980s. The scope of the Islamic resurgence has been worldwide, embracing much of the Muslim world from the Sudan to Indonesia. Heads of Muslim governments as well as opposition groups increasingly appealed to religion for legitimacy and to mobilize popular support. Islamic activists have held cabinet-level positions in Jordan, the Sudan, Iran, Malaysia, and Pakistan. Islamic organizations constitute the leading opposition parties and organizations in Egypt, Tunisia, Algeria, Morocco, the West Bank and Gaza, and Indonesia. Where permitted, they have participated in elections and served in parliament and in city government. Islam has been a significant ingredient in nationalist struggles and resistance movements in Afghanistan, the Muslim republics of the former Soviet Central Asia, and Kashmir, and in the communal politics of Lebanon, India, Thailand, China, and the Philippines.

Islamically oriented governments have been counted among America's staunchest allies (Saudi Arabia and Pakistan) and most vitriolic enemies (Libya and Iran). Islamic activist organizations have run the spectrum from those who work within the system—such as the Muslim Brotherhoods in Egypt, Jordan, and the Sudan—to radical revolutionaries like Egypt's Society of Muslims (known more popularly as Takfir wal-Hijra, Excommunication and Flight) and al-Jihad (Holy War), or Lebanon's Hizbullah (Party of God) and Islamic Jihad, which have resorted to violence in their attempts to overthrow prevailing political systems.

Yet to speak of a contemporary Islamic revival can be deceptive, if this implies that Islam had somehow disappeared or been absent from the Muslim world. It is more correct to view Islamic revivalism as having led to a higher profile of Islam in Muslim politics and society. Thus what bad previously seemed to be an increasingly marginalized force in Muslim public life reemerged in the seventies—often dramatically—as a vibrant sociopolitical reality. Islam's resurgence in Muslim politics reflected a growing religious revivalism in both personal and public life that would sweep across much of the Muslim world and have a substantial impact on the West in world politics.

The indices of an Islamic reawakening in personal life are many: increased attention to religious observances (mosque attendance, prayer, fasting), proliferation of religious programming and publications, more emphasis upon Islamic dress and values, the revitaliztion of Sufism (mysticism). This broader-based renewal has also been accompanied by Islam's reassertion in public life: an increase in Islamically oriented governments, organizations, laws, banks, social welfare services, and educational institutions. Both governments and opposition movements have turned to Islam to enhance their authority and muster popular support. Governmental use of Islam has been illustrated by a great spectrum of leaders in the Middle East and Asia: Libya's Muammar Qaddafi, Sudan's Gaafar Muhammad Nimeiri, Egypt's Anwar Sadat, Iran's Ayatollah Khomeini, Pakistan's Zia ul-Haq, Bangladesh's Muhammad Ershad, Malaysia's Muhammad Mahathir. Most rulers and governments, including more secular states such as Turkey and Tunisia, becoming aware of the potential strength of Islam, have shown increased sensitivity to and anxiety about Islamic issues. The Iranian Revolution of 1978–79 focused attention on "Islamic fundamentalism" and with it the spread and vitality of political Islam in other parts of the Muslim world. However, the contemporary revival has its origins and roots in the late sixties and early seventies, when events in such disparate areas as Egypt and Libya as well as Pakistan and Malaysia contributed to experiences of crisis and failure, as well as power and success, which served as catalysts for a more visible reassertion of Islam in both public and private life.

THE EXPERIENCE OF FAILURE AND THE QUEST FOR IDENTITY

Several conflicts (e.g., the 1967 Arab–Israeli war, Chinese–Malay riots in Malaysia in 1969, the Pakistan–Bangladesh civil war of 1971, and the Lebanese civil war of the midseventies) illustrate the breadth and diversity of these turning points or catalysts for change. For many in the Arab and broader Muslim world, 1967 proved to be a year of catastrophe as well as a historic turning point. Israel's quick and decisive defeat of Arab forces in what was remembered as the Six-Day War, the Israeli capture and occupation of the Golan Heights, Sinai, Gaza, the West Bank, and East Jerusalem, constituted a devastating blow to Arab/Muslim pride, identity, and self-esteem. Most important, the loss of Jerusalem, the third holiest city of Islam, assured that Palestine and the liberation of Jerusalem would not be regarded as a regional (Arab) issue but rather as an Islamic cause throughout the Muslim world. The defense of Israel is dear to many Jews throughout the world. Likewise, for Muslims who retain a sense of membership in a transnational community of believers (the *ummah*), Palestine and the liberation of Jerusalem are strongly seen as issues of Islamic solidarity. As anyone who works in the Muslim world can attest, Israeli control of the West Bank, Gaza, and Jerusalem as well as U.S.–Israeli relations are topics of concern and bitter debate among Muslims from Nigeria and the Sudan to Pakistan and Malaysia, as well as among the Muslims of Europe and the United States.

The aftermath of the 1967 war, remembered in Arab literature as the "disaster," witnessed a sense of disillusionment and soul-searching that gripped both Western-oriented secular elites as well as the more Islamically committed, striking at their sense of pride, identity, and history. Where had they gone wrong? Both the secular and the Islamically oriented sectors of society now questioned the effectiveness of nationalist ideologies, Western models of development, and Western allies who had persisted in supporting Israel. Despite several decades of independence and modernization, Arab forces (consisting of the combined military might of Egypt, Jordan, and Syria) had proved impotent. A common critique of the military, political, and sociocultural failures of Western-oriented development and a quest for a more authentic society and culture emerged—an Arab identity less dependent upon the West and rooted more indigenously in an Arab/Islamic heritage and values. Examples from Malaysia, Pakistan, and Lebanon reflect the turmoil and soul-searching that occurred in many parts of the Muslim world....

FROM FAILURE TO SUCCESS

During the seventies Islamic politics seemed to explode on the scene, as events in the Middle East (the Egyptian–Israeli war and the Arab oil embargo of 1973, as well as the Iranian Revolution of 1978–79) shocked many into recognition of a powerful new force that threatened Western interests. Heads of state and opposition movements appealed to Islam to enhance their legitimacy and popular support; Islamic organizations and institutions proliferated.

In 1973 Egypt's Anwar Sadat initiated a "holy war" against Israel. In contrast to the 1967 Arab–Israeli war which was fought by Gamal Abdel Nasser in the name of Arab nationalism/socialism, this war was fought under the banner of Islam. Sadat generously employed Islamic symbols and history to rally his forces. Despite their loss of the war, the relative success of Egyptian forces led many Muslims to regard it as a moral victory, since most had believed that a U.S.-backed Israel could not be beaten.

Military vindication in the Middle East was accompanied by economic muscle, the power of the Arab oil boycott. For the first time since the dawn of colonialism, the West had to contend with and acknowledge, however begrudgingly, its dependence on the Middle East. For many in the Muslim world the new wealth, success, and power of the oil-rich countries seemed to indicate a return of the power of Islam to a community whose centuries-long political and cultural ascendence had been shattered by European colonialism and, despite independence, by second-class status in a superpower-dominated world. A number of factors enhanced the Islamic character of oil power. Most of the oil wealth was located in the Arab heartland, where Muhammad had received the revelation of the Quran and established the first Islamic community-state. The largest deposits were found in Saudi Arabia, a self-styled Islamic state which had asserted its role as keeper of the holy cities of Mecca and Medina, protector of the annual pilgrimage (*hajj*), and leader and benefactor of the Islamic world. The House of Saud used its oil wealth to establish numerous international Islamic organizations, promote the preaching and spread of Islam, support Islamic causes, and subsidize Is-

lamic activities undertaken by Muslim governments.

No event demonstrated more dramatically the power of a resurgent Islam than the Iranian Revolution of 1978–79. For many in the West and the Muslim world, the unthinkable became a reality. The powerful, modernizing, and Western-oriented regime of the Shah came crashing down. This was an oil-rich Iran whose wealth had been used to build the best-equipped military in the Middle East (next to Israel's) and to support an ambitious modernization program, the Shah's White Revolution. Assisted by Western-trained elites and advisers, the Shah had governed a state which the United States regarded as its most stable ally in the Muslim world. The fact that a revolution against him and against the West was effectively mounted in the name of Islam, organizing disparate groups and relying upon the mullah–mosque network for support, generated euphoria among many in the Muslim world and convinced Islamic activists that these were lessons for success to be emulated. Strength and victory would belong to those who pursued change in the name of Islam, whatever the odds and however formidable the regime.

For many in the broader Muslim world, the successes of the seventies resonated with an idealized perception of early Islam, the Islamic paradigm to be found in the time of the Prophet Muhammad, the Golden Age of Islam. Muhammad's successful union of disparate tribal forces under the banner of Islam, his creation of an Islamic state and society in which social justice prevailed, and the extraordinary early expansion of Islam were primal events to be remembered and, as the example of the Iranian Revolution seemingly verified, to be successfully emulated by those who adhered to Islam. Herein lies the initial attraction of the Iranian Revolution for many Muslims, Sunni and Shii alike. Iran provided the first example of a modern Islamic revolution, a revolt against impiety, oppression, and injustice. The call of the Ayatollah Khomeini for an Islamic revolution struck a chord among many who identified with his message of anti-imperialism, his condemnation of failed, unjust, and oppressive regimes, and his vision of a morally just society.

By contrast, the West stood incredulous before this challenge to the Shah's "enlightened" development of his seemingly backward nation, and the resurrection of an anachronistic, irrational medieval force that threatened to hurtle modern Iran back to the Middle Ages. Nothing symbolized this belief more than the black-robed, bearded mullahs and the dour countenance of their leader, the Ayatollah Khomeini, who dominated the media, reinforcing in Western minds the irrational nature of the entire movement.

THE IDEOLOGICAL WORLDVIEW OF ISLAMIC REVIVALISM

At the heart of the revivalist worldview is the belief that the Muslim world is in a state of decline. Its cause is departure from the straight path of Islam; its cure, a return to Islam in personal and public life which will ensure the restoration of Islamic identity, values, and power. For Islamic political activists Islam is a total or comprehensive way of life as stipulated in the Quran, God's revelation, mirrored in the example of Muhammad and the nature of the first Muslim community-state, and embodied in the comprehensive nature of the Sharia, God's revealed law. Thus the revitalization of Muslim gov-

ernments and societies requires the reimplementation of Islamic law, the blueprint for an Islamically guided and socially just state and society.

While Westernization and secularization of society are condemned, modernization as such is not. Science and technology are accepted, but the pace, direction, and extent of change are to be subordinated to Islamic belief and values in order to guard against the penetration of Western values and excessive dependence on them.

Radical movements go beyond these principles and often operate according to two basic assumptions. They assume that Islam and the West are locked in an ongoing battle, dating back to the early days of Islam, which is heavily influenced by the legacy of the Crusades and European colonialism, and which today is the product of a Judaeo-Christian conspiracy. This conspiracy is the result of superpower neocolonialism and the power of Zionism. The West (Britain, France, and especially the United States) is blamed for its support of un-Islamic or unjust regimes (Egypt, Iran, Lebanon) and also for its biased support for Israel in the face of Palestinian displacement. Violence against such governments and their representatives as well as Western multinationals is legitimate self-defense.

Second, these radical movements assume that Islam is not simply an ideological alternative for Muslim societies but a theological and political imperative. Since Islam is God's command, implementation must be immediate, not gradual, and the obligation to do so is incumbent on all true Muslims. Therefore individuals and governments who hesitate, remain apolitical, or resist are no longer to be regarded as Muslim. They are atheists or unbelievers, enemies of

God against whom all true Muslims must wage jihad (holy war)....

As some dream of the creation of a New World Order, and many millions in North Africa, the Middle East, Central Asia, and southern and Southeast Asia aspire to greater political liberalization and democratization, the continued vitality of Islam and Islamic movements need not be a threat but a challenge. For many Muslims, Islamic revivalism is a social rather than a political movement whose goal is a more Islamically minded and oriented society, but not necessarily the creation of an Islamic state. For others, the establishment of an Islamic order requires the creation of an Islamic state. In either case, Islam and most Islamic movements are not necessarily anti-Western, anti-American, or anti-democratic. While they are a challenge to the outdated assumptions of the established order and to autocratic regimes, they do not necessarily threaten American interests. Our challenge is to better understand the history and realities of the Muslim world. Recognizing the diversity and many faces of Islam counters our image of a unified Islamic threat. It lessens the risk of creating self-fulfilling prophecies about the battle of the West against a radical Islam. Guided by our stated ideals and goals of freedom and self-determination, the West has an ideal vantage point for appreciating the aspirations of many in the Muslim world as they seek to define new paths for their future.

NO

Albert Hourani

A HISTORY OF THE ARAB PEOPLES

Among educated and reflective men and women [of Arab countries in the late 1960s], there was a growing awareness of the vast and rapid changes in their societies, and of the ways in which their own position was being affected by them. The increase of population, the growth of cities, the spread of popular education and the mass media were bringing a new voice into discussion of public affairs, a voice expressing its convictions, and its grievances and hopes, in a traditional language. This in its turn was arousing consciousness among the educated of a gap between them and the masses, and giving rise to a problem of communication: how could the educated élite speak to the masses or on their behalf? Behind this there lay another problem, that of identity: what was the moral bond between them, by virtue of which they could claim to be a society and a political community?

To a great extent, the problem of identity was expressed in terms of the relationship between the heritage of the past and the needs of the present. Should the Arab peoples tread a path marked out for them from outside, or could they find in their own inherited beliefs and culture those values which could give them a direction in the modern world? Such a question made clear the close relationship between the problem of identity and that of independence. If the values by which society was to live were brought in from outside, would not that imply a permanent dependence upon the external world, and more specifically western Europe and North America, and might not cultural dependence bring with it economic and political dependence as well? The point was forcefully made by the Egyptian economist Galal Amin (b.1935) in *Mihnat al-iqtisad wa'l-thaqafa fi Misr* (*The Plight of the Economy and Culture in Egypt*), a book which tried to trace the connections between the *infitah* and a crisis of culture. The Egyptian and other Arab peoples had lost confidence in themselves, he maintained. The *infitah,* and indeed the whole movement of events since the Egyptian revolution of 1952, had rested on an unsound basis: the false values of a consumer society in economic life, the domination of a ruling élite instead of genuine patriotic loyalty. Egyptians were importing whatever foreigners persuaded them that they should want, and this made for a permanent dependence. To be healthy, their political and economic life should be derived from their own moral values, which themselves could have no basis except in religion.

In a rather similar way, another Egyptian writer, Hasan Hanafi, wrote about the relationship between the heritage and the need for renewal. Arabs like other human beings were caught up in an economic revolution, which could not be carried through unless there were a 'human revolution'. This did not involve an abandonment of the heritage of the past, for which the Arabs were no less responsible than they were for 'people and land and wealth', but rather that it should be reinterpreted 'in accordance with the needs of age', and turned into an ideology which could give rise to a political movement. Blind adherence to tradition and blind innovation were both inadequate, the former because it had no answer to the problems of the present, and the latter because it could not move the masses, being expressed in a language alien from that which they understood. What was needed was some reformation of religious thought which would give the masses of the people a new definition of themselves, and a revolutionary party which would create a national culture and so change the modes of collective behaviour.

Much of the contemporary Arab thought revolved around this dilemma of past and present, and some writers made bold attempts to resolve it. The answer given by the Syrian philosopher Sadiq Jalal al-'Azm (b. 1934) sprang from a total rejection of religious thought. It was false in itself, he claimed, and incompatible with authentic scientific thought in its view of what knowledge was and its methods of arriving at truth. There was no way of reconciling them; it was impossible to believe in the literal truth of the Qur'an, and if parts of it were discarded then the claim that it was the Word of God would have to be rejected. Religious thought was not only false, it was also dangerous. It supported the existing order of society and those who controlled it, and so prevented a genuine movement of social and political liberation....

At the other end of the spectrum were those who believed that the Islamic heritage by itself could provide the basis for life in the present, and that it alone could do so, because it was derived from the Word of God. This was the attitude expressed in increasingly sharp terms by some of those associated with the Muslim Brothers in Egypt and elsewhere....

Somewhere in the middle of the spectrum were those who continued to believe that Islam was more than a culture: it was the revealed Word of God, but it must be understood correctly, and the social morality and law derived from it could be adapted to make it the moral basis of a modern society. There were many forms of this reformist attitude. Conservatives of the Wahhabi school, in Saudi Arabia and elsewhere, believed that the existing code of law could be changed slowly and cautiously into a system adequate to the needs of modern life; some thought that only the Qur'an was sacred, and it could be freely used as the basis of a new law; some believed that the true interpretation of the Qur'an was that of the Sufis, and a private mystical devotion was compatible with the organization of society on more or less secular lines.

A few attempts were made to show how the new moral and legal system could be deduced from Qur'an and Hadith in a way which was responsible but bold. In the Sudan, Sadiq al-Mahdi

(b. 1936), the great-grandson of the religious leader of the later nineteenth century, and himself an important political leader, maintained that it was necessary to have a new kind of religious thought which would draw out of the Qur'an and Hadith a *shari'a* which was adapted to the needs of the modern world. Perhaps the most carefully reasoned attempt to state the principles of a new jurisprudence came from beyond the Arab world, from the Pakistani scholar Fazlur Rahman (1919–88). In an attempt to provide an antidote to the 'spiritual panic' of Muslims at the present time, he suggested a method of Qur'anic exegesis which would, he claimed, be true to the spirit of Islam but provide for the needs of modern life. The Qur'an was a 'divine response, through the Prophet's mind, to the moral–social situation of the Prophet's Arabia'. In order to apply its teaching to the moral and social situation of a different age, it was necessary to extract from that 'divine response' the general principle inherent in it. This could be done by studying the specific circumstances in which the response had been revealed, and doing so in the light of an understanding of the Qur'an as a unity. Once the general principle had been extracted, it should be used with an equally clear and meticulous understanding of the particular situation in regard to which guidance was needed. Thus the proper interpretation of Islam was a historical one, moving with precision from the present to the past and back again, and this demanded a new kind of religious education.

One of the signs of the new dominant position of governments in Arab societies was that they were able to appropriate to themselves the ideas which could move minds and imaginations, and extract

from them a claim of legitimate authority. By this time, any Arab government which wished to survive had to be able to claim legitimacy in terms of three political languages—those of nationalism, social justice and Islam.

The first to emerge as a potent language was that of nationalism. Some of the regimes which existed at the beginning of the 1980s had come to power during the struggle for independence, or could claim to be the successors for those who had; this kind of appeal to legitimacy was particularly strong in the Maghrib, where the struggle had been bitter and memories of it were still fresh. Almost all regimes made use too of a different kind of nationalist language, that of Arab unity; they gave some kind of formal allegiance to it, and spoke of independence as if it were the first step towards closer union, if not complete unity; connected with the idea of unity was that of some concerted action in support of the Palestinians. In recent years there had taken place an extension of the idea of nationalism; regimes claimed to be legitimate in terms of economic development, or the full use of national resources, both human and natural, for common ends.

The second language, that of social justice, came into common political use in the 1950s and 1960s, the period of the Algerian revolution and the spread of Nasirism, with its idea of a specifically Arab socialism expressed in the National Charter of 1962. Such terms as socialism and social justice tended to be used with a specific meaning; they referred to reform of the system of land-tenure, extension of social services and universal education, for girls as well as boys, but in few countries was there a systematic attempt to redistribute wealth by means of high taxation of incomes.

The latest of the languages to become powerful was that of Islam. In a way, of course, it was not new. There had always existed a sense of common destiny among those who had inherited the religion of Islam—a belief, enriched by historical memories, that the Qur'an, the Traditions of the Prophet and the *shari'a* could provide the principles according to which a virtuous life in common should be organized. By the 1980s, however, Islamic language had become more prominent in political discourse than it had been a decade or two earlier. This was due to a combination of two kinds of factor. On the one hand, there was the vast and rapid extension of the area of political involvement, because of the growth of population and of cities, and the extension of the mass media. The rural migrants into the cities brought their own political culture and language with them. There had been an urbanization of the migrants, but there was also a 'ruralization' of the cities. Cut off from the ties of kinship and neighbourliness which made life possible in the villages, they were living in a society of which the external signs were strange to them; the sense of alienation could be counterbalanced by that of belonging to a universal community of Islam, in which certain moral values were implicit, and this provided a language in terms of which they could express their grievances and aspirations. Those who wished to arouse them to action had to use the same language. Islam could provide an effective language of opposition: to western power and influence, and those who could be accused of being subservient to them; to governments

regarded as corrupt and ineffective, the instruments of private interests, or devoid of morality; and to a society which seemed to have lost its unity with its moral principles and direction.

It was factors of this kind which produced such movements as the Muslim Brothers, of which the leaders were articulate and educated men, but which appealed to those who were shut out of the power and prosperity of the new societies; and it was partly in self-defense against them or in order to appeal to a wider segment of their nations that most regimes began to use the language of religion more than before. Some regimes, it is true, used the language of Islam spontaneously and continuously, in particular that of Saudi Arabia, which had been created by a movement for the reassertion of the primacy of God's Will in human societies. Others, however, appeared to have been driven into it. Even the most secularist of ruling groups, those for example of Syria, Iraq and Algeria, had taken to use using it more or less convincingly, in one way or another. They might evoke historical themes, of the Arabs as the carriers of Islam; the rulers of Iraq, caught in their struggle with Iran, appealed to a memory of the battle of Qadisiyya, when the Arabs had defeated the last Sasanian ruler and brought Islam to Iran. In most countries of mixed population, the constitution laid down that the president should be a Muslim, so linking the religion of Islam with legitimate authority. In legal codes there might be a reference to the Qurán or the *shari'a* as the basis of legislation. Most governments which took this path tended to interpret the *shari'a* in a more or less modernist way, in order to justify the innovations which were inevitable for societies living in the modern world; even in Saudi Arabia, the principles of Hanbali jurisprudence were invoked in order to justify the new laws and regulations made necessary by the new economic order. Some regimes, however, resorted to certain token applications of the strict letter of the *shar'a*: in Saudi Arabia and Kuwait, the sale of alcohol was forbidden; in the Sudan, a provision of the *shari'a* that persistent thieves should have their hands cut off was revived in the last years of Numayri's period of rule. In some countries strict observance of the fast of Ramadan, which had been spreading spontaneously, was encouraged by the government; an earlier attempt by the Tunisian government to discourage it, because it interfered with the efforts needed for economic development, had met with widespread opposition.

THE FRAGILITY OF REGIMES

... If more radical changes took place, it seemed more likely in the 1980s that they would take place in the name of an Islamic idea of the justice of God in the world than in that of a purely secular ideal. There was not one idea of Islam only, but a whole spectrum of them. The word 'Islam' did not have a single, simple meaning, but was what Muslims made of it. For 'traditional' villagers, it might mean everything they thought and did. For more concerned and reflective Muslims, it provided a norm by which they should try to shape their lives, and by which their acts could be judged, but there was more than one norm. The term 'fundamentalism', which had become fashionable, carried a variety of meanings. It could refer to the idea that Muslims should try to return to the teaching and practice of the Prophet and the first generation of his followers, or to

the idea that the Qurán alone provided the norm of human life; this could be a revolutionary idea, if Muslims claimed— as the Libyan leader Qadhafi appeared to do—that they had the right to interpret the Qur'an freely. The word could also be used of an attitude which might better be called 'conservative': the attitude of those who wished to accept and preserve what they had inherited from the past, the whole cumulative tradition of Islam as it had in fact developed, and to change it only in a cautious and responsible way. This was the attitude of the Saudi regime and its supporters, and of the Iranian revolutionary regime, although the cumulative traditions they accepted were very different from each other.

The circumstances of the different Arab countries varied greatly. An Islamic movement in one country could have a different meaning from what might appear to be the same movement in another. For example, the Muslim Brothers in Syria did not have the same role as those in Egypt; to a great extent they served as a medium for the opposition of the Sunni urban population to the domination of a regime identified with the 'Alawi community. Similarly, the fact that the Iranian revolution had taken a certain form did not mean that it would take the same form in other countries. In part at least, the revolution could be explained in terms of factors which were specific to Iran: certain powerful social classes were particularly responsive to appeals expressed in religious language, and there was a religious leadership which was able to act as a rallying point or all movements of opposition; it was relatively independent of the government, generally respected for its piety and learning, and had always acted as the spokesman of the collective consciousness.

Such a situation did not exist in the Arab countries. In Iraq, where Shi'is formed a majority, their men of learning did not have the same intimate connection with the urban masses or the same influence on the government as in Iran. Sunni *'ulama* had a less independent position. Under Ottoman rule they had become state functionaries, close to the government and compromised by their relations with it; by tradition and interests they were linked with the upper bourgeoisie of the great cities. Leadership of Islamic movements therefore tended to be in the hands of laymen, converted members of the modern educated élite. Such movements did not have the sanctity conferred by leaders of inherited and recognized piety and learning; they were political parties competing with others. On the whole they did not have clear social or economic policies. It seemed likely that they would be important forces of opposition, but would not be in a position to be able to form governments.

An observer of the Arab countries, or of many other Muslim countries, in the mid-1980s might well have come to the conclusion that something similar to the Iranian path would be the path of the future, but this might have been a hasty conclusion, even so far as Iran was concerned. In a sense the rule of men of religion was a reaffirmation of tradition, but in another sense it went against tradition. The inherited wisdom of the *'ulama* was that they should not link themselves too closely with the government of the world; they should keep a moral distance from it, while preserving their access to the rulers and influence upon them: it was dangerous to tie the eternal interests of Islam to the fate of a transient ruler of the world. This attitude was reflected in a certain popular suspicion of men of religion who took too prominent a part in the affairs of the world; they were as susceptible as others to the corruptions of power and wealth, and perhaps they did not make very good rulers.

It might happen too that, at a certain stage of national development, the appeal of religious ideas—at least of ideas sanctified by the cumulative tradition— would cease to have the same force as another system of ideas: a blend of social morality and law which were basically secular, but might have some relationship to general principles of social justice inherent in the Qur'an.

POSTSCRIPT

Does Islamic Revivalism Threaten a Secular World Order?

Understanding how Islam sees itself and its place in the world might make us fearful or hopeful. If Islam cannot accommodate to Western, secular values, as Esposito points out, does it challenge a stable world order? Hourani seems more hopeful that, through the process of political maturation, Islamic states may come to find in the Qur'an inspiration rather than literal law for governing their societies. In either case, the West must understand its own image in the Muslim world and not expect a commitment to secularism that would appear to Muslims as blasphemy. Whether deeper dialogue will bring Islam and the West closer together or further apart is not yet clear.

A fascinating survey of how people have perceived God from the time of Abraham to the present can be found in Karen Armstrong's *History of God* (Ballantine Books, 1993). Since Judaism exists in its own right and is the foundation for both Christianity and Islam, this "4000-year quest" provides insight into key similarities and points of difference. Any good text on religions of the world will provide an introduction to Islam; particularly accessible is Huston Smith's *Illustrated World's Religions: A Guide to Our Wisdom Traditions* (Harper-SanFrancisco, 1994), which is also available on videocassette. Students who have not read the Qur'an might like to explore these scriptures, which are available in paperback.

The dilemma of becoming modern without becoming Western is addressed by Bernard Lewis in "The West and the Middle East," *Foreign Affairs* (January/February 1997). Other books by Lewis include *Islam and the West* (Oxford University Press, 1993) and *The Middle East: A Brief History of the Last 2,000 Years* (Scribner, 1995).

Professor of history Richard Bulliet has written an account of Islam's success among people who live far from the political center, such as those in Iran. In *Islam: The View from the Edge* (Columbia University Press, 1994), Bulliet argues that the origins of today's Islamic resurgence are to be found in the eleventh century. Other books of note are *Orientalism* by Edward Said (Pantheon, 1978) and *Islam and the Cultural Accommodation to Social Change* by Bassam Tibi (Westview Press, 1991). In Francis Fukuyama's influential book *The End of History and the Last Man* (Free Press, 1992), the chapter entitled "The Worldwide Liberal Revolution" considers Islam as an alternative to liberalism and communism. Finally, *The Turban and the Crown: The Islamic Revolution in Iran* by Said Amir Arjomand (Oxford University Press, 1988) explores the conflicts between the authority structures in Shi'ite institutions and the mechanisms of the modern bureaucratic state.

ISSUE 14

Will History Look Favorably Upon Mikhail Gorbachev?

YES: Archie Brown, from *The Gorbachev Factor* (Oxford University Press, 1996)

NO: Robert G. Kaiser, from *Why Gorbachev Happened: His Triumphs and His Failure* (Simon & Schuster, 1991)

ISSUE SUMMARY

YES: Professor of politics Archie Brown asserts that Mikhail Gorbachev deserves credit for reforming the Soviet Union and ending the cold war and that he may have had a greater impact on the twentieth century than any other individual.

NO: Robert G. Kaiser, a member of the Council of Foreign Relations, contends that Gorbachev ultimately failed in his efforts to remake the Soviet Union because he shrank from the drastic, thoroughgoing changes that complete reform required.

In 1985 Mikhail Gorbachev became general secretary of the Communist Party in the Soviet Union. As the first general secretary born after the Bolshevik Revolution of 1917, Gorbachev's accession to power symbolized the emergence of a new generation of Soviet leaders. Determined to preserve the system of Soviet communism, Gorbachev understood that he needed to institute numerous reforms. Wasting no time, Gorbachev announced soon after taking power that he intended to follow a policy of *glasnost* (openness and honesty) and *perestroika* (restructuring of the Soviet economy and society).

Over the next five years, Gorbachev and his colleagues introduced a measure of capitalism into the Soviet economy by allowing the establishment of small private businesses. They also reduced the degree of centralized control of the economy, firing hundreds of incompetent bureaucrats and giving managers of factories and farms increased authority to run their enterprises. In the political arena, Gorbachev convinced the Communist Party to surrender its monopoly of power; in 1989 multiparty elections were held for the first time in more than 70 years. Dissidents were released from prison, newspapers were permitted to publish articles critical of the government, and corrupt party officials were dismissed.

Gorbachev's reforms, however, unleashed long-suppressed forces of change that quickly moved beyond his control. In Eastern Europe, nationalists demanded independence from Soviet control. Violence flared in the Baltic states, particularly when Gorbachev sent Red Army units to put down a rising of Lithuanian rebels in January 1991. Other reformers in the Soviet Union grew frustrated by the measured pace of Gorbachev's changes. Opposition came also from the Right. Angered by Gorbachev's reforms, Communist Party hard-liners launched a coup against Gorbachev in the summer of 1991. When the coup failed, Gorbachev banned the Communist Party from all political activity within the Soviet Union. Finally, leaders of the provincial governments of Russia, Belarus, and the Ukraine declared their independence in December 1991, effectively withdrawing from the Soviet Union. Initially rejecting their claims of independence, Gorbachev finally agreed to dissolve the Soviet Union. On December 25, 1991, he resigned as president of the Soviet Union.

In the following selection, Archie Brown admits that Gorbachev did not plan the dissolution of the Soviet Union; indeed, his main objective was to restore the Soviet Union as "a great and prosperous power." Judged by the narrow standard of whether or not he achieved this goal, Gorbachev would seem to have failed dramatically. Nevertheless, Brown contends that Gorbachev's accomplishments far outweigh his failures. During the course of six years, the Soviet leader succeeded in liberalizing the Soviet political system, reducing the size of the bloated and incompetent Soviet bureaucracy, reestablishing civilian control of the Soviet military, replacing Soviet military dominance of Eastern Europe with a sounder policy of cooperation, and effectively ending the cold war. Given the forces aligned in opposition to him and the powerful inertia built into the Soviet system, Brown finds it truly remarkable that Gorbachev succeeded in achieving these goals, and he ranks the former president as one of the great reformers in Russian history.

In the second selection, Robert G. Kaiser (whose analysis of Gorbachev was written several years earlier than Brown's) concedes the breadth of the Soviet leader's reforms, but he maintains that Gorbachev ultimately failed because he could not see beyond—or move beyond—the Stalinist system he inherited. For Kaiser, Gorbachev was a flawed reformer, a man whose overconfidence led him to believe that he could control the forces he unleashed and whose ambitions led him to betray the reform movement at a critical juncture; that is, the assault upon the Lithuanian nationalists in 1991, an event that cost Gorbachev his claim to moral superiority over his domestic opponents. Further, Gorbachev failed to understand that a substantial segment of the Soviet people had no desire to perpetuate the communist system or even the Soviet Union itself. In the end, Kaiser concludes, Gorbachev succeeded in throwing off the yoke of Stalinism but failed to provide any viable alternative to the Soviet system he had dismantled.

YES

Archie Brown

THE GORBACHEV FACTOR

It is quite common in Russia today, and even in some quarters in the West, to regard Gorbachev as a political failure. Superficially, such a view seems entirely plausible. Nothing was further from Gorbachev's mind in 1985 than that the Soviet Union should cease to exist. On the contrary, he wanted it to enter the next millennium 'as a great and prosperous power'. He wished to reform the Soviet system, not to destroy it, and he had a particular desire to achieve qualitative improvement in its economic performance. In these very important respects outcomes were far removed from Gorbachev's intentions.

Thus, the case for viewing Gorbachev as a failure rests, above all, on a comparison between his goals when he became General Secretary of the Soviet Communist Party and what actually happened during his years at the top of the Soviet political system. Even by these criteria, however, things are not so simple. . . . Gorbachev was a more serious reformer as early as 1984–5 than was generally appreciated at the time either in the Soviet Union or in the West, and he was interested not only in economic reform but also in glasnost (although, then, more as an instrument of reform than as a desirable end in itself), in a liberalization of the political system (for which he used the term 'democratization', although that became fully appropriate only from 1988), in replacing Soviet hegemony over other Communist parties and systems by co-operation, in reducing the size and political weight of the military-industrial complex, in bringing Soviet troops back from Afghanistan, and in ending the Cold War between East and West. Those goals were far from easy to attain, but Gorbachev realized them.

More fundamentally, however, it may be asked why Gorbachev's success or failure should be judged by the limitations on his political horizons at a particular point in time, even the moment at which he became General Secretary. Why 1985 and not 1988? By the summer of 1988 Gorbachev had accepted the need for contested elections and had . . . laid the foundations for the development of political pluralism In the Soviet Union. He had discarded much of Marxist-Leninist ideology and was moving closer to a social demo-cratic vision of socialism. He realized that eventually the Communist Party would have to compete with other political parties in Russia and he had come increasingly to admire what he saw of West European political and economic systems and became correspondingly more critical of the Soviet Communist heritage. He had comprehensively rethought the nature of the Soviet Union's relations with the outside world and had welcomed President Ronald Reagan to Moscow. Reagan had responded by saying that he no longer regarded the USSR as an 'evil empire' and by the end of 1988 the American Secretary of State, George Shultz, was convinced that the Cold War was over. That this was, indeed, so had become still clearer by the end of the following year, by which time most of the countries of Eastern Europe had, one by one, rejected Communism and the Soviet connection and Gorbachev had preferred the disappearance of what had been 'the Soviet bloc' to a return to military intervention and the politics of repression. But already in 1988, in his speeches to the Nineteenth Party Conference and to the United Nations, Gorbachev had paved the way for the independence of the countries of Eastern Europe by recognizing sovereign states' 'freedom to choose' their political and economic system.

If we consider the four transformations... which were required if the Soviet Union was to make the transition from a highly repressive Communist system to some form of democracy and of a market economy, two of the four had by the end of the 1980s been successful beyond the dreams of Soviet dissidents or the most optimistic of Western observers at the time when Gorbachev came to power. That is to say, the political system had become substantially pluralist and partially democratized and international relations had been still more comprehensively transformed. In both cases, the

initiative had come from Gorbachev, although Western leaders, on the whole, reacted sympathetically to the dramatic scale of the change in both Soviet domestic and foreign policy. If the attitudes of the second Reagan administration were significantly different from the first, this was in response to the fundamentally new challenge and opportunities presented by Moscow. The initial scepticism of the Bush administration also had before long to give way to recognition that Gorbachev had changed Soviet foreign policy fundamentally. It had long been taken for granted in Western capitals that, while amelioration of Communist regimes in Eastern Europe might be possible, the Soviet Union regarded the fruits of its victory in the Second World War in the shape of East European Communist regimes to a greater or lesser degree dependent on Moscow as non-negotiable. But this, too, had changed.

Economic reform and nationalities policy—along with some thoroughly bad appointments—were, in contrast, areas of relative failure for Gorbachev. Yet, even the economic system changed in several important respects... and Gorbachev had acquiesced in a substantial devolution of power from the all-union central authorities to the constituent republics of the Soviet Union before the process, from his point of view, got out of hand and resulted in the breakup of the USSR.... [H]owever, it is possible that a smaller and different union might have been preserved but for the actions of Yeltsin and his supporters both before and after the August 1991 *putsch* and, still more, the self-defeating activity of Kryuchkov and his fellow plotters. While the liberalization and partial democratization of the Soviet Union made highly unlikely the preservation of a union covering the entire territory Gorbachev inherited from his predecessors, the total collapse of the union owed more to Yeltsin—and, of course, to the *putschists* —than to Gorbachev.

Yeltsin had moved into political space created by Gorbachev and but for Gorbachev's reforms would have remained a little-known Communist Party official in the Urals. But he used his opportunities effectively, making at times a highly positive contribution to the peaceful transformation of the Soviet Union and of Russia more particularly. For Yeltsin, however, the pursuit of personal power took precedence over construction of a new federation or confederation. While a great many factors brought about the collapse of the statehood of the Soviet Union, it is appropriate to see Yeltsin, in Alexander Dallin's words, as 'the final catalyst of the collapse'. More fundamentally, of course, the Soviet Union disintegrated because of the virtually insuperable difficulties imposed by attempting simultaneously a fourfold transformation of the system, although such were the interconnections between them that a staged sequencing of these transformations was not a realistic alternative.

Gorbachev's success or failure as a politician should, then, be judged not simply on the basis that, contrary to his wishes and notwithstanding his strenuous political efforts to avoid such an outcome, the Soviet Union gave way to fifteen independent successor states. Indeed, the fact that he refused to resort to the only means capable by 1990–1 of holding the entire USSR together—namely, widespread and sustained repression— is entirely to his credit. Even on the national question, moreover... his views developed. It was, above all, because the Union Treaty Gorbachev negotiated, in the course of the Novo-Ogarevo process, gave very substantial powers to the republics that so many leading all-union officials rebelled against him in August 1991 and attempted to undo his conciliatory policy.

Defining Gorbachev's success or failure by reference to his thinking at a particular time is open also to the more basic objection that he was an evolutionary rather than revolutionary by conviction, someone who rejected utopian grand designs on principle, a pragmatist and not an ideologue, and a politician who combined the temperament of a reformer with an extraordinary capacity for learning and adjustment. He has been described by a Russian writer as 'a figure very rare in our history—a principled evolutionist'. The same author underlines the point that 'Gorbachev was the main force, holding in check over a long period potential *putschists*'. For almost the whole of his first five years as Soviet leader, Gorbachev was both in the vanguard of reform and the guarantor of its continuity. For much of 1990–1, in contrast, he was on the defensive as a polarization of politics which he had sought to avoid overtook him, but even then he did not resort to traditional Communist methods to reassert his control. The idea that Gorbachev might have become the dictator in the 'coming dictatorship' of which Shevardnadze warned in December 1990 was inherently absurd, for dictatorial methods were foreign both to his personality and to his intellectual conviction.

Indeed, it was Gorbachev's awareness of the importance of means as well as of ends in politics which distinguished him from all of his Communist predecessors as well as from his *de facto* successor, Boris Yeltsin. Gorbachev's mind-set was far removed from the Bolshevik psychology of *kto kogo* (who will crush whom). He did not see politics as a zero-sum-game. Whether in foreign policy or domestic politics, he combined consensus-seeking with pushing forward increasingly fundamental change.... [H]e moved from being a reformer of the Soviet system to a systemic transformer and, as I underline below, he went on—quite consciously during the second half of his General Secretaryship—to dismantle the pillars of Communism....

What could not be expected of any General Secretary of the Soviet Communist Party was that he would undertake reforms so far-reaching than they would turn the system into something different in kind. It is to Gorbachev's lasting credit that when he found that reform led to resistance from all the vested interests which it threatened, and he was, accordingly, faced with the choice of restoring the status quo ante or moving on to accept the risk of system-transformative change, it was the latter course he adopted. For the decision to move to contested elections and to create a legislature with real powers, taken by Gorbachev in 1988 (before there was any mass pressure for such a fundamental change, and at a time when Yeltsin was still sidelined in the State Construction Committee), was *the* crucial move towards making the Soviet system something different in essence from what it had been before.

THE DISMANTLING OF COMMUNISM

Of the fact that the Soviet political system changed fundamentally under Gorbachev there is no doubt and, at least from the summer of 1988 onwards, there was a *conscious* aim on Gorbachev's part to *transform* it, even if he could

not always move at his own preferred pace, which would sometimes have been faster than that forced on him and sometimes slower. Instead, he had, especially during his last two years in office, to respond to pressures and events beyond his control which were, nevertheless, in large part a result of the new freedoms he had opened up. There are two points in 1991, at one or other of which it is conventionally assumed that Communism in the Soviet Union ended. One is when Yeltsin suspended the activities of the Communist Party on Russian soil on 23 August 1991 following the failure of the attempted *putsch*. The other is when the Soviet flag was lowered from the Kremlin on 25 December of the same year and Gorbachev resigned and formally handed power over to Yeltsin— and to Russia as the major successor state to the Soviet Union (or 'continuer state', as Russian officials called it, thus setting it apart from the fourteen other successor states).

However, although there was a Communist Party of the Soviet Union until August 1991, and though its General Secretary was also President of the country, it had ceased to be a ruling party in anything like the sense it had been throughout Soviet history. That was clearly the case at the centre—and it was because the party had lost control over the General Secretary (and, with that, their decisive influence over the fate of the USSR) that some of its leading figures launched the *putsch*—although there were many rural areas, in particular, where the local party boss still held sway. Yet, from the spring of 1989 it is scarcely meaningful to describe the Soviet Union as a *Communist system*. It is not only that the greater part of Marxist-Leninist dogma had been abandoned by then—and by the party leader himself—but also that the most important defining characteristics of a Communist system, whether structural or ideological, had ceased to apply as a result of the policies introduced during the period of radical reform which got seriously under way in 1987 and became more fundamental in 1988....

The dramatic changes which Gorbachev introduced, and which had, of course, unintended as well as intended consequences, had made the Soviet political system even by the spring of 1989 —and, still more clearly, a year later— different in kind from the polity Gorbachev inherited in 1985. Although far from fully democratic, it had become *pluralist* as a result of the introduction of contested elections and the existence of relatively autonomous political organizations whose activities could not be prevented even by the state authorities except at a cost higher than they, under Gorbachev's leadership, were prepared to pay. It had attained a level of political freedom, together with political (and religious) tolerance, unheard of throughout the earlier Soviet period. In effect, well before Yeltsin took over Gorbachev's offices in the Kremlin and the old Central Committee building, the system had ceased to be Communist.

GORBACHEV'S PLACE IN HISTORY

What applies to the system is still more true of Gorbachev himself. Nothing could be further removed from an understanding of Gorbachev than the description offered of him at the beginning of 1995 by Richard Pipes as 'a typical product of the Soviet nomenklatura, a man who to this day affirms his faith in the ideals of communism'. The former Chairman of the Soviet Council of Ministers, Nikolay Ryzhkov—who criticized Gorbachev for his unwillingness to use to the full the power he possessed and for his excessive liking for listening to a great many opinions and arguments before making up his mind—perceptively remarks: 'Gorbachev—long before all our native parliamentary games began—was a leader of a parliamentary type. How this formation took place in a party-bureaucratic system, God alone knows. But so he was formed, although from his post-student youth he had risen up the traditional career ladder of Komsomol and party.' Contrary to the view of Pipes, Gorbachev was a highly untypical product of the Soviet *nomenklatura* and the only leader of the Soviet Communist Party to come to reject, while he still held the office of General Secretary, the most distinctive features of Communism. Gorbachev has appositely described himself as 'a product of that very *nomenklatura* and at the same time its antiproduct—its "grave digger", so to speak'.

Gorbachev could, of course, have achieved nothing if there had not been within the Soviet system people who were deeply dissatisfied with it, whether specialists within the research institutes or a minority of senior officials (among the latter, such important political actors of the Gorbachev era as Yakovlev, Shevardnadze, Chernyaev, and Shakhnazarov) who had occupied high positions within the party apparatus. There had also been crucial changes in Soviet society which... made the Soviet Union when Gorbachev came to power a very different place from what it had been immediately after the death of Stalin, although in 1985 it remained far removed from being a civil society. If political change in Poland was, in large measure, a result of the struggle of autonomous forces within the society against the power of the party-state, this was not how change was initiated in the Soviet Union.

Social changes and the availability of enlightened (as well as a more numerous category of unenlightened) party officials notwithstanding, individuals desperate for radical reform remained highly dependent on change at the top of the party hierarchy. Political power was concentrated to a remarkable degree in the Central Committee building and the tone of political life set to a surprising extent by the party General Secretary. This meant that would-be reformers, especially over the period of approximately twenty years between the fall of Khrushchev and the death of Chernenko, had found themselves frustrated by the strict limits of Soviet official political discourse and the narrow bounds of all sanctioned political activity. They needed a Gorbachev even more than he needed them. Thus, Alexander Yakovlev, who is today rightly regarded as an important reformer, would have made little mark on Russian history had Gorbachev not brought him into the inner circle of power and given him great opportunities to exercise influence over policy. Yakovlev himself, speaking in March 1995—by which time, partly as a result of their very different assessments of a number of actions of Yeltsin, he had become estranged from Gorbachev —said: 'I consider Gorbachev to be the greatest reformer of the century, the more so because he tried to do this in Russia where from time immemorial the fate of reformers has been unenviable.'

In a political system which concentrates great power in the hands of the political leader, the character, intelligence, courage, and relative open-mindedness of the person at the apex of that system becomes crucially important. Yet... a Soviet leader was accorded great power provided he did not engage in actions which posed a threat to the system. Since Gorbachev did present such a threat, he was always in danger of being removed and the fact that he survived for almost seven years while transforming the system is a tribute to his exceptional political finesse. Almost three decades ago Samuel Huntington wrote:

> The revolutionary must be able to dichotomize social forces, the reformer to manipulate them. The reformer, consequently, requires a much higher order of *political skill* than does the revolutionary. Reform is rare if only because the political talents necessary to make it a reality are rare. A successful revolutionary need not be a master politician; a successful reformer always is.

These words apply especially forcefully in the Soviet and Russian context. Social scientists may resist an emphasis on the element of contingency and particularity in the coming to power of a reformer in 1985. It is tempting to see Gorbachev as the handmaiden of history or the embodiment of social forces which, if Gorbachev rather than Dmitry Ustinov had died in December 1984, would have brought forth an alternative leader in the mid-1980s whose policies would have been broadly the same as Gorbachev's, producing similar results. This, however, is a temptation which should be resisted, for it has got little but a 'retrospective determinism' to commend it.

No scholar predicted in 1985 the actual sequence of events whereby the Soviet system was reformed, then transformed, whereupon the Soviet state itself collapsed. Certainly this provided further evidence to support the view that *reform communism* was an unstable and temporary expedient, although that is not at all the same thing as saying that it was pointless to embark on radical reform in the Soviet Union (however unlikely even such an attempt appeared to most observers before Gorbachev undertook it). On the contrary, a process of ever more radical reform was the *only* way in which the Communist system could have been peacefully transformed in a country where—in sharp contrast with East-Central Europe—Communist institutions and norms were deeply entrenched. Reform of the Soviet system could, however, have been either a stage on the path to more thoroughgoing change (not necessarily to democracy, possibly to a non-Communist authoritarian regime) or a transient liberalization before more orthodox Communist norms were restored. There was nothing inevitable either about the timing of the end of the Soviet state or about the way in which, under Gorbachev's leadership, the system was transformed.

Taking all his mistakes and some undoubted failures into account—along, however, with the almost insuperable obstacles he had to overcome—Gorbachev has strong claims to be regarded as one of the greatest reformers in Russian history and as the individual who made the most profound impact on world history in the second half of the twentieth century. He played the decisive part in allowing the countries of Eastern Europe to become free and independent. He did more than anyone else to end the Cold War between East and West. He went along with, encouraged, and (in important respects) initiated fundamental rethinking about politics—radically new thinking in the Soviet context about the political and economic system he inherited and about

better alternatives. He presided over, and facilitated, the introduction of freedom of speech, freedom of the press, freedom of association, religious freedom, and freedom of movement, and left Russia a *freer country* than it had been in its long history.

For Olga Chaykovskaya, Gorbachev is 'the one great Russian reformer'. Focusing precisely on his contribution to Russian freedom, she compares him favourably in this respect with Peter the Great, Catherine the Great, and even Alexander II (although the last-named 'made a huge step forward on the path to freedom'). But Gorbachev, she says, *succeeded:* he inherited 'a moribund, slavish country and made it alive and free'. Similarly, Alexander Tsipko has emphasized as perhaps the greatest of Gorbachev's achievements that he 'delivered us from fear—from fear of thought and speech' and gave people the possibility for the first time in seventy years to state their convictions out loud.

There are other Russian intellectuals who cannot forgive Gorbachev for the fact that he gave them freedom when their self-esteem suggests they should have won it for themselves. Similarly, for a General Secretary of the Soviet Communist Party to have played the most decisive part in dismantling the Communist system was not a script much to the liking of a number of Western observers and they have done their best to rewrite it. Yet the Gorbachev factor *was* the most crucial of all. Gorbachev must be judged in his political context —not by the purely intellectual criteria of total consistency of word and thought, but as the inheritor of the most powerful post in a highly repressive regime who abandoned both the means and the ends of Communism. In his own words he was 'a man who led a colossal military force, a deadly police and surveillance apparatus, and a state that was the sole great master of all'. But 'I started to dismantle all that, to rid myself of that power, and now Russia is a different country'—although one which has gone through great turmoil and in which it will remain for future generations to appreciate fully Gorbachev's historic role.

NO

Robert G. Kaiser

TRIUMPH AND FAILURE

How could so much happen in so short a time? The world that Gorbachev destroyed in five years had taken decades to construct, and until he started to dismantle it, there was no obvious sign that it was as fragile as it proved to be. And yet it did crumble, as if shaken by a gigantic earthquake.

The amazing pace of change was an important clue. It was possible because energies had accumulated beneath the surface comparable to the natural forces that build up where two plates of the earth's crust meet, finally erupting in a shattering earthquake. Once the first tremors were felt, the Soviet Union's stale and rigid economic and political structures began to shake. Eastern Europe's false front—a slapdash façade of Stalinism forcibly and unnaturally attached to ancient Central European cultures—crumbled under the temblor's strength.

Events could only move so fast because as long as he was dismantling the Stalinist system, Gorbachev was working with the forces of history, not against them. He understood this himself, more clearly as he went along. He knew from the outset that his country was in dire straits—this knowledge was the source of his urge to reform. The more he tried to put things right, the better he grasped how bad things were. We've seen him say time and again that plans had to be changed after he and others understood the seriousness of the problems they faced. What they thought they knew repeatedly turned out to be less than the full truth. At the Central Committee plenum of April 1989 Gorbachev admitted: "None of us had a good knowledge of the country we live in."

The truth was that the Stalinist model had long outlived its utility and was nearing collapse after doing immeasurable damage to the country. The idea that a huge industrial economy could effectively be planned and controlled by relatively few officials in Moscow had proven false. The system this idea created was static, not dynamic, and was based on a simple-minded distinction between pre-industrial and industrial life. The planned economy would take Russia from backwardness to modernity—that was its authors' vision. But their vision left no room for the actual dynamics of technological innovation, improvisation, market mechanisms, and so on. It was the vision of economic illiterates. It created a hapless economic monster that was backward, inefficient, and clumsy. Its managers did not know how to manage, its workers did not know how to work, its currency was worthless in any competitive marketplace. This was the Stalinist legacy.

Despite the inherent disadvantages of their system, Soviet leaders from Stalin to Chernenko, had sought to compete for power and influence with the Americans and their allies, a formidable group of free societies and strong economies. Operating from a position of profound weakness, they tried to establish the Soviet Union as a superpower equal to the United States. They could succeed only in the realm of military might. For a time in the 1970s Brezhnev and his cronies exulted in the achievement of strategic parity with the Americans, and launched several new international adventures, particularly in Africa, to show off what they considered their improving superpower credentials. But that hubris also led Brezhnev into Afghanistan, a catastrophic blunder. Then Ronald Reagan initiated his Strategic Defense Initiative—in effect, a declaration of his willingness to recommence the arms race in an entirely new arena, outer space. Suddenly the Soviets' accomplishments of the seventies began to pale.

The cost of sustaining superpower status was immense. Shevardnadze acknowledged in the summer of 1990 that Soviet governments routinely spent a quarter of their resources on their military establishment—and more to sustain alliances with ne'er-do-well third world allies like Cuba, Nicaragua, and Ethiopia. The actual number may have been even higher. This squandering of the nation's wealth over more than forty years certainly hastened the collapse of the Stalinist system.

So did the worsening corruption of Soviet society. The corruption of a nation is a dynamic process; once begun, it tends to gain momentum and accelerate. I watched this happen in the Soviet Union over the last twenty years as bribe takers became ever bolder and everyday survival increasingly depended on corrupt relationships with black marketeers of many kinds. By the time Gorbachev came to power it was common for a Soviet citizen to be asked for a bribe for the most basic services, even health care. The high-minded principles of the Bolshevik Revolution has lost all relevance; the society was rotting from within. This was obvious just from the statistics on life expectancy and consumption of alcohol, which showed a country that was killing itself.

The reasons of Gorbachev's revolution were similar to the causes of the first revolution of 1917: stubborn retention of an outmoded social and economic structure —the monarchy then, the Stalinist system in the 1980s—and reckless commitments to ruinously expensive foreign ambitions had caused a crisis for the old order. By the time Gorbachev became general secretary his country's economy could no longer grown, and was falling farther and farther behind the developed world. Conditions of life were deteriorating ominously. The people were alienated and isolated from their so-called leaders. Either there would be change, or there would be disaster.

The nature of the change that had to be made was widely understood—not as a blueprint for specific reforms, but as a set of general principles. Sakharov laid out many of them in his 1968 essay. Some had been obvious as early as

1956. Gorbachev's generation included thousands of intelligent people who realized that the Soviet system had to loosen up, had to allow more freedom, and had to connect work to rewards and prices to values.

The modernization of the Soviet Union and the breakdown of its isolation actually began in the early 1970s, in the time of the Nixon-Brezhnev détente, when thousands of Soviet citizens first saw the West and realized how far their country lagged behind. Stalinism required isolation; only in ignorance would successive generations continue to accept the myths that propped it up. In the seventies Soviet young people discovered and joined the international youth culture; large numbers of Western tourists began to visit the U.S.S.R.; Soviet scientists caught on to the computer revolution and what it might mean, though because of the country's inability to produce the hardware, they could not easily take part in it.

As Alexander Bovin put it to me in the spring of 1990: "Understanding Gorbachev means understanding the Soviet Union." It is important to see Gorbachev in the context of Soviet history and society. "We are all children of our times," as Gorbachev said often during his first five years in power. His times did not begin in 1985. Nor did the ideas for change that he embraced suddenly fall from the heavens after he became general secretary.

Similarly, the trouble Gorbachev encountered at the end of 1990 and the tragic events of early 1991 can also be understood only in the context of Soviet history. His reforms crashed into the realities of the Stalinist inheritance: an unnatural multinational state, a pathetic economy, and the enduring power of the core groups that had made the old system work, however feebly. The army, the KGB, the police, the still hidden but still powerful military-industrial complex, and remnants of the Party apparatus pushed Gorbachev off course at the very moment when he seemed to be triumphant.

They pushed him toward a new, hard line that led directly to the clumsy showdown with the Baltic states and then to tragedy in January 1991. Not that those conservative forces could be blamed for what happened. It was Gorbachev's own fear and ambition that made him susceptible to their pressure. The blood of the fourteen Lithuanians killed when army troops stormed the television station in Vilnius was blood on Gorbachev's hands. For nearly six years he had avoided this; he had built a great international reputation and collected the Nobel Prize as an implacable foe of violence. Even as he plotted to bring the Lithuanians to heel, violently if necessary, he was working feverishly in the diplomatic arena to avoid was in the Persian Gulf—trying to fulfill the noble aspirations of his United Nations speech of December 1988. But that was window dressing. The real test of his moral position came at home, and he failed it. The wild, bucking horse he had been riding for seventy months finally threw him. When the paratroopers opened fire in Vilnius, the hopeful, high-minded Gorbachev era ended.

It ended with the shooting and clubbing in Vilnius, but that was a manifestation of Gorbachev's failure, not the cause of it. The cause was Gorbachev's inability to go beyond the dismantling of Stalinism to the creation of something new and successful to replace it. Dismantling the old was an enormous accomplishment, but it was quite literally not enough....

Many of Gorbachev's supporters among the liberal intellectuals hoped he would turn against the Party to prove that he had truly buried the past. But he wouldn't do that. He continued to call himself a "convinced Communist" and a socialist even when he was embracing economic reforms that looked more like capitalism than socialism. "Socialism... is entrenched among the people," he said at the end of November 1990, "and I don't think it is necessary to destroy it, as some are trying to do.

"Yes," he went on, "we have bid farewell to the past—an agonizing process." He acknowledged that young people without roots in the earlier phases of Soviet experience might not feel as he did about socialism. "But we are all from those times," he said in the speech to intellectuals when he first disclosed the arrests of his grandfathers, "and it is not so simple for us. Should we renounce things? What shall I do, renounce my grandfather, who was dedicated to everything right until the end and who, having returned [from prison, apparently], spent another seventeen years as chairman of the collective farm?... I cannot go against my grandfather. I cannot go against my father, who fought [the Germans] in the Kursk salient, who crossed the Dnepr, flowing with blood...." He was happy to reject "the barracks-like mentality of Stalinism," Gorbachev said, but he would not "renounce my grandfather and what he did. This would mean rejecting generations and what they did. Well then, did they live in vain?" He was certain they did not, and he would respect "the memory of those who gave their all, who believed that if it wasn't for themselves [that they sacrificed], then it was for the country, for the motherland."

In other words, if we had to admit that the whole Bolshevik experiment was a terrible mistake, we would have nothing to live for. That, I think, is what Gorbachev believes: Don't take away the very essence of our cause, lest we have nothing at all.

Here, perhaps, is a clue to the flaw in Gorbachev's character that threatens to turn his revolution from a great crusade into something horrific. In the end he perceived his very identity as part of a contiuum that began with Lenin. He believed that the Bolsheviks had produced something important, something worth salvaging. I was struck by two sentences of his April 1990 speech on Lenin: "It is high time we put an end to the absurd idolization of Lenin," he said, then added: "But we condemn wholeheartedly the desecration of his memory, whatever form it takes...." Don't make Lenin a golden idol, but revere him! It was thin line to tread.

Gorbachev's insistence on trying to preserve his communism ultimately undermined his position in the country, which by 1990 was in full flight away from the political doctrine that had done so much damage during the previous seventy-three years. Relatively few of his countrymen shared his concern with redeeming Lenin's revolution —they wanted something to eat, some sign of progress toward a normal society, and normal lives.

Although Gorbachev held on to his Communist identity, he was never hidebound. Once he committed himself to "revolutionary change," he was willing to accept wholesale revision of Party tradition, and to break nearly all the old rules that governed Soviet society. But there were limits—I suspect they were limits that were literally part of his image of himself.

He was overhauling Soviet communism to create a better Soviet Union, and better communism—that's how Gorbachev has seen his historical role. But communism held no appeal for large numbers of people, and the idea of the Soviet Union held no appeal for many, probably more, of the non-Russian citizens of the U.S.S.R.

Yet, as I hope I have made clear, there has been much more to Gorbachev's revolution than an effort to preserve communism and the Soviet Union. At certain moments there are nobility, even morality....

* * *

From 1985 onward Gorbachev was hobbled by his own shortcomings. One... was his inability to choose the right aides and associates, a serious disability for a political revolutionary trying to push a giant nation in a new direction. Apart from Yakovlev and Shevardnadze, Gorbachev never found reliable, resourceful peers who could help him achieve his goals. In the end, he even fell out with those two friends. He made many bad appointments, from Ligachev as his first number-two man, to Ryzhkov as his premier, to Yazov as his minister of defense, and Murakhovsky, his first patron in Stavropol, as minister of the agricultural superministry created in 1986. Yeltsin, when he became president of Russia in 1990, quickly surrounded himself with bright young men in their thirties and forties, but Gorbachev never built a staff of younger associates. Nor did he establish close working relationships with the new political figures his reforms had thrown up, people like Stankevich and Popov in Moscow and Sobchak in Leningard. He stuck to Party *apparatchiks* with a loyalty that exasperated his liberal intellectual supporters.

Was this tactics, or genuine preference? I suspect the latter. Gorbachev never seemed comfortable with unconventional people who might be in his intellectual class—he preferred good Party men. But his preference suited his tactics: Party men would have been alarmed if Gorbachev had suddenly embraced a retinue of liberal intellectuals with no Party backgrounds.

One reason why Gorbachev did not reach out for more talented associates may have been his excessive confidence in himself. At the outset Gorbachev seemed overconfident of his ability to carry the Party apparatus with him as he initiated reforms. His overconfident belief that he could deal with the Yeltsin affair in the fall of 1987 led to the horrendous display of Stalinist discipline at the Moscow Party plenum, an event that gravely undermined Gorbachev's efforts at the time. He overconfidently thought he could win a majority of the delegates to the 19th Party Conference of 1988 by instituting democratic selection procedures, which proved easy for his opponents to manipulate. In 1989 and 1990 he seemed to think he could overcome Yeltsin's great popularity and head off his election first to the Congress, then to the Russian presidency. In both cases Gorbachev's intervention seems to have helped Yeltsin, not hurt him.

Perhaps the most egregious example of his overconfidence was his failure to confront the need to create a new system to replace the one he was so successfully destroying. Gorbachev seemed to convince himself that he could postpone this task for three years, then four, then five. In the sixth year his procrastination caught up with him.

Vanity has also tripped him up. A senior Soviet journalist who had long been a staunch supporter complained when Gorbachev came to Washington in June 1990, "He has succumbed to narcissistic tendencies." This was a common reaction to the long and fruitless speeches Gorbachev made that spring to try to block Yeltsin and calm the population after a run on consumer goods when Ryzhkov announced his reform plan that would triple bread prices. Gorbachev's first years were such a great triumph at home and abroad that when the country began to turn against him late in 1989 (pushed initially by disappearing food supplies and deteriorating economic conditions), he could not adjust. In 1990, when it became clear that the Soviet Union was in real danger of falling apart, Gorbachev allowed himself to become one of the very people he spent his first five years struggling against—a stubborn officeholder determined above all to retain power. By late 1990 it was obvious that love of power for its own sake was motivating Gorbachev—which isn't surprising. This was the man who invested twenty-three years in Stavropol to get his shot at power in Moscow. Power was important to him long before democratization was....

The fact that Gorbachev was unable to brag of any positive economic results was disastrous for his standing in the country. This failure to produce goods that people wanted to eat and buy was also an incentive to the old guard reactionaries who felt defeated by the first five years of Gorbachev's rule. They revived themselves in the sixth year when they realized that they could discredit all Gorbachev's liberalizing reforms by blaming them for food shortages and worsening economic conditions.

Ultimately, the facts of Soviet life—objective reality, as a Marxist might put it—were Gorbachev's greatest enemy. He could open up the Soviet Union, restore its history, initiate debate on fundamental issues, even convert a nation of sheeplike followers into a vibrant new political organism, but he could not overcome the fundamental terms of existence in his country. So, after nearly six years, he had succeeded brilliantly, but also failed. He had thrown off the yoke of Stalinism, as astounding accomplishment; but even without the yoke the country was crippled by the consequences of its past.

I don't think Gorbachev's failures are surprising. Consider what he proposed to do: take a huge, multinational empire that had been created by force and coercion; give it a large measure of democracy, while loosening all the traditional bonds that held it together—thus encouraging the rebirth of long-suppressed local nationalisms; allow its citizens to travel quite freely around the world, but at home fail to give them attractive consumer goods, food, housing, and so on—fail worse and worse, while proclaiming the benefits of your reforms; do all this in a backward land whose citizens have little training and less experience useful for building a democratic society of self-reliant citizens, a country whose economic infrastructure is collapsing. This is obviously no formula for success. It may actually be a formula for disaster....

As he dismantled the old system, Gorbachev never eliminated the mechanisms that make dictatorship possible. The army shrank but never lost its influence, and the Soviet version of the military-industrial complex apparently retained its ability to commandeer the most desirable economic resources. The KGB survived at full strength—hundreds of thousands of agents. Many of the hard-nosed Party hacks who maintained discipline for the old regime remained available for service. Censors never forgot how to censor. Prosecutors and judges still know how to take arbitrary orders from above, and probably don't know how to resist them. As the dismaying events of January 1991 made clear, Gorbachev himself never fully overcame the authoritarian instincts that he grew up with....

At the beginning of 1991 the future is unpredictable, but the situation in some respects is clear. The country is collapsing, economically and politically. Nationalistic popular fronts have won the allegiance of majorities in many republics. The restoration of dictatorship might eliminate the continuing chaos, but it offers no prospect of solving the country's problems. The army and its friends would find reviving the economy even harder than Gorbachev did. They would have no practical solution to nationalist tensions. They would be unable to stop the rot. That is why Shevardnadze was right when he said, at the close of his dramatic resignation speech, that "the dictatorship will not succeed." I hope he was also right when he added that "the future belongs to democracy and freedom."

Gorbachev has thought a good deal about his place in history. Once, when asked to which earlier Russian leaders he compared himself, he listed three reformer czars: Peter the Great, Catherine the Great and Alexander II. But of course, he added, the one I feel closest to is Lenin.

Lenin won the revolution and destroyed the old order, but he died in 1924 at age fifty-three, long before a new order was established. Stalin established it several years later.

Gorbachev will also have left the scene before the next new order is established. Like Lenin, Gorbachev was a missionary figure who could lead a crusade to a new Russia. He has the personality of a missionary—zealous, utterly self-confident, solemn to a fault. His determination to turn away from the past and start afresh was his greatest strength. But his zealotry and his self-confidence were confining. He could begin the process of reinventing his country, but at the critical moment he could not reinvent himself.

Perhaps Gorbachev will be remembered as the leader of the prologue to true *perestroika*—the real renewal of Russia. This is no small accomplishment. On the contrary, his is a heroic achievement, because Machiavelli was right: nothing is more difficult than taking the lead in the introduction of a new order of things.

POSTSCRIPT

Will History Look Favorably Upon Mikhail Gorbachev?

Turmoil in the Soviet Union's successor states has not ended with the resignation of Mikhail Gorbachev. The ongoing conflict between Russia and ethnic groups along the republic's borders flared into open warfare when Russian troops invaded the separatist region of Chechnya in December 1994. The resulting bloodshed damaged the reputation of Russian president Boris Yeltsin, hitherto regarded as one of Russia's foremost reformers, and aroused popular discontent with his government.

Economic problems continue to plague Russia and its neighboring republics. The gross domestic product has declined steadily since 1991, albeit at a slower rate in recent years. Budget deficits continue to rise, and unemployment remains a significant problem. Politically, the Communist Party staged a resurgence in Russia in 1995–1996, winning more than one-third of the seats in the legislature. In the summer of 1996 Yeltsin narrowly won a plurality of the voting in the Russian presidential campaign, but subsequent concerns about Yeltsin's health and emotional stability have raised doubts about Russia's political future.

Before the election, Yeltsin managed to reestablish Russian supremacy over most of its neighboring republics through the establishment of a "community" of states with shared political institutions and a common currency. Whether the region continues to experience turmoil, or whether new institutions and personalities emerge to restore a measure of stability, will go far toward determining history's judgment on the accomplishments of Mikhail Gorbachev, the man most responsible for the dismantling of the Soviet Union.

For a contemporary Russian perspective on Gorbachev, see Zhores A. Medvedev, *Gorbachev* (W. W. Norton, 1986). Two Western accounts may be found in *The Gorbachev Phenomenon: A Historical Interpretation* by Moshe Lewin (University of California Press, 1988) and *Russia and the West: Gorbachev and the Politics of Reform* by Jerry Hough (Simon & Schuster, 1988). Finally, Michael Beschloss, one of the foremost experts on late-twentieth-century American foreign policy, provides an excellent overview in *At the Highest Levels: The Inside Story of the End of the Cold War* (Little, Brown, 1993).

ISSUE 15

Should Africa's Leaders Be Blamed for the Continent's Current Problems?

YES: George B. N. Ayittey, from *Africa Betrayed* (St. Martin's Press, 1992)

NO: Ali A. Mazrui, from *The Africans: A Triple Heritage* (Little, Brown, 1986)

ISSUE SUMMARY

YES: Economics professor George B. N. Ayittey contends that since achieving independence, many African countries' interests have been betrayed by their own incompetent, corrupt, power-hungry leaders.

NO: Political science professor Ali A. Mazrui argues that colonialism's legacy is at the root of many of the problems facing African countries today.

To say that Africa has been exploited by outsiders throughout its history is an understatement. Beginning with the East and West African slave trades and continuing through the age of imperialism, it is difficult to fathom the price that Africa has had to pay for its geographic location and richness of resources.

When European imperialists invaded Africa in the late nineteenth century, the exploitation was blatant and all-encompassing. Every conceivable reason —economic, political, social, cultural, religious—was used by Europeans to justify their actions. By the time the imperialists were finished carving up the continent, only two states, Ethiopia and Liberia, could be called free and independent nations.

The post–World War II era marked the end of worldwide imperialism. Gradually, most of the continent's nations achieved independence, some peacefully, some through armed resistance or the threat of it. As these former colonies entered nationhood, hopes were high that Africa's future would be a bright and glorious one.

One only needs to look at the continent today, almost a half-century since the demise of colonialism, to see that Africa's problems far outweigh the continent's promise. In regard to this, several questions need to be answered. One of the most important is this: Who or what is responsible for Africa's state of affairs?

It would be hard to find anyone who would state that colonialism was a positive force in the development of Africa or that its negative impact was minimal. Therefore, the standard argument is that many of the continent's problems are part and parcel of the colonial legacy. Recently, however, the focus of attention has turned to many African leaders, who some argue have betrayed their people's trust and exploited their country's wealth in the name of power and self-aggrandizement. Today, the continent seems to be filled with military dictators and political tyrants who refuse to serve anyone but themselves and their cronies and who neglect to share power with anyone, including their own people. Some feel that the fact that aid programs from Western nations often went to staunch anticommunists rather than solid, prodemocratic leaders exacerbated the problems.

The authors of the following selections—George B. N. Ayittey, a native Ghanian, and Ali A. Mazrui, born in Kenya—agree that the colonial legacy was damaging to Africa's people and their interests. Their differences lie in determining who or what is responsible for the continent's current problems. For Ayittey, the answer is simple: African leaders who have come to power since independence have betrayed their own people through usurpation of power, political corruptness, and a failure to enact democratic principles. He finds that the continent today is generally worse off than it was under colonial rule. The policies of the outside world toward Africa have not helped the situation, maintains Ayittey, but the problems that the continent faces today are more internal than external.

Mazrui argues that a "triple heritage" has influenced the development of Africa: indigenous African cultures, Western colonialism, and Islam. He sees Western colonialism as being responsible for Africa's problems because it has forced African culture to declare war against itself in order to survive. Islam, he feels, has been a positive force in the development of the continent, but its influence on African affairs seems to be declining rather than increasing. Mazrui contends that Western colonialism continues to plague Africa today because of the legacy it has bequeathed to the continent.

The question of responsibility for Africa's current problems is an important one, for these problems cannot be solved until it is understood what has caused them.

YES

George B. N. Ayittey

ALUTA CONTINUA!
(*THE STRUGGLE CONTINUES!*)

This [is an attempt] to present the true story about Africa's postcolonial experience. It is a grisly picture of one betrayal after another: economic disintegration, political chaos, inane civil wars, and infrastructural and institutional decay. These were not what Africans hoped for when they asked for their independence from colonial rule in the 1960s. It is difficult to convey their outrage and sense of indignation at the leaders who have failed them.

By the beginning of the 1990s economic and political conditions in Africa had become intolerable. African socialism has been a dismal failure, one-party rule has been a disaster, and international blindness to the nearly universal corruption of the continent's leaders has made matters immeasurably worse.

Various actors, foreign as well as domestic, participated, wittingly or not, in the devastation of Africa. It is easy for African leaders to put the blame somewhere else; for example, on Western aid donors or on an allegedly hostile international economic environment. But as the World Bank observed in its 1984 report, *Toward Sustained Development in Sub-Saharan Africa*, "genuine donor mistakes and misfortunes alone cannot explain the excessive number of 'white elephants'" (p. 24). Certainly, donor blunders and other external factors have contributed to the crisis in Africa, but in my view the internal factors have played a far greater role than the external ones.

Of the internal factors, the main culprit has been the failure of leadership. In many cases African leaders themselves created "black elephants" and state enterprises that were dictated more by considerations of prestige than by concerns for economic efficiency. Mobutu Sese Seko of Zaire once declared, "I know my people. They like grandeur. They want us to have respect abroad in the eyes of other countries" (*The Wall Street Journal*, Oct 15, 1986). Accordingly, half of Zaire's foreign debt of $6 billion went to build two big dams and the Inga-Shaba powerline, as well as a $1 billion double-decked suspension bridge over the Congo River. The upper level is for a railroad that does not exist. In many other cases elite *bazongas* (raiders of the public treasury) blatantly squandered part of the foreign aid money. Does Africa need more foreign aid?

From George B. N. Ayittey, *Africa Betrayed* (St. Martin's Press, 1992). Copyright © 1992 by George B. N. Ayittey. Reprinted by permission of St. Martin's Press, Inc. Notes omitted.

In truth, Africa needs less—not more —foreign aid. David Karanja of Kenya wrote: "Foreign aid has done more harm to Africa than we care to admit. It has led to a situation where Africa has failed to set its own pace and direction of development free of external interference. Today, Africa's development plans are drawn thousands of miles away in the corridors of the IMF and World Bank" (*New African,* Jun 1992; p. 20).

Moreover, there are a number of ways that aid resources Africa desperately needs can be found in Africa itself. Maritu Wagaw wrote: "Let Africa look inside Africa for the solution of its economic problems. Solutions to our predicament should come from within not from outside" (*New African,* Mar 1992; p. 19). Indeed.

First, in 1989 Africa was spending $12 billion annually to import arms and to maintain the military. Second, the elites illegally transferred from Africa at least $15 billion annually during the latter part of the 1980s. Third, at least $5 billion annually could be saved if Africa could feed itself. Foreign exchange saved is foreign exchange earned. Fourth, another $5 billion could be saved from waste and inefficiencies in Africa's 3,200-odd state enterprises. This might entail selling off some of them or placing them under new management. Fifth, the civil wars raging in Africa exact a heavy toll in lost output, economic development, and destroyed property. If Angola's civil war alone cost the country $1 billion annually, $10 billion would not be an unreasonable estimate of the average annual cost of civil wars throughout the continent. Adding up these savings and the foreign exchange generated from internal sources would yield at least $47 billion annually, compared with the $12.4

billion in aid Africa received from all sources in 1990.

A bucket full of holes can only hold a certain amount of water for a certain amount of time. Pouring in more water makes little sense as it will all drain away. To the extent that there are internal leaks in Africa—corruption, senseless civil wars, wasteful military expenditures, capital flight, and government wastes—pouring in more foreign aid is futile. As a first order of priority, the leaks should be plugged to ensure that the little aid that comes in, stays. But African dictators, impervious to reason, continue to wage destructive wars.

In 1990 the OAU [Organization of African Unity] finally began to show signs of awakening from its slumber. Delegates to the OAU summit in July of that year, which Nelson Mandela addressed, observed that the summit demonstrated realism and a laudable determination to make progress in the resolution of Africa's intractable problems. Delegates realized that if Africa is to resist Western pressure for reforms and find its own solutions, it must first put its house in order. There was a genuine desire to end civil wars and disputes between neighbors, to increase regional cooperation, and to advance development.

The delegates signed a declaration, pledging to establish more democracy on the continent. According to the *Washington Times,* the incoming OAU chairman, President Yoweri Museveni of Uganda, averred, "Africa must find African solutions to its problems." Emphasizing that democracy could take many forms, he said that all states must have regular, free elections, a free press, and respect for human rights. In addition, the *Washington Times* reported that Nigerian President Ibrahim Babangida told the assembly that

Africa's leaders had failed their people. "Ever since the majority of our countries became independent in the 1960s we have conducted our lives as if the world owes us a living," he said. According to one African political analyst, the delegates realized that "unless they change they won't be coming to any other summits because they will no longer be in power" (*Washington Times*, Jul 13, 1990; p. A11). But rhetoric is one thing and action another.

While the delegates were speaking, the Babangida administration was continuing its crackdown on journalists and anyone suspected to be involved in the abortive April 22, 1990, coup attempt. In Uganda it may be recalled that journalists who put tough questions to visiting President Kaunda were arrested in spite of the free press that President Museveni called for.

If Africa is in a mess, the fault does not lie in any innate inferiority of the African people but rather in the alien, defective political systems instituted across much of the continent. It is not the charisma or the rhetoric of African leaders which makes a political system democratic and accountable. The *institutional approach* ... is far superior.

Kwame Nkrumah, Julius Nyerere, Kenneth Kaunda and other nationalists were all great heroes with charisma. But they all established regimes which lacked the institutions of a free press, an independent judiciary, freedom of political association, and the most basic standards of accountability. Political systems which lack these institutions have the tendency to produce despots.... [V]irtually all African regimes have been characterized by an enormous concentration of both economic and political power in the hands of the state and, therefore, one individual.

Africa has more than its share of civilian autocrats, military dictators, and rapacious elites.... Africa's indigenous system of government produced few tyrants. The modern leadership is a far cry from the traditional. In fact, by Africa's indigenous standards the modern leadership in much of Africa has been a disgraceful failure. They refuse to learn and keep repeating not only their own mistakes but those of others as well.

In an address to the Rotary International in Accra, retired Lt. Gen. Emmanuel Erskine, former commander of the United Nations Forces in Lebanon, remarked: "The fact that some African leaders get themselves emotionally identified with their country which they consider their personal property and that they and their minority ethnic clientele should lead the country and that they should rule until death is the single major phenomenon creating serious political crisis on the continent. Not even bulldozers can dislodge some of these leaders from office" (West Africa, May 6–12, 1991; p. 722).

WHY AFRICAN DICTATORS CLING TO POWER

Recall from Chapter 6 that between 1957 and 1990, there were more than 150 African heads of state and only six relinquished power voluntarily. There are three main reasons why African heads of state refuse to step down when their people get fed up with them. First, they somehow get this absurd notion that the country belongs to them and them alone. Witness their pictures on the currency and in every nook and cranny in the country. Every monument or building of some significance is named after them: Houphouet-Boigny this, Houphouet-Boigny that, Moi National Park, and on and on. In Malawi, "President Hastings Kamuzu Banda's face is everywhere, from the buttons on Youth League uniforms to the dresses of dancers. Highways, stadiums and schools are named for him. A national holiday honors him. It is forbidden to call him by his last name; only 'Ngwazi,' meaning lion or protector, or 'the life president' are allowed (*Washington Post,* May 5, 1992; p. A22).

Second, insecure African heads of state surround themselves with loyal supporters, often drawn from their own tribes: the late Doe from the Krahn tribe, Mobutu of Zaire from the Gbande, Biya of Cameroon from the Bamileke, Moi of Kenya from the Kalenjin and Babangida of Nigeria from the Muslims. In Togoland, about 70 percent of General Eyadema's army were drawn from his own Kabye tribe (*Africa Report,* Jan–Feb 1992; p. 5).

Other supporters are simply bought: soldiers with fat paychecks and perks; urban workers with cheap rice and sardines ("essential commodities"); students with free tuition and hefty allowances; and intellectuals, opposition leaders and lawyers with big government posts and Mercedes-Benzes.

Even when the head of state is contemplating stepping down, these supporters and lackeys fiercely resist any cutbacks in government largesse or any attempt to open up the political system. This was precisely the case in The Gambia when Sir Dawda Jawara—in power since the country's independence in 1965—announced in March 1992 his intention to step down. Freeloaders and patronage junkies urged him to stay on! In Sierra Leone, Mr. Musa Gendemeh, the deputy

agriculture minister, was quite explicit. On the BBC "Focus on Africa" program (Apr 24, 1990), he declared that,

"He won't give up his present privileged position for the sake of a multiparty system nor would one expect a policeman or soldier to give up his one bag of rice at the end of every month for the same. . . .

He warned that anyone talking about another party would be committing treason . . . that ministers and MPs suspected of having something to do with the multiparty movement are now under surveillance . . . and that whenever there has been trouble in the country, his people, the Mende, have suffered the most and he warned them to be careful" (*West Africa,* Jun 4–10, 1990; p. 934).

To protect their perks and benefits, these sycophants lie, deceive, and misinform the head of state. They continually praise him to the sky, even when his own tail is on fire! Kenneth Kaunda was informed that he would have "no problem" winning the October 1991 elections as he had 80 percent of the popular vote and "everything else had been taken care of." But when the actual voting took place, he was resoundingly humiliated, garnering a pitiful 25 percent of the vote. Ghanaians would recall that "party stooges" and "sycophants" also misled Nkrumah. African leaders should remember that "it is better to have wise people reprimand you than have stupid people sing you praises" (Ecclesiastes 7:5).

The third reason why African heads of state are reluctant to relinquish power is *fear.* Many of them have their hands so steeped in blood and their pockets so full of booty that they are afraid all their past gory misdeeds will be exposed. So they cling to power, regardless of the cost and consequences. But eventually they are dislodged, and only few subsequently are able to live peacefully in their own countries, much less to enjoy the loot.

Three Ways of Removing African Tyrants

In the ouster of Africa's dictators, three scenarios have emerged since 1990. By the "Doe scenario," those leaders who foolishly refused to accede to popular demands for democracy only did so at their own peril and at the destruction of their countries: Doe of Liberia, Traore of Mali, Barre of Somalia and Mengistu of Ethiopia. (Doe was killed in September 1990; Barre fled Mogadishu in a tank in January 1991; and Mengistu to Zimbabwe in February 1991.) African countries where this scenario is most likely to be repeated are Algeria, Cameroon, Djibouti, Equatorial Guinea, Libya, Malawi, Sudan, Tunisia, and Uganda.

In the "Kerekou scenario," those African leaders who wisely yielded to popular pressure managed to save not only their own lives but their countries as well: Kerekou of Benin, Kaunda of Zambia, Sassou-Nguesso of Central African Republic, and Pereira of Cape Verde Islands. Unfortunately, they are the exceptions.

The "Eyadema scenario," the third, is by far the most common. In this scenario, they yield initially after considerable domestic and international pressure but then attempt to manipulate the rules and the transition process to their advantage, believing that they could fool their people. In the end, they only fool themselves and are thrown out of office in disgrace. African countries likely to follow this route are: Angola, Burkina Faso, Burundi, Ghana, Ivory Coast, Kenya, Mozambique, Nigeria, Rwanda, Sierra Leone, Tanzania, Zaire, Zambia, and Zimbabwe. Recent events in Togo and Zaire also show that the outcome of the Eyadema scenario is highly unpredictable and its impact on economic development deleterious. Political uncertainty discourages business investment and trade....

Education of Opposition Leaders

It is sad and painful to admit that the level of political sophistication and intellectual maturity of some of our opposition leaders is disgustingly low. All opposition groups and leaders must recognize that the political arena is a free marketplace and they are like merchants, peddling political ideas and solutions. If they demand the right to propagate their political philosophy, they cannot deny anyone else the right to do so. If their philosophy has any merit, the people will buy it. If not, they will reject it. It is not up to the opposition leaders to make this determination, but the people.

Furthermore, most opposition leaders define "democracy" only in terms of their right to form political parties, to hold rallies, and to criticize foolish government policies.... [I]nstitutions such as the rule of law, freedom of expression, and an independent judiciary are far more important.

Focus

The primary focus of all opposition groups in Africa should be on removing the tyrant in power and establishing a level political playing field. If the tyrant is crafting a dubious transition process, the focus should be on halting or changing that process. All other issues (such as who should be president, what type of ideology the country should follow, a political platform, whether the country should have a new currency or flag) are secondary.

The Covenant

Quite clearly, the opposition in Africa needs to "get its act together." One effective way of doing this is to draw up a covenant, a set of rules by which all opposition groups agree to abide. At a meeting of all opposition leaders, a covenant should be signed containing the following stipulations:

1. Politics is a competitive game, and therefore the rules of competition must be established and respected by all. The term of the president will be limited to two terms (of four years each) in office.

2. All must agree on the safeguards and the necessary structures to be adopted to ensure free and fair elections. Political maturity requires accepting electoral defeat graciously and congratulating the winner. Political violence and voter intimidation must be eschewed. Severe sanctions, such as disqualification or heavy fines, must be imposed against any political party that is guilty of murder of political opponents.

3. Ultimately, it is the African people themselves who must determine what is best for them; not what one person imposes upon them. To do this, the African people need the means and the forum as well as the freedom to participate in the decisionmaking process.

4. Each opposition leader must agree to respect and honor the OAU's Charter of People's and Human Rights. This Charter is explicit on freedom of expression, freedom from arbitrary arrests, press freedoms, and so forth.

5. No one person or party shall monopolize the means or the forum by which the people can participate. All leaders will undertake to respect the right of every African to air his opinion freely, without harassment or intimidation, even if his view diverges from that of the head of state. Tolerance of diversity of opinion is a sign of intellectual maturity.

6. The media shall be taken out of the hands of the government. Religion and foreign ideology must be kept out of government. All leaders must pledge to build on or improve Africa's indigenous institutions and culture.

7. All must agree on sanctions to be applied against any leader or political party acting in violation of this covenant. Such sanctions must be determined by the leaders themselves.

After all is said and done, it becomes apparent that it is the educated elites—the leaders and the intellectuals—who have failed Africa. The Vai of Liberia have a proverb most appropriate for this situation. If after spending their meager savings to educate a child, he returns to the village an ignoramus, Vais elders may look upon him and ruefully remark: "The moon shines brightly but it is still dark in some places." Doesn't this describe postcolonial Africa and its elites?

Common sense has probably been the scarcest commodity among the elite in postcolonial Africa. Most of the "educated" leaders lacked it, intellectuals flouted it, and the opposition, in many cases, was woefully deficient in it. The peasants may be "illiterate and backward," but at least they can use their common sense. Obviously, a *common sense revolution* is what is urgently needed in African government. ...

While battling current despots, Africans should be vigilant, think ahead, and formulate strategies against the next buffoon. Since the winds of democratic change began sweeping across Africa in 1990, all sorts of intellectual crackpots, corrupt former politicians, charlatans, and unsavory elements have suddenly jumped on to the "democracy bandwagon" to hijack the democratic revolution. In 1992, Kaunda, and Nyerere, for example, were all preaching multiparty democracy. Where were they back in 1985 when true democrats were laying their lives on the line to demand political pluralism?... The African story is one of betrayal—by one buffoon after another.

NO

Ali A. Mazrui

A CELEBRATION OF DECAY?

WESTERNISATION AND DECAY

The ancestors of Africa are angry. For those who believe the power of the ancestors, the proof of their anger is all around us. For those who do not believe in ancestors, the proof of their anger is given another name. In the words of Edmund Burke, 'People will not look forward to posterity who never look backward to their ancestors.

But what is the proof of the curse of the ancestors? Things are not working in Africa. From Dakar to Dar es Salaam, from Marrakesh to Maputo, institutions are decaying, structure are rusting away. It is as if the ancestors had pronounced the curse of cultural sabotage. This generation of Africans is hearing the ancestral voice in no uncertain terms proclaiming,

> Warriors will fight scribes for the control of your institutions; wild bush will conquer your roads and pathways; your land will yield less and less while your offspring multiply; your houses will leak from the floods and your soil will crack from the drought; your sons will refuse to pick up the hoe and prefer to wander in the wilds; you shall learn ways of cheating and you will poison the cola nuts you serve your own friends. Yes, things will fall apart.

If this is the curse of the ancestors, what is the sin? It is the compact between Africa and the twentieth century and its terms are all wrong. They involve turning Africa's back on previous centuries—an attempt to 'modernize' without consulting cultural continuities, an attempt to start the process of 'dis-Africanizing' Africa. One consequence takes on the appearance of social turbulence, of rapid social change let loose upon a continent.

Franklin D. Roosevelt once said to Americans, when faced with the economic crisis of the 1930s, 'The only thing we have to fear is fear itself.' For my turn I am tempted to say to fellow Africans, facing a series of severe political, economic, social and cultural crises in the 1980s, 'The main thing we need to change is our own changeability.'

African states since independence have experienced a bewildering and rapid sequence of military coups and economic shifts and turns. In addition, over the last generation or two there has been a remarkable pace of

From Ali A. Mazrui, *The Africans: A Triple Heritage* (Little, Brown, 1986). Copyright © 1986 by Greater Washington Educational Telecommunications Association; text copyright © 1986 by Ali A. Mazrui. Reprinted by permission of Little, Brown and Company. Notes omitted.

cultural dis-Africanisation and Westernisation. If the Jews in the Diaspora had scrambled to change their culture as fast as Africans in their own homelands seemed to be doing until recently, the miracle of Jewish identity would not have lasted these two or three additional millennia in the wilderness. Many Africans even today seem to be undergoing faster cultural change in a single generation than the Jews underwent in the first 1000 years of dispersal.

Yet there may be hope in the very instability which Africa is experiencing in the wake of this unnatural dis-Africanisation. The fate of African culture may not yet be irrevocably sealed. With every new military coup, with every collapse of a foreign aid project, with every evidence of large-scale corruption, with every twist and turn in opportunistic foreign policy, it becomes pertinent to ask whether Western culture in Africa is little more than a nine-day wonder.

Africa is at war. It is a war of cultures. It is a war between indigenous Africa and the forces of Western civilisation. It takes the form of inefficiency, mismanagement, corruption and decay of the infrastructure. The crisis of efficiency in the continent is symptomatic of the failure of transplanted organs of the state and the economy. Indigenous African culture is putting up a fight. It is as if the indigenous ancestors have been aroused from the dead, disapproving of what seems like an informal pact between the rulers of independent Africa (the inheritors of the colonial order) and the West—a pact which allows the West to continue to dominate Africa. It is as if the ancestors are angry at the failure of Africans to consult them and to pay attention to Africa's past and usage. It is as if the apparent breakdown and decay in Africa today is a result of the curse of the ancestors. Or is it not a curse but a warning, a sign from the ancestors calling on Africans to rethink their recent past, their present and their future and calling on them to turn again to their traditions and reshape their society anew, to create a modern and a future Africa that incorporates the best of its own culture?

What is likely to be the outcome of this drama? Is the Westernisation of Africa reversible? Was the European colonial impact upon Africa deep or shallow? Was the colonial impact a cost or a benefit to Africa?

THE EPIC OF COLONIALISM

Let us take the epic school first, the insistence that these last 100 years were not a mere century but a revolution of epic proportions. The arguments for this school include a number of apparently decisive turning points.

First, there is the argument that colonialism and the accompanying capitalism effectively incorporated Africa into the world economy, for good or ill. It started with the slave trade, which dragged African labour itself into the emerging international capitalist system. This was the era of the *labour* imperative in relations between Africa and the West.

But colonialism was the era of the *territorial* imperative, as the West demanded from Africa not just labour but territory and its promise in all its dimensions. Capitalism had come knocking on the doors of the continent and enticed the host into the wider world of the international economy.

Then there was Africa's admission into the state system of the world emanating from the European Peace of Westphalia of 1648. It was that particular set of treaties which has been regarded widely as the beginnings of the modern system of sovereign states. Africa might have been dragged screaming into the world of capitalism, but it was not dragged unwillingly into the world of the sovereign state system. On the contrary, one colonial society after another framed its agitation and anti-imperialism in terms of seeking admission to the international community whose rules had grown out of European diplomatic history and statecraft. Independence for every African country was in fact a voluntary entry into the sovereign state system.

Then there is Africa's incorporation into a world culture which is still primarily Eurocentric. The major international ideologies—liberalism, capitalism, socialism, Marxism, communism and indeed fascism—have all been European-derived. To that extent, the world of ideology is in part the world of European dominance in the field of values and norms.

Another aspect of Africa's incorporation into world culture concerns the role of European languages in Africa. The significance of English, French and Portuguese especially in Africa's political life can hardly be overestimated, at least in the short run. Rulers are chosen on the basis of competence in the relevant imperial language. Nationwide political communication in the majority of African countries is almost impossible without the use of the relevant imperial medium.

Then there is Africa's incorporation into the world of international law, which is again heavily Eurocentric in origin. Many aspects of international law are named after European cities—the Geneva Convention, the Vienna Convention and the like. One looks in vain in the body of international law for conventions named after such Third World cities as

Bombay, Maiduguri or Rio de Janeiro. But nevertheless African states *seem* to be firmly and irrevocably tied to the body of legal precepts governing international diplomacy in the twentieth century.

Also part of the epic theory of the significance of colonialism is the technological variable. It is quite clear that the West has been in the lead in scientific and technological change for at least 300 years. Western colonisation of Africa could therefore be interpreted as an invitation to Africa to be incorporated into the modern technological age. At first glance this ranges from medical science to the automobile, from the tractor in African agriculture to the missile in African military establishments. Again, this would seem to be an incorporation into a global system which is basically of epic proportions and seemingly irreversible.

INFORMATION FLOWS AND THE MORAL ORDER

Next is the issue of information and data. Africa has been swallowed by the global system of dissemination of information. What Africa knows about itself, what different parts of Africa know about each other, have been profoundly influenced by the West. Even in the field of the mass media, Africa is overwhelmingly dependent on the wire services of the Western world for information about itself. What Nigerians know about Kenya, or Zambians know about Ghana, is heavily derived from the wire services of the Western world transmitting information across the globe. African newspapers and radios subscribe to these wire services and receive data for their news bulletins from Western sources.

Also apparently epic in significance was the *moral* order which had come with colonialism and Christianity. Important Western and Christian ethical factors entered the domain of African systems of restraint. Can a man have more than one wife? Is female circumcision morally legitimate? Is there such a thing as an illegitimate child if the father admits paternity and the mother acknowledges the child? How sinful was sexuality outside marriage?

All these were major moral dilemmas for Africa, *implying* a permanent change as a result of colonisation and Christianisation. How then could their impact be anything but an epic drama? How then could European influence be anything but a totally transformative force?

COLONIALISM AS AN EPISODE

Yet there is an alternative case for regarding the European impact as no more than an episode in millennia of African history.

There are two main versions of this idea. One insists that Africa could have entered the world economy and the international state system without being colonized by Europe. After all, Japan is now a major power in the world economy and has at times been a major figure in the international state system without having undergone the agonies of European colonisation and imperialism. Japan was able to acquire Western tools without succumbing to Western subjugation. But Africa was denied that option.

Related to this is the argument that modern science and technology were bound to convert the whole world into a global village. Twentieth-century science and technology had become too expansionist to have left Africa untouched. If this body of expertise could reach the Moon without colonizing it, why could

it not have reached Africa without subjugating it?

What follows from this is the conclusion that European colonisation of Africa was not the only way of Africa's entry into the global system of the twentieth century. Africa could have made such an entry without suffering either the agonies of the slave trade, or the exploitation of colonialism or the humiliation of European racism.

The second version of the episodic school asserts that the European impact on Africa has been shallow rather than deep, transitional rather than long-lasting. It is not often realised how brief the colonial period was. When Jomo Kenyatta was born, Kenya was not yet a crown colony. Kenyatta lived right through the period of British rule and outlasted British rule by fifteen years. If the entire period of colonialism could be compressed into the life-span of a single individual, how deep was the impact?

The kind of capitalism which was transferred to Africa was itself shallow. Western consumption patterns were transferred more effectively than Western production techniques, Western tastes were acquired more quickly than Western skills, the profit motive was adopted without the efficient calculus of entrepreneurship, and capitalist greed was internalised sooner than capitalist discipline.

All this is quite apart from the anomaly of urbanisation without industrialisation. In the history of the Western world the growth of cities occurred partly in response to fundamental changes in production. Urbanisation followed in the wake of either an agrarian transformation or an industrial revolution. But in the history of Africa urbanisation has been under way without accompanying growth of productive capacity. In some African countries there is indeed a kind of revolution—but it is a revolution in urbanisation rather than in industrialisation, a revolution in expanding numbers of people squeezed into limited space, rather than a transformation in method and skill of economic output. It is these considerations which have made capitalism in Africa, such as it is, lopsided and basically shallow.

But alongside this phenomenon is the post-colonial state in Africa, which is also quite often in the process of decaying. The African state since independence has been subject to two competing pressures —the push towards militarisation and the pull towards privatisation. In the capitalist Western world state ownership is regarded as an alternative to or even the opposite of private ownership. The privatisation of the steel industry (its return from state nationalisation to private ownership) in England, for example, is an alternative to state ownership and state control.

In post-colonial Africa, on the other hand, the question arises whether the state in itself can be privatized or become privately owned. Is there a new echo in Africa of Louis XIV's notorious dictum, 'I am the state'?

There is an echo of a sort, but with distinctive African variations. What must be remembered is that the pressure of privatisation in Africa are accompanied by pressures towards militarisation. The pull towards privatisation is partly a legacy of greed in the tradition of Shylock, Shakespeare's creation in *The Merchant of Venice*. The push towards militarism, on the other hand, is a legacy of naked power in the tradition of Shaka, the founder of the Zulu kingdom and empire. Africa is caught between Shylock and Shaka, between greed and naked power—and the decay of the post-colonial state is one consequence of that dialectic.

In Nigeria between 1979 and 1984 the two tendencies of privatisation and militarisation appeared to be alternatives. Under civilian rule from 1979 privatisation gathered momentum. The resources of the nation were, to all intents and purposes, deemed to be the private hunting ground of those in power and of their supporters. Lucrative contracts for trade or construction were handed out on the basis of personal considerations. Foreign exchange was privately allocated and arbitrarily distributed. Millions of dollars and naira disappeared into the private accounts of key figures abroad.

This rampant unofficial and unlegislated privatisation of the state's resources seemed to have set the stage for the state's militarisation. Nigeria's armed forces— restive for a variety of reasons—found additional grounds for impatience with the civilian politicians. On 31 December 1983 the soldiers once again intervened and took over power. The push towards militarisation had triumphed over the pull towards privatisation of the Nigerian state. The soldiers justified their intervention on the basis of ending the private pillage of the country's resources. The action of the soldiers this time seemed calculated to arrest the decay of both the Nigerian economy and state....

IS THE CRESCENT ALSO DECAYING?

The first thing to note is that the most serious forms of decay seem to be occurring in the institutions inherited from the Western world, rather than those bequeathed by Islam.

But this very decomposition of the Western heritage has complex consequences for Islam in Africa. It is arguable that where Islam is already established, the decline of the West is advantageous for Islam. After all, the most important threat to Islam in Africa is not a revival of indigenous culture but the triumph of Western secularism. The materialism of Western civilisation, the superiority of Western science and technology at their home base in the West, the declining moral standards in at least certain areas of Western culture, and the glitter and temptations of Western life-styles, have all combined to pose a significant threat especially to the younger generations of the Muslim world. As these Western institutions grind to a standstill in Africa, causing new areas of poverty and deprivation, the glitter of Western civilisation begins to dim.

But while established Islam is indeed stabilised by this Western decay, Islamic expansion to new areas is probably hindered by the same decay. For example, the economic decline in West Africa has resulted in reduced traffic of Muslim traders and other migrants, many of whom have been unofficial missionaries for the Islamic faith. Also reducing the expansion of Islam are the decaying roads and railways, which reduce social and economic mobility.

To summarize the argument so far: where Islam is already established, the decay of Western civilisation is good for Islam since it helps to neutralise a major threat. On the other hand, where Islam has not yet arrived, the disintegration of African communications and the decline in commercial traffic across African borders has reduced the pace of Islamic expansion....

CONCLUSION

European colonial rule in Africa was more effective in destroying indigenous African *structures* than in destroying African *culture*. The tension between new imported structures and old resilient cultures is part of the post-colonial war of cultures in the African continent. The question has therefore arisen as to whether Africa is reclaiming its own.

As we have indicated, the shallowness of the imported *economic* institutions from the West was partly due to the lopsided nature of colonial acculturation. Western consumption patterns prevailed more quickly than Western production techniques, thus promoting Western tastes without developing Western skills.

As for the shallowness of the imported *political* institutions, this was partly due to the moral contradictions of Western political tutelage. After independence these political contradictions took their toll, for the transferred institutions simply did not take root. Africa was torn between the forces of anarchy on one side, in the sense of decentralised violence, and the forces of tyranny, on the other side, in the sense of orchestrated centralised repression. The post-colonial state was in turn torn between the forces of privatisation and the forces of militarism. Privatisation puts a state outside the public sector, as it denationalises it. Militarisation, by definition, abolishes the principle of civilian supremacy.

But in the final analysis, the shallowness of the imported institutions is due to that culture gap between new structures and ancient values, between alien institutions and ancestral traditions.

Africa can never go back completely to its pre-colonial starting point but there may be a case for at least a partial retreat, a case for re-establishing contacts with familiar landmarks of yesteryear and then re-starting the journey of modernisation under indigenous impetus.

In many parts of Africa there is, as we indicated, a war between Islam and Westernism. The decay of Western civilisation is good for Islam in those parts of the continent. But the decay of the infrastructure and the decline of African economies may be bad for Islamic expansion in west Africa.

But when all is said and done, the most important cultural conflict occurring in Africa is between Western civilisation and indigenous forces. If instability in the continent is a symptom of cultures at war, perhaps Africa's identity may survive the ravages of Westernisation after all. It is still true to say that Africans in the twentieth century are becoming acculturated faster than were, for example, the Jews in the first millennium of their dispersal. But the war of cultures is by no means over in Africa. It is almost as if the indigenous ancestors have been aroused from the dead, and are fighting back to avert the demise of Africanity. In their immediate consequences decay and instability are a matter of lament. But in their longer term repercussions, they may be a matter for celebration.

But what is the way out? How can Africa's compact with the twentieth century be amended? How can the ancestors be appeased?

Two broad principles should influence and inform social reform in Africa in the coming decades. One is the imperative of looking inwards towards ancestry; the other is the imperative of looking outward towards the wider humanity. The inward imperative requires a more systematic investigation into the cultural preconditions of the success of each project, of each piece of legislation, of each system of government. Feasibility studies should be much more sensitive to the issue of 'cultural feasibility' than has been the case in the past. Africa's ancestors need to be consulted through the intermediary of consulting African usage, custom and tradition.

But since the world is becoming a village, Africa cannot just look inward to its own past. The compact with the twentieth century has to include a sensitivity to the wider world of the human race as a whole. . . .

Islam and Westernism have been part of Africa's response to the imperative of looking outward to the wider world. But Africa's own ancestors are waiting to ensure that Africa also remembers to look inward to its own past.

Before a seed germinates it must first decay. A mango tree grows out of a decaying mango seed. A new Africa may be germinating in the decay of the present one—and the ancestors are presiding over the process.

POSTSCRIPT

Should Africa's Leaders Be Blamed for the Continent's Current Problems?

Although Ayittey and Mazrui disagree on the causes of Africa's current problems, they agree on what is needed to improve conditions there—the rediscovery and promotion of the African traditions and institutions that have been misplaced or discarded since colonialism's end. The West can play a role in this process, but it must be a supportive rather than a directive role. The time has come to let Africans solve Africa's problems—using uniquely African solutions, if they are deemed necessary.

Besides the two sources from which this issue's readings were taken, there are many fine books on the subject of Africa since World War II. Robert W. July, in *An African Voice: The Role of the Humanities in African Independence* (Duke University Press, 1987), concentrates on Africa's struggles against cultural imperialism, a subject that is eloquently dealt with in Mazrui's book. Basil Davidson, Europe's most sensitive and prolific writer on African history and culture, surveys the continent's recent history in *The Black Man's Burden: Africa and the Curse of the Nation-State* (Random House, 1992). Davidson's *Search for Africa: History, Culture, Politics* (Random House, 1994) is more historical in coverage but nevertheless complementary to *Black Man's Burden*.

For a history of the African continent and its people, see Robert W. July, *A History of the African People* (Waveland Press, 1992) and Roland Oliver, *The African Experience: Major Themes in African History from Earliest Times to the Present* (HarperCollins, 1992). Finally, two videotape series are recommended: Mazrui's *Africans: A Triple Heritage* and Davidson's *Africa: A Voyage of Discovery With Basil Davidson*.

ISSUE 16

Has the United Nations Outlived Its Usefulness?

YES: Saadia Touval, from "Why the U.N. Fails," *Foreign Affairs* (September/October 1994)

NO: Rosemary Righter, from *Utopia Lost: The United Nations and World Order* (Twentieth Century Fund Press, 1995)

ISSUE SUMMARY

YES: Saadia Touval, a Peace Fellow at the United States Institute of Peace, maintains that the United Nations contains inherent defects that severely limit its effectiveness as a mediator and peacekeeper.

NO: Editorial writer Rosemary Righter argues that the increasing dependence upon multilateral action among the world's nations will enhance the United Nations' effectiveness.

In June 1945, 50 nations gathered in San Francisco, California, to sign the charter of the United Nations. Clearly, different countries had diverse motives for establishing the UN at the end of World War II, but for the victorious Allies the United Nations offered a forum for the peaceful resolution of international disputes and, therefore, for maintaining the existing world order with only gradual, managed change. Publicly, the UN charter stated that the organization's members would "work with renewed vigor and effectiveness in promoting peace, development, equality and justice, and understanding among the peoples of the world."

Initially, officials expected the most significant bodies within the United Nations to be the General Assembly and the Security Council. The rivalry among Security Council members—and the existence of a veto power that made unanimity necessary—soon eviscerated the council as a viable means of keeping world peace. And the explosion of membership in the General Assembly during the late 1950s and early 1960s, when numerous nations in Africa and Asia gained their independence and were admitted to the UN, made it possible for nations with small populations to block action in that body, too.

Although the UN played a significant peacekeeping role in Cyprus, Pakistan, and India in the immediate postwar years, it failed to stop Soviet aggression in Hungary in 1956 and in Czechoslovakia in 1968. The United Nations also could not prevent the spread of nuclear weapons. The organization did, however, enable nations to work effectively in such areas of social improvement as education, health reform, and environmental protection.

In the following selection, Saadia Touval maintains that the United Nations has never fulfilled the promise of its founders and that it never will. According to Touval, the UN cannot solve international disputes because it lacks credibility as a mediator and possesses little effective leverage to force disputants to accept its findings. Moreover, the fact that the UN's actions must reflect a consensus among dozens of nations means that it can rarely pursue a consistent or cohesive strategy over a prolonged period of time. Touval suggests that the United Nations should encourage member states to resolve problems in their own areas of strategic interest and influence. Unless its member states voluntarily surrender a considerable measure of sovereignty and agree to abide by majority votes within the organization, Touval concludes that the UN will never be an effective peacekeeping force.

In the second selection, Rosemary Righter concedes that the United Nations has not lived up to its potential, but she insists that it possesses the potential to act more effectively in the twenty-first century. For Righter, the key to the UN's capabilities resides in the increasingly multilateral character of international relations. As the world grows more interdependent, individual nations will find that they must, in fact, rely upon coalitions and cooperation to achieve their strategic goals. And as nations realize that they may no longer act with as much autonomy as they have in the past, Righter argues, they will become more amenable to turning problems over to the United Nations. And if the major powers restructure the United Nations' collective security functions, they may find cooperation within the organization a viable alternative to chaos and conflict.

YES

Saadia Touval

WHY THE U.N. FAILS

IT CANNOT MEDIATE

Only a few years ago it was widely expected that the end of the Cold War would lead to the rebirth of the United Nations. Between 1987 and 1991, the United Nations mediated a series of agreements that helped end fighting between Iran and Iraq, led to the withdrawal of Soviet forces from Afghanistan, established a broad-based coalition government in Cambodia, and ended El Salvador's chronic civil war. This brief window of success encouraged the view that it was the Cold War that had prevented the United Nations from being an effective mediator. The East-West standoff, many surmised, had made the collective security mechanism, envisaged by the U.N. Charter and premised on great power cooperation, a dream deferred.

That dream has already lost much of its promise. In hindsight, those successes clearly stemmed from unique circumstances. Successful U.N. mediation was made possible by the exhaustion of local parties and the unwillingness of external powers to continue supporting clients whose usefulness had expired with the Cold War. Iran and Iraq accepted a U.N.-brokered cease-fire only after they had spent themselves in an eight-year battle of attrition. The Soviet Union was eager to withdraw from a losing venture in Afghanistan, and U.N. mediation provided it with the face-saving mechanism to do so. Once denied Soviet backing, the Vietnamese desired to reduce their commitments in Cambodia, as did the Chinese who, in the wake of the Tiananmen Square massacre, wished to dissociate themselves from the Khmer Rouge and improve their international image. In El Salvador, both superpowers wanted to disengage and pressured their respective allies, themselves discouraged by an inconclusive war, to modify their positions.

Those heady days inspired the false hope that the United Nations could be an effective mediator of international disputes. Since then, U.N. negotiators, however talented and experienced, have tried for years to resolve or reduce conflicts in Afghanistan, Angola, Haiti, Somalia, and the former Yugoslavia, all without success. In fact, U.N. mediation seems to have extended or aggravated many of those disputes, as belligerents have been able to manipulate the organization's obvious weaknesses. And today none of those U.N. failures can be blamed on the Cold War.

It is increasingly apparent that the United Nations possesses inherent characteristics that make it incapable of effectively mediating complex international disputes. Yet because of its brief period of success, an egregious gap has grown between popular expectations and U.N. abilities. As currently constituted, the United Nations has great difficulty performing many basic functions required of an effective mediator. It does not serve well as an authoritative channel of communication. It has little real political leverage. Its promises and threats lack credibility. And it is incapable of pursuing coherent, flexible, and dynamic negotiations guided by an effective strategy.

Those limitations are ingrained. They are embedded in the very nature of intergovernmental organizations, and no amount of upgrading, expansion, or revamping of U.N. powers can correct those flaws. Rather, it is time to recognize U.N. shortcomings and to quit dumping on the organization tasks that it cannot perform. It is urgent instead to devise a mechanism whereby the United Nations can encourage individual states, under their own flags, to assume the risky and thankless task of mediating those conflicts that they have the best chance of resolving. Sponsored by the United Nations, unilateral mediation by great powers or other states who have a vested interest in conflicts within their sphere of influence offers the best chance to salvage waning U.N. prestige and to secure for many regions the peace that has been so elusive in recent years.

THE RISE OF THE LAST RESORT

Former Secretary General U Thant has offered part of the explanation for the disappointing U.N. record as a peacemaker: "Great problems usually come to the United Nations because governments have been unable to think of anything else to do about them. The United Nations is a last-ditch, last resort affair, and it is not surprising that the organization should often be blamed for failing to solve problems that have already been found to be insoluble by governments."[1]

It is this category of "orphan" conflicts, which states will not mediate on their own, either because they have more urgent priorities or because they are loath to commit their prestige and resources to a risky or peripheral endeavor, that are placed in the public charge, thrown into the lap of the United Nations or other international organizations. By their very nature they are the most intractable disputes and require effective mediation, especially as they are often among the most costly in terms of lives and human suffering. This was the case during the Cold War, and it remains so in the present era, with the difference being that the number of orphan conflicts is growing.

States make the primary decisions about mediation. They decide whether to exert efforts to help settle a conflict and, if so, whether to act alone or through the United Nations. A state external to a dispute typically initiates mediation for self-interested reasons. The stakes of the Cold War usually prompted states to mediate on their own rather than through the United Nations. The United States, for example, mediated between disputing NATO allies Greece and Turkey. It mediated between its allies and anticolonial forces, as in the Anglo-Iranian and Anglo-Egyptian disputes. It also mediated between newly independent states in order to prevent Soviet gains, for example, between Indonesia and Malaysia, and Egypt and Israel. Other states have launched mediation efforts for similar self-interested reasons. The Soviets mediated between India and Pakistan at Tashkent; France mediated between Mali and Senegal and recently between Cameroon and Nigeria; India mediated in Sri Lanka; and Saudi Arabia has frequently mediated between disputing Arab parties.

Disputants often accept such interventions because they hope a mediator can help them win better terms than they could attain on their own, or because they fear that rejecting mediation might lead the third party to support their enemy. Mediation may, of course, also be driven by altruism. But self-interest is a useful working assumption, helping to explain much of the mediation in contemporary international politics.

The number of orphan conflicts, which includes those in Bosnia and Somalia, has grown in the post–Cold War era. States have seemingly broadened their perceptions of self-interest, perhaps in response to the pressure of public opinion, to include issues such as stemming refugee flows and humanitarian abuses. This broader range of concerns has prompted states to refer to the United Nations the mediation of conflicts in Haiti, Liberia, Nagorno-Karabakh, Rwanda, Somalia, and the former Yugoslavia. At the same time, however, the great powers have become more reluctant to expend blood, treasure, and prestige to resolve this longer list of disputes that are nettlesome but do not directly threaten their security.

It is not necessarily the fault of the United Nations that it has been asked to mediate an increasing number of disputes. While the United Nations has certain institutional interests of its own, it is primarily an instrument of its membership. The secretary general is constrained by the views and interests of the Security Council's five permanent members. To accomplish any significant intervention, he needs their active support. This fact is demonstrated by Boutros Boutros-Ghali's efforts to engage the United Nations in Somalia and Rwanda. The United Nations mediates only to the extent that its membership desires and provides it with the necessary material and diplomatic resources. Unfortunately, states have become more likely to want the United Nations to mediate in situations where the organization has less chance of success than bolder and more persistent action by states themselves. Moreover, states have often become less forthcoming with the kinds of military or monetary support that might enable greater success....

THE BAD MEDIATOR

Granted, the United Nations is saddled With the most intractable disputes, but its poor mediation record is nonetheless troubling. The reason is that the United Nations possesses inherent qualities tha. render it ill-suited to the task. One need only look at tne functions that mediators must perform, then look at the United Nations, to sketch a stark contrast.

Mediators must offer their "good offices" to help disputants communicate. They try to persuade each party to change its image of the adversary or to interp.et the adversary's behavior in a manner that will facilitate a settlement. Mediators can help a party understand its adversary's concerns and constraints. They also suggest compromises and help parties save face in making concessions. Disputants, for example, often believe that it is less damaging to their reputations to accept a proposal made by a mediator than an adversary.

Mediation stands a better chance of succeeding when a conflict is "ripe"— that is, when adversaries feel exhausted and understand that the continued pursuit of their goals through other means would be costly or dangerous. But mediators can induce ripeness and contribute to the making of a "hurting stalemate." They help create a disposition among the disputants to settle the conflict. Having an interest in a settlement, mediators sometimes bargain with the parties, offer them incentives, or subject them to pressure in order to induce them to accept specific settlement terms. Finally, if an agreement is reached, mediators may provide guarantees that its terms will be honored and implemented.

Thus a successful mediator must be able to influence disputants to modify their positions. Foremost, it needs leverage. Some of a mediator's leverage derives from the very nature of a three-sided process. Like any triangle, the shape of a mediated negotiation contains the potential for a coalition to be formed. The possibility of the mediator lending support to one's adversary makes each disputant more dependent on the mediator and endows the mediator with bargaining power and influence. Such concerns, for example, were very much on the minds of Greek and Turkish leaders when the United States tried to mediate the Cyprus conflict in 1964 and 1967. But leverage also derives from military and economic resources, which great powers have in abundance. For example, by offering Egypt and Israel economic and military assistance, the United States was able to induce them to make important concessions leading to the Camp David accords.

Part of the U.N. problem is that it has no readily accessible military or economic resources of its own. It is entirely dependent on member states, or at least some of them, to provide the resources necessary for a successful mediation. The United Nations cannot even harness the assets of international financial and trading institutions. Doing so depends yet again on the decisions of member states. A U.N. mediator cannot commit the International Monetary Fund or World Bank to provide credits to reluctant disputants. While U.N. member states might theoretically be able to pool their resources and enhance the organization's bargaining power, that type of cooperation seldom comes about. Governments are usually reluctant to commit resources to such a venture, negotiations for such commitments are slow and cumbersome, and the resources states do make available are often inadequate.

These U.N. weaknesses are perceived by disputants. Parties are likely to doubt that U.N. promises of assistance or threats of punishment will actually be fulfilled. The same holds true for other international organizations. When Jacques Delors, president of the EC Commission, tried to mediate between the disputing Yugoslav parties in the spring of 1991, he promised that the EC would provide financial assistance and conclude a favorable trade agreement if the Yugoslavs compromised on restructuring the federation and avoided a breakup. But the promise carried little weight because Delors did not have the authority to commit EC states and could not credibly deliver.

Leverage is, of course, also a matter of legitimacy and credibility. This is the main U.N. asset: the aura of legitimacy its actions carry as representing the consensus of the international community. But U.N. credibility is consistently eroded by its inability to formulate and pursue the kind of coherent policy essential to mediation. A mediator must be able to pursue a dynamic negotiation, reacting to events quickly, seizing opportunities, and having the necessary flexibility to adjust positions and proposals as the situation unfolds. States often have difficulty in meeting those demanding requirements. For the United Nations, it is nearly impossible.

That kind of policymaking, even for a state, requires constant trade-offs between inconsistent goals and compromises among multiple participants. Policymaking within an international organization does not merely add another layer of bargaining and trade-offs. It is qualitatively different. There is no ultimate authority empowered to decide between competing proposals. Voting rules give the appearance of effective decision-making capacity. Security Council decisions, for example, are made when 9 of 15 members vote in favor, provided that none of the permanent members casts a veto. In reality, however, those rules do not eliminate the need for consensus. When pursuing mediation, intergovernmental organizations adopt only those measures on which consensus is possible. Issues and measures on which unanimity cannot be achieved are usually excluded. Even those decisions that are adopted are likely to be hedged and balanced. They are often ambiguous, re-

flecting a compromise based on the lowest common denominator.

This tortuous decision-making process saps the United Nations of necessary dynamism and flexibility in pursuing mediation. Once the United Nations agrees on a mediating proposal or framework, it cannot easily be modified in response to changing circumstances. Modification requires renegotiation among U.N. members, an often lengthy process that delays mediation. Thus the U.N.-EU commitment to the Vance-Owen plan constrained their ability to adapt to new conditions once the Serbs rejected it in the summer of 1993.

U.N. decisions are further weakened in the practice of day-to-day diplomacy. U.N. representatives need to be backed filly by the member states. But inevitably member states speak with different voices, and mediation efforts lack a coherent strategy. Again, the Vance-Owen plan serves as an example. While official mediators and some states were trying to persuade parties to accept the proposal, the United States indicated that it did not support it. Such discord undermines a coherent mediating position. It reduces the mediator's leverage and strengthens the hand of disputants. It provides an opening for a disputant to divide both the mediator from its adversary and the mediators among themselves.

The United Nations comes to mediation encumbered. It is bound not only by its own general principles but also by specific resolutions reflecting the membership's consensus about the principles upon which a settlement should be based. Such resolutions "instead of being pointers to a settlement... become a prison," restricting the mediators' room to maneuver.[2] For example, the admission of Bosnia-Herzegovina to the United

Nations, and the subsequent resolutions affirming its sovereignty, territorial integrity and political independence, restricted the ability of U.N. and EU mediators to trade territory for peace. Besides hindering the bargaining process, a lack of credibility can be fatal once negotiators must construct guarantees for implementing and observing an agreement. After the often incoherent U.N. negotiating process, disputants will have greater difficulty putting their faith in U.N. guarantees. Guarantees by great powers, motivated by a transparent self-interest, are likely to be more credible. It required an American presence in Sinai, unencumbered by U.N. auspices, to assure Egypt and Israel that their accord would be respected. An American commitment of ground troops to serve as a buffer between contending parties in Bosnia may similarly be required to lend credibility to any future settlement.

RENDER UNTO STATES ...

The problems in using the United Nations as a mediator are ingrained in the nature of intergovernmental organizations. No degree of devolution to less cumbersome multilateral organizations or U.N. restructuring is likely to improve U.N. performance. Moreover, member states are unlikely to agree to the kinds of reform required for the slimmest hope of making a significant difference in U.N. abilities.

Decentralizing mediation efforts by making greater use of regional organizations might ease the plight of the overburdened U.N. Security Council and Secretariat. It might also place greater responsibility on those states closest to the conflicts and presumably most interested in their resolution. Unfortunately, such a course is unlikely to be an improvement. Most of the problems that hamper the United Nations also impede regional organizations. They, too, are hindered by complex decision-making procedures, the inability to effectively commit usually scant state resources, and hence insufficient flexibility and leverage. By their very nature as intergovernmental organizations, they are incapable of pursuing coherent, flexible, and dynamic negotiations guided by an effective strategy.

To transform the United Nations into an effective mediator, states would have to agree to binding decisions by majority vote. U.N. mediators would have to be authorized to commit the membership to a course of action and to harness the resources of international financial and trade institutions as sticks and carrots. Member states, moreover, would have to learn to speak with one voice and refrain from any action that might undercut mediation efforts. But any of these ambitious reforms is difficult to imagine in the foreseeable future.

NOTES

1. U Thant, *View from the U.N.*, Garden City, NY: Doubleday & Co., 1978, p. 32.

2. Sydney D. Bailey, *How Wars End: The United Nations and the Termination of Armed Conflict, 1946–1964*, Oxford: Clarendon Press, 1982, vol. 1, p. 168.

NO

Rosemary Righter

UTOPIA LOST: THE UNITED NATIONS AND WORLD ORDER

There is an analogy between reform of the UN and the restructuring of national economies. Governments generally have to be convinced that there is no alternative before they embark on radical surgery—and even then the decisions are usually made long after the process should have begun and implemented less than resolutely. Tinkering with the UN will do no good. If the UN has reached a watershed, it is not in the last analysis for want of deciding what it "can and cannot do," as Pérez de Cuéllar put it, but because organizations of states, formally wedded to absolute respect for national sovereignty, are out of step. As we shall see, aspects of contemporary multilateralism inevitably blur the edges of sovereignty. Modernizing the UN will thus involve far more than streamlining—however indispensible it may be to shake out its bureaucracies.

Yet, at the same time, the circumstances for regenerating certain aspects of global cooperation ought to be propitious in the 1990s, and at least some UN organizations should be capable of catching the tide. There are several grounds for optimism. The apparent readiness of both Washington and Moscow to use the UN as one of the vehicles of diplomacy may be a passing phase. But even partial recourse to the UN provides an opportunity to rethink collective security. In a world in which the typical conflict is undeclared and, or internal, and the UN's conventional peacekeeping techniques fit only a minority of cases, such rethinking is in any case overdue.

The bloc politics that have been a dreary feature of UN debate appear to be on the way out, at least in the old East, South, West format. Constructive engagement in the UN forms part of the post-Communist world's insurance against political uncertainties; and for Russia, its neighboring republics and the Eastern Europeans alike, the International Monetary Fund, the World Bank, and the General Agreement on Tariffs and Trade regime are important assets in the hard task of modernizing their economies and integrating them with the outside world. The collapse of the "Eastern bloc" will inevitably disrupt old, ritualized allegiances and voting patterns. The myth of the "South," like nonalignment, required East-West rivalry as its foil. The "North-South"

From Rosemary Righter, *Utopia Lost: The United Nations and World Order* (Twentieth Century Fund Press, 1995). Copyright © 1995 by The Twentieth Century Fund. Reprinted with permission from The Twentieth Century Fund, New York. Notes omitted.

divide was of course a misnomer: it was a South-West divide, exploited by the East. Some pessimists anticipate that ideological divisions will be replaced by a *genuinely* North-South divide between "haves" and "have-nots." But the real world fits less and less readily into such neat divisions. Countries such as Mexico can no longer be counted even as reliable members of the "South" and even India, for so long a standard-bearer of Third World solidarity, is developing a robust streak of pragmatism. And in the poorest countries, the great wave of nationalism that accompanied decolonization has passed its euphoric phase; the demythification of sovereignty has begun and, with that, there may gradually be less inclination to use the global organizations as an anti-Western grandstand. Where states have a genuine stake in the outcome of a negotiation, the Uruguay Round of the General Agreement on Tariffs and Trade (GATT) talks revealed a new determination to put practical self-interest before theatricals. There is no "Third World interest." The breakup of the Soviet empire produced a resurgence of nationalism from the Baltic to Mongolia and—accompanied by vicious fighting—south to the Illyrian Coast; but for states in the throes of headlong change, functioning global institutions are a source of stability and external support.

Finally, in what constitutes as profound a political mutation as the collapse of communism, countries of all political hues are questioning the efficacy of state *dirigisme* and central planning. And this coincides with the growing importance of problems such as environmental management, which ought to cut across conventional political and ideological allegiances, although Third World "solidarity" was going strong in the United Na-

tions long after developing countries had abandoned the pretense in non-global diplomacy, and the UN will be its last bastion....

THE SHIFTING PARADIGM

To think back to Roosevelt's voyage to Yalta is to realize how automatic has come to seem the schedule of regional tours, international conferences, and summits that bulks out the diaries of ministers of foreign affairs, finance, trade, and industry of even medium-sized countries. The density and variety of international dialogue greatly exceed anything the architects of the United Nations could have anticipated, and most of it is multilateral in character. The most restricted of these encounters has a broader dimension—even bilateral summits have invisible participants, just as agreements reached their influence larger gatherings. A government's domestic political standing is increasingly profoundly and publicly connected with its success in handling the matter-of-fact business of managing interdependence.

This new multilateralism is driven by what is, not what ought to be. It responds to the globalization of banking and financial markets, the transnational integration of investment and manufacturing strategies by the major corporations, and the increasing vulnerability of each national body politic to political, environmental, or economic mismanagement elsewhere. As with all efforts to adjust to extremely rapid change, the building of these new networks of debate, competition, and cooperation is a halting and unevenly successful process, but it is continuous and multifaceted. And it is flexible, taking account both of an individual country's level of integration with the international economy and, still more importantly, of the need to involve the commercial and financial actors whose decisions increasingly constrain governmental choices. The UN will continue, selectively, to be used for the maintenance of international peace, but for purposes of economic and social cooperation, it will have to hook up with the "hot circuits" of multilateralism—international banking and financial flows, regional trading partnerships, chambers of commerce, and research centers.

Governments in the late twentieth century must balance diminished sovereignty with a lively sense of nationhood. The language of politics is still couched in terms of national units, and national interest, but these interests can be served only by coming to terms with an increasingly transnational world. The meaning of economic integration is that corporations and financial markets are leaving behind the nineteenth-century concept of international relations, to operate across frontiers. The switch by large manufacturers from international trade to direct foreign investment and multi-country production is one symptom of this "globalization"—albeit a selective globalization that tends to bypass countries without attractive domestic markets or developed regional trading networks. Governmental organizations that are remote from this real world of political constraints and economic opportunities are not much use to politicians.

The political machinery of cooperation, based as it is on the nation-state, has to take into account these wider dimensions of global change. If the new multilateralism is largely subuniversal, this will not so much dignify a retreat from the global dimensions of policy-making as imply a recognition that the principles on which the existing global organizations operate are impractical. The romantic view that all interests coincide and all countries are equally to be involved in decisions because all are affected may have some Platonic allure, but has little relevance to political or economic life. And, with the partial exception of the International Labor Organization (ILO), the financial, corporate, and intellectual communities are barely tolerated in UN forums—and then only as "nongovernmental observers." Since outside the UN, governments have to take these constituencies into account, this helps to explain the gap between what they say at the UN and what they do outside. Even the World Bank and the IMF, much the most innovative in this respect, have yet to integrate the private sector adequately into their operational planning and consultative mechanisms —although the Bank's International Finance Corporation, a joint investment corporation to promote the development of the private sector in developing countries, was expanding its activities by the late 1980s to offer advice on company restructuring, the development of local stock markets, and the development of an underwriting service to enable creditworthy Third World companies to borrow direct on the international capital markets.

A senior Scandinavian official describes this aloofness as

the UN's most insuperable credibility gap. We sit there, paper tiger governments, discussing principles and theories. They, meanwhile, have created their own economic space, where they talk about how to make things work. Our discussions are falling behind in this new, fascinating world, because these corporations are creating multilateralism and we are still playing with what it might, in a properly ordered world, mean. There is a role for governments, but it is only by working with and through the market approach that we can discover the market imperfections which need to be addressed.

The government-oriented bias of most UN activity is one reason why the driving impulses of the new multilateralism are coming from outside the global frameworks. New geographical, functional, and organizational coalitions are forming —and reforming, for the strongest characteristic of these groups is their fluidity.

The war to drive Iraq out of Kuwait put the fashionable theses about the decline of U.S. power of the late 1980s into perspective, but paradoxically emphasized how greatly any future Pax Americana would depend on supporting coalitions. The active involvement of other countries was a precondition of U.S. public support for U.S. engagement in the Gulf. The U.S. war effort was financed largely from allied contributions, and had to be: the U.S. budget deficit was heading toward $350 billion as the war ended. The United States, heavily dependent on foreign investors and financial markets, cannot afford to shoulder alone what George Bush once called "the hard work of freedom." The coalition must include the marketplace, too, since even the most powerful governments have understood the limits of the traditional tools of macroeconomic policy. The postindustrial revolution is well launched. Access on a global scale to instantly processed information is having a profound effect, not only on individual lives but on the world economy, and political institutions are beginning to catch up with these changes. Rules are needed to provide fairness and predictability, but the scope for effective government intervention has to be finely judged.

It is difficult to assess the future of the United Nations organizations without taking these transformations into account. Regional cooperation is being redefined in the light of them, in ways that will profoundly influence what demands are made on global structures. So is international negotiation. What may be emerging is a "multilateralism of the North." But the "North" is simultaneously being forced to redefine itself not only in East-West terms, but in response to a growing continuum of interest between the old industrialized world and energetic newcomers. Previous assumptions about the technology gap are becoming rapidly outdated by the globalization of research and development networks, by transnational agreements between companies and between branches of the same company that give developing countries' companies direct access to data, markets and finance, patents, and consultancy services. The quantum leap in communication flows and the tendency of corporations to maximize different countries' comparative advantage in a "global market" further reduce geographical barriers to technological innovation. The artificiality of "North" and "South" is giving way to a practical distinction between insiders and outsiders, hot circuits and cold. And the outsiders, immensely disparate in most respects, have this in common: for want of alternatives, they rely more than others on the universal forums. Yet these are of limited practical use to them. The remarkable growth of regional and interregional cooperation between the richer countries —networks that involve not just governments but businessmen and bankers— has created emerging patterns of reciprocity from which the poor are largely excluded. Governments in the most dynamic economies are wrestling with the disruptive effects of the transition to a world driven by microchips and telecommunications, and are disinclined to include mere passengers, countries outside the mainstream, in their joint efforts to adjust.

Ironically, this has not been without benefit to the poorest countries. In some ways their special needs are being more firmly addressed. There was considerable progress in the 1980s, for example, toward forgiving or sharply reducing sub-Saharan Africa's unpayable official debt. The most isolated countries were those that were not "basket countries, which the GATT began to produce in 1988 as a step toward preparing for the WTO, will make it harder for governments to fall short of their obligations. Breaking with the UN's "common system" would provide some safeguard against bureaucratic mediocrity, with the rigidities that engenders. Meetings of trade minister ought, in principle, to have as high a profile as the annual Bank IMF meetings. The challenge for the WTO will be to involve multilateral cooperation and investors in the GATT's work, and to build strong domestic constituencies for liberal and nondiscriminatory trading rules.

The importance of preventing growth-inhibiting exclusive regional deals does not mean that trading patterns will not change over the next decades. Open-ended trading agreements between smaller groups of countries are already developing. A strong international regime is the best insurance that they will indeed be open ended—free for others to join—and nondiscriminatory. Trade is genuinely a matter for governments because they set the rules. Unwatched by other governments able to point to the rule-book, they have an historical tendency to set them to the disadvantage of the majority of their citizens: the power of protectionist lobbies distorts political judgment.

Stabilizers for the volatile worlds of capital flows and financial services may be a different matter. Banking is beginning to be regulated on a worldwide basis, through capital adequacy accords negotiated between governors of the leading central banks. And it will only be a matter of time before there is an international regime for the securities industry. "Uniform trading, accounting, capital and disclosure standards for major markets and institutions" are recognized by such influential market participants as Henry Kaufman of Salomon Brothers as essential, if major disruption on global markets operating around the clock is to be prevented. The market-makers need such regulation; this is a case of experience creating political will.

The hallmark of tomorrow's forms of dialogue will be careful attention to detail, progress toward reasonably well-defined and achievable objectives, and growing realism about what governments can, and cannot, expect to control. Differing perspectives are useful. The Greek poet Archilochus observed that foxes know many things and the hedgehog knows one big thing; in the business of making the world "safe for diversity," foxes are better equipped than hedgehogs. The powerful will pay attention only to those global organizations that take this rich world of cooperation into proper account.

But with increasing mobility of capital have come new kinds of trading competition. Wide ranges of manufactured goods compete not on the traditional basis of price advantage, but on product differentiation, style, and marketing. Countries short of investment and technology have been unable either to develop the industries that have been at the forefront of trade expansion, or to participate in the trade flows within the advanced industrial sectors. They have also lost out in the active trading between the subsidiaries of a typical multinational corporation. There may, in the post-Cold War world, be some scope for pragmatic experiments with dialogue on economic policy within the United Nations, however, as one way of ensuring that the concerns of these "outsiders," who are excluded from the flourishing multilateral networks developing between the world's more prosperous countries, are taken into account. Several groups in the late 1980s put forward proposals for an Economic Security Council, whose authority in economic and social questions would parallel that of the Security Council. The idea was that such a body would have limited membership, with permanent seats for more traditional producers out of these staple markets. And, above all in Africa, rapidly growing populations put enormous pressures on land, health and education facilities, job markets, and urban centers, greatly complicating the difficult task of adjustment.

In the postwar generation, albeit with generous external finance and assisted by very rapid growth in global trade, countries like South Korea broke through odds that seemed as formidable. And South Korea, unlike some of the poorest countries in the 1990s, did not have considerable natural wealth—although natural resources (take copper, for example) are no longer the automatic base of wealth they once were. There were no *inevitable* basket cases in these decades. Blessed were the microstates of the East that took to microcircuits: in theory at least, why

should not barren Djibouti or tragically anarchic Haiti be one day of their number? Yet a study of the odds suggested that the future does not belong to the countries that will enter the twenty-first century poor.

Technology is "heating up" the world in other, more positive ways that still put new strains on established institutions. The process of "structural adjustment," at first thought of as a finite program of reforms to streamline and modernize a country's administration and liberalize its economy, is now seen as a necessary constant. To change as rapidly as did Western European countries in the 1950s would be not much better than treading water in the 1990s. The pyramid gets taller, and consequently wider at the base. Even in the industrialized world, the race is to the innovative, not the merely productive, and this has created profound changes in official thinking about the priorities for government action. Gone, in practice, is the goal of full employment; governments are thinking instead about tomorrow's jobs, emphasizing public investment in frontier technologies while they move to "free up" the current working environment through reforms to tax regimes and financial markets. "Flexible" labor markets may be essential, but some will benefit and some will not. Within every country, there is considerable fumbling and uncertainty about where and how to compensate the dropouts from the information society. On a global scale, we are still more perplexed: how can we help the marginalized"? One of the most difficult challenges for bodies dedicated to multilateral cooperation will be to harness the opportunities created by technical change to enhance the prospects for those outside the mainstream. But institutionalized global dialogue on such matters will become a realistic possibility only when and if the UN wins back its long-lost reputation for political responsibility and organizational effectiveness, bridging the gap between global rhetoric and the pragmatic incrementalism of the world outside its corridors.

There is a sense in which the colossal institution-building effort of the past half-century may have weakened our natural radar. There is an understandable temptation to let an institution be, simply because it exists, even when it is neither efficient nor honorable nor even safe to do so. We need international institutions, but we need to cooperate in more flexible and sensitive ways than we have come to do in many of them. If the United Nations is to be relevant to the rule-making and management problems of the twenty-first century, its organizations face an enormous task of adaptation: to subuniversal approaches to problem solving, and to working with wide constituencies. And some will fail. That does not matter. The polycentric structure of the UN should be treated as an asset, not a defect, because the considerable autonomy enjoyed by different organizations enables the best of them to innovate. The myth of the UN "system," as we have seen, has been worse than a misdescription of the way these organizations actually function: it has been an obstacle to making the best of what exists. Coordination has been the pursuit of utopia masked in the language of the boardroom; what the best of these organizations require is encouragement to set fresh route maps of their own, to experiment, and to question every facet of their current operations. They need to be freed of the conceptual carapace of the utopian construct, the systemic ideal.

Outside the UN, we have begun to innovate—through special task forces, through regional and subregional associations, through the commercial networks for which cooperation is, happily, not a luxury but a banal necessity, through increasingly courageous human rights organizations. As national networks become richer, they complement the flourishing international dimension. And this approach to world order, inductive and spreading in concentric circles, seems more likely to set the pattern of the twenty-first century than global plans of action that are like uncut jigsaws, grand strategies that are imposed from the top and rarely stand the test of implementation at local level. We should not be concerned if a good deal of the political and economic machinery of the 1940s looks, in these conditions, in need of more than cosmetic surgery. That is not a reason for jettisoning all of it, but it is a reason for applying to these organizations the same criteria we would apply to any national institution, for insisting that the United Nations be judged by competitive standards.

This more realistic view of global organizations is in prospect. It is only a question of time. Already, a generation gap is apparent in thinking about multilateralism. The United Nations bulks large for those now nearing retirement, for whom its creation marked the rebirth of the rule of law, and even of those in mid-career, who were brought up to regard it as the guarantor of what limited stability the postwar world has known. But younger generations have diminished expectations for the power of governments to organize their lives and are considerably more skeptical about the desirability of their doing so. The original animating impulses behind the myth of the United Nations make us reluctant to jettison what was created, and this is prudent

But it would be mistaken to assume that the global agenda of a "new world order" necessarily requires global initiatives, international bureaucracies, or the guiding hand of the state. The withering away of the state may be as remote as the end of history, but the civil society through which it operates is vastly more dynamic, and more complex, than the world of the United Nations yet allows.

The preoccupations, the "great general questions," may remain constant. But myths can outlive the temples of their cult. In a world transformed since 1945, so long as UN forums are perceived as intractable hidebound clubs of diplomatic generalists, bet on asserting the dignity of 180-plus stubbornly separate sovereignties, increased public awareness of the need for effective cooperation could paradoxically erode public support for the global organizations. It is not just a question of refusing to accept the old excuse that the UN is "only the mirror of mankind." It is a question of a spreading, and largely salutary, challenge to the right of governments to shape the mirror in the first place.

Events may conspire to create richer tissues of multilateral cooperation, without precipitating the reforms of which the UN stands so deeply in need. The universal character of the global organizations will need to be modified—through steering committees, weighted voting, selective participation in negotiations, and so on—if they are to function; but such measures to improve efficiency will not be enough to assure them a future. They have to overcome the skepticism of the young, for whom World War II or colonialism or even the Holocaust has diminished resonance, but who do care about fairness, are many of them passionately concerned about the destruction of the environment, who believe in the indivisibility of human rights and who see the toleration of atrocities as an abdication of responsibility. Directly or indirectly, as a result of the communications revolution, pressure is being put on governments by citizens who are more aware of these rights, and more able to compare the records of their leaders with those of others. In Africa, the fall of each dictator weakens the throne of another. Seen in Rangoon, television images of life in Thailand hold out, in all its relativity, the promised land. Generations that have grown up with incompetent and unaccountable dictatorships are not fooled by "international development strategies," or impressed by a United Nations that is seen to protect the rights of rulers against the ruled.

Issue-based coalitions are beginning to emerge, inside and outside the UN. The test for the global organizations will be to make the most of them. It may be that the reassessment by the major powers of the UN's collective security functions, coupled with a more sophisticated approach to international stability, will begin to weaken the foundations of sovereign autonomy on which the global organizations are so unrealistically constructed. And that may make it possible to integrate the UN's activities more closely with those of the other multilateral circuits that criss-cross the world. And some at least of the UN organizations may rediscover their original, creatively subversive role as hairshirts for governments, reminding them of their domestic and international obligations and subjecting their conduct to independent scrutiny. But it will not be the end of multilateralism if they do not. Neither pessimism nor optimism about the institutions should obscure the matter-offactness with which we have come to accept the realities—the tensions as well as the opportunities—of interdependence.

Thomas Kuhn has observed that the great changes that sometimes occur in science take place when an old paradigm of scientific thinking is, through experimental discovery of another means of analysis, replaced by a new one. Before that "paradigm shift" occurs, the solutions to problems may run in circles, on the tracks of the old model. Beyond it, a new form of thought must shape itself. Human institutions, multiple, diffuse, and shapeless as they are, hardly lend themselves to such formal analysis. But it is reasonable to ask whether or not a kind of watershed may be close, a point at which institutions that seem to frame present realities may very quickly seem to belong to the past. Not that they will vanish, or like legendary states wither away, but that they will no longer suggest political means that we can creatively use. The developments sketched [here] are at best uncertain indications. By no means do all of them point away from the global institutions. But they do point to a rapid process of experimental discovery, however piecemeal in character, through which a new multilateral world is being constructed. The paradigm shift has not fully declared itself. A fuller understanding of that world lies in future. But the laboratory has about it the excitement and tension of imminent discovery.

POSTSCRIPT

Has the United Nations Outlived Its Usefulness?

In October 1995 the largest gathering of government leaders in history came together in New York City to celebrate the 50th anniversary of the founding of the United Nations. At the same time, UN peacekeeping forces struggled vainly to bring an end to the mutually destructive warfare in the former Yugoslav republics—particularly Serbia, Croatia, and Bosnia and Herzegovina. Not until troops from the North Atlantic Treaty Organization stepped in to force a settlement did the ethnic conflicts cease. Several years earlier, however, the United Nations had worked effectively to help force Iraqi troops out of Kuwait.

The checkered record of the UN as a peacekeeping force seems to bear out Touval's contention that the organization cannot mediate an end to the sort of intractable, long-standing conflicts that are often turned over to it as a last resort. On the other hand, when individual states discern a common goal through multilateral action, the United Nations continues to provide an effective means for implementing what President Woodrow Wilson called "the organized opinion of mankind."

Nevertheless, in June 1996 the world's seven richest industrialized nations issued a communique calling for the reformation of the United Nations' operations. Specifically, these nations' leaders recommended that the UN focus its activities on the areas of health, education, elimination of poverty, protection of women and children, employment, and humanitarian assistance. Meanwhile, there appeared to be growing sentiment in the U.S. Senate that the United States should pull out of the United Nations, or at least significantly reduce American funding of the organization. If Righter's scenario is to prevail, there must first occur a significant shift in sentiment among government officials throughout the world.

Additional historical perspectives on the United Nations can be found in Thomas M. Franck, *Nation Against Nation: What Happened to the U.N. Dream and What the United States Can Do About It* (Oxford University Press, 1985) and Stanley Maisler, *United Nations: The First Fifty Years* (Atlantic Monthly Press, 1995).

ISSUE 17

Is Western Civilization in a State of Decline?

YES: Samuel P. Huntington, from *The Clash of Civilizations and the Remaking of World Order* (Simon & Schuster, 1996)

NO: Francis Fukuyama, from *The End of History and the Last Man* (Free Press, 1992)

ISSUE SUMMARY

YES: Samuel P. Huntington, a professor of the science of government, maintains that due to internal weaknesses and threats from potential rivals organized along civilizational lines, the West is in danger of losing its status as the world's preeminent power base in the twenty-first century.

NO: Francis Fukuyama, a former deputy director with the U.S. State Department, argues that with the end of the cold war and the absence of alternatives to liberal democracy, the West is in a position to maintain and expand its role as the world's primary power base.

For almost 50 years the cold war has occupied the attention of most of the world's nations. Beginning in the last years of World War II—when it became obvious that the two major powers to emerge from the war, the United States (and its Western allies) and the Soviet Union, had different plans for the future of the postwar world—the cold war turned into an ideological conflict between two dominant superpowers, each of which attempted to export its influence in search of the upper hand in this power struggle. The possession of nuclear arsenals by both the United States and the Soviet Union raised the stakes to the potential of total war and annihilation. It made for a very uneasy, unsettling half century.

The cold war also produced its own language—Iron Curtain, containment, nuclear proliferation, massive retaliation, flexible response, regional alliances—as well as a long list of interesting personalities, all of whom lent their names to this colorful yet dangerous era. It also threatened to involve all of the world's nations, whether they wished it or not. With world dominance the prize, both sides sought to obtain the most favorable situation in which to push their different agendas. Sometimes the cold war developed into armed conflict, endangering the delicate balance-of-power politics that it had created.

Suddenly, the cold war was over. With the crumbling of the Soviet Empire and the disintegration of the Soviet Union into a number of separate republics, the West was faced with a novel situation: there was no major power to threaten hegemony or well-being. A collective sigh of relief emanated from the West's citizens and leaders.

What does all this mean to today's world? What will conditions and circumstances be like in the post–cold war era? Will the world be in any less danger? Are there any potential enemies who can replace the Soviet Union and create a new cold war, or worse? And, most important, what will be the position of the West in world affairs as we move into the new millennium?

Diplomatic historians and foreign policy experts seem to be divided with regard to the state of the West today and its ability and willingness to shoulder the responsibilities of world leadership. They also differ in their analysis of the twenty-first century's new world order. Who will be the new major players in the world arena, and what effect will they have on the body politic? Will the twenty-first century be a more peaceful one than the twentieth?

In the selection that follows, Samuel P. Huntington argues that in the future, civilizations (with core states) rather than nations will be the twenty-first century's power brokers. He lists nine such civilizations that he predicts may play a role in the future world order: Japanese, Buddhist, Orthodox (Russia), Hindu (India), Sinic (Chinese), Islamic, African, Latin American, and Western. If the West is to compete with its civilizational rivals in the future, says Huntington, it will have to unify and develop the strength and will to maintain its status as the world's leading power base. If it fails to do so, the decline of the West will become a reality.

On the other hand, argues Francis Fukuyama in the second selection, with the defeat of enemies on both the political Left and Right, the West's liberal democracy is in an enviable position to provide the only viable alternative for the nations of the world in their search for a just and profitable life for their citizens. If the West succeeds in spreading its systems throughout the world, Fukuyama asserts, it will be able to extend its power status well into the twenty-first century.

YES

Samuel P. Huntington

THE FADING OF THE WEST: POWER, CULTURE, AND INDIGENIZATION

WESTERN POWER: DOMINANCE AND DECLINE

Two pictures exist of the power of the West in relation to other civilizations. The first is of overwhelming, triumphant, almost total Western dominance. The disintegration of the Soviet Union removed the only serious challenger to the West and as a result the world is and will be shaped by the goals, priorities, and interests of the principal Western nations, with perhaps an occasional assist from Japan. As the one remaining superpower, the United States together with Britain and France make the crucial decisions on political and security issues; the United States together with Germany and Japan make the crucial decisions on economic issues. The West is the only civilization which has substantial interests in every other civilization or region and has the ability to affect the politics, economics, and security of every other civilization or region. Societies from other civilizations usually need Western help to achieve their goals and protect their interests. Western nations, as one author summarized it:

- Own and operate the international banking system
- Control all hard currencies
- Are the world's principal customer
- Provide the majority of the world's finished goods
- Dominate international capital markets
- Exert considerable moral leadership within many societies
- Are capable of massive military intervention
- Control the sea lanes
- Conduct most advanced technical research and development
- Control leading edge technical education
- Dominate access to space
- Dominate the aerospace industry
- Dominate international communications
- Dominate the high-tech weapons industry

The second picture of the West is very different. It is of a civilization in decline, its share of world political, economic, and military power going down relative to that of other civilizations. The West's victory in the Cold War has produced not triumph but exhaustion. The West is increasingly concerned with its internal problems and needs, as it confronts slow economic growth, stagnating populations, unemployment, huge government deficits, a declining work ethic, low savings rates, and in many countries including the United States social disintegration, drugs, and crime. Economic power is rapidly shifting to East Asia, and military power and political influence are starting to follow. India is on the verge of economic takeoff and the Islamic world is increasingly hostile toward the West. The willingness of other societies to accept the West's dictates or abide its sermons is rapidly evaporating, and so are the West's self-confidence and will to dominate. The late 1980s witnessed much debate about the declinist thesis concerning the United States. In the mid-1990s, a balanced analysis came to a somewhat similar conclusion:

[I]n many important respects, its [the United States'] relative power will decline at an accelerating pace. In terms of its raw economic capabilities, the position of the United States in relation to Japan and eventually China is likely to erode still further. In the military realm, the balance of effective capabilities between the United States and a number of growing regional powers (including, perhaps, Iran, India, and China) will shift from the center toward the periphery. Some of America's structural power will flow to other nations; some (and some of its soft power as well) will find its

way into the hands of nonstate actors like multinational corporations.

Which of these two contrasting pictures of the place of the West in the world describes reality? The answer, of course, is: they both do. The West is overwhelmingly dominant now and will remain number one in terms of power and influence well into the twenty-first century. Gradual, inexorable, and fundamental changes, however, are also occurring in the balances of power among civilizations, and the power of the West relative to that of other civilizations will continue to decline. As the West's primacy erodes, much of its power will simply evaporate and the rest will be diffused on a regional basis among the several major civilizations and their core states. The most significant increases in power are accruing and will accrue to Asian civilizations, with China gradually emerging as the society most likely to challenge the West for global influence. These shifts in power among civilizations are leading and will lead to the revival and increased cultural assertiveness of non-Western societies and to their increasing rejection of Western culture.

The decline of the West has three major characteristics.

First, it is a slow process. The rise of Western power took four hundred years. Its recession could take as long. In the 1980s the distinguished British scholar Hedley Bull argued that "European or Western dominance of the universal international society may be said to have reached its apogee about the year 1900." Spengler's first volume appeared in 1918 and the "decline of the West" has been a central theme in twentieth-century history. The process itself has stretched out through most of the century. Conceivably, however, it could accelerate. Economic growth and other increases in a country's capabilities often proceed along an S curve: a slow start then rapid acceleration followed by reduced rates of expansion and leveling off. The decline of countries may also occur along a reverse S curve, as it did with the Soviet Union: moderate at first then rapidly accelerating before bottoming out. The decline of the West is still in the slow first phase, but at some point it might speed up dramatically.

Second, decline does not proceed in a straight line. It is highly irregular with pauses, reversals, and reassertions of Western power following manifestations of Western weakness. The open democratic societies of the West have great capacities for renewal. In addition, unlike many civilizations, the West has had two major centers of power. The decline which Bull saw starting about 1900 was essentially the decline of the European component of Western civilization. From 1910 to 1945 Europe was divided against itself and preoccupied with its internal economic, social, and political problems. In the 1940s, however, the American phase of Western domination began, and in 1945 the United States briefly dominated the world to an extent almost comparable to the combined Allied Powers in 1918. Postwar decolonization further reduced European influence but not that of the United States, which substituted a new transnational imperialism for the traditional territorial empire. During the Cold War, however, American military power was matched by that of the Soviets and American economic power declined relative to that of Japan. Yet periodic efforts at military and economic renewal did occur. In 1991, indeed, another distinguished British scholar, Barry Buzan, argued that "The deeper reality is that

the centre is now more dominant, and the periphery more subordinate, than at any time since decolonization began." The accuracy of that perception, however, fades as the military victory that gave rise to it also fades into history.

Third, power is the ability of one person or group to change the behavior of another person or group. Behavior may be changed through inducement, coercion, or exhortation, which require the power-wielder to have economic, military, institutional, demographic, political, technological, social, or other resources. The power of a state or group is hence normally estimated by measuring the resources it has at its disposal against those of the other states or groups it is trying to influence. The West's share of most, but not all, of the important power resources peaked early in the twentieth century and then began to decline relative to those of other civilizations.

Territory and Population. In 1490 Western societies controlled most of the European peninsula outside the Balkans or perhaps 1.5 million square miles out of a global land area (apart from Antarctica) of 52.5 million square miles. At the peak of its territorial expansion in 1920, the West directly ruled about 25.5 million square miles or close to half the earth's earth. By 1993 this territorial control had been cut in half to about 12.7 million square miles. The West was back to its original European core plus its spacious settler-populated lands in North America, Australia, and New Zealand. The territory of independent Islamic societies, in contrast, rose from 1.8 million square miles in 1920 to over 11 million square miles in 1993. Similar changes occurred in the control of population. In 1900 Westerners composed roughly 30 percent of the world's population and Western governments ruled almost 45 percent of that population then and 48 percent in 1920. In 1993, except for a few small imperial remnants like Hong Kong, Western governments ruled no one but Westerners. Westerners amounted to slightly over 13 percent of humanity and are due to drop to about 11 percent early in the next century and to 10 percent by 2025. In terms of total population, in 1993 the West ranked fourth behind Sinic, Islamic, and Hindu civilizations.

Quantitatively Westerners thus constitute a steadily decreasing minority of the world's population. Qualitatively the balance between the West and other populations is also changing Non-Western peoples are becoming healthier, more urban, more literate, better educated. By the early 1990s infant mortality rates in Latin America, Africa, the Middle East, South Asia, East Asia, and Southeast Asia were one-third to one-half what they had been thirty years earlier. Life expectancy in these regions had increased significantly, with gains varying from eleven years in Africa to twenty-three years in East Asia. In the early 1960s in most of the Third World less than one-third of the adult population was literate. In the early 1990s, in very few countries apart from Africa was less than one-half the population literate. About fifty percent of Indians and 75 percent of Chinese could read and write. Literacy rates in developing countries in 1970 averaged 41 percent of those in developed countries; in 1992 they averaged 71 percent. By the early 1990s in every region except Africa virtually the entire age group was enrolled in primary education. Most significantly, in the early 1960s in Asia, Latin America, the Middle East, and Africa less than one-third of the appropriate age group was enrolled in

secondary education; by the early 1990s one-half of the age-group was enrolled except in Africa. In 1960 urban residents made up less than one-quarter of the population of the less developed world. Between 1960 and 1992, however, the urban percentage of the population rose from 49 percent to 73 percent in Latin America, 34 percent to 55 percent in Arab countries, 14 percent to 29 percent in Africa, 18 percent to 27 percent in China, and 19 percent to 26 percent in India.

These shifts in literacy, education, and urbanization created socially mobilized populations with enhanced capabilities and higher expectations who could be activated for political purposes in ways in which illiterate peasants could not. Socially mobilized societies are more powerful societies. In 1953, when less than 15 percent of Iranians were literate and less than 17 percent urban, Kermit Roosevelt and a few CIA operatives rather easily suppressed an insurgency and restored the Shah to his throne. In 1979, when 50 percent of Iranians were literate and 47 percent lived in cities, no amount of U.S. military power could have kept the Shah on his throne. A significant gap still separates Chinese, Indians, Arabs, and Africans from Westerners, Japanese, and Russians. Yet the gap is narrowing rapidly. At the same time, a different gap is opening. The average ages of Westerners, Japanese, and Russians are increasingly steadily, and the larger proportion of the population that no longer works imposes a mounting burden on those still productively employed. Other civilizations are burdened by large numbers of children, but children are future workers and soldiers.

Economic Product. The Western share of the global economics product also may have peaked in the 1920s and has clearly been declining since World War II. In 1750 China accounted for almost one-third, India for almost one-quarter, and the West for less than a fifth of the world's manufacturing output. By 1830 the West had pulled slightly ahead of China. In the following decades, as Paul Bairoch points out, the industrialization of the West led to the deindustrialization of the rest of the world. In 1913 the manufacturing output of non-Western countries was roughly two-thirds what it had been in 1800. Beginning in the mid-nineteenth century the Western share rose dramatically, peaking in 1928 at 84.2 percent of world manufacturing output. Thereafter the West's share declined as its rate of growth remained modest and as less industrialized countries expanded their output rapidly after World War II. By 1980 the West accounted for 57.8 percent of global manufacturing output, roughly the share it had 120 years earlier in the 1860s.

Reliable data on gross economic product are not available for the pre-World War II period. In 1950, however, the West accounted for roughly 64 percent of the gross world product; by the 1980s this proportion had dropped to 49 percent. By 2013, according to one estimate, the West will account for only 30% of the world product. In 1991, according to another estimate, four of the world's seven largest economies belonged to non-Western nations: Japan (in second place), China (third), Russia (sixth), and India (seventh). In 1992 the United States had the largest economy in the world, and the top ten economies included those of five Western countries plus the leading states of five other civilizations: China, Japan, India, Russia, and Brazil. In 2020 plausible projections indicate that the top five economies will be in five different civilizations, and the top ten economies will include only three Western countries. This relative decline of the West is, of course, in large part a function of the rapid rise of East Asia.

Gross figures on economic output partially obscure the West's qualitative advantage. The West and Japan almost totally dominate advanced technology industries. Technologies are being disseminated, however, and if the West wishes to maintain its superiority it will do what it can to minimize that dissemination. Thanks to the interconnected world which the West has created, however, slowing the diffusion of technology to other civilizations is increasingly difficult. It is made all the more so in the absence of a single, overpowering, agreed-upon threat such as existed during the Cold War and gave measures of technology control some modest effectiveness.

It appears probable that for most of history China had the world's largest economy. The diffusion of technology and the economic development of non-Western societies in the second half of the twentieth century are now producing a return to the historical pattern. This will be a slow process, but by the middle of the twenty-first century, if not before, the distribution of economic product and manufacturing output among the leading civilizations is likely to resemble that of 1800. The two-hundred-year Western "blip" on the world economy will be over.

Military Capability. Military power has four dimensions: quantitative—the numbers of men, weapons, equipment, and resources; technological—the effectiveness and sophistication of weapons and equipment; organizational—the coherence, discipline, training, and morale of the troops and the effectiveness of command and control relationships; and societal—the ability and willingness of the society to apply military force effectively. In the 1920s the West was far ahead of everyone else in all these dimensions. In the years since, the military power of the West has declined relative to that of other civilizations, a decline reflected in the shifting balance in military personnel, one measure, although clearly not the most important one, of military capability. Modernization and economic development generate the resources and desire for states to develop their military capabilities, and few states fail to do so. In the 1930s Japan and the Soviet Union created very powerful military forces, as they demonstrated in World War II. During the Cold War the Soviet Union had one of the world's two most powerful military forces. Currently the West monopolizes the ability to deploy substantial conventional military forces anywhere in the world. Whether it will continue to maintain that capability is uncertain. It seems reasonably certain, however, that no non-Western state or group of states will create a comparable capability during the coming decades.

Overall, the years after the Cold War have been dominated by five major trends in the evolution of global military capabilities.

First, the armed forces of the Soviet Union ceased to exist shortly after the Soviet Union ceased to exist. Apart from Russia, only Ukraine inherited significant military capabilities. Russian forces were greatly reduced in size and were withdrawn from Central Europe and the Baltic states. The Warsaw Pact ended. The goal of challenging the U.S. Navy was abandoned. Military equipment was either disposed of or allowed to deteri-

orate and become nonoperational. Budget allocations for defense were drastically reduced. Demoralization pervaded the ranks of both officers and men. At the same time the Russian military were redefining their missions and doctrine and restructuring themselves for their new roles in protecting Russians and dealing with regional conflicts in the near abroad.

Second, the precipitous reduction in Russian military capabilities stimulated a slower but significant decline in Western military spending, forces, and capabilities. Under the plans of the Bush and Clinton administrations, U.S. military spending was due to drop by 35 percent from $342.3 billion (1994 dollars) in 1990 to $222.3 in 1998. The force structure that year would be half to two-thirds what it was at the end of the Cold War. Total military personnel would go down from 2.1 million to 1.4 million. Many major weapons programs have been and are being canceled. Between 1985 and 1995 annual purchases of major weapons went down from 29 to 6 ships, 943 to 127 aircraft, 720 to 0 tanks, and 48 to 18 strategic missiles. Beginning in the late 1980s, Britain, Germany, and, to a lesser degree, France went through similar reductions in defense spending and military capabilities. In the mid-1990s, the German armed forces were scheduled to decline from 370,000 to 340,000 and probably to 320,000; the French army was to drop from its strength of 290,000 in 1990 to 225,000 in 1997. British military personnel went down from 377,100 in 1985 to 274,800 in 1993. Continental members of NATO also shortened terms of conscripted service and debated the possible abandonment of conscription.

Third, the trends in East Asia differed significantly from those in Russia and the West. Increased military spending and force improvements were the order of the day; China was the pacesetter. Stimulated by both their increasing economic wealth and the Chinese buildup, other East Asian nations are modernizing and expanding their military forces. Japan has continued to improve its highly sophisticated military capability. Taiwan, South Korea, Thailand, Malaysia, Singapore, and Indonesia all are spending more on their military and purchasing planes, tanks, and ships from Russia, the United States, Britain, France, Germany, and other countries. While NATO defense expenditures declined by roughly 10 percent between 1985 and 1993 (from $539.6 billion to $485.0 billion) (constant 1993 dollars), expenditures in East Asia rose by 50 percent from $89.8 billion to $134.8 billion during the same period.

Fourth, military capabilities including weapons of mass destruction are diffusing broadly across the world. As countries develop economically, they generate the capacity to produce weapons. Between the 1960s and 1980s, for instance, the number of Third World countries producing fighter aircraft increased from one to eight, tanks from one to six, helicopters from one to six, and tactical missiles from none to seven. The 1990s have seen a major trend toward the globalization of the defense industry, which is likely further to erode Western military advantages. Many non-Western societies either have nuclear weapons (Russia, China, Israel, India, Pakistan, and possibly North Korea) or have been making strenuous efforts to acquire them (Iran, Iraq, Libya, and possibly Algeria) or are placing themselves in a position quickly to acquire them if they see the need to do so (Japan).

Finally, all those developments make regionalization the central trend in mili-

tary strategy and power in the post-Cold War world. Regionalization provides the rationale for the reductions in Russian and Western military forces and for increases in the military forces of other states. Russia no longer has a global military capability but is focusing its strategy and forces on the near abroad. China has reoriented its strategy and forces to emphasize local power projection and the defense of Chinese interests in East Asia. European countries are similarly redirecting their forces, through both NATO and the Western European Union, to deal with instability on the periphery of Western Europe. The United States has explicitly shifted its military planning from deterring and fighting the Soviet Union on a global basis to preparing to deal simultaneously with regional contingencies in the Persian Gulf and Northeast Asia. The United States, however, is not likely to have the military capability to meet these goals. To defeat Iraq, the United States deployed in the Persian Gulf 75 percent of its active tactical aircraft, 42 percent of its modern battle tanks, 46 percent of its aircraft carriers, 37 percent of its army personnel, and 46 percent of its marine personnel. With significantly reduced forces in the future, the United States will be hard put to carry out one intervention, much less two, against substantial regional powers outside the Western Hemisphere. Military security throughout the world increasingly depends not on the global distribution of power and the actions of superpowers but on the distribution of power within each region of the world and the actions of the core states of civilizations.

In sum, overall the West will remain the most powerful civilization well into the early decades of the twenty-first century. Beyond then it will probably continue to have a substantial lead in scientific talent, research and development capabilities, and civilian and military technological innovation. Control over the other power resources, however, is becoming increasingly dispersed—among the core states and leading countries of non-Western civilizations. The West's control of these resources peaked in the 1920s and has since been declining irregularly but significantly. In the 2020s, a hundred years after that peak, the West will probably control about 24 percent of the world's territory (down from a peak of 49 percent), 10 percent of the total world population (down from 48 percent) and perhaps 15–20 percent of the socially mobilized population, about 30 percent of the world's economic product (down from a peak of probably 70 percent), perhaps 25 percent of manufacturing output (down from a peak of 84 percent), and less than 10 percent of global military manpower (down from 45 percent).

In 1919 Woodrow Wilson, Lloyd George, and Georges Clemenceau together virtually controlled the world. Sitting in Paris, they determined what countries would exist and which would not, what new countries would be created, what their boundaries would be and who would rule them, and how the Middle East and other parts of the world would be divided up among the victorious powers. They also decided on military intervention in Russia and economic concessions to be extracted from China. A hundred years later, no small group of statesmen will be able to exercise comparable power; to the extent that any group does it will not consist of three Westerners but leaders of the core states of the world's seven or eight major civilizations. The successors to Reagan, Thatcher, Mitterrand, and Kohl will be rivaled by those of Deng Xiaoping, Nakasone, Indira Gandhi, Yeltsin, Khomeini, and Suharto. The age of Western dominance will be over....

At various times before the nineteenth century, Byzantines, Arabs, Chinese, Ottomans, Moguls, and Russians were highly confident of their strength and achievements compared to those of the West. At these times they also were contemptuous of the cultural inferiority, institutional backwardness, corruption, and decadence of the West. As the success of the West fades relatively, such attitudes reappear. People feel "they don't have to take it anymore." Iran is an extreme case, but, as one observer noted, "Western values are rejected in different ways, but no less firmly, in Malaysia, Indonesia, Singapore, China, and Japan." We are witnessing "the end of the progressive era" dominated by Western ideologies and are moving into an era in which multiple and diverse civilizations will interact, compete, coexist, and accommodate each other.

NO

Francis Fukuyama

THE WORLDWIDE LIBERAL REVOLUTION

The distant origins of the present [selection] lie in an article entitled "The End of History?" which I wrote for the journal *The National Interest* in the summer of 1989. In it, I argued that a remarkable consensus concerning the legitimacy of liberal democracy as a system of government had emerged throughout the world over the past few years, as it conquered rival ideologies like hereditary monarchy, fascism, and most recently communism. More than that, however, I argued that liberal democracy may constitute the "end point of mankind's ideological evolution" and the "final form of human government," and as such constituted the "end of history. That is, while earlier forms of government were characterized by grave defects and irrationalities that led to their eventual collapse, liberal democracy was arguably free from such fundamental internal contradictions. This was not to say that today's stable democracies, like the United States, France, or Switzerland, were not without injustice or serious social problems. But these problems were ones of incomplete implementation of the twin principles of liberty and equality on which modern democracy is founded, rather than of flaws in the principles themselves. While some present-day countries might fail to achieve stable liberal democracy, and others might lapse back into other, more primitive forms of rule like theocracy or military dictatorship, the *ideal* of liberal democracy could not be improved on.

The original article excited an extraordinary amount of commentary and controversy, first in the United States, and then in a series of countries as different as England, France, Italy, the Soviet Union, Brazil, South Africa, Japan, and South Korea. Criticism took every conceivable form, some of it based on simple misunderstanding of my original intent, and others penetrating more perceptively to the core of my argument. Many people were confused in the first instance by my use of the word "history." Understanding history in a conventional sense as the occurrence of events, people pointed to the fall of the Berlin Wall, the Chinese communist crackdown in Tiananmen Square, and the Iraqi invasion of Kuwait as evidence that "history was continuing," and that I was *ipso facto* proven wrong.

And yet what I suggested had come to an end was not the occurrence of events, even large and grave events, but History; that is, history understood as a single, coherent, evolutionary process, when taking into account the experience of all peoples in all times. This understanding of History was most closely associated with the great German philosopher G. W. F. Hegel. It was made part of our daily intellectual atmosphere by Karl Marx, who borrowed this concept of History from Hegel, and is implicit in our use of words like "primitive" or "advanced," "traditional" or "modern," when referring to different types of human societies. For both of these thinkers, there was a coherent development of human societies from simple tribal ones based on slavery and subsistence agriculture, through various theocracies, monarchies, and feudal aristocracies, up through modern liberal democracy and technologically driven capitalism. This evolutionary process was neither random nor unintelligible, even if it did not proceed in a straight line, and even if it was possible to question whether man was happier or better off as a result of historical "progress."

Both Hegel and Marx believed that the evolution of human societies was not open-ended, but would end when mankind had achieved a form of society that satisfied its deepest and most fundamental longings. Both thinkers thus posited an "end of history": for Hegel this was the liberal state, while for Marx it was a communist society. This did not mean that the natural cycle of birth, life, and death would end, that important events would no longer happen, or that newspapers reporting them would cease to be published. It meant, rather, that there would be no further progress in the development of underlying principles and institutions, because all of the really big questions had been settled....

* * *

We stand at the gates of an important epoch, a time of ferment, when spirit moves forward in a leap, transcends its previous shape and takes on a new one. All the mass of previous representations, concepts, and bonds linking our world together are dissolving and collapsing like a dream picture. A new phase of the spirit is preparing itself. Philosophy especially has to welcome its appearance and acknowledge it, while others, who oppose it impotently, cling to the past.

—G. W. F. Hegel, in a lecture on
September 18, 1806

On both the communist Left and the authoritarian Right there has been a bankruptcy of serious ideas capable of sustaining the internal political cohesion of strong governments, whether based on "monolithic" parties, military juntas, or personalistic dictatorships. The absence of legitimate authority has meant that when an authoritarian government met with failure in some area of policy, there was no higher principle to which the regime could appeal. Some have compared legitimacy to a kind of cash reserve. All governments, democratic and authoritarian, have their ups and downs; but only legitimate governments have this reserve to draw on in times of crisis.

The weakness of authoritarian states of the Right lay in their failure to control civil society. Coming to power with a certain mandate to restore order or to impose "economic discipline," many found themselves no more successful than their democratic predecessors in stimulating steady economic growth or in creating a sense of social order. And those that were successful were hoisted on their own petard. For the societies on top of which they sat began to outgrow them as they became better educated, more prosperous, and middle class. As memory of the specific emergency that had justified strong government faded, those societies became less and less ready to tolerate military rule.

Totalitarian governments of the Left sought to avoid these problems by subordinating the whole of civil society to their control, including what their citizens were allowed to think. But such a system in its pure form could be maintained only through a terror that threatened the system's own rulers. Once that terror was relaxed, a long process of degeneration set in, during which the state lost control of certain key aspects of civil society. Most important was its loss of control over the belief system. And since the socialist formula for economic growth was defective, the state could not prevent its citizens from taking note of this fact and drawing their own conclusions.

Moreover, few totalitarian regimes could replicate themselves through one or more succession crises. In the absence of commonly accepted rules of succession, it would always be a temptation for some ambitious contender for power to throw the whole system into question by calls for fundamental reform in the struggle against his rivals. The reform card is a powerful trump because dissatisfaction with Stalinist systems is high everywhere. Thus Khrushchev used anti-Stalinism against Beria and Malenkov, Gorbachev used it against his Brezhnev-era competitors, and Zhao Ziyang used it against the hard-line Li Peng. The question of whether the individuals or groups contending for power were real

democrats was in a sense irrelevant, since the succession process tended to undermine the old regime's credibility by exposing its inevitable abuses. New social and political forces, more sincerely committed to liberal ideas, were unleashed and soon escaped the control of those who planned the first limited reforms.

The weakness of strong states has meant that many former authoritarianisms have now given way to democracy, while the former post-totalitarian states have become simple authoritarianisms, if not democracies. The Soviet Union has devolved power to its constituent republics, and while China continues to be a dictatorship, the regime has lost control of significant parts of society. Neither country possesses any longer the ideological coherence once given them by Marxism-Leninism: the conservatives opposed to reform in the Soviet Union are as likely to place an Orthodox icon on their wall as a picture of Lenin. The would-be makers of the August 1991 coup resembled a Latin American military junta, with army officers and police officials playing a major role.

In addition to the crisis of political authoritarianism, there has been a quieter but no less significant revolution going on in the field of economics. The development that was both manifestation and cause of this revolution was the phenomenal economic growth of East Asia since World War II. This success story was not limited to early modernizers like Japan, but eventually came to include virtually all countries in Asia willing to adopt market principles and integrate themselves fully into the global, capitalist economic system. Their performance suggested that poor countries without resources other than their own hardworking populations could take advantage of the openness of the international economic system and create unimagined amounts of new wealth, rapidly closing the gap with the more established capitalist powers of Europe and North America. The East Asian economic miracle was carefully observed around the world, nowhere more than in the communist bloc. Communism's terminal crisis began in some sense when the Chinese leadership recognized that they were being left behind by the rest of capitalist Asia, and saw that socialist central planning had condemned China to backwardness and poverty. The ensuing Chinese liberalizing reforms led to a doubling of grain production in five years and provided a new demonstration of the power of market principles. The Asian lesson was later absorbed by economists in the Soviet Union, who knew the terrible waste and inefficiency that central planning had brought about in their own country. The Eastern Europeans had less need to be taught; they understood better than other communists that their failure to reach the living standards of their fellow Europeans in the West was due to the socialist system imposed on them after the war by the Soviets.

But students of the East Asian economic miracle were not restricted to the communist bloc. A remarkable transformation has taken place in the economic thinking of Latin Americans as well. In the 1950s, when the Argentine economist Raul Prebisch headed the United Nations Economic Committee for Latin America, it was fashionable to attribute the underdevelopment not only of Latin America but of the Third World more generally to the global capitalist system. It was argued that early developers in Europe and America had in effect structured the world economy in their favor

and condemned those who came later to dependent positions as providers of raw materials. By the early 1990s, that understanding had changed entirely: President Carlos Salinas de Gortari in Mexico, President Carlos Menem in Argentina, and President Fernando Collor de Mello in Brazil, all sought to implement far-reaching programs of economic liberalization after coming to power, accepting the need for market competition and openness to the world economy. Chile put liberal economic principles into practice earlier in the 1980s under Pinochet, with the result that its economy was the healthiest of any in the Southern Cone as it emerged from dictatorship under the leadership of President Patricio Alwyn. These new, democratically elected leaders started from the premise that underdevelopment was not due to the inherent inequities of capitalism, but rather to the insufficient degree of capitalism that had been practiced in their countries in the past. Privatization and free trade have become the new watchwords in place of nationalization and import substitution. The Marxist orthodoxy of Latin American intellectuals has come under increasing challenge from writers like Hernando de Soto, Mario Vargas Llosa, and Carlos Rangel, who have begun to find a significant audience for liberal, market-oriented economic ideas.

As mankind approaches the end of the millennium, the twin crises of authoritarianism and socialist central planning have left only one competitor standing in the ring as an ideology of potentially universal validity: liberal democracy, the doctrine of individual freedom and popular sovereignty. Two hundred years after they first animated the French and American revolutions, the principles of liberty and equality have proven not just durable but resurgent.

Liberalism and democracy, while closely related, are separate concepts. Political liberalism can be defined simply as a rule of law that recognizes certain individual rights or freedoms from government control. While there can be a wide variety of definitions of fundamental rights, we will use the one contained in Lord Bryce's classic work on democracy, which limits them to three: civil rights, "the exemption from control of the citizen in respect of his person and property"; religious rights, "exemption from control in the expression of religious opinions and the practice of worship"; and what he calls political rights, "exemption from control in matters which do not so plainly affect the welfare of the whole community as to render control necessary," including the fundamental right of press freedom. It has been a common practice for socialist countries to press for the recognition of various second- and third-generation economic rights, such as the right to employment, housing, or health care. The problem with such an expanded list is that the achievement of these rights is not clearly compatible with other rights like those of property or free economic exchange. In our definition we will stick to Bryce's shorter and more traditional list of rights, which is compatible with those contained in the American Bill of Rights.

Democracy, on the other hand, is the right held universally by all citizens to have a share of political power, that is, the right of all citizens to vote and participate in politics. The right to participate in political power can be thought of as yet another liberal right—indeed, the most important one—and it is for this reason that liberalism has been closely associated historically with democracy.

In judging which countries are democratic, we will use a strictly formal definition of democracy. A country is democratic if it grants its people the right to choose their own government through periodic, secret-ballot, multi-party elections, on the basis of universal and equal adult suffrage. It is true that formal democracy alone does not always guarantee equal participation and rights. Democratic procedures can be manipulated by elites, and do not always accurately reflect the will or true self-interests of the people. But once we move away from a formal definition, we open up the possibility of infinite abuse of the democratic principle. In this century, the greatest enemies of democracy have attacked "formal" democracy in the name of "substantive" democracy. This was the justification used by Lenin and the Bolshevik party to close down the Russian Constituent Assembly and proclaim a party dictatorship, which was to achieve substantive democracy "in the name of the people." Formal democracy, on the other hand, provides real institutional safeguards against dictatorship, and is much more likely to produce "substantive" democracy in the end.

While liberalism and democracy usually go together, they can be separated in theory. It is possible for a country to be liberal without being particularly democratic, as was eighteenth-century Britain. A broad list of rights, including the franchise, was fully protected for a narrow social elite, but denied to others. It is also possible for a country to be democratic without being liberal, that is, without protecting the rights of individuals and minorities. A good example of this is the contemporary Islamic Republic of Iran, which has held regular elections that were reasonably fair by Third World standards, making the country more democratic than it was in the time of the Shah. Islamic Iran, however, is not a liberal state; there are no guarantees of free speech, assembly, and, above all, of religion. The most elementary rights of Iranian citizens are not protected by the rule of law, a situation that is worse for Iran's ethnic and religious minorities.

In its economic manifestation, liberalism is the recognition of the right of free economic activity and economic exchange based on private property and markets. Since the term "capitalism" has acquired so many pejorative connotations over the years, it has recently become a fashion to speak of "free-market economics" instead; both are acceptable alternative terms for economic liberalism. It is evident that there are many possible interpretations of this rather broad definition of economic liberalism, ranging from the United States of Ronald Reagan and the Britain of Margaret Thatcher to the social democracies of Scandinavia and the relatively statist regimes in Mexico and India. All contemporary capitalist states have large public sectors, while most socialist states have permitted a degree of private economic activity. There has been considerable controversy over the point at which the public sector becomes large enough to disqualify a state as liberal. Rather than try to set a precise percentage, it is probably more useful to look at what attitude the state takes *in principle* to the legitimacy of private property and enterprise. Those that protect such economic rights we will consider liberal; those that are opposed or base themselves on other principles (such as "economic justice") will not qualify.

The present crisis of authoritarianism has not necessarily led to the emergence of liberal democratic regimes, nor are all the new democracies which have emerged secure. The newly democratic countries of Eastern Europe face wrenching transformations of their economies, while the new democracies in Latin America are hobbled by a terrible legacy of prior economic mismanagement. Many of the fast developers in East Asia, while economically liberal, have not accepted the challenge of political liberalization. The liberal revolution has left certain areas like the Middle East relatively untouched. It is altogether possible to imagine states like Peru or the Philippines relapsing into some kind of dictatorship under the weight of the crushing problems they face.

But the fact that there will be setbacks and disappointments in the process of democratization, or that not every market economy will prosper, should not distract us from the larger pattern that is emerging in world history. The apparent number of choices that countries face in determining how they will organize themselves politically and economically has been *diminishing* over time. Of the different types of regimes that have emerged in the course of human history, from monarchies and aristocracies, to religious ·theocracies, to the fascist and communist dictatorships of this century, the only form of government that has survived intact to the end of the twentieth century has been liberal democracy.

What is emerging victorious, in other words, is not so much liberal practice, as the liberal *idea*. That is to say, for a very large part of the world, there is now no ideology with pretensions to universality that is in a position to challenge liberal democracy, and no universal principle of legitimacy other than the sovereignty of the people. Monarchism in its various forms had been largely defeated by the beginning of this century. Fascism and communism, liberal democracy's main competitors up till now, have both discredited themselves. If the Soviet Union (or its successor states) fails to democratize, if Peru or the Philippines relapse into some form of authoritarianism, democracy will most likely have yielded to a colonel or bureaucrat who claims to speak in the name of the Russian, Peruvian, or Philippine people alone. Even non-democrats will have to speak the language of democracy in order to justify their deviation from the single universal standard.

It is true that Islam constitutes a systematic and coherent ideology, just like liberalism and communism, with its own code of morality and doctrine of political and social justice. The appeal of Islam is potentially universal, reaching out to all men as men, and not just to members of a particular ethnic or national group. And Islam has indeed defeated liberal democracy in many parts of the Islamic world, posing a grave threat to liberal practices even in countries where it has not achieved political power directly. The end of the Cold War in Europe was followed immediately by a challenge to the West from Iraq, in which Islam was arguably a factor.

Despite the power demonstrated by Islam in its current revival, however, it remains the case that this religion has virtually no appeal outside those areas that were culturally Islamic to begin with. The days of Islam's cultural conquests, it would seem, are over: it can win back lapsed adherents, but has no resonance for young people in Berlin, Tokyo, or Moscow. And while nearly a billion people are culturally Islamic— one-fifth of the world's population—they cannot challenge liberal democracy on its own territory on the level of ideas. Indeed, the Islamic world would seem more vulnerable to liberal ideas in the long run than the reverse, since such liberalism has attracted numerous and powerful Muslim adherents over the past century and a half. Part of the reason for the current, fundamentalist revival is the strength of the perceived threat from liberal, Western values to traditional Islamic societies.

We who live in stable, long-standing liberal democracies face an unusual situation. In our grandparents' time, many reasonable people could foresee a radiant socialist future in which private property and capitalism had been abolished, and in which politics itself was somehow overcome. Today, by contrast, we have trouble imagining a world that is radically better than our own, or a future that is not essentially democratic and capitalist. Within that framework, of course, many things could be improved: we could house the homeless, guarantee opportunity for minorities and women, improve competitiveness, and create new jobs. We can also imagine future worlds that are significantly worse than what we know now, in which national, racial, or religious intolerance makes a comeback, or in which we are overwhelmed by war or environmental collapse. But we cannot picture to ourselves a world that is *essentially* different from the present one, and at the same time better. Other, less reflective ages also thought of themselves as the best, but we arrive at this conclusion exhausted, as it were, from the pursuit of alternatives we felt *had* to be better than liberal democracy.

The fact that this is so, and the breadth of the current worldwide liberal revolution, invites us to raise the following question: Are we simply witnessing a momentary upturn in the fortunes of liberal democracy, or is there some longer-term pattern of development at work that will eventually lead all countries in the direction of liberal democracy?

It is possible, after all, that the present trend toward democracy is a cyclical phenomenon. One need only look back to the late 1960s and early 70s, when the United States was undergoing a crisis of self-confidence brought on by its involvement in the Vietnam War and the Watergate scandal. The West as a whole was thrown into economic crisis as a result of the OPEC oil embargo; most of Latin America's democracies were overthrown in a series of military coups; and un- or anti-democratic regimes seemed to be prospering around the world, from the Soviet Union, Cuba, and Vietnam to Saudi Arabia, Iran, and South Africa. What reason, then, do we have to expect that the situation of the 1970s will not recur, or worse yet, that the 1930s, with its clash of virulent anti-democratic ideologies, can not return?

Can it not be argued, moreover, that the current crisis of authoritarianism is a fluke, a rare convergence of political planets that will not recur for the next hundred years? For careful study of the different transitions away from authoritarianism in the 1970s and 80s will yield a plethora of lessons concerning the accidental nature of these events. The more one knows about a particular country, the more one is aware of the "maelstrom of external contingency" that differentiated that country from its neighbors, and the seemingly fortuitous circumstances that led to a democratic outcome. Things could have worked out very differently: the Portuguese Communist party could have emerged victorious in 1975, or the Spanish transition might not have re-sulted in democracy had King Juan Carlos not played so skillful and moderating a role. Liberal ideas have no force independent of the human actors who put them into effect, and if Andropov or Chernenko had lived longer, or if Gorbachev himself had a different personality, the course of events in the Soviet Union and Eastern Europe between 1985 and 1991 would have been quite different. Following the current fashion in the social sciences, one is tempted to say that unpredictable political factors like leadership and public opinion dominate the democratization process and ensure that every case will be unique both in process and outcome.

But it is precisely if we look not just at the past fifteen years, but at the *whole scope of history*, that liberal democracy begins to occupy a special kind of place. While there have been cycles in the worldwide fortunes of democracy, there has also been a pronounced secular trend in a democratic direction.... [T]he growth of democracy has not been continuous or unidirectional; Latin America had fewer democracies in 1975 than it did in 1955, and the world as a whole was less democratic in 1940 than it was in 1919. Periods of democratic upsurge are interrupted by radical discontinuities and setbacks, such as those represented by nazism and Stalinism. On the other hand, all of these reverses tended to be themselves reversed eventually, leading over time to an impressive overall growth in the number of democracies around the world. The percentage of the world's population living under democratic government would grow dramatically, more-over, should the Soviet Union or China democratize in the next generation, in whole or in part. Indeed, the growth of liberal democracy, together with its companion, economic liberalism, has been the most remarkable macropolitical phenomenon of the last four hundred years.

It is true that democracies have been relatively rare in human history, so rare that before 1776 there was not a single one in existence anywhere in the world. (The democracy of Periclean Athens does not qualify, because it did not systematically protect individual rights.) Counted in the number of years they have existed, factory production and automobiles and cities with multiple millions of inhabitants have been equally rare, while practices like slavery, hereditary monarchies, and dynastic marriages have persisted for enormous periods of time. What is significant, however, is not the frequency or length of occurrence, but the trend: in the developed world, we would as little expect to see the disappearance of cities or cars in the near future as we would the re-emergence of slavery.

It is against this background that the remarkable worldwide character of the current liberal revolution takes on special significance. For it constitutes further evidence that there is a fundamental process at work that dictates a common evolutionary pattern for *all* human societies —in short, something like a Universal History of mankind in the direction of liberal democracy. The existence of peaks and troughs in this development is undeniable. But to cite the failure of liberal democracy in any given country, or even in an entire region of the world, as evidence of democracy's overall weakness, reveals a striking narrowness of view. Cycles and discontinuities in themselves are not incompatible with a history that is directional and universal, just as the existence of business cycles does not negate the possibility of long-term economic growth.

Just as impressive as the growth in the number of democracies is the fact that democratic government has broken out of its original beachhead in Western Europe and North America, and has made significant inroads in other parts of the world that do not share the political, religious, and cultural traditions of those areas. The argument was once made that there was a distinct Iberian tradition that was "authoritarian, patrimonial, Catholic, stratified, corporate and semi-feudal to the core." To hold Spain, Portugal, or the countries of Latin America to the standards of the liberal democracy of Western Europe or the United States was to be guilty of "ethnocentrism." Yet those universal standards of rights were those to which people in the Iberian tradition held *themselves*, and since the mid-1970s Spain and Portugal have graduated to the ranks of stable democracies, tied ever more tightly to an economically integrating Europe. These same standards have had meaning for peoples in Latin America, Eastern Europe, Asia, and many other parts of the world as well. The success of democracy in a wide variety of places and among many different peoples would suggest that the principles of liberty and equality on which they are based are not accidents or the results of ethnocentric prejudice, but are in fact discoveries about the nature of man as man, whose truth does not diminish but grows more evident as one's point of view becomes more cosmopolitan.

The question of whether there is such a thing as a Universal History of mankind that takes into account the experiences of all times and all peoples is not new; it is in fact a very old one which recent events compel us to raise anew. From the beginning, the most serious and systematic attempts to write Universal Histories saw the central issue in history as the development of Freedom. History was not a blind concatenation of events, but a meaningful whole in which human ideas concerning the nature of a just political and social order developed and played themselves out. And if we are now at a point where we cannot imagine a world substantially different from our own, in which there is no apparent or obvious way in which the future will represent a fundamental improvement over our current order, then we must also take into consideration the possibility that History itself might be at an end.

POSTSCRIPT

Is Western Civilization in a
State of Decline?

Both Huntington and Fukuyama agree that the West is the main power in the world today and will continue to be so well into the twenty-first century. They disagree, however, over what the long-term future will bring. Huntington believes that the United States must solve its internal problems (multicultural conflicts, economic stagnation, social decay, and a decline in morality and moral values) and then reinvigorate the Atlantic Community to present a united front against the other civilizations. Convincing Latin America to join would bring added strength.

Fukuyama offers a concise analysis of his thesis in his article "The End of History," *The National Interest* (Summer 1989). Critiques of this article appeared in subsequent 1989 issues of *The National Interest*, and Fukuyama's rebuttal appeared in the Winter issue. We have likely not seen the last word on this debate. The optimism that Fukuyama expressed in his 1989 article is tempered somewhat in his later book *The End of History and the Last Man* (Free Press, 1992), from which his selection was excerpted. Despite this, he still sees the West's liberal-capitalist democracy as the only road to a fair and just world.

The book from which Huntington's selection was excerpted, *The Clash of Civilizations and the Remaking of World Order* (Simon & Schuster, 1996), is a must read for anyone interested in the world's future. Huntington repeats the need for Western unity in "The West and the World," *Foreign Affairs* (November/December 1996). Criticism of Huntington's work can be found in the September/October 1993 issue of *Foreign Affairs*; his rebuttal is contained in the publication's November/December 1993 issue.

Needless to say, Huntington and Fukuyama are not the first to speculate about the future of the West. Earlier in the twentieth century, Oswald Spengler's *Decline of the West* (Alfred A. Knopf, 1926–1928) explored the inevitability of the West's decline, with its place of power being taken by a Eurasian nation. A comparison of Spengler's conclusions with those of Fukuyama and Huntington would be a fruitful endeavor.

CONTRIBUTORS TO THIS VOLUME

EDITORS

JOSEPH R. MITCHELL is a history instructor at Howard Community College in Columbia, Maryland, and an educational consultant for *U.S. News and World Report*. He is also an educational consultant for Summer Productions (educational programmers for the Discovery Channel and the Learning Channel). He received an M.A. in history from Loyola University and an M.A. in African American history from Morgan State University.

HELEN BUSS MITCHELL is a professor of philosophy and director of the women's studies program at Howard Community College in Columbia, Maryland. She is the author of *Roots of Wisdom: Speaking the Language of Philosophy* (Wadsworth, 1996) and *Roots of World Wisdom: A Multicultural Reader* (Wadsworth, 1997). She has received numerous degrees, including a Ph.D. in women's history from the University of Maryland.

WILLIAM K. KLINGAMAN is an instructor at the University of Maryland in Baltimore County. He is the author of many publications, including *1929: The Year of the Great Crash* (Harper & Row, 1989); *The First Century: Emperors, Gods, and Everyman* (HarperCollins, 1991); and *Encyclopedia of the McCarthy Era* (Facts on File, 1996). He received an M.S. and a Ph.D. in history from the University of Virginia.

R. K. McCASLIN is a teacher at the Maryland public schools in Howard County. He also teaches Scottish history under the aegis of the St. Andrew's Society of Maryland. He has published many articles on Scottish history, and he has a B.A. and an M.A. in history from the University of Maryland.

STAFF

David Dean   List Manager
David Brackley   Developmental Editor
Ava Suntoke   Developmental Editor
Tammy Ward   Administrative Assistant
Brenda S. Filley   Production Manager
Juliana Arbo   Typesetting Supervisor
Diane Barker   Proofreader
Lara Johnson   Graphics
Richard Tietjen   Publishing Systems Manager

AUTHORS

GAR ALPEROVITZ is a senior research scientist at the University of Maryland. He is the author of *The Decision to Use the Atomic Bomb and the Architecture of an American Myth* (Alfred A. Knopf, 1995).

GEORGE B. N. AYITTEY is a professor of economics at the American University in Washington, D.C. He is the author of *Indigenous African Institutions* (Transnational, 1991).

ARCHIE BROWN is a professor of politics at the University of Oxford and subwarden of St. Antony's College, where he has been a fellow since 1971. He has also taught at Glasgow University. He is the author of numerous publications on Soviet and Russian politics, including *The Cambridge Encyclopedia of Russia and the Former Soviet Union* (Cambridge University Press, 1994).

HERBERT BUTTERFIELD taught for many years at Cambridge University. He is the author of several works, including *The Englishman and His History* (Archon Books, 1970) and *Herbert Butterfield on History* (Garland, 1985).

ALICE DENNY is coauthor, with Ronald Robinson and John Gallagher, of *Africa and the Victorians: The Official Mind of Imperialism* (Macmillan, 1981).

EDWARD L. DREYER has been a professor of history at the University of Miami since 1970. His areas of interest are Chinese, German, and military history, and he is a specialist in Asian studies. He is the author of *China at War, 1901–1949* (Longman, 1995).

JOHN L. ESPOSITO is a professor of religion and international affairs at George-town University in Washington, D.C., and director of the Center for Muslim-Christian Understanding at Georgetown University's Edmund A. Walsh School of Foreign Service. His publications include *Islam and Democracy* (Oxford University Press, 1996).

JOHN KING FAIRBANK taught modern Chinese history at Harvard University from 1936 to 1977.

SIDNEY BRADSHAW FAY was a prominent revisionist historian in the 1920s and 1930s who became the first American scholar to write a dispassionate study of the causes of World War I when he published *The Origins of the World War* in 1928.

STEVEN FEIERMAN is a professor in and chair of the department of the history and sociology of science at the University of Pennsylvania in Philadelphia. He is the author of many works, including *Peasant Intellectuals* (University of Wisconsin Press, 1990) and *The Social Basis of Health and Healing in Africa* (University of California Press, 1991).

FRANCIS FUKUYAMA, a former deputy director of the U.S. State Department's policy planning staff, is a senior researcher at the RAND Corporation in Santa Monica, California. He is also a fellow of the Johns Hopkins University School for Advanced International Studies' Foreign Policy Institute and director of its telecommunications project.

JOHN GALLAGHER is the Vere Harmsworth Professor of Imperial and Naval History and a late fellow of Trinity College at the University of Cambridge. He is the author of *The Decline, Revival, and Fall of the British Empire* (Cambridge University Press, 1981).

DANIEL JONAH GOLDHAGEN is a professor of government and social studies at Harvard University. He is the author of *Hitler's Willing Executioners: Ordinary Germans and the Holocaust* (Alfred A. Knopf, 1996), for which he was awarded the Democracy Prize by Germany's *Journal for German and International Politics*.

J. A. HOBSON (1858–1940) was a British journalist and social reformer. His book *Imperialism: A Study* (Ann Arbor, 1965) is considered by historians of imperialism to be the classic discussion of the economic motives for imperialism. He is also the author of *The Economics of Distribution* (Clifton, 1972).

ALBERT HOURANI is an emeritus fellow of St. Antony's College at the University of Oxford. His publications include *The Emergence of the Modern Middle East* (University of California Press, 1981) and *Islam in European Thought* (Cambridge University Press, 1991).

SAMUEL P. HUNTINGTON is the Eaton Professor of the Science of Government in and director of the John M. Olin Institute for Strategic Studies at Harvard University. He is the author of *Political Order in Changing Societies* (Yale University Press, 1968).

ROBERT G. KAISER served as Moscow bureau chief for the *Washington Post* from 1971 to 1974. A former visiting professor at Duke University, Kaiser remains a member of the Council of Foreign Relations, and he has authored numerous works on the Soviet Union and the cold war.

GEORGE F. KENNAN is a professor emeritus in the School of Historical Studies at the Institute for Advanced Study in Princeton, New Jersey. A member of the first American delegation to the USSR in 1933, Kennan is a prolific author with more than 20 books to his credit, including his Pulitzer Prize–winning *Memoirs, 1925–1950* (Little, Brown, 1967).

PETER KROPOTKIN (1842–1921) was a Russian revolutionary who wrote his autobiography *Memoirs of a Revolutionist* in 1899.

DUN J. LI was a professor of history at the William Paterson College in Wayne, New Jersey. He has also taught at the University of Dubuque, Oklahoma State University, and the University of Political Science in Nanking, China. He is the editor of *The Road to Communism: China Since 1912* (Van Nostrand Reinhold, 1969).

ALI A. MAZRUI is director of the Institute of Global Cultural Studies at the State University of New York at Binghamton, as well as the Ibn Khaldun Professor-at-Large at the School of Islamic and Social Sciences in Leesburg, Virginia. His books include *Cultural Forces in World Politics* (Heinemann, 1990).

WILLIAM H. McNEILL taught history at the University of Chicago from 1947 to 1987. He served as president of the American Historical Association in 1981 and received the Erasmus Prize from the Dutch government in 1996.

FRANÇOISE NAVAILH is a Russian film historian at the University of Paris. She teaches Russian language and is a specialist in Russian cinema.

EDWIN O. REISCHAUER (1910–1990) attended Harvard University and also studied in Paris, Japan, Korea, and China. He was the American ambassador to Japan from 1961 to 1966, and he is the author of *Japan, Past and Present* (Alfred

A. Knopf, 1964) and *Transpacific Relations* (C. E. Tuttle, 1969).

ROSEMARY RIGHTER is chief editorial writer for *The Times* of London.

RONALD ROBINSON is the Beit professor of the History of the British Commonwealth and a fellow of Balliol College at the University of Oxford. He is the author of *The Ending of Apartheid in Zimbabwe* (East Carolina University, 1989).

SIMON SCHAMA is a professor of art and art history at Columbia University. He is the author of *The Embarrassement of Riches: An Interpretation of Dutch Culture During the Golden Age* (Alfred A. Knopf, 1987) and *Landscape and Memory* (Alfred A. Knopf, 1995).

JOAN W. SCOTT is a professor of social science at Princeton University's Institute for Advanced Study. She is the author of *Gender and the Politics of History* (Columbia University Press, 1988).

STEVEN SHAPIN is a professor of sociology at the University of California, San Diego. He has written extensively on the social history of science and the sociology of scientific knowledge. He is the author of *Leviathan and the Air-Pump: Hobbes, Boyle, and the Experimental Life* (Princeton University Press, 1985).

EDWARD SHORTER directs the history of medicine program at the University of Toronto. He is the author of *From the Mind into the Body* (Free Press, 1996) and *Psychiatry: From the Era of the Asylum to the Age of Prozac* (John Wiley & Sons, 1997).

THOMAS C. SMITH is an expert on the origins of modern Japan and the author of *The Aristocratic Revolution in Japan*

(1965). He taught at Stanford University from 1948 to 1971 and then served as a professor of history at the University of California, Berkeley.

JONATHAN D. SPENCE is the George Burton Adams Professor of History at Yale University. His published works include *To Change China* (Little, Brown, 1969) and *God's Chinese Son* (W. W. Norton, 1996).

FRITZ STERN is a professor of history at Columbia University. He has written many books on German history, including *Dreams and Delusions: National Socialism in the Drama of the German Past* (Vintage Books, 1987).

RICHARD STITES is a professor of history at Georgetown University. He is the author of *Revolutionary Dreams* (Oxford University Press, 1989) and *Russian Popular Culture* (Cambridge University Press, 1992).

LOUISE A. TILLY is an assistant professor of history and director of the women's studies program at the University of Michigan. She is the author of numerous articles on social history.

SAADIA TOUVAL is currently a Peace Fellow at the United States Institute of Peace in Washington. He is a former professor of political science and dean of the faculty of social sciences at Tel Aviv University.

HARTMUT POGGE VON STRANDMANN is the British Academy Wolfson Research Reader in Modern History at and is a fellow of University College in Oxford. He is coeditor, with R. J. W. Evans, of *The Coming of the First World War* (Oxford University Press, 1988).

INDEX

DATE DUE

ILL			
4593937			
1 27 99			
NO 27 '01		WITHDRAWN	
GAYLORD			PRINTED IN U.S.A